Adobe InDesign Interactive Digital Publishing

Tips, Techniques, and Workarounds for Formatting Across Your Devices

Ted Padova

Apress®

Adobe InDesign Interactive Digital Publishing: Tips, Techniques, and Workarounds for Formatting Across Your Devices

Ted Padova
Davao City
Philippines

ISBN-13 (pbk): 978-1-4842-2438-0   ISBN-13 (electronic): 978-1-4842-2439-7
DOI 10.1007/978-1-4842-2439-7

Library of Congress Control Number: 2017931398

Managing Director: Welmoed Spahr
Editorial Director: Todd Green
Acquisitions Editor: Natalie Poe
Development Editor: Gary Schwartz
Technical Reviewer: Keith Gilbert
Coordinating Editor: Jessica Vakili
Copy Editor: Kezia Endsley
Compositor: SPi Global
Indexer: SPi Global
Artist: SPi Global
Cover Image: Designed by Freepik

Distributed to the book trade worldwide by Springer Science+Business Media New York, 233 Spring Street, 6th Floor, New York, NY 10013. Phone 1-800-SPRINGER, fax (201) 348-4505, e-mail orders-ny@springer-sbm.com, or visit www.springeronline.com. Apress Media, LLC is a California LLC and the sole member (owner) is Springer Science + Business Media Finance Inc (SSBM Finance Inc). SSBM Finance Inc is a Delaware corporation.

For information on translations, please e-mail rights@apress.com, or visit http://www.apress.com/rights-permissions.

Apress titles may be purchased in bulk for academic, corporate, or promotional use. eBook versions and licenses are also available for most titles. For more information, reference our Print and eBook Bulk Sales web page at http://www.apress.com/bulk-sales.

Any source code or other supplementary material referenced by the author in this book is available to readers on GitHub via the book's product page, located at www.apress.com/9781484224380. For more detailed information, please visit http://www.apress.com/source-code/.

Printed on acid-free paper

For Robz

Contents at a Glance

Contents

About the Author

Ted Padova owned and operated a digital imaging center in Ventura, California for over 15 years. He taught classes part-time over 19 years for the University of California at Santa Barbara and UCLA in a variety of application software programs, digital imaging, prepress and printing, and digital photography.

He is the author of over 60 computer books. His work primarily involves Adobe Acrobat and Adobe Creative Suite applications. In addition to writing, he teaches classes in Graphic Design and Adobe Creative Suite applications at the Philippine Center for Creative Imaging in Manila, Philippines.

About the Technical Reviewer

Keith Gilbert is a digital publishing consultant and educator, Adobe Certified Instructor and Community Professional, conference speaker, lynda.com author, and contributing writer for various publications. His work has taken him throughout North America, Africa, Europe, and Asia. During his 30+ years as a consultant, his clients have included Adobe, Apple, Target, the United Nations, Best Buy, General Mills, and Lands' End. Follow him on Twitter @gilbertconsult, at blog.gilbertconsulting.com, and at lynda.com/keithgilbert.

Acknowledgments

First, I want to thank the staff at Apress for their assistance in bringing this publication to fruition. Many thanks to my Acquisitions Editor, Natalie Pao. If it weren't for Natalie, I would never have been able to complete this work for Apress. A special thank you to my absolutely wonderful developmental editor, Gary Schwartz. Gary added polish to this work and made it so much better than my original manuscript. I'd also like to thank Jessica Vakili, my Coordinating Editor, for keeping me on track and assisting me throughout this project. Many thanks to the rest of the Apress staff for being such a delight to work with.

A very special thank you goes to Keith Gilbert, my Technical Reviewer. Keith is undeniably the best technical reviewer I've had on any book I've written. His vast knowledge of Adobe InDesign and digital publishing made this book so much better and certainly more technically accurate. Thank you, Keith, for a great job.

A big thank you to makeup artists Juliet Berenguer and Gerelyn Galo for their photo contributions from photographers Rommel Balcita and Primo Salinas and models Rose Magtana and Mylene Bacus.

Some special thanks go to Anne-Marie Concepcion of Seneca Design and Training (http://www.senecadesign.com), InDesign Secrets (https://indesignsecrets.com), and Creative Pro (http://creativepro.com). Also, many thanks to my friend of many years David Blatner, who together with Anne Marie hosts many blogs and web sites all related to Adobe InDesign, EPUBs, and publishing. If you're looking for wonderful tips and tricks for using Adobe InDesign, log on to the InDesign Secrets web site.

Introduction

This book is all about creating digital publishing documents with interactivity using Adobe InDesign CC 2017. I begin this publication talking about Adobe InDesign and some core essentials that you need to know first to create InDesign documents that eventually are converted to a format for viewing on computers and devices such as tablets and smartphones.

In Part I, we start with essentials such as creating a workspace, working with preferences, creating palettes, and using some InDesign tools that you'll find handy when working on any kind of document.

In Part II, we look at working with text and graphics. We explore font handling and setting type attributes. We look at using the various panels associated with formatting text, using the Story Editor, and spell checking documents. Also in this part, I talk about importing and working with graphics, creating tables, and creating and applying styles for paragraphs, characters, graphics, tables, and table cells.

In Part III, we come to adding interactive elements to your designs. I cover adding hyperlinks, cross-references, and bookmarks. We thoroughly work through the many different animations available to you in InDesign, and then we move on to changing object and text views using multi-state objects. The final chapter in this part is dedicated to rich media, where we look at using audio and video in documents.

Part IV covers exporting documents from InDesign to a number of different formats. We look at creating reflowable and fixed layout EPUBs, creating interactive PDF documents, and using the marvelous new InDesign feature Adobe Publish Online. For each of the different file exports, we look at how to format text and graphics and what kinds of animations and interactivity can be added to each format, and we discover a few workarounds to add interactive elements that are not traditionally supported by one format or another. Each chapter in Part IV also covers viewing the different file formats on desktop computers and on devices. In addition, I cover issues related to content hosts and what you need to know to prepare files for hosting your documents with content providers.

Part V covers some tips that I provide for creating digital publishing documents and various project ideas for you to explore.

When it comes to Adobe InDesign digital publishing, there are five different document types you can create—documents designed for Reflowable EPUBs, Fixed Layout EPUBs, Interactive PDFs, Adobe Publish Online (Preview), and Adobe Digital Publishing System/ Solution (DPS)/AEM.

All but the latter is addressed in this book. What you won't find in the chapters ahead is any discussion about DPS. DPS is a marvelous tool for creating interactive magazines. However, the licensing fees are extraordinary for individual users. DPS is designed for large publishing houses creating magazines like *Time, Sports Illustrated,* Condé Nast publications, and so forth. The majority of readers of this book are no doubt more interested in serving smaller client bases or using the tools to self-publish content. Therefore, I have eliminated DPS from this book.

What you find when creating interactive digital publishing documents is a number of ways that you can help clients broaden their reach. You can take InDesign documents designed for print and repurpose the files for hosting online on web sites and social media sites. You can make documents more dynamic and engaging that offer consumers a richer experience. Once you begin exploring the opportunities InDesign provides you for more creative expressions, you'll likely incorporate digital publishing as another avenue for additional client services.

Part I: Fundamentals of Digital Publishing

Part I covers in some detail digital publishing documents and fundamentals for using Adobe InDesign. I talk about setting preferences, using workspaces, creating new documents, using master pages, and how to import assets. I also cover creating font and color palettes for your designs, and I throw in a little bit about customizing keyboard shortcuts.

Part II: Creating Documents in Adobe InDesign

This part is all about creating InDesign documents and essentials that you need to know in preparing files containing interactive elements for export.

In Chapter 3, I cover formatting text. We look at working with text frames, using glyphs, and creating drop caps. We look at formatting paragraphs, adding strokes to characters, using the Story Editor, creating type on paths, and creating text wraps. I cover using the spell checker and correcting misspelled words in documents.

Chapter 4 is all about graphics. I cover importing graphics, using strokes and creating custom strokes, creating art objects inside InDesign, transforming and aligning objects, and adding effects and transparency.

In Chapter 5, we look at creating tables in InDesign. I cover some table basics, various methods for how to create tables, explore the table tools and commands, and create a variety of custom tables.

Chapter 6 deals with styles. I talk about creating character, paragraph, object, cell, table, and GREP styles. We look at cell overrides and formatting cell styles within paragraph styles to eliminate overrides. I cover creating drop caps and nested styles, managing lists, and working with bullets and number styles.

Part III: Adding Interactivity

In Part III, we look at adding interactive elements to your InDesign documents.

In Chapter 7, I talk about creating hyperlinks and linking to URLs and pages within documents. We look at using the Hyperlinks Panel and the various options that you have when working with hyperlinks.

Chapter 8 introduces you to the world of animations and the huge number of opportunities that you have in creating and managing InDesign animations. We look at several animation presets and how to modify the presets and set various animation attributes. We look at using buttons to show/hide animations and use the Timing Panel. We look at creating animations with scrolling text, motion paths, adding sounds to animations, and using animations with multi-state objects. Finally, I introduce you to a few different animation projects.

Chapter 9 covers working with multi-state objects (MSOs). We look at the Object States Panel, how to create MSOs, adding/deleting different object states in an MSO, adding button events for viewing different states, nesting MSOs, and hiding various states.

Chapter 10 covers working with rich media. I begin by explaining some basics for video files, compressing video, and using the InDesign Media Panel. We look at importing video, adding video masks, and using MSOs with video.

Part IV: Publishing Documents

Part IV covers creating the final documents that you will publish for viewing on a variety of devices.

In Chapter 11, I begin this section with a short chapter on how to upload your published documents to various devices. I talk about uploading files to devices and URLs, copying files via URLs, and using Dropbox for file exchanges.

In Chapter 12, we look at creating and exporting to reflowable EPUB format. I cover specifics related to formatting files properly for export to reflowable EPUB, using various export options, and tagging styles. We look at how to open EPUB files and examine the contents. I cover adding interactivity to reflowable EPUBs and some workarounds that you need to use with certain interactive assets. We look at viewing EPUBs and using content hosts and providers.

In Chapter 13, we switch from reflowable EPUBs to fixed layout EPUBs, where most of the interactivity that you create in InDesign can be exported and viewed as you design the material. I start this chapter by examining the differences between reflowable EPUBs and fixed layout EPUBs. We look at how to prepare graphics, introduce interactive elements, and create a TOC, and look at a number of different export options available to you when exporting to fixed layout EPUBs. I also cover viewing the exports on a variety of devices.

In Chapter 14, we look at Adobe Publish Online. This is one of the best features found in InDesign for publishing interactive documents. You can add Publish Online documents to Facebook, Twitter accounts, and web sites. I cover how to export to Publish Online and how to manage your documents.

In Chapter 15, I cover creating Interactive PDF files. We look at setting up the Acrobat workspace, exporting documents from InDesign to Adobe Interactive PDF, working with Acrobat layers, creating hyperlinks inside Acrobat, working with media files, working with SWF files, and creating interactive tables. Many of the interactive tasks that you can perform in InDesign won't work in Acrobat. I offer several workarounds to maximize exporting interactive documents to Adobe Interactive PDF.

Part V: Tips and Techniques

The last two chapters provide you with tips and ideas for creating interactive documents.

In Chapter 16, I cover ten tips for creating digital publishing documents.

In Chapter 17, I offer some project ideas.

What lays ahead is a detailed view for tips, techniques, and instructions in setting up interactive InDesign layouts and exporting documents to reflowable and fixed layout EPUBs, Adobe Publish Online, and Interactive PDFs. Come join me in a journey through the world of interactive digital publishing.

PART I

Fundamentals of Digital Publishing

CHAPTER 1

■ ■ ■

Understanding Digital Publishing

There's much to understand when working with digitally published documents. There are several kinds of file formats and many different reading devices. And every time you turn around, something new appears on the horizon. It's enough to make your head spin.

Before you begin creating documents, you need to know what kind of publication you want to work with and what kind of device you want to use to display your work. That being said, you then need to do some research to be certain that what you create conforms to online publisher requirements.

In this chapter, I begin by defining the term *digital publishing* so that we have a mutual understanding of what lies ahead in the rest of the chapters. I also talk about file formats and reading devices. I try to offer you many reasons for why Adobe InDesign is the program of choice for any kind of published document, and I suggest the workflow that you need to follow to create well-formed and valid EPUBs.

As you read this chapter and move forward through the remaining chapters, keep in mind that you do not have to master every item discussed in this book. You may only be interested in Kindle books, and therefore you can just skim over non-Kindle related discussion. Or you may only be interested in Apple iBooks and can similarly just skim over all of the content not related to iBooks. My effort is to offer you a broad spectrum of digital publishing creations and distribution. I leave it up to you to decide what specific areas of interest pertain to your work.

1.1 Defining Digital Publishing

For the purposes of this book, let's break apart the term digital publishing. First let's look at publishing in general, and then we'll look at what digital means.

Publishing is defined as the process of production and dissemination of literature, music, or information—the activity of making information available to the general public.

© Ted Padova 2017

T. Padova, *Adobe InDesign Interactive Digital Publishing*,
DOI 10.1007/978-1-4842-2439-7_1

When we look at the term digital, it typically refers to numerical data. However, a broader definition includes information that is available in electronic form, readable and manipulable by computer.

Quite simply, we look at the term digital publishing as content (text, graphics, and images) made available for viewing on electronic devices such as smartphones, tablets, smart TVs, computers, and any other electronic device that can display content designed for human consumption.

What's familiar to us today as electronic content includes web pages, magazines, articles, books, brochures, briefs, manuals, and so on, all the way down to single-page items such as greeting cards and invitations.

1.2   Understanding File Formats

To understand the file types that are used with digital publishing, we also need to know what kinds of devices display our content. These go hand in hand, and it's difficult to talk about one without the other. To make this clear, take a look at Table 1-1.

Table 1-1. *File Formats and Display Devices*

File Format	File Type	Display Devices
HTML	.html, text	Desktop, cell phones, tablets
EPUB (reflowable)	.epub, .mobi*	eReaders, desktop, cell phones, tablets
EPUB (Fixed layout)	.epub, .kf8	eReaders, desktop, cell phones, tablets
PDF (interactive and static)	.pdf	Desktop, cell phones, tablets
Adobe Publish Online	HTML, Adobe Proprietary**	Desktop, cell phones, tablets

* MOBI is a format used by Amazon Kindle for viewing EPUBs on Kindle readers.
** Adobe Proprietary is listed here because the Publish Online content is uploaded to Adobe's servers, and you don't have access to the final files.

1.3   Getting Familiar with the Display Devices

You have many different choices for the software and/or devices that can display your content. You can view content on desktop or laptop computers to test results and be relatively certain that the content will display properly on a given device. In some cases, you can connect a device to your computer and view content directly on the given device.

1.3.1   Previewing Content in Desktop Applications

You can download a number of different viewing applications to your computer for the purpose of previewing your work. I highly recommend doing this before you upload anything to a content provider.

Among your choices include the following:

- *HTML*: Most of us are familiar with web viewing applications such as MS Edge, Internet Explorer, Firefox, Safari, Google Chrome, and others. These applications are designed to view web pages. For some work with EPUBs, you might want to install Google Chrome because Chrome can preview EPUB documents with the help of the free Readium app for Google Chrome.

- *EPUB*: There are two types of EPUB3 documents: reflowable and fixed layout. Reflowable EPUBs are used with eReaders that support font size changes and reflow text (and sometimes images) as font size increases or decreases. Fixed layout EPUBs are similar to PDF documents that provide a complete WYSIWYG (what you see is what you get) view.

  Applications for desktop previews of EPUBs include Adobe Digital Editions (version 4 and above), as shown in Figure 1-1, Apple iBooks, and Readium (launched from Google Chrome). In addition, there are an assortment of eReaders available for both iOS and Android devices.

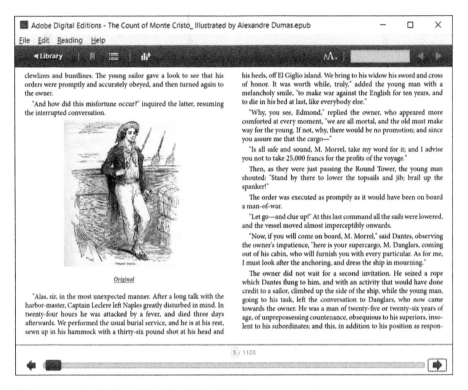

Figure 1-1. *eBook shown in Adobe Digital Editions*

■ **Note**   The EPUB market is continually changing. More eReaders are being introduced and more applications that support EPUB creation are continually being announced. If you're serious about publishing EPUBs, routinely search the Internet for new products to help you develop and display your creations.

- *MOBI*: Kindle EPUBs require a different kind of viewer. You can download Kindle Preview from Amazon and install it on your computer. The Kindle Previewer displays your EPUBs as they would be viewed on a Kindle device.

- *PDF*: Desktop viewers include Adobe Reader and Adobe Acrobat and Preview on the Mac as well as an assortment of third-party applications. When you move to smartphones and tablets, there are many choices for viewing PDFs. Some applications offer you features such as adding comment notes, form filling, EPUB support, and support for multimedia viewing. Adobe distributes a free Adobe Reader for PDF documents. Others are free or are sold for nominal fees.

1.3.2   Acquiring EPUB Content on Computers

As a first step in your digital publishing workflow, you should acquire the tools that are needed to preview EPUBs on your computer and/or devices. The ones that I recommend include the following:

- *Kindle Previewer*: Download the Kindle Previewer application for Mac or Windows at http://www.amazon.com/gp/feature. html?docId=1000765261.

- *Apple iBooks*: Unfortunately, iBooks is Mac only and there is no way to simulate the iBooks reader on Windows. For Mac users, you can use iTunes and connect an iPad to your computer via a USB cable and preview content directly on the device. However, if you have many books in your library, you need to wait until your iPad syncs with iTunes.

  An easier way is to use Dropbox. You can upload EPUBs to Dropbox and access eBooks on Windows, Android devices, and iPads. Visit Dropbox.com and download a version for your devices.

- *Kobo Readers*: Kobo is one of the fastest growing eReaders available today. You can download desktop readers for Kobo from https://www.kobo.com/desktop.

- *Android File Transfer*: You can transfer files for Android devices using the Android File Transfer utility that you can find at http://android-file-manager.en.softonic.com.

- *Adobe Digital Editions*: ADE version 4 and above now support the EPUB 3 format for previewing both reflowable and fixed layout EPUBs. ADE is available for both Windows and Macintosh. You can download the free application from http://www.adobe.com/ solutions/ebook/digital-editions/download.html.

- *Readium*: Readium is a plugin for the Google Chrome browser. Install Google Chrome from https://support.google.com/chrome/ answer/95346?hl=en. After you install Chrome, visit the Chrome web store at https://chrome.google.com/webstore/category/apps and search for Readium. Download and install the plugin.

1.3.3   Previewing EPUB Content on eReading Devices

Desktop previewing applications generally work well; however, they are not perfect and you may not get an exact view of your documents when using a desktop application. Typically, you would use a desktop application to preview edits that you make on InDesign files and then later preview the entire publication on a device. Devices that you may have available include the following:

- *Apple iPads*: You can connect an iPad directly to your computer with a USB cable, and in iTunes you can drag and drop an EPUB for previewing (see Figure 1-2) or use Dropbox to upload an EPUB and download it to your iPad.

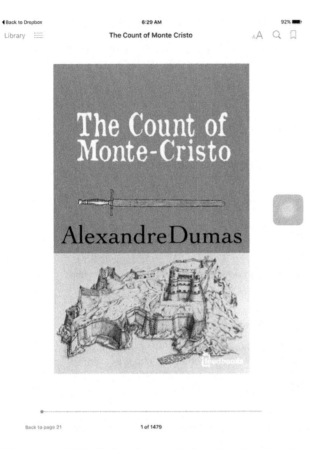

Figure 1-2. EPUB displayed on an iPad via Dropbox download

- *Kobo Readers*: You can connect a Kobo reader to your computer
  and preview an EPUB directly on the Kobo via a USB cable. If you
  don't have a Kobo reader, you can use the Kobo Desktop Reader
  (see Figure 1-3).

Figure 1-3. *EPUB displayed on the Kobo Desktop Reader*

- *Kindle*: You can convert an EPUB to the Kindle .mobi format and use Kindle Previewer to preview the Mobi-formatted file. Unfortunately, you can't connect your Kindle Reader to your computer to preview directly on the device before submitting the final file to Amazon. To convert EPUB to MOBI, you can use KindleGen, which you can download free from Amazon at http://www.amazon.com/gp/feature.html?docId=1000765211. KindleGen is run from a command line on Mac or Windows. For a more user-friendly converter, you can download the free eBook Converter for Windows from Softonic at http://ebook-converter.en.softonic.com. For a Macintosh version, visit http://ebook-converter-mac.en.softonic.com/mac/download?ex=SWH-1608.6. This converter permits you to convert to MOBI and also convert PDF documents to the MOBI format.

- *Barnes & Noble Nook*: Connect your Nook tablet to your computer and locate the folder (Mac Finder or Windows Explorer): My Nook > My Files > Books. Drag and drop an EPUB file to the folder to view it on the device.

Just about all devices permit you to preview pubs on your computer before submitting to online hosts.

1.4   Why InDesign?

This book is all about designing your creations in Adobe InDesign. The reason we use InDesign instead of any other application is that InDesign gives you so many tools that enable you to create dynamic and engaging documents. Among the things you can do with InDesign include:

- *Add animations*: Animations are supported in fixed layout EPUBs, Interactive PDF files only on desktop computers (with some workarounds), and Adobe Publish Online. I talk about creating InDesign animations in Chapter 8.

- *Use multi-state objects*: You may use multi-state objects (MSO) for slideshows, and button events are supported in fixed layout EPUBs, Interactive PDFs (only on desktop computers with workarounds), and Adobe Publish Online. I cover all that you need to know about MSOs in Chapter 9.

- *Include rich media*: Audio and video files are supported in Reflowable EPUBs, Fixed Layout EPUBs, PDF files (with some limitations), and Adobe Publish Online. Look over Chapter 10 for how to include video and sound in your publications.

- *Create cross-references and hyperlinks*: Supported in all formats. Chapter 7 covers hyperlinks and cross-references.

- *Organize content flow*: With InDesign's Articles Panel, you can make sure that your objects and text frames appear in a reflowable EPUB exactly as you want them to appear.

- *Use styles*: InDesign supports style sheets (which are critical in creating any EPUB) for not only character and paragraph styles, but also for table and cell styles.

- *Export directly to EPUB3*: InDesign CC 2015 and above supports exporting to the EPUB3 format for both reflowable and fixed layout EPUBs.

There are many more tools and commands available to you with InDesign. You have marvelous opportunities using the Object Export Options, tagging styles with HTML tags, using layers (essential for complex pages), applying special effects, and importing assets from a vast array of sources.

Adobe InDesign is a fabulous program that provides you with a huge toolset to create just about any kind of digital publishing document.

1.5   Setting Up an EPUB Workflow

EPUB content providers distribute elaborate guidelines that you need to follow before uploading your content. You'll want to know if a given host supports rich media, drop caps, drop shadows on images and objects, cover images as separate files or contained within the publication, structure of the table of contents, and more.

For EPUBs, your workflow is much more elaborate than when publishing PDF documents and using Adobe Publish Online (APO). With PDF and APO, you preview the work and no validation is necessary. Most often what you see is what you get and if it looks good to you on your computer, you can often upload the file to a content provider. With EPUBs, you have several additional steps, as shown in Figure 1-4.

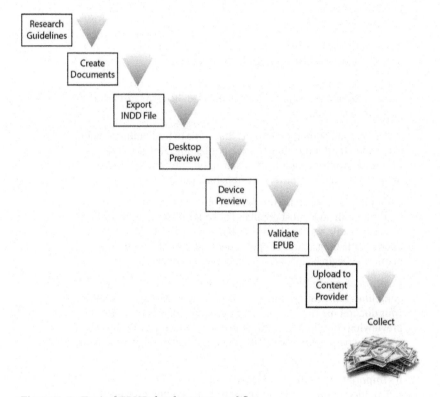

Figure 1-4. *Typical EPUB development workflow*

Let's look at each step in more detail:

- *Research*: If you intend to distribute an EPUB on Apple, Amazon, or other content provider, the provider typically has guidelines that you need to follow. For Apple's iBooks, as of this writing, the Apple Asset Guide 5.1, Revision 2 document is hosted as a PDF file at https://itunesconnect.apple.com/docs/iBooksAssetGuide5.1Revision2.pdf.

  For Kindle books, as of this writing, the Amazon Kindle Publishing Guidelines version 2015.2 can be downloaded from http://kindlegen.s3.amazonaws.com/AmazonKindlePublishingGuidelines.pdf.

11

The Kobo User Guide can be downloaded from
`http://download.kobobooks.com/writinglife/en-US/KWL-User-Guide.pdf`.

For Barnes & Noble Nook, you can find out more information by logging on to Nook Press at `https://www.nookpress.com/ebooks`.

For Sony eReader guidelines, check out `https://docs.sony.com/release/PRST2.pdf`.

The Smashwords Style Guide can be downloaded from `https://www.smashwords.com/books/view/52`.

For ISSUU, you can find a video and guidelines at `http://help.issuu.com/hc/en-us/articles/204816098-How-to-upload-and-publish-on-issuu`.

There are many other documents that you can find online to help you understand more about eBook publishing. You can find how-to guides, formatting guidelines, self-publishing guides, and so on. Just search the Internet for publishing guidelines.

Rather than look over many different content hosts, narrow the list down to the two most popular. The top two distributors are Amazon Kindle and Apple iBooks. If you're just getting started with eBook publishing, read the Apple and Kindle guidelines thoroughly before you begin laying out your document in InDesign.

- *Create documents*: When you're familiar with the publishing guidelines from your publishers of choice, you can begin creating your document. This process requires many toggles between previewing content and editing the document. You typically will work on a page, export to EPUB, and return to InDesign to make edits.

  It's important to understand what an eBook is comprised of. EPUB documents are like an entire web site contained within a zipped file. There are tools that you can use to unzip the files, open the HTML and CSS documents, and make some changes to the HTML. I cover editing HTML and CSS in Chapter 12. At this point, don't be concerned if you're not a programmer or familiar with writing code. We simply address making some edits to the documents with easy steps for you to follow.

- *Export to EPUB*: With InDesign CC, you have two choices for EPUB exports: reflowable text and fixed layout. Use the export option from the File ➤ Export menu (shown in Figure 1-5) for the type of EPUB you want to distribute. You need to review all of the options in the various panes in the Export window to create the final document.

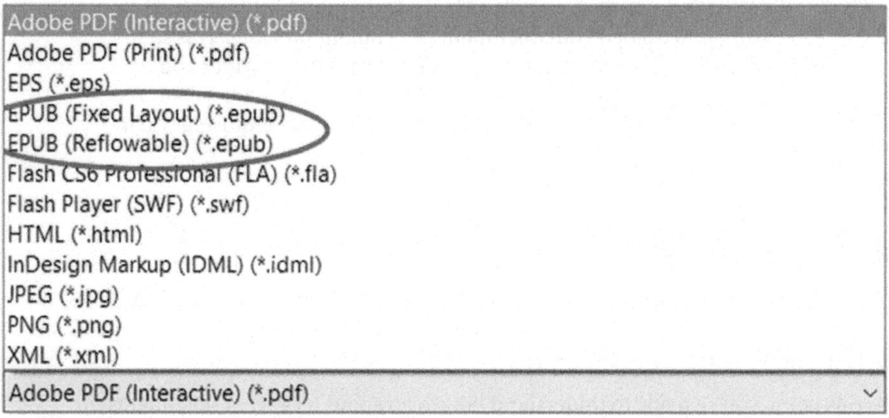

```
Adobe PDF (Interactive) (*.pdf)
Adobe PDF (Print) (*.pdf)
EPS (*.eps)
EPUB (Fixed Layout) (*.epub)
EPUB (Reflowable) (*.epub)
Flash CS6 Professional (FLA) (*.fla)
Flash Player (SWF) (*.swf)
HTML (*.html)
InDesign Markup (IDML) (*.idml)
JPEG (*.jpg)
PNG (*.png)
XML (*.xml)

Adobe PDF (Interactive) (*.pdf)                      ⌄
```

Figure 1-5. *The InDesign Export options*

- *Preview the EPUB*: Preview in desktop applications for all of the devices that you intend to use.

- *Preview on Devices*: Hook up an iPad, Android tablet, Kobo Reader, or any other device that permits previewing your work.

- *Validate your EPUB*: Some validation occurs when you export from InDesign. For a final check to be certain that your EPUB is valid, use a validation checker or a validation service to validate your document.

  You can download an EPUB checker from https://github.com/IDPF/epubcheck, which is run from a command line. If you want an easier solution, check out the few listed here.

  The International Digital Publishing Forum hosts a web site where you can upload an EPUB for validation. Navigate to http://validator.idpf.org.

  Sigil is a desktop application that enables you to edit HTML and CSS code. It can also validate EPUBs. You can download the free application for Windows and Mac from http://sigil.en.softonic.com.

  Mac users can download the free AppleScript ePubCheck from https://code.google.com/p/epub-applescripts/downloads/detail?name=ePubCheck_3.0b5.zip&can=2&q=. Just drag and drop your EPUB on top of this script.

  A pricey application for editing HTML and validating EPUBs is Oxygen. If you're willing to pay $200 or more for one of the Oxygen apps, visit http://www.oxygenxml.com/download.html.

- *Upload to a content provider*: The last step in publishing your work is to upload your document to a content provider. This step presumes that you acquired an account with the provider and supplied all of the necessary identifier and payment information as well as acquired an ISBN number for providers requiring you to obtain one.

1.6   Summary

This chapter served as an introduction to EPUBs, EPUB formats, and viewing EPUBs on various reading devices. Once you know the target for the final product, it's much easier to begin the development process.

At this point, you're ready to understand how to go about laying out documents for viewing on various devices. The program of choice, of course, is Adobe InDesign, and we begin our journey on EPUB creation with an understanding of some of the basics related to working in Adobe InDesign.

CHAPTER 2

■ ■ ■

Getting Started in InDesign

Some readers may be new to InDesign, so I will use this chapter to talk briefly about some important features in InDesign that can help you get up to speed. This is simply an overview of some of the tools and commands that you need to know to move around the program for creating your designs.

If you intend to work with EPUBs, animations, interactive elements, and export your InDesign files to EPUB, Interactive PDF, or use Adobe Publish Online (Preview), you'll definitely want to personalize InDesign so that tools, menus, panels, and preferences are set up for the kind of work you do.

In this chapter, I talk about creating custom workspaces, modifying preferences and keyboard shortcuts, creating templates, and customizing presets to personalize the work environment for general needs. What I suggest may or may not include all of the options that you want for your particular work, but I provide a starting point. Feel free to modify some settings as you follow along in this chapter.

I also cover some of the basics for working with important features such as using fonts, master pages, creating grids, and what you need to know about importing assets in InDesign. I don't have enough space in this book for a thorough explanation for using all that InDesign provides. If you want to know even more about using InDesign, I suggest that you take a look at *Adobe InDesign CS for Dummies* or the *Adobe InDesign CS Bible* from Wiley publishing.

2.1   Setting Up the Digital Publishing Workspace

All of the changes that you make to workspace panel locations and keyboard shortcuts can be saved as a custom workspace. When you start InDesign and choose a workspace, all of the settings you made to customize your work environment change back to your saved settings. If you move panels around and mess up the workspace, you can easily change it back to your original saved settings. As you look at the many different options that you have for workspace choices, you'll save the settings and overwrite the saved workspace settings several times to create the final workspace.

© Ted Padova 2017
T. Padova, *Adobe InDesign Interactive Digital Publishing*,
DOI 10.1007/978-1-4842-2439-7_2

2.1.1   Locating Workspace Choices

Open InDesign and look in the top-right corner of the InDesign window. By default, you may see Essentials listed with a down-pointing arrow, as shown in Figure 2-1. If workspaces are not available in your InDesign window, your Application Bar will not be visible (Mac only). Choose Window ➤ Application Bar, and the Workspaces menu is shown. Click the arrow to open the menu, and you will find several workspaces that Adobe has provided for you. Notice that you have a menu option for New Workspace and Delete Workspace. I'll get to these a little later. For now, be aware of the workspaces and options that you have in the menu.

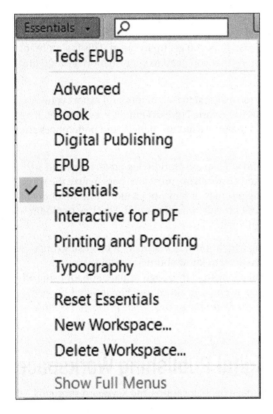

Figure 2-1. *Click the down arrow next to Essentials to open the Workspaces menu*

2.1.2   Organizing Panels

To begin creating a personal workspace for Digital Publishing, notice that Adobe has provided a Digital Publishing workspace for you. However, all of the panels you'll use throughout this book are not contained in the Digital Publishing Workspace. You need to start somewhere, so select Digital Publishing from the Workspace menu. This will give you an excellent starting place.

When you select a workspace, the first thing that you see as a change in the interface are panels on the right side of the InDesign window. We'll add some panels a little later. For now, be aware that you can undock panels by dragging them away from the Panel Dock. Click Liquid Layout and drag the panel away from the Panel Dock, as shown in Figure 2-2. It becomes a floating panel, and you can move it around the InDesign window. Using floating panels can help you work on some specific items as you create your documents. For our purposes, we'll dismiss the panel by clicking the X in the top-right corner (Windows) or top-left corner (Macintosh).

Figure 2-2. *Click the X in a floating panel to dismiss it*

The Liquid Layout options are helpful when you want to repurpose documents created for print and change the design suited for an EPUB or Publish Online. But for the rest of your work, it won't be useful.

You can open the panels to reveal the panel icon and the panel name. By default, the interactive panels are displayed with an icon and panel name. To reveal the panel names along the right side of the Panel Dock, move the cursor over the division line and drag left.

Another panel that you won't use often is the Preflight Panel. Move it away from the Panel Dock and dismiss it.

You can reorder the panel list by clicking a panel and dragging up or down. Likewise, if you have two columns of panels, you can drag a panel from one list to the other. When you drag a panel to a new location, notice the blue bar appearing above the panel name. This bar shows you where the panel will be placed.

2.1.3   Adding Panels to the Workspace

InDesign has a vast number of panels that are all listed in the Window menu either as separate items or nested in groups. To open a panel, choose Window ➤ `<panel name>` such as Articles appearing first in the Window menu (see Figure 2-3).

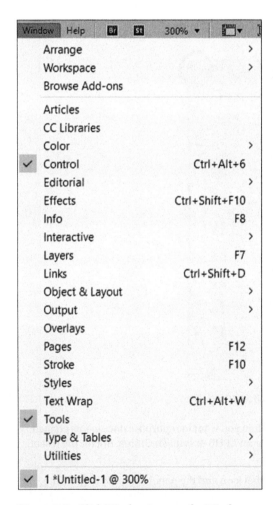

Figure 2-3. *Click Window to open the Window menu*

Notice in Figure 2-4 that Articles is bundled with two other panels. To remove just the Articles Panel, click the name and drag away from the bundle. Separate all of the individual panels by dragging away from the nested group. Then drag each panel to the Panel Dock. You can always organize the panels in an order that you prefer by dragging up or down in the Panel Dock or across the individual columns in the Panel Dock.

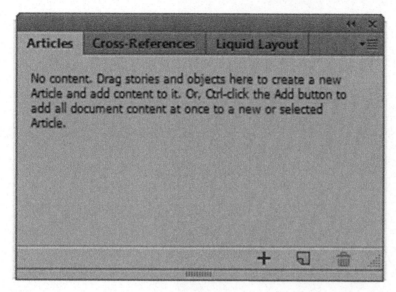

Figure 2-4. *The Articles Panel is bundled with two other panels*

Notice in the Window menu that several panes appear with a right chevron indicating a submenu, such as the Type and Tables menu command. When you place the cursor over Type and Tables, a submenu appears with options beginning with Character through Table at the bottom of the submenu. When you select one of these items, the panel opens as a floating panel and you can move it around the InDesign Workspace or dock it in the Panel Dock.

You should have an idea now for how to access panels and move them to the Panel Dock. In Figure 2-5, you can see the panels that I recommend for creating a custom workspace, which you might use for EPUBs and Digital Publishing documents. The panels include the following:

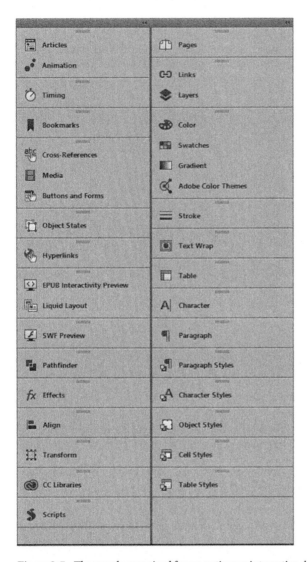

Figure 2-5. *The panels organized for an optimum interactive document development workflow*

- *Articles*: If you export to reflowable EPUBs from InDesign and choose the layout order, typically all images appear at the end of the document. Before InDesign CS 5.5 and the introduction of the Articles Panel, it was a challenge to get images appearing between paragraphs of text in a reading order similar to your design. The Articles Panel made this process much easier and together with Anchored objects (see Chapter 12 for more on the Articles Panel and anchoring objects), you can easily create reflowable EPUBs in reading orders that mimic your layouts.

- *Color*: The Color group contains several panels that you may want to add to your workspace. These include the following:

  - *Swatches*: The Swatches Panel enables you to apply color to text and objects.

  - *Gradient*: This is a personal choice. If your documents contain objects with gradients, add the panel to the Panel Dock. If you don't use gradients, then don't add it.

  - *Adobe Color Themes*: This panel accesses what was formerly known as Adobe Kuler. You can create various color palettes and add them to your Swatches Panel. I cover this later in this chapter in the section, "Creating a Color Palette".

- *Effects*: The Effects Panel, among other things, enables you use blend modes with objects and add transparency to text and objects.

- *Interactive*: The Interactive menu item in the Window menu contains panels for creating works with interactivity, such as fixed layout EPUBs, Interactive PDFs, and Adobe Publish Online (Preview). Add these panels to your workspace. They include the following:

  - *Animation*: You can animate text and objects in a number of ways that are covered in Chapter 8. Animations can be viewed in Fixed Layout and Adobe Publish Online. With Interactive PDFs, you need a workaround, as I explain in Chapter 14.

  - *Bookmarks*: Bookmarks can be helpful when using an alternative to a Table of Contents in EPUBs and Interactive PDFs.

  - *Buttons and Forms*: Buttons are used to trigger events in fixed layout EPUBs, Interactive PDFs, and Adobe Publish Online. Form fields are used only with PDF documents.

- *EPUB Interactivity Preview*: This is a preview panel that permits you to preview EPUB layouts by page and by document as well as animations.

- *Hyperlinks*: Hyperlinks can be set up to link to pages, anchors, and URLs in EPUBs, Interactive PDFs, and Adobe Publish Online.

- *Media*: The Media Panel is used to preview video and sound and add poster images to a video either from within the video or from an external document. You can also trigger a video to play on a page load.

- *Object States*: This panel is used with multi-state objects (MSOs) that can be viewed in Fixed Layout EPUBs, Interactive PDFs (only on desktop computers using a workaround), and Adobe Publish Online. For a thorough explanation of MSOs, see Chapter 10.

- *SWF Preview*: Adobe Flash SWF files are not used with most interactive documents today, but SWF is still supported with Interactive PDFs except on iOS devices. If your work includes Interactive PDF, add this panel to the Panel Dock.

- *Timing*: The Timing Panel is used in conjunction with the Animation Panel.

- *Layers*: Using layers is essential for almost any kind of document that you create. When you use animations and MSOs, the Layers Panel is a blessing.

- *Links and Pages*: These panels are critical with just about any design. The Links Panel helps you identify missing links and update links. The Pages Panel permits you to add/delete pages from a document.

- *Align*: In the Object and Layout Panel, you find Align in the submenu. This panel is useful when you need to align and distribute objects. It's particularly helpful when working with MSOs.

- *Stroke*: The Stroke Panel permits you to change line widths and styles.

- *Styles*: A number of different panels appear in the submenu. You should add several from the list that includes the following:

  - *Character Styles*: Both Character and Paragraph Styles are a must for EPUB creations or for any other document that you create in InDesign. With EPUBs, you need to identify all of the body text and display type using styles. The styles will get exported in the HTML and CSS files, where you can easily make edits in an HTML editor.

  - *Paragraph Styles*: Same reasons for Character Styles. You need to use them, particularly for EPUBs.

  - *Object Styles*: When you want to apply effects to objects and match the same effects settings to other objects, the Object Styles will save you much time.

  - *Cell and Table Styles*: If you use tables in your document, you should create Cell and Table Styles.

- *Text Wrap*: The Text Wrap Panel permits you to wrap text around objects and set offset distances.

- *Tools*: The Tools Panel displays the tools along the left side of the InDesign window. This panel is essential for all documents.

- *Application Frame (Mac Only)*: For Macintosh users, you may want to choose Application Frame. The Application Frame eliminates any distracting background from the desktop. By default, the Application Frame is always used when you launch InDesign on Windows.

2.1.4   Saving a New Workspace

Inasmuch as you may make some other adjustments that require revising your custom workspace, once you set up the panels you should save the workspace. Open the Workspace menu and choose New Workspace. In the dialog box that opens, provide a name for the workspace. In this example, since Digital Publishing is already a workspace, let's call our new custom workspace EPUB. Type the name in the Name text field and click OK. By default, Panel Locations are saved with the workspace.

During a work session, you may move panels out of the Panel Dock and arrange them around the InDesign window. If you want to return to your saved workspace, open the Workspace menu and choose Reset [*workspace name*], where workspace name is the name that you used when you saved the workspace.

If you make other adjustments to your workspace, use the same menu commands. There is no option to update the workspace, so you need to choose New Workspace and type the same name to overwrite the last one you saved.

2.2   Modifying Preferences

A *preference choice* is something that applies to an item or the user interface each time you open a new document or within a document, and addresses applying something that affects the item or interface. For example, if you want a given font, such as Palatino, to be the default font each time you use the Type tool, you can choose to make Palatino as your default font. When you click the cursor, Palatino is automatically selected in the font menu. This prevents you from having to open the Font menu and choosing the font each time you type new text.

There are two kinds of preferences in InDesign: Application preferences and Document preferences. *Application preferences* are used with each new document that you create. *Document preferences* adhere only to the open document. Using a font choice as an example, if you don't have a document open and choose Palatino as your default font, each time that you create a new document, Palatino will be the default font. On the other hand, if you want to override the default font and choose another font, choose the font without an insertion cursor in an open document, and that font becomes the default for only the current open document. Hence, if Palatino is the default font for a given document and you want Myriad Pro to be the default font for the document, choose Myriad Pro from the font menu. Be certain that the text cursor is not active on a page and that Myriad Pro becomes the default font for only the current open document.

When you choose preference options from the Preferences Panel, the options shown in Figure 2-6 (Edit ➤ Preferences (Windows) or InDesign ➤ Preferences (Macintosh)) are available. All of the choices that you make to the "General" preferences are application preferences and therefore apply to each new document you open.

2.2.1   Changing Some Important Application Preferences

Most of the preferences Adobe has supplied for you when you install InDesign work well for creating digital designs. There are a few though that you might want to change. These include the following:

- *Interface*: This option is a personal choice. Open the Preferences Panel (Ctrl+K (Windows) or ⌘+K (Macintosh)) and click Interface in the left pane. Where you see Color Theme, you can choose from Light to Dark when you click Color Theme to open the menu. On the right side of the panel, click the right chevron to open a slider and you can move the slider left and right to adjust the InDesign overall brightness. Choose a setting that's comfortable for you.

- *Units*: Much of what you do will be measured in Points. If you prefer inches as a unit of measure, make the choice in the Units and Increments pane. Likewise, if you prefer Picas or Points, make the change from the menus for Horizontal and Vertical in the same pane. When creating EPUBs, your best choice is to set up the Units for points.

- *Guides & Pasteboard*: By default, InDesign has a narrow pasteboard (the area around your page). You may want to add some more space for the vertical height of your pasteboard. As a personal default, I add about 4 inches (288 points) for the vertical pasteboard.

- *Display Performance*: By default, InDesign sets the display quality for vector art and images to Typical, which often displays images and objects pixelated. The lower the quality, the faster you can move around in InDesign. However, since low-res images are often used for digital designs, you won't find InDesign slowing down if you change the Default View and Adjust View Settings options to High Quality in the Display Performance preferences (see Figure 2-6). High Quality renders the images with the best quality and without pixilation.

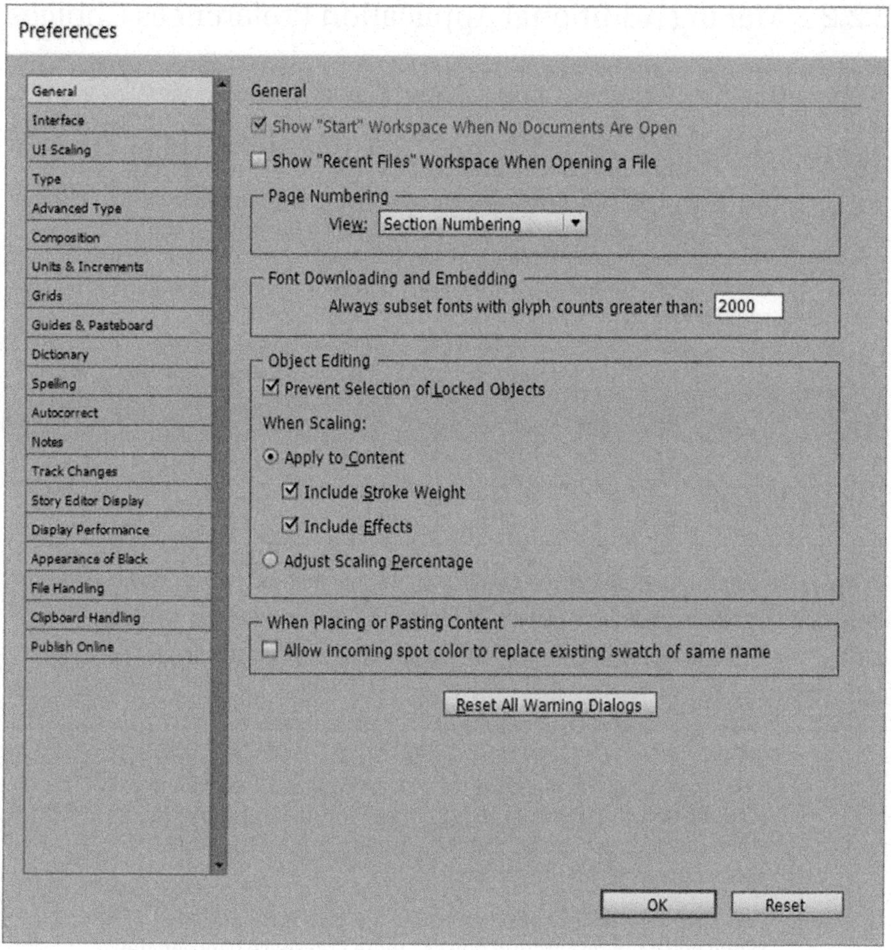

Figure 2-6. *The Preferences Panel has a list on the left with corresponding panes on the right*

- *Publish Online*: By default, the Disable Publish Online checkbox is not checked. Leave this setting at the default.

Once you make a change in the Preferences dialog box, click OK and the new preference settings are saved. Just to be careful, quit InDesign and reopen the application. If InDesign crashes during a work session, you'll lose all of your new preference settings. By quitting and relaunching InDesign, your new settings will remain intact.

2.2.2   Making Additional Application Preferences Choices

While InDesign is open and no document is in view, you can make some changes that apply to all new documents. A few things that you may want to change include the following:

- *Fonts*: Choose the font that you want to use as your default font. This should be a Text font (used for body copy) and not a Display font (used for headlines and captions). Open the Font menu and make a choice for Font, choose a font size from the Control Panel, shown in Figure 2-7, at the top of the InDesign window, and make a choice for Leading (distance between the lines of type) from the same panel.

Figure 2-7. *The InDesign Control Panel*

■ **Tip**   The Control Panel changes depending on the tool that you have selected in the Tools Panel. When you click the Type tool, all of the settings apply to type. If you click another tool, the Control Panel changes and displays options that you use for paragraphs or objects.

- *Strokes*: You may want to have the size for strokes appear different than the default 1-point. I use .5 points for my default stroke size. Open the Strokes Panel and make a choice for the size of the strokes that you want as a default.

- *Text Wrap*:The default offset for text wraps is 0 (zero) points. When you wrap text around objects, there's no space between the edges of objects and text. You would rarely want a wrap to show text against an object. Open the Text Wrap Panel (Window ➤ Text Wrap or press Ctrl/⌘+Alt+W). Be certain that the link icon is active and type 1p6 (or 18 points) or another value that you want for the offset distance. In Figure 2-8, I set the offset value to 1p6 or 18 points. Note that every object that you add to a design will have a text wrap applied to the objects. If you want to disable text wraps, set the text wrap panel to 0 for the offsets without selecting an object. This will change the default to no wrap for the current open document.

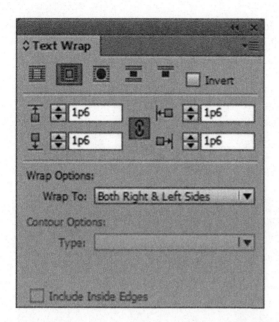

Figure 2-8. *Set the Text Wrap offset value to offset text wrapped around objects*

2.2.3   Changing Document Preferences

Document preferences are specific to the document that you have open in InDesign. When you close the document, the application preferences prevail. You can change items such as fonts, font sizes and leading, stroke weights, and any other panel setting where you can make an adjustment. Just keep in mind that nothing should be selected in the document window if you want to change a preference.

2.3   Modifying Keyboard Shortcuts

A keyboard shortcut applies to an edit when you strike a modifier key with a keystroke. For example, pressing Ctrl/⌘+N opens the new document window. Many of the default keyboard shortcuts work well for your design creations. There are a few though that you may want to change in a custom Keyboard Shortcuts list.

To open Keyboard Shortcuts, choose Edit ➤ Keyboard Shortcuts. The Keyboard Shortcuts window opens, as shown in Figure 2-9.

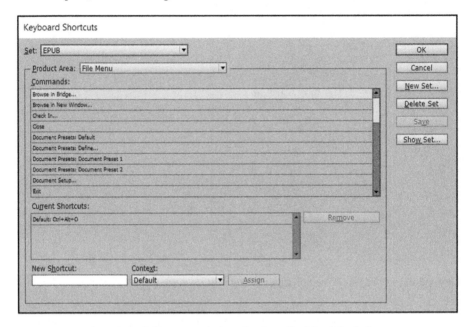

Figure 2-9. *The Keyboard Shortcuts window displays all of the default shortcuts*

To create a new list, click the New Set button on the right side of the window. Provide a name for your custom keyboard shortcuts and click OK. This action just duplicates the defaults, but you can delete or add shortcuts in the new set.

At the top of the window, you have a Product Area menu. Open the menu and you will find a list of the top-level menus, panel menus, tools, scripts, and an assortment of other areas where you can add or change a keyboard shortcut.

2.3.1   Reassigning Paste

Choose the Edit menu from the list and scroll down to the Paste options. Click Paste and remove the Ctrl/⌘+V command by selecting it in the Current Shortcuts list, then click the Remove button. We'll replace Paste (that pastes any object on the clipboard to the center of your document) with Paste in Place, which pastes a copied element directly on top of the copied item. You'll find this shortcut a more frequent operation than Paste, especially when working with Multi-State Objects.

After removing Paste, click Paste in Place in the list and press Ctrl/⌘+V. The old shortcut is still in the current shortcuts list, so click on the old shortcut (Ctrl/Alt+V or ⌘/⌥+V) and click the Remove button. After completing the steps, your window should appear as shown in Figure 2-10.

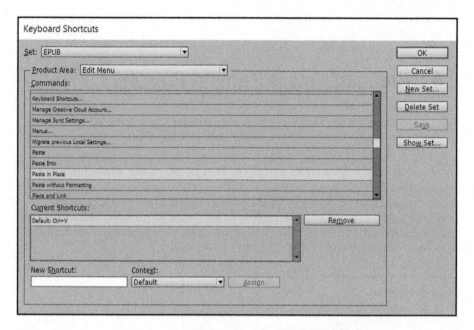

Figure 2-10. *A custom shortcut is added to the menu command Paste in Place*

■ **Note** When you make a change to a panel view, you need to resave your workspace to capture the new size for a window adjustment.

I offered a few shortcuts here that I use often. There are many other choices that you can make and modify shortcuts for the kind of work you do. Rather than modifying a huge number of shortcuts, start with just a few that you can easily remember; then later you can return to the Keyboard Shortcuts window and make additional edits to your custom set.

2.3.2 Adding a Shortcut for Tabbing in a Table Cell (Windows only)

If you work with tables often, you'll want to move around the table quickly without having to access menu commands. When you press the Tab key in a table, the cursor moves to the next cell. On the Macintosh if you want to tab within a cell, you press Option+Tab. On Windows, if you press Alt+Tab, you get the System Application Switcher.

The way you can tab within a cell in InDesign with a menu command is to choose Type ➤ Insert Special Character ➤ Tab.

To add a keyboard shortcut to tab within a table cell, you might open the Type Menu in the Product area of the Keyboard Shortcuts dialog box and scroll down to Insert Special Character: Other: Tab. Use something like Alt+F1 (the Function key) or whatever

Function key you want to use. If you do a lot of tabbing within table cells, a keyboard shortcut will help speed up your work.

2.4   Creating New Document Presets

When you chose File ➤ New Document, the default is set to create a document for Print—hardly something we're interested in when creating digital publications. You can change the default, or you can add a custom preset in the New Document window.

Press Ctrl/⌘+N to open the New Document window. Choose Mobile from the Intent menu. For Page size, you can make a choice for iPad, Kindle Fire, or Android, or set up a custom page size. For our purposes, we'll add iPad as our choice. Choose an Orientation by clicking Landscape or Portrait. For Margins, click the Lock icon to unlock the four adjustments. Add 44 points to the top, left, and right and 88 points to the bottom. This will be a good margin size for documents on an iPad so that the content stays away from the scroll bars. Uncheck Primary Text Frame (see Figure 2-11).

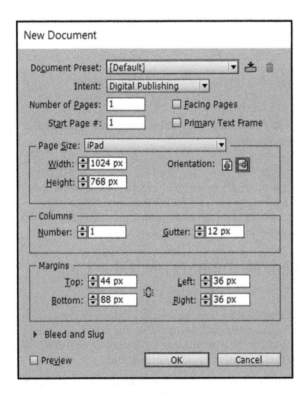

Figure 2-11. *Custom settings for an iPad*

▓ **Note**   Figure 2-11 is a screen shot from InDesign CC 2017. If you use earlier versions of InDesign, choose Digital Publishing from the Intent menu.

At this point you can assign these settings to a new default. Every time you open the New Document, the default will be the settings that you apply here. If you have several types of publications, you may not want the settings to be a new default, but you may want to retrieve the settings from time to time.

Click the Save Preset button adjacent to the Document Preset menu. When the window opens, you can type [Default] to make the new settings the default choice for new documents. Click OK and an alert dialog opens informing you that the name already exists. Click Yes to overwrite the previous default.

▓ **Tip**   If you want to use the Default New Document and bypass the New Document window, press Ctrl+Alt+N (Windows) or ⌘+Option+N (Macintosh).

If you want to create a new preset, provide a name in the Save Preset dialog box and click OK.

2.5   Creating Palettes

Designers know the importance of creating a color palette for a new project, but some readers may be authors who want to publish their own eBooks and who have no design background. Therefore, I want to cover briefly some essential design tips for creating a color palette and using type in your design projects.

2.5.1   Creating a Color Palette

You have a fabulous opportunity using InDesign to create color palettes made up of various tones, complementary, analogous, triadic, pastel colors, and much more. I won't delve into a long discussion on color theory here. I just want to guide you in a direction to follow skilled designers and famous artists.

In InDesign, open the Adobe Color Theme Panel. If you don't have your workspace set up to display the Color Theme Panel, choose Window ➤ Color ➤ Color Themes. For users of earlier versions of Adobe software prior to Creative Cloud applications, this panel was referred to as Adobe Kuler.

You have three tabs in the panel, as shown in Figure 2-12. The first tab is Create. Here you can create colors based on a number of options that you choose from the menu where you see Analogous appear. Open the menu and make a choice for one of the color relationships listed. Move the sliders to select a hue and you see a set of five colors.

You can click the circles appearing on top of the color spectrum and move them around to change the vibrance and saturation. When you decide on a set, you can add the colors to your Swatches Panel by typing a name at the bottom of the panel and click Save. The Save to Library dialog appears. Select a Library or create a New Library and click Save. To access the colors, click the My Themes tab.

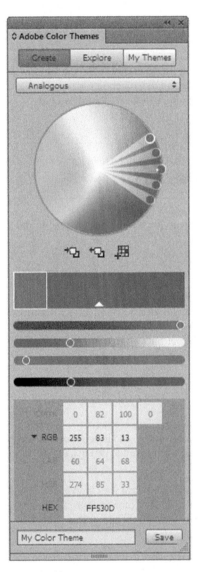

Figure 2-12. *The Create tab in the Color Themes Panel enables you to create a custom color set*

■ **Note**   You must have an Adobe ID to save color swatches. If you don't have an Adobe ID, log on to www.adobe.com and click the Sign In button. When the page changes, click Get an Adobe ID. This ID enables you to take advantage of many Adobe services, and it is essential for the work you do in creating digital publishing documents.

You may want to add swatches from your libraries to the InDesign Swatches Panel. To add a color group to the Swatches Panel, open a library from the My Themes Panel and scroll the window to locate the colors that you want to add to swatches. Place the cursor over Actions and a pop-up menu opens. Click Add to Swatches in the pop-up menu, and the colors are added to a new folder in the Swatches Panel.

The really cool thing about Color Themes is the Explore tab. Here you can search for a variety of different options. You may want a palette of earth tones or sky tones. Simply type text in the Search field and press Enter/Return. Typically, you'll see a long list of search results.

One of my favorite search items is searching for master painters. If you want a color set of vibrant colors, you might search some of the impressionist artists by name such as Monet or Van Gogh. If you want something in the post impressionist era, such as strong vivid colors combined with a clear lucid structure as was used by Cézanne, just type Cezanne in the search text box in the Explore tab. After pressing Enter/Return, a list is returned to you and you can add various color sets to the InDesign Swatches Panel. In Figure 2-13, you can see the results of searching for Cezanne. If you want something more contemporary, just search for contemporary artists. The possibilities are endless. And just poking around in the Adobe Color Themes Panels is a lot of fun.

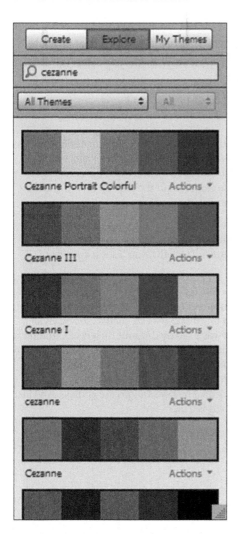

Figure 2-13. The results of searching for Cezanne in the Explore tab

Using the Color Themes Panel won't make you a master at color theory and usage, but it's a starting point and especially helpful to those without a design background. One of the nice things about using the Color Theme Panel is that you have the same panel available to you in Adobe Photoshop and Adobe Illustrator. If you create assets in these applications, you can easily synchronize your color palettes.

2.5.2   Creating a Font Palette

If you're not a designer, then it will serve you well to obtain a basic understanding of fonts and what choices you might want to make for fonts used in your designs. There's a ton of information available to you on the Internet regarding fonts that work well together and font matches you should avoid. You're safe when choosing multiple fonts within a single large typeface library such as Univers or Helvetica Neue.

When choosing fonts for a publication, you might look at typefaces from the same historical period, typefaces from the same designer, typefaces with similar body heights, and in many cases you can choose typefaces that are very different and opposites. What you want to avoid is stylistic conflicts such as using Eurostile and Cochin in the same work.

You should carefully consider the typefaces you use for Text type (body copy) and Display Type (headlines and section heads). You can search the Internet to find out more about what typefaces work well together. If you introduce a third font in a design piece, perhaps a slab serif such as Rockwell or Museo Slab would do the trick or a formal script such as Bickham Script or calligraphic typeface such as Zapfino.

2.5.2.1   Using the Right Font Types

Font selection isn't as important when creating reflowable EPUBs since the end readers can choose from a limited number of installed fonts on their reading devices. But all other types of publications do require that you make some good font choices.

The type of fonts you want to use in your publications are True Type and OpenType fonts. Stay away from other type fonts, as you may have some problems when the document is viewed on a device.

You also need to be certain that you have the right to embed fonts in a document. This is important for fixed layout, Interactive PDF, and Adobe Online publications. Font foundries may provide you with permission to use the font in a design but not license you for embedding the font. For more information on licensing and embedding fonts, see Chapter 13.

2.5.2.2   Using Adobe Typekit

If you're a Creative Cloud user (and I recommend for any serious document developer that you obtain a subscription to Adobe Creative Cloud), you have access to fonts using Adobe Typekit. Adobe Typekit fonts can be embedded in your publications, and they are free to use for Creative Cloud users.

To access Typekit, open the Font menu from the Control Panel and click Add Fonts from Typekit (see Figure 2-14).

Figure 2-14. *Adobe's Typekit web site enables you to sync fonts from an impressive library of typefaces*

Once in Typekit, you can search for typefaces by Classification and Properties. Click one of the Classification items in the right panel and look over the Weight, Width, xHeight, contrast, and so forth, and click the font attributes that you like for a given typeface.

When you find a typeface that you want to use, mouse over the typeface in the left panel. A pop-up menu opens where you can click Use Fonts. When you click Use Fonts, a window opens where you can check the fonts within the typeface with which you want to sync on your computer. Click Sync Selected Fonts, as shown in Figure 2-15. When the fonts complete syncing to your computer, a message window informs you that the fonts are ready to use.

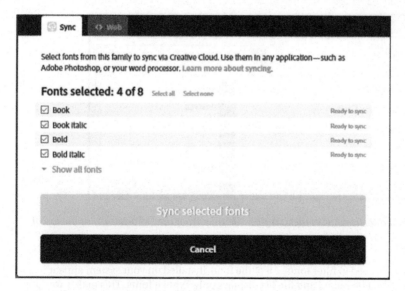

Figure 2-15. *Click Sync Selected Fonts to sync the fonts with your computer*

■ **Note**   You must have an active Internet connection to sync a Typekit font with your computer, and you must connect to the Internet once every 30 days to maintain your CC license.

Back in InDesign when you open the Font menu, you find Filter at the top-left of the menu with two icons adjacent to the text. Select a font and click the Star icon to add the font to a Favorites list. The Favorites list appears at the top of the font menu. If you have a lot of fonts installed, the Favorites list prevents you from having to scroll through a long list to find a font. Notice that when you open the Font menu, you see some stars with fills and no fills. When a font name appears adjacent to a star with a fill, the font is part of the Favorites list. If you want to remove a font from the Favorites list, click the star. When the star has no fill, the font is removed from the Favorites list (see Figure 2-16).

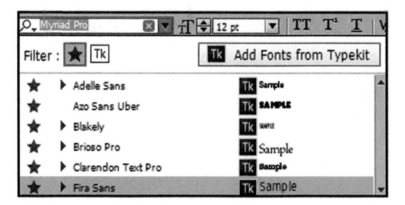

Figure 2-16. *Fonts listed with the Star filled in are part of the Favorites list at the top of the menu*

The other icon is used to filter fonts. All of the fonts installed on your system appear in the font list. Click the Filter icon, and the list displays only Typekit fonts. This makes working on a design project easy when using only Typekit fonts and you need to toggle fonts in your layout.

2.6   Getting Familiar with the Layers Panel

Using the Layers Panel is essential with complicated designs. If you use Animations and nested multi-state objects (MSOs), you may need to isolate items to make your work easier. There are just a few things that you need to know about using layers in your design work.

2.6.1   Naming Layers

When you create new layers, it's important to name each layer as you create it. Provide a descriptive name so that you can easily find a layer associated with content. To create a new layer, press the Alt/‾ key and click the new layer icon at the bottom of the Layers Panel. This opens the New Layer window, where you can add a name as you create the layer.

2.6.2   Selecting Objects on Layers

When you have objects on a layer and you want to select an item, use the Layers Panel. Open any nested group and click on an object or text. To select the item, click the square adjacent to the right of the layer name to select the object. If you want to select multiple objects, press Shift or Ctrl/⌘ and click for contiguous and noncontiguous selections.

2.6.3   Moving Objects Between Layers

If you want to move an object from one layer to another, open the Layers Panel, click the square icon to the right of the object name, and drag it to the target layer. When you add a new object, the object appears on the active layer (selected in the Layers Panel). If you accidently create an object on the selected layer and want it on another layer, simply drag the square in the Layers Panel to the target layer.

2.6.4   Pasting Objects

More often than not when you copy an item and want to paste it into your document, you'll want to paste on the layer from which you copied the item. To paste on the same layer, open the Layers Panel menu and select Paste Remembers Layers.

2.6.5   Hiding and Locking Layers

If you have a complicated design, it may be easier to hide a layer from view or lock a layer to be certain additional content is not added to undesired layers. In the Layers Panel, to hide a layer click the Eye icon. To lock a layer, click in the column between the Eye icon and the layer name (see Figure 2-17).

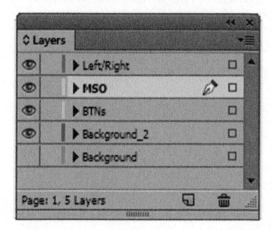

Figure 2-17.   Click adjacent to the Layer name the Eye icon for showing/hiding

---

■ **Tip**   To hide or lock all layers except the selected layer, hold the Alt/⌥ key down and click the Eye (show/hide) icon or the column between the Eye icon (lock/unlock) and the layer name. To reveal all layers or unlock the layers, use the same shortcut.

If you haven't worked in a program using layers, following these simple steps can help get you up to speed when creating your designs.

2.7   Using Master Pages

When an object is placed on a Master Page, the object appears on all pages assigned to the master. For example, if you have Master A, Master B, and Master C, and pages 1–3 are all assigned to Master A, any object that you place on the A master will appear on pages 1–3.

Master Page items will not appear in reflowable EPUBs, but the other types of digital publications can benefit by placing items such as page numbers, folios, logos, and so on on a Master Page.

To add page numbers to Master Pages, open the Master Page from the Pages Panel. Double-click on the master that you want to use for all pages with page numbers. Create a text frame and choose Type ➤ Insert Special Character ➤ Markers ➤ Current Page Number. Format the text for font and size, and page numbers appear on all pages assigned to the master.

▓ **Note**   Master Page items won't appear in reflowable EPUBs.

If you want to create a new Master Page but you also want to use page numbers on pages assigned to the new master, open the Pages menu and choose New Master. In the New Master dialog box, choose from the Based on Master menu the master containing page numbers (see Figure 2-18). InDesign uses the content from the first master, and it permits you to add additional items on the new master that will appear on all pages assigned to the second master.

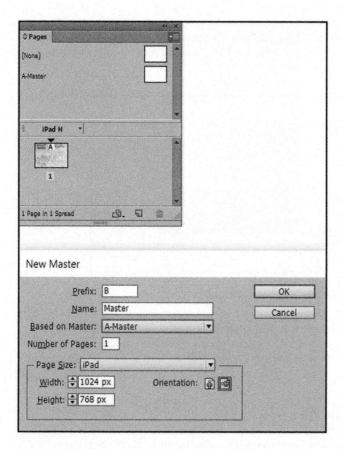

Figure 2-18. *Choose Based on Master to add all content for a given master on a new master page*

2.8   Working with Grids

Use grids to help you add structure and order in your design work. When you create a grid, you'll find that laying out a document is much easier than randomly placing text, images, and objects on a page. Grids help you develop clarity and polish in a design, and they help you create order and consistency in your document.

Grids can be added to Master Pages, and you can also add grids on individual pages. When applying a grid to a given page that has a grid on a master, the page grid dismisses the master and the grid applied to the page takes precedence. In other words, a page grid overrides the Master Page grid. For example, you may add a seven-column grid to a Master Page where all pages follow the same grid. However, on page 3 in a document, you might want to use a two-column grid. When you apply the two-column grid to a page, the seven-column grid disappears.

Adding grids either on Master Pages or individual pages is handled with the same menu command. Choose Layout ➤ Margins and Columns to open the Margins and Columns dialog box, as shown in Figure 2-19. In the section where you see Columns, enter the number of columns that you want for a grid.

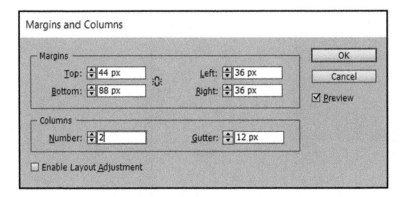

Figure 2-19. *Set up a grid in the Margins and Columns dialog box*

Keep in mind that when you create a grid, for example a nine-column grid, all your elements don't need to be contained within individual columns. You may have text frames spanning two columns, an image spanning five columns, and a sidebar spanning one column.

2.9　Importing Assets

Most of the assets that you add to a design are handled by using the File ➤ Place command. You can import photos, objects, videos, audio files, PDF pages, and pages from other InDesign files, all with a single menu command.

In some cases, you may paste an object in InDesign. Generally, it's best to use File ➤ Place to import your images. In other cases though, pasting objects might be a better choice. If you have an Adobe Illustrator file, for example, and you want to access individual objects, select the objects in Illustrator and choose Edit ➤ Copy. Open InDesign and choose Edit ➤ Paste. When you paste Illustrator art, you can select each element individually and you can change attributes such as fills, strokes, and transformations (see Figure 2-20).

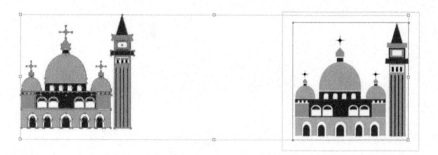

Figure 2-20. *Pasted Illustrator artwork (left) and placed Illustrator artwork (right)*

If you place an Illustrator file in InDesign, the contents are grouped and you can't ungroup the artwork in InDesign to isolate and change attributes of individual objects.

2.10   Using Find/Change

InDesign has one of the best Find/Change tools of any software program. Finding a word and changing it to another word is straightforward, and it doesn't need much explanation. However, the Find/Change dialog box in InDesign offers you much more than finding words. You can also find and change items such as whitespace, line breaks, carriage returns, metadata and other variables, symbols and markers, and much more. In addition, InDesign allows you to search and replace GREP patterns and styles.

2.10.1   Changing Type Formatting

Assume that you added some line breaks in a document (Shift+Enter/Return) instead of carriage returns (Enter/Return). Reflowable EPUBs can't interpret line breaks like other kinds of documents, and you want to avoid using them.

If you want to replace line breaks with carriage returns, open Find/Change by choosing Edit ➤ Find/Change. In the Find/Change dialog box, click the @ symbol to the right of the text box in Find What. Select Forced Line Break, as shown in Figure 2-21.

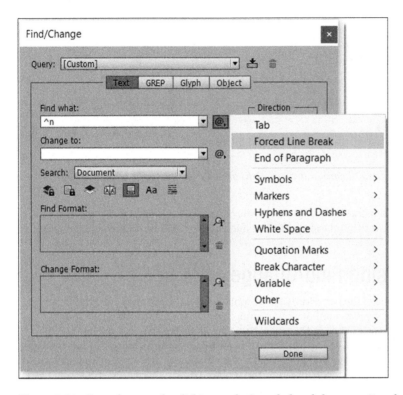

Figure 2-21. *Open the menu by clicking on the @ symbol and choose an item for finding the type formatting*

In the Change To area, click the @ symbol and choose End of Paragraph. If you want to replace all instances in the entire document, choose Document from the Search menu. Click Change All on the right side of the panel, and InDesign changes all instances of line breaks to carriage returns.

2.10.2   Searching GREP Patterns

GREP stands for *globally search* a *regular expression* and *print*. In the Find/Change window, you see a tab for GREP. When you search using this tab, InDesign searches for patterns and expressions.

Suppose that you added fractions in a layout using superscripts and subscripts. You want to change the fractions to glyphs from a font that supports fractions. In the Find/Change window in the GREP tab, you can search for all fractions where superscripts and subscripts have been used.

In the Find What text box, type: \d+/\d+ (see Figure 2-22).

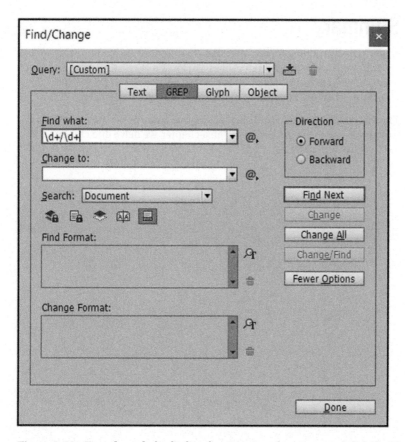

Figure 2-22. *Type the code for finding fractions in a document and click the Find Next button*

This simple line of code will find any fraction within your document. Click the Find Next button, and InDesign offers the first occurrence of the searched expression.

There are many different GREP codes available to you on the Internet. Just search for GREP patterns, and you'll find a number of expressions that you can use in InDesign. For more information on using GREP, see Chapter 6.

2.10.3   Saving Queries

At the top of the Find/Change dialog box you see Query. Click the default item to open the menu, and you will find some searches that have been saved as presets. When you perform searches and you use a given search many times, add the search to create a new query.

Click the Save Query button to the left of the Trash icon, and the Save Query dialog box opens. Type a name and click OK. Your newly-saved query now appears as a menu choice in the Query menu.

2.11 Summary

In this chapter, we looked at setting up the InDesign environment and customizing tools and features for your individual design preferences. We looked at creating color and font palettes, creating grids and folios, and how to use the Layers Panel. You learned how to import assets, perform searches, and how to find/change text and formatting.

You should view this chapter as a general introduction into some of the important tasks that you need to perform using InDesign. In the next chapter, we delve into creating documents and how to format text.

PART II

■ ■ ■

Creating Documents in Adobe InDesign

CHAPTER 3

Formatting Text

All publications, both for print and digital publishing, contain text as well as graphics. Text is critical for any document intended for viewing as printed material or on any device. The appearance and design of the text is equally important as the overall physical layout and appearance of a publication. Quite simply, you just can't go anywhere in InDesign without adding text to your document pages.

When it comes to handling text, InDesign is a powerhouse. You can layout text and format it in just about every imaginable way. And InDesign provides you with an abundant set of tools and commands, all designed to help you set type and achieve a typesetting masterpiece.

In this chapter, we explore the many ways that you can set type and how to manage and format it. Along with managing and formatting text in your documents, you'll need to know much about creating styles for characters and paragraphs. These are essential for any document that you create. I'll cover styles in Chapter 6. For now, let's look at some of the essential things that you need to know about setting type in InDesign.

3.1   Using Text Frames

The first thing to understand about type in InDesign is that all text lives in a text frame. If you select the Type tool in the Tools Panel and click on a document page, nothing happens. InDesign requires a text frame. Unlike word processing programs, text editors, illustration programs such as Adobe Illustrator, and image editing programs like Adobe Photoshop, where you click a type tool and the cursor starts blinking ready for you to type text, InDesign behaves differently. InDesign needs a text frame that you create or that InDesign creates for you, depending on how you add text to a document.

3.1.1   Creating Text Frames

To add text to a document, you need either to create a text frame or import text, in which case InDesign creates the text frame for you. If you begin with a new document and want to add text, there are several ways to create text frames.

© Ted Padova 2017
T. Padova, *Adobe InDesign Interactive Digital Publishing*,
DOI 10.1007/978-1-4842-2439-7_3

- *Create a text frame:* Use the Type tool and click and drag to open a rectangle. This action creates a text frame. When you release the mouse button, the familiar blinking cursor appears by default at the top-left corner of the frame.

- *Create a frame:* Select the Rectangle Frame, Ellipse Frame, or Polygon Frame tool in the Tools Panel and draw a frame. Click the Type tool in the Tools Panel and click inside the frame. The Frame now becomes a text frame.

- *Create a shape:* Click the Rectangle, Ellipse, or Polygon tool and create a shape. Click the Type tool in the Tools Panel and click on the shape. The frame is now a text frame.

- *Create a line:* Use the Line tool or the Pen tool and create a line. Click and hold the mouse button down on the Type tool in the Tools Panel to reveal the pop-up Type toolbar, choose the Type on a Path tool, and type text.

- *Paste text in a document:* Take any text that you copy in another program and choose Edit ➤ Paste (Ctrl/⌘+V). This action pastes the clipboard contents in the InDesign document. When pasted, InDesign creates a text frame containing the pasted text.

- *Import text:* When you choose File ➤ Place and select a text file, the text is imported and InDesign creates a text frame.

3.1.2   Understanding the Anatomy of a Text Frame

Text frames have several common attributes with which you should become familiar when adding text to your publications. As shown in Figure 3-1, these include the following:

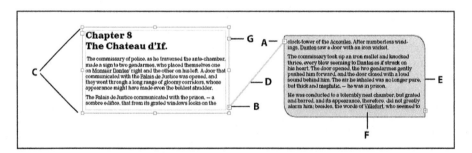

Figure 3-1. *Two selected text frames*

A.   *Inports:* The inports show you, by the appearance of the small square in the top-left corner of the frame, if text is threaded or if the text passage is the beginning of a thread. The frame on the left side of Figure 3-1 shows an empty square. This indicates no text is threaded at the beginning of the frame. In other words, the frame shows you that the text is the beginning of a passage. On the right you see the Inport showing a tiny arrowhead indicating that a text frame precedes the text. In other words, the second frame is a continuation of a passage.

B.   *Outports:* The square at the lower-right side of the text frame is the outport. This shows you either the end of a passage of text or if more text is threaded to another text frame. In Figure 3-1, you see an arrowhead on the left and a + symbol on the right outports. The arrowhead indicates that the passage is threaded to another text frame, and the + symbol indicates that there is more text in the passage that has not yet been placed in the document. This is commonly called *overset text.* Anytime you see a + symbol in a text frame, InDesign informs you that there is more text in the passage. When you export to PDF or preflight a file, InDesign informs you in an error dialog box that the document contains overset text.

C.   *Handles:* When you select a text frame, handles appear at the corners and midpoints along the sides of the frame. Click and drag a handle using the Selection tool to resize the frame.

D.   *Thread lines:* You can turn on and off the lines that show text threads by choosing View ➤ Extras ➤ Show(Hide) Text Threads. The text thread lines show you the linking order of the text frames and how the frames are linked together.

E.   *Strokes:* The text frame on the left in Figure 3-1 shows a frame with no border. On the right you see a frame with a border. You can add a border around a text frame by making choices in the Strokes Panel.

F.   *Fills:* Text frames can be filled like any other object. Select the frame and open the Swatches or Color Panel. Click a color with the frame selected, and the frame is filled with the selected color.

G.   *Corner adjustment:* The little yellow box on the right side of the text frame is used to change corner options. Click the yellow box and four yellow diamonds appear on the frame. Click and drag a diamond left or right to make a corner adjustment to all four corners. Press the Shift key and drag to adjust a single corner.

3.1.3   Using Text Frame Options

When you select the Type tool in the Tools Panel and click inside a text frame containing text, you see the familiar blinking cursor. Click and drag and you can select text. Type on your keyboard and you can add text to the frame.

If you choose the Selection tool and click a frame, the frame is interpreted as an object. If you want to change attributes for text, use the Type tool and click in the text frame. You then choose options from the Type menu. If you want to change attributes for the frame, you again switch to the Selection tool and click the frame. As an object, you find options in the Object menu. Once you select a frame, choose Object ➤ Text Frame Options. The Text Frame Options dialog box opens, as shown in Figure 3-2.

■ **Tip**   Double-click a text frame with the Selection arrow tool and the tool changes to the Type tool, where you can select text or type new text in the frame.

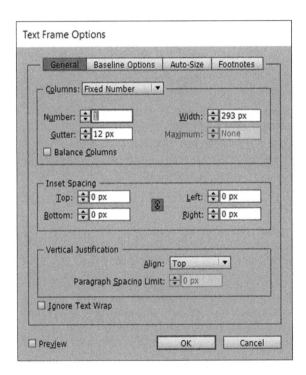

Figure 3-2. *Select a text frame with the Selection tool and choose Object ➤ Text Frame Options*

In the Text Frame Options dialog box, you can divide the frame into multiple columns by changing the Number from the default 1 column to any number you desire. You can change the gutter (space between columns) by typing new values in the Gutter text box.

■ **Caution**   Text frames with multiple columns will revert to single columns when exported to reflowable EPUBs.

If you want to create some space between the text and the frame (something like a padding setting) edit the Inset text box. The link icon in the Inset area is used to set the inset values evenly on all sides when the link is active. If you want to adjust each side differently, click the link so that the icon appears as a broken chain and set each side individually.

To align text vertically in a frame, choose options from the Align menu. If you want to avoid having overset text when you resize the text frame, click the Auto-Size option in the Text Frame Options dialog box. Options you have for auto-sizing are shown in the menu in Figure 3-3.

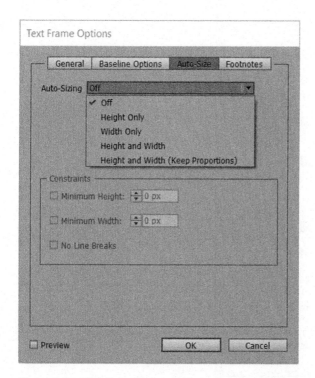

Figure 3-3. Click Auto-Size and choose an option from the Auto-Sizing menu

When you adjust the handles and resize the text frame, or edit the text, the frame snaps to a size that accommodates all of the text in the frame. In other words, you won't be able to size the frame lower than a size that can display all of the text.

3.2   Using the Character Panel

Like so many things in InDesign, you have several ways to change attributes. The same holds true for changing options for setting type. For example, you select fonts by opening the Type menu and choosing the desired font. The Font menu shows you all of the fonts accessible in InDesign. You can also open the Fonts menu in the Control Panel. The third way to choose a font is by opening the Font menu in the Character Panel, as shown in Figure 3-4.

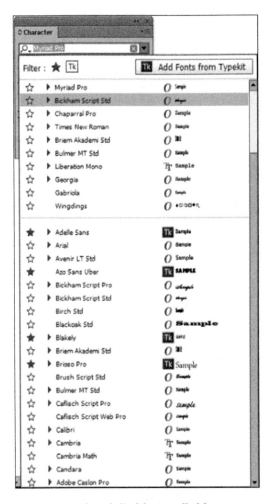

Figure 3-4. *A list of all of the installed fonts in your system appears in the Character Panel Font menu*

The difference between using the Type ➤ Font menu and the other two methods is that both the Control Panel and Character Panel provide you with the option for filtering fonts. If you click the Tk icon in either the Control Panel or the Character Panel, only Typekit fonts are shown (see Figure 3-5). Click again and you see all of the fonts loaded in your system.

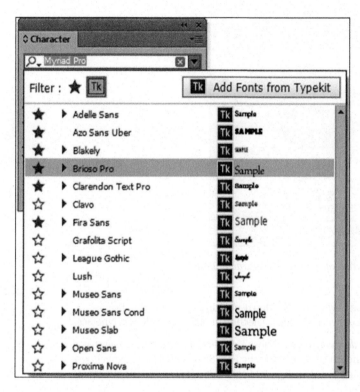

Figure 3-5. *Click the Tk icon and only Typekit fonts are shown in the menu*

The Control Panel and Character Panel offer many identical choices. Feel free to use the one that works well for you. When you select the Type tool, notice in the Control Panel that you have two icons at the top left—the A character and a ¶ (pilcrow) symbol. Click the A character and the palette changes displaying options for character attributes. Click the pilcrow ¶ and the Control Panel changes displaying options for paragraph attributes.

■ **Tip**   The Control Panel is a quick and easy way to access tools for characters and paragraphs. Get familiar with its options and use it frequently. Setting options in the Control Panel is much faster than using menu commands.

3.2.1   Using Character Panel Options

The basic typesetting options that you find in the Character Panel (shown in Figure 3-6) and the Control Panel include the following:

Figure 3-6. *Typesetting options in the Character Panel*

- *Typeface menu:* Click the down-pointing arrow to open the Typeface menu. Making a selection in this menu selects a typeface.

- *Font Style menu:* If you choose Helvetica in the Typeface menu, you select the entire typeface. In the Font Style menu, you might choose something like Helvetica Bold, which is a font within the Helvetica typeface.

- *Font size:* Choose the point size for the selected font.

- *Leading:* Leading represents the distance between the baseline of one line of text and the baseline of the next line of text. When you choose Auto, the leading will be 120% of the font size (or two points larger than the font size). You can choose other values to increase or decrease the leading.

- *Kerning:* Kerning is the distance between characters. Many fonts have kerning pairs built into the fonts. For example, when you type a Ty, Wa, Ke, Va, and similar characters, the second character in each pair is tucked under the capital letters. You also have a choice for Optical and Metrics. If you choose Optical, the kerning is tightened up just a bit.

- *Tracking:* This setting is the distance between all characters in a selection, a line of type, a paragraph, or a passage depending on what text you select when you change the tracking. You can bring all of the characters closer together or farther apart by choosing values in the menu or by typing custom values in the text box.

- *Vertical Scale:* Used for scaling the text vertically.

- *Horizontal Scale:* Used for scaling type horizontally.

- *Baseline Shift:* You can shift the text above or below the baseline by clicking the arrows or by typing values in the text box.

- *Skew:* Using this option will artificially italicize type.

- *Language:* From the Language menu, choose a language to be used for spell checking and hyphenation.

SCALING AND SKEWING TYPE

Sometimes you may be tempted to use the Horizontal and Vertical scaling or the Skew option in the Character Panel. My advice is *NEVER* use these controls.

Typography is much more than graphic design or illustration with some text thrown in. Typefaces are carefully crafted pieces of artwork with precise detail as to character sizes, widths, x-heights, ascenders and descenders, and so forth. A type designer spends a lot of time creating a new typeface, and much attention is paid to how the characters appear together in size and form.

When you scale or skew type, it's like throwing some paint on a Picasso or Kandinsky painting.

3.2.2   Using the Character Panel Menu

Like other panels in InDesign, the Character Panel has a menu where you can choose more options. Click the menu icon (top-right corner) in the Character Panel and the menu opens, as shown in Figure 3-7.

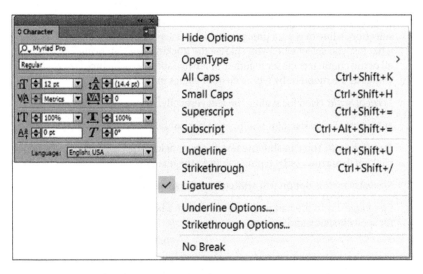

Figure 3-7. *Click the menu icon in the Character Panel to open the menu*

The menu offers you choices for All Caps, Small Caps, Superscript/Subscript, Underline, Strikethrough, using *Ligatures* (character pairs such as fl, fi, ffi, and so forth where the combination of characters is a single character itself), and some options for formatting Underline and Strikethrough. When applied to selected text, No Break will not break a word. This is useful for keeping certain word pairs together, preventing long URLs from wrapping, or preventing hyphenation in a specific word.

The other menu item in the Character Panel menu is OpenType. The options for OpenType fonts are shown when you select the OpenType command in the Character Panel menu. As you can see in Figure 3-8, you have many choices when using OpenType fonts. I won't explain each of these choices here. To become familiar with the options, play a little with OpenType fonts and see the results. Many of the options are self-descriptive.

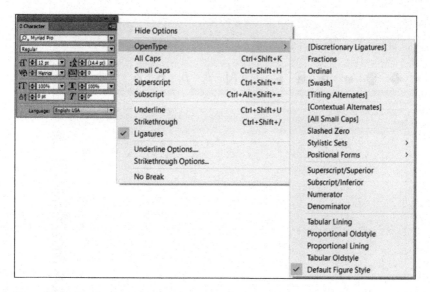

Figure 3-8. *You have many more options when using OpenType fonts*

As a general rule, avoid typing text in all caps. Instead, if you want a subhead to display as all caps, for example, type the subhead in lowercase and use the All Caps command instead.

3.3   Using the Glyphs Panel

A *glyph* is an individual character in a given font. The number of different glyphs within a font is dependent upon the type of font you use. For OpenType fonts, you have standard fonts with a more limited set of characters. You also have Pro fonts that offer you many more glyphs. If you want to choose from a number of different special characters, use a Pro font like Clarendon Text Pro, Adobe Caslon Pro, Myriad Pro, Minion Pro, Warnock Pro, or any other font where the word Pro is part of the font name.

To see all of the characters in a font, open the Glyphs Panel by choosing Window ➤ Type & Tables ➤ Glyphs, or open the Type menu and choose Glyphs. If the Glyphs Panel is part of your workspace, click Glyphs in the Panel Dock. The Glyphs Panel opens, as shown in Figure 3-9.

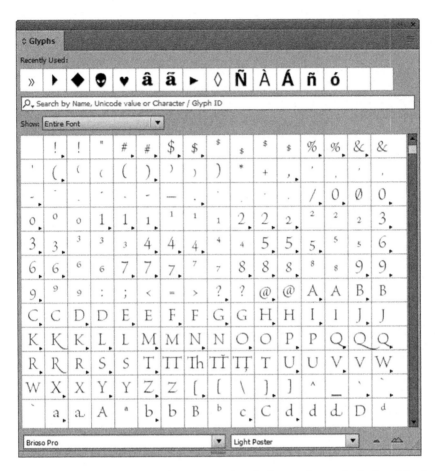

Figure 3-9. Choose Type ➤ Glyphs or click the Glyphs Panel name in the Panel Dock to open the Glyphs Panel

The current active font is displayed in the Glyphs Panel. If you want to change the font, open the Font menu at the bottom left of the panel. From the Show menu, you can choose to display the Entire Font or make a menu choice for a number of different options, such as Math Symbols, Currency, Proportional Figures, Small Caps, and much more. Making a choice in the menu narrows down the display so that you can easily target special characters in the selected font.

In the lower-right corner of the Glyphs Panel, you have options for zooming in or out of the characters. If the characters appear too small and it's hard to see them, click the Zoom In icon (represented by the two large mountain peaks icon).

Let's say that you want to add a character that you want for a bullet in a bulleted list. Choose Symbols from the Show menu, and the display is reduced to show you only the symbol characters in the font. Locate the symbol you want to use and double-click it. The symbol is added to the current cursor location in your document, and it also appears in the Recently Used bar along the top of the Glyphs Panel, as shown in Figure 3-10.

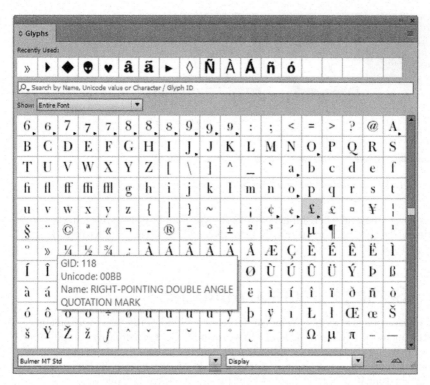

Figure 3-10. *Double-click a character to insert it at the cursor location, and the character is automatically added to the Recently Used list*

By using the Glyphs Panel, you don't need to memorize keystrokes to type characters like trademarks, copyright symbols, and any other special characters that you need when setting type.

3.4   Adding Strokes to Characters

I won't say that you should never add strokes to characters. In fact, in some cases, adding strokes can work quite well. An example of some beautiful typography where several strokes are applied to characters is the *Sports Illustrated* masthead. When the masthead was created, the artists for *Sports Illustrated* needed to come up with a masthead that could be used with any kind of photo for the cover. Since the sports coverage included nighttime sporting events, skiing on white slopes, photo shoots at dawn and dusk, and so on, the masthead had to be seen on backgrounds of all shades and colors.

The traditional masthead was type with a white fill. The type had a large medium gray stroke, a thin black stroke, a heavy black drop shadow, and a soft black drop shadow. Several strokes and drop shadows were applied. The end result was a beautifully designed masthead that contrasted well with any photo for the cover (see Figure 3-11).

Figure 3-11. *Strokes added to a character that contrasts with any color background*

What you want to avoid when applying strokes to type is adding heavy black strokes or ornamental designs that don't do anything for the characters. The golden rule is "keep it simple and elegant."

3.5   Setting Paragraph Attributes

So far we have looked at formatting individual characters and words. Let's move on and review the many options with which InDesign provides us for formatting paragraphs. You can use the Paragraph Panel to set options for Paragraph formatting, and you can also use the Control Panel to make a number of the same choices as you have in the Paragraph Panel. When using the Control Panel, click the Paragraph (¶) symbol (pilcrow).

3.5.1   Using the Paragraph Panel

If the Paragraph Panel is part of your workspace, click Paragraph in the Panel Dock. If you don't see the Paragraph Panel, choose Window ➤ Type & Tables ➤ Paragraph, and the Paragraph Panel opens, as shown in Figure 3-12.

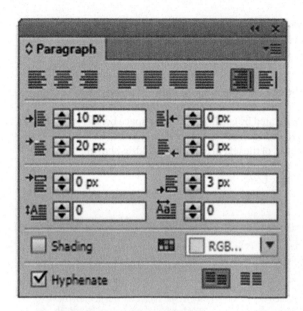

Figure 3-12. Click Paragraph in the Panel Dock, or choose Window ➤ Type & Tables ➤ *Paragraph, to open the Paragraph Panel*

Options that you will find in the Paragraph Panel include:

- *Alignment:* Across the top row, you will find options for a range of alignment functions. The first three are left, center, and right alignment. The next four are various alignment options that you have for justified text. The last two are alignment towards the spine (left and right).

- *Left Indent:* The entire paragraph is indented according to the value you add to the text box.

- *Right Indent:* Indents the paragraph from the right.

- *First Line Left Indent:* Indents the first line in a paragraph.

- *Last Line Right Indent:* Indents the last line in a paragraph to the right.

- *Space Before:* Adds space before a paragraph.

- *Space After:* Adds space after a paragraph.

- *Drop Cap Number of Lines:* Sets the number of lines for a drop cap.

- *Drop Cap One or More Characters:* If you want to use a whole word or several characters for a drop cap, enter the number in the text box and be sure that you set the number of lines (see "Drop Cap Number of Lines").

- *Shading:* Check the box for Shading to shade individual paragraphs with a color. Choose a color from the drop-down menu. If you have several paragraphs separated by carriage returns or space before/after, only the text area shows shading, as shown in Figure 3-13 on the left. If you want all of the text in a frame shaded, as shown in Figure 3-13 on the right, you need to make adjustments in the Paragraph Shading dialog box.

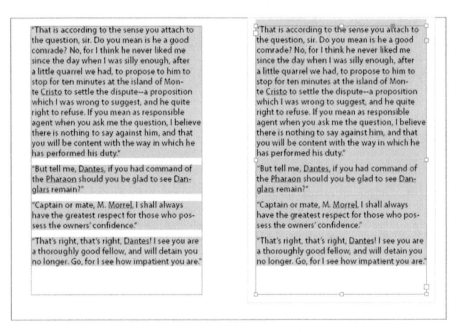

Figure 3-13. *Default Paragraph Shading (left) and Paragraph Shading as edited in the Paragraph Shading dialog box*

- To open the Paragraph Shading dialog box, choose Paragraph Shading from the Paragraph Panel menu. The Paragraph Shading dialog box opens, as shown in Figure 3-14. To continue the shading in the text frame shown in Figure 3-14, first click the chain icon to break the link for the left, right, top, and bottom settings. Add the amount in the Top text box to cover the distance between the paragraphs. In my example, the space after the first paragraph is set to 14 points; therefore, 14 points in the Top text box covers the gap adequately.

- While in the Paragraph Shading dialog box, move the dialog adjacent to the text frame you edit and check Preview. After making an edit, press the Tab key to preview the results (see Figure 3-14).

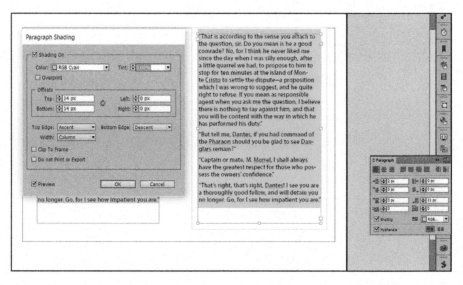

Figure 3-14. *Make edits in the Paragraph Shading dialog box and check Preview*

- *Hyphenate:* Enable the Hyphenate check box to apply hyphenation.

- *Alignment to baseline grid:* Clicking the first icon turns off alignment to the baseline grid. Clicking the second icon turns alignment to the baseline grid on. Grids and Guides are set in the InDesign Preferences. If you need to change the gridline subdivisions, press ⌥/Alt and click on one of the icons. The Grids preference options open in the Preferences dialog box. Make adjustments here, and click OK to change the grid size.

3.5.2   Using the Paragraph Panel Menu

Just as the Character Panel offers you a wealth of options for character settings, the Paragraph Panel provides you with yet another set of choices for formatting paragraphs, as shown in Figure 3-15.

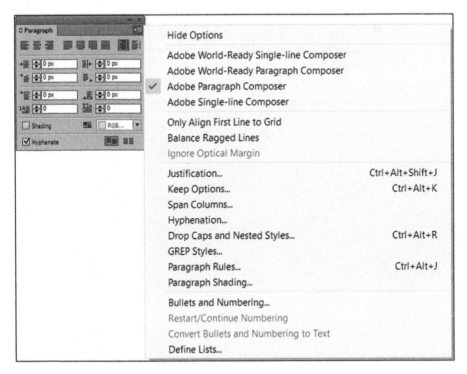

Figure 3-15. Click the icon in the top-right corner of the Paragraph Panel to open the panel menu

Once again, I won't explain all of the options that you have in the panel. Consult the Adobe InDesign Help documents to delve into the various options. Some of the more frequent settings with which you might work include Span Columns, Paragraph Rules, and Bullets and Numbering.

When choosing one of the options, InDesign opens a dialog box where you make choices for how you want a given setting represented. For Span Columns, you can choose single, multiple, or split columns in the Span Columns dialog box. For Paragraph Rules, you have choices for setting rules above and/or below a paragraph, specifying line styles and weight, line color, and the distance you want the rules to appear relative to the paragraph. For Bullets and Numbering, you make choices for choosing either a bullet or a number (for numbered lists), characters, and alignment.

The typesetting options you have for both character and paragraph formatting are enormous. Most people don't use all that InDesign provides for you. People tend to pick and choose the options consistent with the kind of work they do. If you're new to InDesign, become familiar with the two panels and the Control Panel, and use the options you need. As you become more sophisticated in your work, explore additional features that help you save time and make your production more efficient.

3.6 Creating Type on a Path

In the Tools Panel, you have two Type tools. The default tool is the Type tool. If you click the Type tool in the Tools Panel and hold the mouse button down, a pop-up toolbar opens and you can see both tools. The second tool is the Type on a Path tool. You use this tool to add type on a path.

A path can be any path that you draw with the Pen tool or the line tool as well as any of the shapes that you can draw with the Shape tools. You can add type to ellipses, rectangles, polygons, other shapes, and free form lines.

In Figure 3-16, you see a few examples of type on a path. When you click a path with the Type on a Path tool, the I-beam cursor starts blinking at the location where you clicked. Type text and the text follows the path.

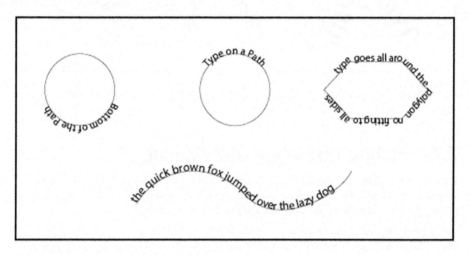

Figure 3-16. *Some examples of type on a path*

You can change some options when using Type on a Path. Select the path and choose Type ➤ Type on a Path ➤ Options to open the Type on a Path Options dialog box.

The default effect is Rainbow. You can choose other options such as Skew, 3D Ribbon, Stair Step, and Gravity. When you change the effect, you see many different results, as shown in Figure 3-17. You also have control over where the type appears relative to the baseline. The default is aligning to the Baseline. You can also choose to align to Ascender, Descender, and Center and make choices in the adjacent To Path menu for Top, Bottom, and Center. The Spacing text box enables you to adjust the character spacing.

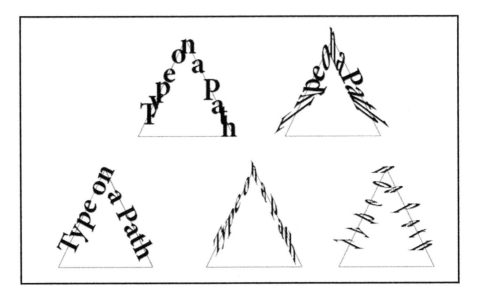

Figure 3-17. *Open the Type on a Path Options dialog box to refine the type relative to the shape*

3.7 Editing Text in the Story Editor

InDesign's Story Editor is like having a word processor inside InDesign. The Story Editor is very simple compared to word processing programs, but it is very powerful and enables you to stay in InDesign without having to exit the program to edit text.

One useful purpose of the Story Editor is editing text in text frames with overset text. You may want to end a text passage at a given text frame but the text is overset so you need to make some edits in order to fit the copy to the frame.

To open the Story Editor, click the Type tool in a text frame and choose Edit ➤ Edit in Story Editor or press Ctrl/⌘+Y. The Story Editor window opens on top of your InDesign document, as shown in Figure 3-18.

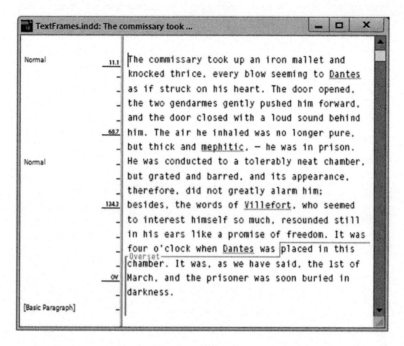

Figure 3-18. *Choose Edit ➤ Edit in Story or press Ctrl/⌘+Y to open text in the Story Editor*

As you can see in Figure 3-18, there is a horizontal line across the bottom of the Story Editor with Overset appearing on the left side of the line. The line indicates all text currently overset in the text frame.

In the Story Editor, you can cut, copy, and paste text. You also can use the Find/Change dialog box to search for text and GREP patterns and replace the text. If you right-click the mouse button inside the Story Editor, you find a number of formatting options in the menu, as shown in Figure 3-19.

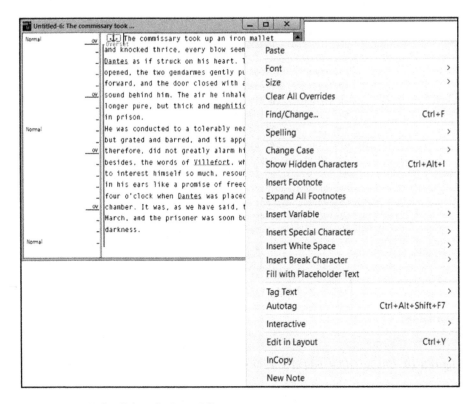

Figure 3-19. *Right-click in the Story Editor to open a context menu*

While laying out documents in InDesign, you may find the Story Editor to be very helpful, especially when you find overset text in text frames.

3.8   Creating Text Wraps

When you place objects in a linear fashion, one after another between text passages, the design can be uninteresting. In some cases, when you wrap text around an image, you create a more interesting design. You can lay out a page where the text flows and becomes part of the image creating a graphic statement, something like Figure 3-20.

Figure 3-20. *Text wrapped around an image*

3.8.1   Using the Text Wrap Panel

To wrap text around images, you need to use the Text Wrap Panel in InDesign. To access the panel, choose Window ➤ Text Wrap or press Ctrl/⌘+Alt/⌥+W. The text Wrap Panel opens, as shown in Figure 3-21.

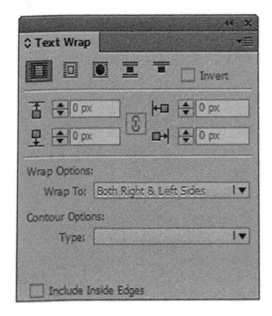

Figure 3-21. *Choose Window ➤ Text Wrap to open the Text Wrap Panel*

The important options that you find in this panel include the following:

- *No Text Wrap:* By default, you find this item selected. No text wrap is applied to the object.

- *Wrap around the bounding box:* This option wraps the text around all sides of the object.

- *Wrap around shape:* Use this option when you want the text to follow the contours of a shape.

- *Jump object:* When you choose this option, the text jumps from the top of the object to the bottom of the object. No wrap occurs on the horizontal sides.

- *Jump to next column:* The text jumps from the top of the image to the next column. The text frames need to be linked for the text to flow to the next column.

- *Offsets:* Click the Link icon to unlink the sides, or click again to link all four sides. Type values in the text boxes to offset the text from the graphic.

Tip Click in an offset text box and press the up arrow key on your keyboard to increment the values. Press the down arrow key to decrement the offset values.

- *Wrap Options:* From the drop-down menu, you can choose to wrap on the right side, the left side, both sides, toward and away from the spine, and the largest area. (If the object is placed close to one side or the other of the column, the largest area is the opposite side, hence the wrap is made to one side only.)

3.8.2   Wrapping Around Shapes

To wrap text around images and objects, you need to move through a few steps. InDesign can't detect edges for images and objects unless you set up the image properly and inform InDesign that you want to wrap around a shape.

With raster images (like Photoshop files), you can use a clipping path or just use an image on a layer with transparency. Save the file as a .psd file and import the image in InDesign. Open the Text Wrap Panel, and click the Wrap around shape icon. You probably won't see the text wrap around the shape.

The reason the text isn't wrapping is that you haven't told InDesign to detect the shape's edges. After clicking the Wrap around shape icon, open the Object drop-down menu and choose Clipping Path ➤ Options. In the Clipping Path dialog box, open the Type menu and choose Detect Edges. The text should now wrap around the shape, as you see in Figure 3-22.

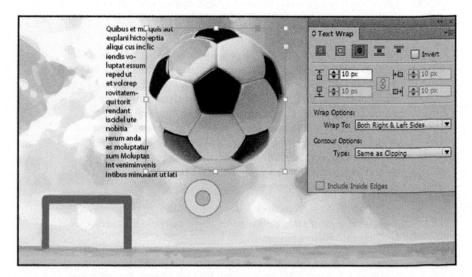

Figure 3-22. Be sure to choose Detect Edges in the Type menu when you want to wrap around a shape

Interestingly enough, if you create text outlines in InDesign such as selecting a word or character and then choose Type ➤ Create Outlines (Ctrl/⌘+Shift+O), the text character(s) is converted to an editable object. If you want to wrap text around a character converted to an object, you simply select the object and then click the Wrap around shape icon in the Text Wrap Panel.

Adobe Illustrator and other vector artwork behaves differently when imported into InDesign. When you select an imported vector object in InDesign and click the Wrap around shape icon in the Text Wrap Panel, you won't get a wrap around the shape. Again you must choose Detect Edges from the Type menu in order for the text to wrap around the shape of the image.

Just remember that if you're not getting the wrap to work as you expect, take a look at the Type menu and be certain that you have Detect Edges selected in the menu.

3.9   Running the Spell Checker

The last step in your design process before you publish a document is to check for spelling errors. I've been using Microsoft Word almost 30 years now, and I continually had problems with the spell checker in Word until I upgraded to Word 2016. With InDesign, spell checking is intuitive and easy to use.

3.9.1   Exploring Spell Checking Options

Spell checking is handled in the Edit menu. When you choose Edit ➤ Spelling, a submenu offers you four choices that include:

- *Check Spelling:* When you choose this option, the Check Spelling dialog box opens. In the Check Spelling dialog box, InDesign reports spelling errors and offers several options for editing the spelling.

- *Dynamic Spelling:* At first glance, you might think that this option corrects errors as you type. That's not what happens when you make this menu selection. InDesign displays a wavy line below words it thinks are misspelled. When the line is red, InDesign interprets the word as misspelled. When the line is green, the spelling is correct but something else is wrong. If you type a sentence with a lowercase letter at the beginning of the sentence, InDesign displays a green line if the word is spelled correctly, but the first word in a sentence should have a capital letter. Therefore, the line shows you some kind of error other than a misspelled word.

- *AutoCorrect:* When you check AutoCorrect, InDesign automatically replaces commonly misspelled and mistyped words with correct spelling while you're typing.

- *User Dictionary:* Click this menu item, and the User Dictionary dialog box opens. You can add words to your user dictionary, import words from a text file, and replace the dictionary with a new dictionary.

3.9.2   Checking Spelling Errors

Choose Edit ➤ Spelling ➤ Check Spelling to open the Check Spelling dialog box shown in Figure 3-23. The first item that you want to select in the dialog is the Search menu at the bottom of the dialog. You can choose All Documents, where InDesign will search through all of the open documents in InDesign. You can search Document, where InDesign will search through all stories in the open document. The next option is Story. When you place the cursor in a text frame and choose Story, InDesign searches through the respective story and ignores other text frames not linked to the selected frame. You can search through the End of Story. If you place the cursor in the middle of a story and choose this option, InDesign searches to the end of the story and then stops the search. The last item in the menu is Selection. If you select text in a frame and choose this option, InDesign searches only the selected text and then halts the search.

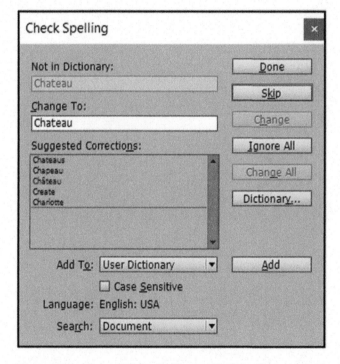

Figure 3-23. *Choose Edit ➤ Spelling ➤ Check Spelling to open the Check Spelling dialog box*

After making a choice for what to search, InDesign lists the first misspelled word in the Not in Dictionary text box. If InDesign can make a suggestion for a correct spelling, the suggestions are shown in the Suggested Corrections box. If you find an appropriate correction, click the correction suggestion in the box and the word is placed in the Change To text box. Click the Change button, and the selected word is replaced with the suggested correction. If you have several occurrences of the same word, click Change All and InDesign corrects all of the misspelled words.

If you use a foreign language word, exit out of the Check Spelling dialog box and place the cursor before the foreign language word. Click the A icon in the Control Panel to select the Character options, and choose a dictionary from the Control Panel, as shown in Figure 3-24.

Figure 3-24. *Choose the language dictionary for words respective to a given language*

Choose Edit ➤ Spelling ➤ Check Spelling to open the Check Spelling dialog box, and if the word is spelled correctly, InDesign passes the word and jumps to the next spelling error. If the word is not spelled correctly, a list of suggested corrections may appear in which case you should select the correct spelling and click Change or Change All.

3.9.3   Correcting Misspellings in the Document

If you right-click the mouse button in a text frame, a pop-up menu opens with a number of different options for changing character attributes and access to several menu commands. If you right-click on a word that is misspelled, the menu changes and offers only choices respective to spelling errors. At the top of the menu is a Suggested Correction. If the suggestion is correct, select it in the menu and InDesign changes the word to the correct spelling.

■ **Note**   In order to see misspelled words (the red wavy line below the word) in the document, you must check Edit ➤ Spelling ➤ Dynamic Spelling and you must be in Normal view (not Preview).

3.10   Summary

In this chapter, we worked with text and looked at setting type, formatting text, using various type features, and setting a variety of attributes. You learned how to choose fonts, use Adobe's Typekit, and some of the do's and don't's when setting type.

In the next chapter, we leave type formatting and look at many of the InDesign features that you have to work with when using graphics and objects.

CHAPTER 4

■ ■ ■

Working with Graphics

In Chapter 3, I talked about many of the features that you have when working with text. Believe me, Chapter 3 only touches the surface of all of the things that you can do with text in InDesign. However, after reading through Chapter 3 you should have a foundation for setting type in InDesign.

In this chapter, I talk about working with graphics that include images, objects, and all assets that are not text. Likewise, I can only scratch the surface of working with graphics in InDesign, as there is so much more to working with graphics than I can share with you here. Hopefully though, it will be enough to get you started on adding graphics to your digital publications and exploring some nifty effects.

Importing a graphic into InDesign is relatively straightforward and thus not much of a challenge. It's what you can do with these images and objects after you get them into InDesign that requires a little more study and mastery.

In this chapter, we take a look at importing graphics in your layouts, creating graphic objects in InDesign, applying color, and marvelous ways to use special effects on objects.

4.1   Importing Graphics

All graphics including images, illustrated artwork, movie files, SWF files, as well as text files and audio files are imported using the same menu command. You choose File ➤ Place to import assets in InDesign. With the exception of short passages of text and some vector art illustrations, you should always use the Place command rather than copying and pasting elements into InDesign. The only exception is when adding Adobe Illustrator artwork to a project. When you copy and paste Illustrator artwork, you have access to all of the individual paths of the Illustrator drawing. When you place Illustrator artwork, you can't break apart the illustration.

4.1.1   Placing a Single Object

When you choose File ➤ Place, the Place dialog box opens, as shown in Figure 4-1. At the bottom of the dialog box, you will find several checkboxes. Show Import Options appears on the left. When you enable this box, another dialog box opens before the object is placed. In the Import Options, you can make some choices for page range, if you

© Ted Padova 2017
T. Padova, *Adobe InDesign Interactive Digital Publishing*,
DOI 10.1007/978-1-4842-2439-7_4

intend to place a document with multiple pages such as a PDF file, image attributes, color profiles, and layers for layered documents.

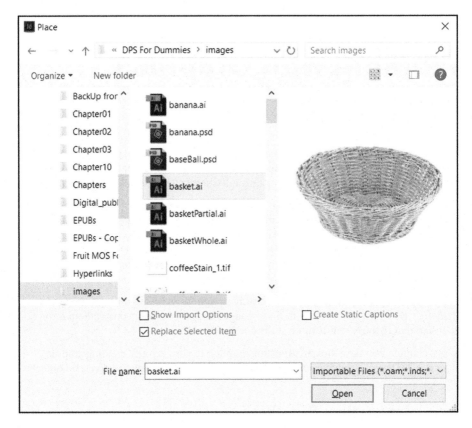

Figure 4-1. Choose File ➤ Place to open the Place dialog box

The next checkbox is Replace Selected Item. If you have an image frame selected and you choose this option, all contents of the frame are replaced with the new import. The last checkbox is Create Static Captions. Use this checkbox to add captions based on file names.

If you select Show Import options before you click Open in the Place dialog box, the Import Options dialog box opens. Depending on the file type, the options change. In Figure 4-2, I selected an Adobe Illustrator file. The options you see are relative to vector art. If you choose an image file, the options change.

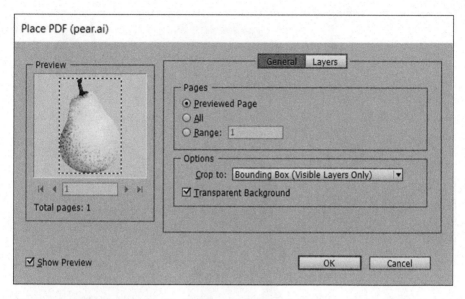

Figure 4-2. *When you click OK in the Place dialog box, the Import Options are shown in another dialog box*

Regardless of the file type, you see a preview of the file being placed. If the file appears as the one you want, click OK and the cursor is loaded with the respective object.

■ **Note** When you use the Place command and import a file, the file is placed inside a frame. Just like text, all graphics live inside frames.

4.1.2 Placing Multiple Objects

If you have several objects and you want to place them in a grid or a layout similar to a table, choose File ➤ Place. Select the objects by pressing Ctrl/⌘+click for non-contiguous selections and click Open. Drag the loaded cursor, and while the mouse button is down, press the Up Arrow key on your keyboard to create rows and the Right Arrow key to create columns. This is known as InDesign's *gridify* feature.

When the guidelines show you the number of rectangles that accommodate the number of objects that you want to import, release the mouse button and all objects are placed in frames arranged in columns and rows, as shown in Figure 4-3.

Figure 4-3. *Click and drag a loaded cursor and press the Up Arrow key for creating rows and the Right Arrow key for adding columns*

4.1.3 Fitting Objects in Frames

All objects you place in InDesign are placed inside frames. In the Control Panel you have several options for how the object fits a frame. In Figure 4-4, you see the Control Panel fitting options that include the following:

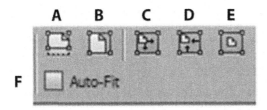

Figure 4-4. *Use the Fitting options in the Control Panel to adjust fitting options*

A. *Fill Frame Proportionally:* Click this item to fill the frame with the object, maintaining the proportions of the object. Either the width or height of the image will fill the frame, and a portion of the image may be cropped.

B. *Fit Content to Frame Proportionately:* Click this item to fit the content to the size of the frame proportionately.

C. *Fit Content to Frame:* When you click this item, the content is fit to the frame but disproportionately. You may see some distortion on the object when using this option.

D. *Fit Frame to Content:* As a matter of practice, you should use this option with most images. The frame is sized to the size of the contents. With text frames, the frame is sized to the text article in the frame. This eliminates potentially oversized frames that may get in the way of other items that you lay out on a page.

E. *Center Content:* Use this item to center the content horizontally and vertically within a frame.

F. *Auto-Fit:* Enable the box to auto fit the content to the frame. See the next section on "Resizing Objects" to understand more thoroughly how Auto-Fit can help you.

4.1.4   Resizing Objects

InDesign is the wildcard among most of the other Creative Cloud programs. In other programs, you press the Shift key and drag a handle to size objects proportionately. If you use this method in InDesign, you size the frame, not the object. If the frame is smaller than the object, you crop the object when moving handles around the frame (see Figure 4-5).

Figure 4-5. *Object Resized (left) using key modifiers or Auto-Fit (see checkbox in Control Panel) on the right, where a corner handle is moved without modifier keys or Auto-Fit enabled*

To resize an object, you can use two methods. If the Auto-Fit checkbox is disabled, press the Ctrl/⌘+Shift key and drag a handle. Be certain to press the keys on your keyboard before moving a handle.

The second method uses the Auto-Fit checkbox. If you enable the Auto-Fit checkbox, you can press the Shift key and drag a handle to resize an object. The object resizes proportionately. You need to enable Auto-Fit for each object if you want to use Shift+drag to resize objects. If you want to size several objects, press Ctrl/⌘+A to select the objects, then enable the Auto-Fit checkbox.

Once you assign Auto-Fit to an object, it remains assigned to the object. If you later want to crop an image, you need to disable the Auto-Fit checkbox and then drag a handle to crop the image inside the frame.

All edits that you make on imported images and objects are non-destructive, meaning that you won't physically change the object permanently. If, for example, you crop an image, save your file, and then open it in another editing session, you can drag out the frame and reveal the cropped area.

4.2 Applying Color to Placed Images

One of the more common uses for colorizing an image is when you want to apply color to a texture. You can find a number of royalty-free texture images on the Internet. Download the files and open them in Photoshop.

There are some rules that you need to follow in order to colorize a raster (image) in InDesign. The file must be grayscale or bitmap (all color needs to be removed from the file). The image must be saved as a flattened (single layer) .psd or .tif file.

Once you import an image, be aware that the image resides inside a frame. By default, the frame is selected when you click with the Selection tool. If you apply color, you apply color to the frame and not the image. Double-click the frame to select the image, and then you can apply color.

■ **Caution**   When you click a frame with the Selection tool, the click selects the frame. When you double-click a frame with the Selection tool, you select what's inside the frame (or the content).

To get a better understanding for how all of this works, lets walk through some steps to colorize an image in InDesign.

1. **Prepare the file in Photoshop.** If the file is an RGB image, you need to convert it to grayscale. Choose Image ➤ Mode ➤ Grayscale or use the Adjustments Panel in Photoshop and click the icon for Create a New Black and White Adjustment Layer. Then flatten the layers and save it as a .psd or .tif file.

2. **Open an InDesign file or create a new document**.

3. **Place the image in InDesign.** Choose File ➤ Place and import the image. Position the image by dragging it to the desired location. In my example, I placed a texture for a background, as shown in Figure 4-6.

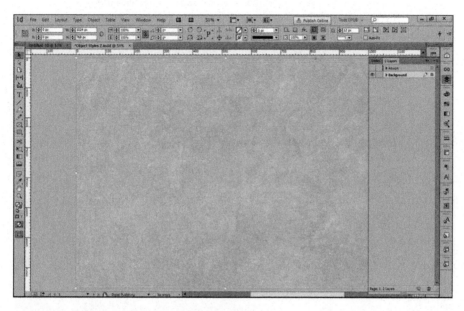

Figure 4-6. Place the image in the InDesign file

4. **Select the Eyedropper tool.** Presuming that you want to use a color applied to an object in your document, click the Eyedropper tool in the Tools Panel or press I on your keyboard. Make sure that you have the Eyedropper tool selected. In the Tools Panel, there are two Eyedropper tools. One is the Eyedropper and the other is the Color Theme tool. The Color Theme tool icon appears with a tiny set of swatches below the Eyedropper icon. If you see this tool selected, press I on your keyboard again and the eyedropper is selected. Alternately, you can click a color in the Swatches Panel.

5. **Click on an object to sample the color.** If your object is a vector file imported from a vector drawing program such as Adobe Illustrator, a warning dialog box opens informing you that the sample is based on a low-resolution proxy of the image. In most cases, you're okay sampling color in vector objects. Click OK in the dialog box, and the color appears as the new default Foreground color in the Tools Panel.

6. **Add the color to your Swatches Panel.** Right-click the
    Foreground color swatch in the Tools Panel and choose Add
    to Swatches.

7. **Apply the color to the imported grayscale image.** You
    should see the Eyedropper icon change appearance with the
    Eyedropper pointing from lower-left to lower-right. Clicking
    an object will apply the selected color. If your image is not
    selected, press the Ctrl/⌘ key and double-click the image to
    select the image and not the frame. Release the modifier key
    and the Eyedropper is still selected. Click on the image.

8. **Change the tint.** Since you added the color to your Swatches
    Panel, you can adjust the color tint. Click the new color and
    click on the Tint right-pointing arrowhead. Move the slider left
    to adjust the color tint, as shown in Figure 4-7.

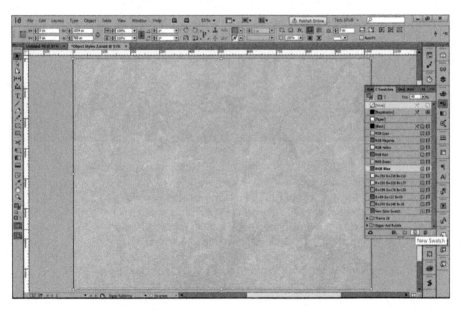

Figure 4-7. *Adjust the color tint*

▦ **Note**   When you move the cursor over a selected image, if you see the Selection Arrow,
the frame is selected. If you see the Grabber Hand icon, the image is selected. When you
apply color to an object, if the color appears opaque and much darker than you expect,
you probably applied color to the frame and not the image. Undo the step, double-click the
image to select it, and then apply the color.

4.3   Drawing Strokes

Years ago, circa the mid to late 1990s, QuarkXPress was the dominant layout program and the main tool for graphic designers and advertising agencies. Designers used the program for everything including creating logos, illustrated artwork, and drawing icons and symbols. When the files got to service bureaus for output to prepress devices, the service bureau technicians went crazy trying to print the files on their high-end devices. Layout programs of the time just weren't suited to handle the many methods designers used to add objects to their documents that looked fine onscreen but soon went awry when printed.

Software developers quickly learned that designers like to stick with one program that they know well and create everything in their program of choice. Some people created multiple page layouts in Adobe Illustrator long before we had support for multiple artboards. Some designers stayed exclusively with Adobe Photoshop when they created posters and brochures. The layout artists used their program of choice when drawing shapes and custom strokes.

As InDesign matured, Adobe offered more sophisticated methods for creating custom strokes and objects. Today, for those creating interactive digital publishing documents, you may never need to leave InDesign when you want custom buttons, fancy borders, 3D objects, perspective drawings, and objects with a variety of special effects. The tools that you find in InDesign for drawing illustrations are extensive and impressive. Moreover, all that you create in InDesign is equally suited for prepress and printing.

4.3.1   Using Stroke Tools

You can draw strokes with the Pen tool, the Pencil tool, and the Line tool. Strokes can also be applied to shapes and frames. In Figure 4-8, you can see strokes drawn with the three drawing tools, strokes applied to shapes, and strokes applied to a text frame.

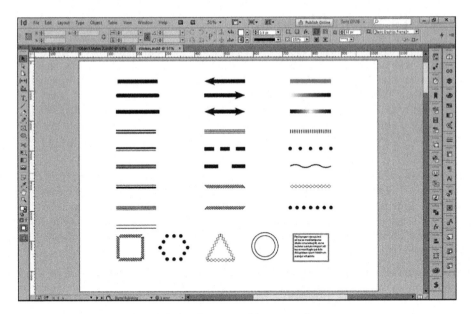

Figure 4-8. *Strokes applied to lines, shapes, and frames with text*

With objects and text, you can also add fills. The strokes appear on the outside of objects, and the fills appear inside the strokes.

4.3.2   Using the Stroke Panel

The Stroke Panel is where you can change stroke attributes. Choose Window ➤ Stroke (F10) to open the Stroke Panel, as shown in Figure 4-9.

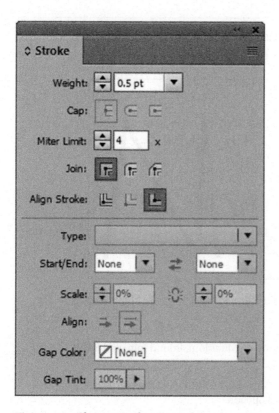

Figure 4-9. *Choose Window ➤ Stroke or press F10 to open the Stroke Panel*

The Stroke Panel offers you several options, including the following:

- *Weight*: Type a value in the text box or choose various sizes for the stroke weight from the drop-down menu.

- *Cap*: Three options exist for the end caps. You can use the default Butt cap where the stroke begins and ends at the same size as the stroke with no cap. Click the second icon for Rounded caps to apply a rounded end on the stroke. Choose the third icon for a Projecting cap where the cap extends beyond the stroke length on each side.

- *Miter Limit*: When you draw lines with the Pen tool or the Pencil tool, the line joins may appear with a Butt cap and a spike on the same path—something like what you see on the left side of Figure 4-11. If you raise the Miter Limit, you can eliminate the Butt cap, as shown on the right side of Figure 4-10. The downside of editing the Miter Limit value is that you end up with spikes of different sizes, as you can see in Figure 4-10.

▪ **Note**   You can only edit the Miter Limit when the Miter Join option is selected.

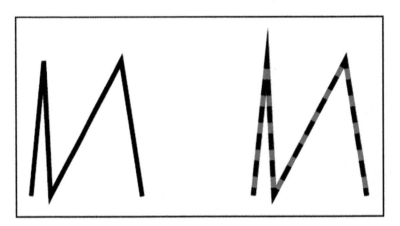

Figure 4-10. *Miter Limit set at the default 4x value (left) and the Miter Limit set to 13x (right)*

- *Joins*: The three options include Miter Join, Round Join, and Bevel Join.

- *Align Stoke*: Choose from Align Stroke to Center, Align Stroke to Inside, and Align Stroke to outside.

- *Type*: Open the drop-down menu, and you can choose from a long list of stroke styles.

- *Start/End*: Choose from different arrowheads and other start/end point options from the drop-down menus.

- *Gap Color*: On occasion, you may want a dashed line and you want to fill the gaps between the dashes with a color or a tint of the same color. This option has no effect if the stroke type is solid.

- *Gap Tint*: Change the tint value of the gap color by typing in the text box or moving the slider that appears when you click the right-pointing arrowhead.

If you find yourself using stokes in a document with the same attributes, use a document preference for the stroke. After you create a new document, don't select anything on the document page. Open the Stroke Panel and set the stroke attributes that you expect to use for strokes you draw or apply to frames. The settings become the new default (for the current open document only), and every time you draw or apply a stroke, you won't need to make other edits in the Stroke Panel.

4.3.3   Creating Custom Strokes

In Adobe Illustrator, you have the Appearance Panel where you can create an object and apply multiple strokes and/or fills to a single object. Unfortunately, InDesign doesn't have an Appearance Panel and, as of this writing, we can't match the power for handling strokes in InDesign as we can in Adobe Illustrator. The good news, however, is that we can use some workarounds and trickery to go beyond the options that you find in the Stroke Panel and create some interesting effects.

To create a new custom stroke, open the Stroke Panel menu and choose Stroke Styles. The Stroke Styles dialog box opens, as shown in Figure 4-11.

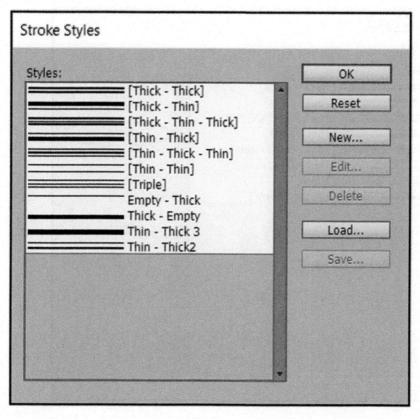

Figure 4-11. *Choose Stroke Styles from the Stroke Panel menu to open the Stroke Styles dialog box*

In the Stroke Styles dialog box, you see a number of default styles that InDesign provides for you. You can modify and edit the styles by clicking on the New button. If you don't have a style selected when you click New, InDesign adds the New Stroke Style name for a new style. If you select a style and click New, InDesign uses the style name and adds *copy* to the end of the name as shown in Figure 4-13. This ensures that you won't overwrite the default styles. The default stroke styles cannot be edited or deleted.

Below the Name field, you see the Type drop-down menu. You can choose to add a Stripe, Dotted, or Dashed stroke. If you choose a style such as Thick – Thin – Thick and click New (see Figure 4-12), you see the current style in the New Stroke Style dialog box.

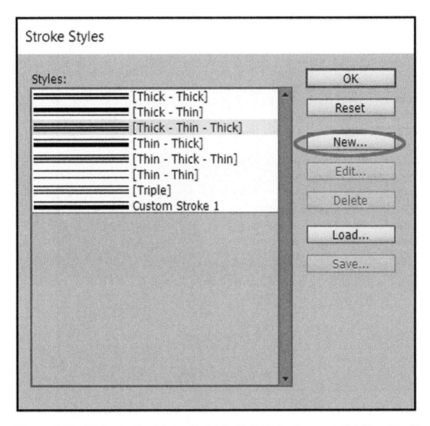

Figure 4-12. *Click a stroke style in the Stroke Style dialog box and click New. The New Stroke Style dialog box opens where you can edit the stroke style*

There are three edits that you can apply to a stroke style:

- *Delete a stroke:* Click a stroke in the Stripe preview area and drag it away from the dialog box. This deletes the stroke from the style.

- *Size a stroke:* Each stroke has a marker to the left of the stroke with a scale measuring from 0% to 100%. To size a stroke, click and drag one of the markers up or down.

- *Add a stroke:* Click the cursor in one of the gaps (between the strokes in the dialog box) to add a new stroke. Drag the marker up or down to size the new stroke.

Type a new name for the new stroke style and click OK. The new style is added to the Type drop-down menu in the Stroke Panel.

CREATING A NEW STROKE STYLE

To make this a little clearer, let's create a new stroke style by walking through the following steps:

1. **Open the Stroke Panel and choose Stroke Styles from the Stroke Panel menu.**

▓ **Note**   You don't need a document open in InDesign to create a new stroke style.

2. **Click Thick – Thin – Thick in the Stroke Styles Panel.**

3. **Click New to open the New Stroke Style dialog box.** The name InDesign adds to the new style name is *Thick – Thin – Thick copy.* In the Stripe area, you see the three strokes for this style, as shown in Figure 4-13.

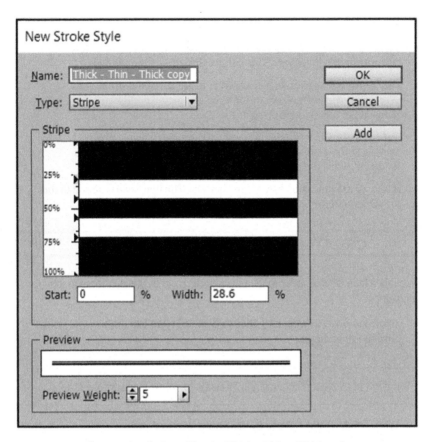

Figure 4-13. *The New Stroke Panel for the Thick – Thin – Thick style*

4. **Click the top stroke and drag it up to make the stroke thinner**.

5. **Move the bottom marker down to size the stroke smaller**.

6. **Click between the strokes to add a new stroke. Make this stroke thicker than the other two**.

7. **Add another stroke, as you can see in Figure** 4-14. Feel free to size the strokes to your liking. In my example, you see the results of the edited stroke sizes in Figure 4-14.

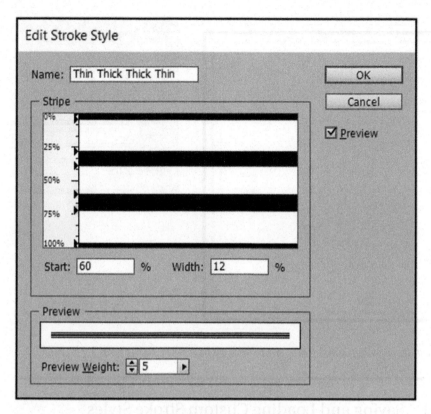

Figure 4-14. *The new style edits after sizing two strokes and adding two*

8. **Type a name for the new style and click OK**.

9. **Apply the stroke**.

10. **You can apply the stroke to a line, a frame, an object, or to type**. In my example, I applied the stroke to a frame, as shown in Figure 4-15.

11. **Apply a color to the stroke (optional)**.

12. **After applying the stroke, open the Swatches Panel and click the color that you want for the stroke color**. Be certain that Stroke is selected in the Swatches Panel when you click a color swatch. The final result is shown in Figure 4-15.

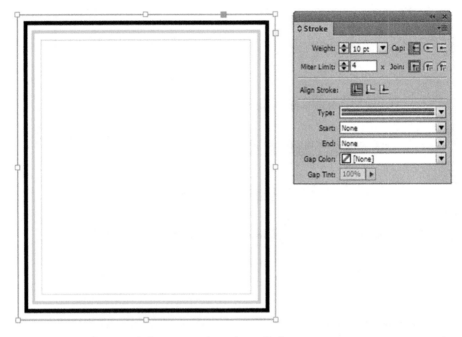

Figure 4-15. *A frame with the new Stroke Style applied*

4.3.4   Saving and Loading Custom Stroke Styles

If you create custom stroke styles when no document is open in InDesign, the custom stroke style is available to you when you create new documents. It's there until you delete it.

However, if you create a stroke style when a document is open, the stroke styles are document specific. When you close the document or create a new document, any stroke style that you added when a previous document was open is lost.

You can save stroke styles to a file and load them when you want to use your custom strokes in any document that you create in InDesign. To save a stroke style or multiple styles when a document is open, choose Stroke Styles from the Stroke Panel menu. The Stroke Style dialog box opens. You must select one or more custom strokes in the Stroke Styles dialog box in order to activate the Save button. Select a stroke and click Save.

InDesign lets you save the stroke styles anywhere on your hard drive. You can add them to a folder where you keep assets for a given design piece or save them to a root folder to use in multiple documents. When you click the Save button, the Save As dialog box opens. Type a name for the custom set, navigate your hard drive for the target location where you want to save the set, and click Save.

When you create a new document and want to use a custom stroke set, open the Stroke Styles dialog box and click Load. The Open a File dialog box opens. Navigate your hard drive and locate the custom set that you want to load. Select the set and click Open. The custom set is now available in the Stroke Panel Type menu.

Once you load a custom set of stroke styles and save a document, you don't need to load the set each time you work on the document. The stroke styles are part of the document after you save it.

4.3.5   Layering Objects with Strokes

One limitation that you have with custom stroke styles is that you cannot use more than one color for the different strokes. If you use Thick – Thin – Thick as a stroke style and click in the Swatches Panel to apply a color, all of the individual strokes accept the same color value. InDesign sees each stroke style as a single stroke. There's no way to make a choice in the Stroke Styles dialog (as of now) to apply different colors to different strokes in the same style.

The way around this problem is to create a stroke style and apply it to an object, such as a frame, and then create a duplicate copy of the object and apply a stroke with a different color.

LAYERING OBJECTS WITH STROKES

Let's take a look at how you would accomplish adding multiple strokes with different color values.

1. **Open the Stroke Panel and choose Stroke Styles from the Stroke Panel menu**.

2. **Click Thin – Thick in the Stroke Styles Panel and click New**. In my example, I want to create a Two strokes the same size but with two different colors. On the outside stroke, I want a solid black color and the inside stroke a red color. I start with the inner stroke colored red.

3. **Delete the top stroke by clicking and dragging away from the dialog box**.

4. **Set the stroke height to 50%**.

5. **Type a name and click OK**. Let's call this style *Empty - Thick*.

6. **Create a new stroke style**. I want to create a new style that's exactly the opposite of my first style. In the first style, I have one stroke at the bottom occupying 50%. Now I want to create a new style that has the bottom empty and the top with a stroke of about 10% (similar to what you see in Figure 4-16). Let's call this style *Thin – Empty*.

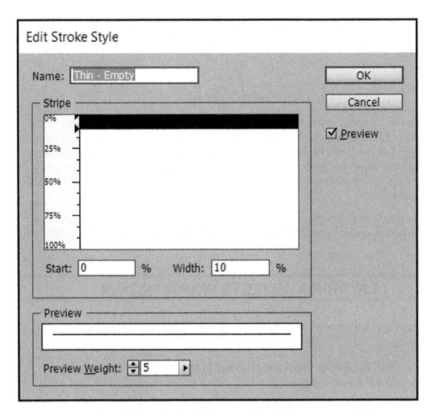

Figure 4-16. *Create a second style and name it Thin - Empty*

7. **Click OK to exit the Stroke Styles dialog box**.

8. **Apply the Empty - Thick style (the first style we created) to a frame**.

9. **Set the stroke Weight in the Stroke Panel to 20 points and set the Alignment to Align Stroke to Outside**.

10. **Apply a color from the Swatches Panel**. In my example, I used a gradient.

11. **Select the frame and choose Edit ➤ Copy (Ctrl/⌘+C)**.

12. **Choose Edit ➤ Paste in Place**. The new copy sits on top of the original frame at the same exact position on the page.

13. **Select the foreground frame and apply the Thin – Empty Stroke Style**.

14. **Set the Weight to 20 points in the Stroke Panel and set the Alignment to Align Stroke to Inside**.

15. **Choose Black in the Swatches Panel for the stroke color**.

The final result is shown in Figure 4-17.

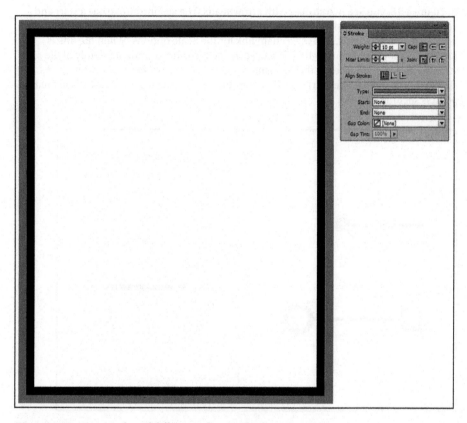

Figure 4-17. *Two strokes of different colors applied to a frame*

You can create multiple strokes by copying and pasting frames and applying different stroke colors and weights to each frame. The thing that you need to keep in mind is that the stroke styles need to be developed with strokes and empty spaces, or gaps that represent the style you want, and the stroke weights need to be the same value.

4.3.6   Sizing Arrowheads

In earlier versions of InDesign prior to InDesign CC 2017, the only way that you could size arrowheads was to size a stroke weight. Arrowheads could not be sized independently of stroke weights. Now in InDesign CC 2017, you can size arrowheads and strokes in tandem and independently.

In Figure 4-18, you see two strokes with arrowheads. The second stroke has a start and end arrowhead. Obviously, the arrowhead sizes are exaggerated to illustrate the point here. In the Stroke Panel, you see a chain link for the Scale options. When the link is broken, as shown in Figure 4-18, you can scale the arrowheads independently of the stroke weight. Type values in the corresponding text boxes to size the arrowheads. As shown in Figure 4-18, the Start arrowhead for the second line is set to 125% while the End point is set to 175%.

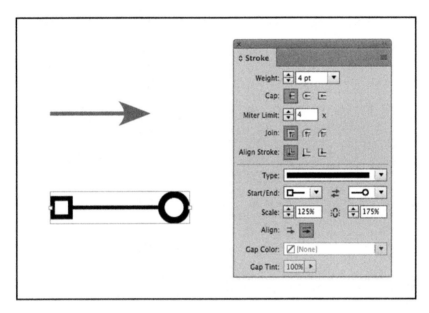

Figure 4-18. *Edit the Scale text boxes to size the arrowheads*

4.4   Drawing Objects

Thus far in this chapter we know how to draw strokes using the Line tool, the Pencil tool, and the Pen tool. Drawing strokes are a fraction of what is available to you when drawing in InDesign. You wouldn't want to create a complex technical drawing or illustration in InDesign. That type of artwork is best performed in Adobe Illustrator. However, creating buttons, icons, logos, and moderately complex shapes are all within the vast capabilities of InDesign's tools for working with objects.

4.4.1   Creating Geometric Shapes

In the Tools Panel, you have three geometric shapes available to you when you click the Rectangle tool and keep the mouse button down to open the hidden tools. Here you find the Rectangle tool, the Ellipse tool, and the Polygon tool.

To draw one of the shapes, select a shape tool in the Tools Panel and click-drag with the tool to create the shape. If you want to draw from center, press the Alt/⌥ key as you draw. If you want to constrain the shape, such as when drawing a perfect square or perfect circle, press the Shift key as you draw. If you begin drawing on a document page and you want to move the shape as you draw, press the Spacebar while the mouse button is pressed and move the shape around the page and continue drawing.

4.4.1.1   Drawing Multiple Shapes

Suppose that you want to create a grid with multiple shapes—something like a calendar design. Click a shape tool in the Tools Panel and drag out by pressing the Shift key and drag open a shape. While the mouse button and Shift key are both pressed, press the Right Arrow key to add a column. Press the Up Arrow key to add a row. Continue pressing the Right and Up Arrow keys to add more columns and rows. In Figure 4-19, you can see the multiple squares using the arrow keys for adding columns and rows.

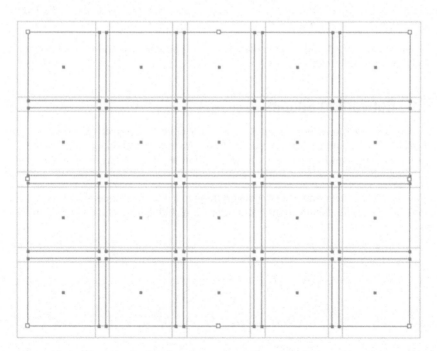

Figure 4-19. Press the Right and Up Arrow keys as you draw to create additional columns and rows

4.4.1.2   Drawing Shapes to Specific Sizes

If you want to draw shapes to a specific size, click the desired shape in the Tools Panel and click in the document. The respective tool dialog box opens. In Figure 4-20, I clicked the Polygon tool in a document and the Polygon dialog box opened.

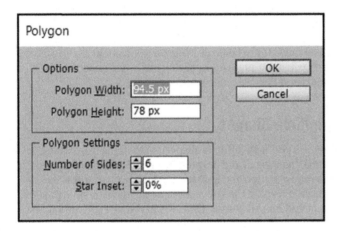

Figure 4-20. *Click a shape tool, and click on a page to open the respective shape dialog box*

Type the Width and Height values in the dialog box and click OK. The shape is created at the size determined in the shape dialog box.

4.4.1.3   Converting Shapes

You can convert shapes to different shapes by using the Object ➤ Convert Shape menu and choosing one of the nine shapes in the submenu. An easier method for converting shapes is found in the Pathfinder Panel. Choose Window ➤ Object & Layout ➤ Pathfinder to open the panel.

If you draw multiple shapes and want to convert them to a different shape, select all of the shapes and click a new shape in the Pathfinder Panel. In Figure 4-21, I converted the shapes shown in Figure 4-19 to triangles.

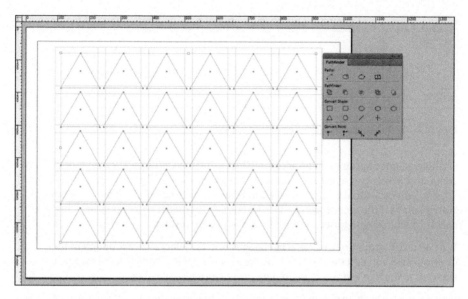

Figure 4-21. *Click one of the Convert Shape options in the Pathfinder Panel*

4.4.1.4   Editing Paths

When drawing paths with the Pen tool, you may want to join paths, close paths, or reverse paths. If you draw a geometric shape, you may want to open a path. In the Pathfinder Panel, you will find options for editing paths.

At the top of the panel, you will find four path options. The first item is Join Paths. The bottom row appears after clicking the Pathfinder paths (left to right) Join Paths, Open a Closed path, Closes an Open Path, and Changes the Direction of a Path (Reverse the Path). When using the Open a Closed Path option, you won't see the object change. InDesign breaks the path, and you need to use the Direct Selection tool to move the point where the path is broken.

4.4.1.5   Editing Corners

You can change corner options on shapes and paths using several methods. InDesign supports five different options for modifying corners. The default is None. When None is selected, the corner appears as you draw the original path. You can change a corner or multiple corners to Fancy, Bevel, Inset, Inverse Rounded, and Rounded. In Figure 4-22, you can see the results of changing corner options to each of the five options.

103

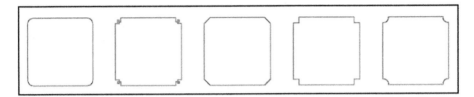

Figure 4-22. *InDesign provides five corner options*

Changing corner options can be accomplished using the Object ➤ Corner Options menu command. When you select the menu command, the Corner Options dialog box opens. You can edit individual corners or all corners and choose one of the five corner options. You can also set the amount applied to the corners to smaller or larger sizes. A Preview checkbox enables you to see a dynamic preview of the results.

You can also use the Control Panel to change corners. Select a corner option in the Control Panel and edit the size text box. Press the Alt/⌥ key and click the square icon adjacent to the size text box to open the Corner Options dialog box.

Perhaps the best way to change corner options is to make edits directly on the path. When you draw a geometric shape, you see handles at the corners and midpoints on each side. These handles are used for scaling and rotating an object. You also find a yellow square close to the top-right corner. Click the yellow square, and InDesign displays four yellow diamonds at each corner, as shown in Figure 4-23.

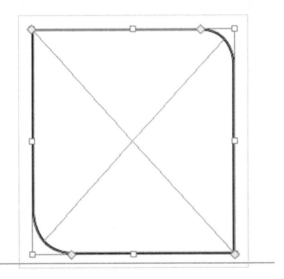

Figure 4-23. *Click the yellow square on a shape, and the corners appear with yellow diamonds*

To modify all corners, click and drag a diamond shape. The default is rounded corners. When you drag a diamond away from the corner, the shape changes to an object with rounded corners. If you want to edit a single corner, press the Shift key and drag the corner. If you want to change the corner style, press the Alt/⌥ key and click a diamond.

Editing corners using the diamonds on a shape offers you the benefit of not having to leave the object when making your edits. You'll find that using this method is faster than opening a dialog box or using the Control Panel.

4.4.2 Creating Starbursts and Ornaments

You can create starbursts and ornaments that you might use for graphic elements and buttons. As objects, you can apply strokes and fills to the items like any other object that you create in InDesign.

4.4.2.1 Creating Starbursts

When you draw a shape with the Polygon tool, you get a hexagon by default. You can change the attributes easily for polygons by double-clicking on the Polygon tool in the Tools Panel. The Polygon Settings dialog box opens, as shown in Figure 4-24.

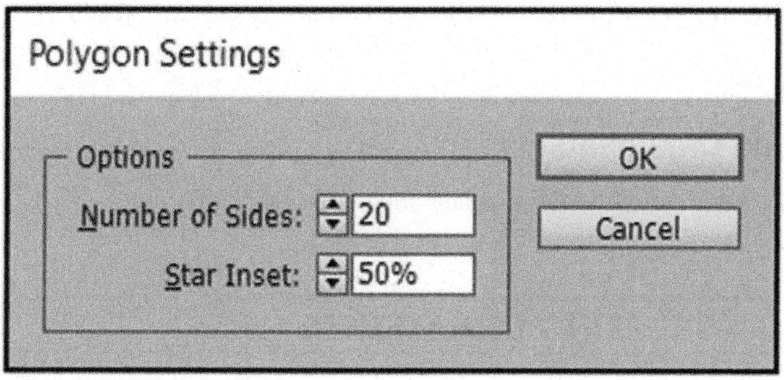

Figure 4-24. *Double-click the Polygon tool in the Tools Panel to open the Polygon Settings dialog box*

In the Polygon Settings dialog box, type a value for the number of sides. For a starburst effect, use an exaggerated number like 20. For the Star Inset value, use a large value like 50%. This setting brings the center inward, which results in large spikes on the ends of the object. Click OK and apply a gradient or color to the object, as you see in Figure 4-25.

Figure 4-25. *A 20-sided polygon with a 50% inset*

The Polygon Settings dialog box doesn't have a Preview option, and you won't see a dynamic preview when you create the object. If you want to change the appearance and add more sides or change the inset, double-click again on the Polygon tool. The last settings you made appear in the Polygon Settings dialog box. Edit the values and click OK. If you need to refine the object, just double-click the Polygon tool again and edit the values.

4.4.2.2   Creating Ornaments

Ornaments are easily created from free-form strokes and with a little help from transformations.

CREATING ORNAMENTS

To create something like a spiral pattern, follow these steps:

1. **Click the Pencil tool and draw a short, rough shape**.

2. **You don't have to be an artist**. The beauty of the end result is that you'll create a beautiful pattern with any kind of rough shape.

3. **Transform the shape**.

4. **Click the lower-middle square at the far left of the Control Panel to set the reference point at the bottom center**. Choose Object ➤ Transform ➤ Rotate. The Rotate dialog box opens.

5. **Set the transformation angle**.

6. **You can type any number in the Angle text box**. Just make sure that the value is equally divided into 360. For my example, I use 10°. Click Copy to create a copy of the shape rotated 10°.

7. **Transform the sequence**.

8. **Choose Object ➤ Transform Again ➤ Transform Sequence Again**. Notice that the Transform Sequence Again menu item has a keyboard shortcut. Press Ctrl/⌘+Alt/⌥+4. Keep striking the keys until the shape rotates back to the first object.

9. **Apply strokes, colors, gradients, and so forth to your liking**.

10. **In Figure 4-26, you can see the original rough shape that I drew with the Pencil tool**. The three patterns to the right of the shape show the shapes with a stroke setting and a stroke color with a gradient.

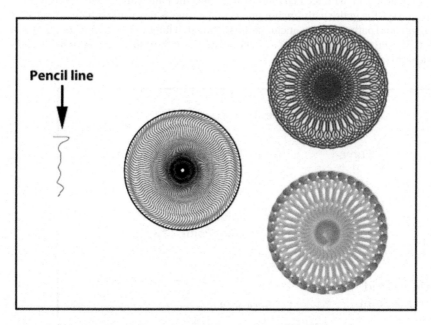

Figure 4-26. Spiral patterns are created from simple rough shapes

The marvelous thing about using these steps is that every time that you create a new free-form shape, you create a new pattern. Play with this a bit and use gradients, bevels, and emboss, as I discuss later in the section "Creating Buttons," and apply some neon effects, as I discuss later in the section "Using the Neon Effect."

■ **Tip** You can share objects that you create in InDesign with other Creative Cloud editing programs, such as Adobe Illustrator and Photoshop. Choose Window ➤ CC Libraries. Drag an object to the CC Libraries Panel. In other Creative Cloud programs, open the Library Panel and drag and drop the object in your document. You can't break apart or expand the object in other programs, but you can use the objects when you want common design elements in other program's layouts.

4.4.3   Using the Pathfinder

In the Pathfinder Panel, you find the Pathfinder options and the Convert point options. For the Pathfinder options, you need two or more objects to use the five options in the panel. For the Convert Point options, you need to select one or more points on a path to apply one of the four options.

To understand the Pathfinder options, you need to have a basic understanding of paths. When you draw a path with the Pen tool (P) and select the path with the Direct Selection tool (A), you see the entire path, anchor points (appearing as tiny white squares along a path), segments (paths between anchor points), direction lines (when an anchor point is selected), the direction point (end of a direction line), and the end point (the point at the end of a path) (see Figure 4-27).

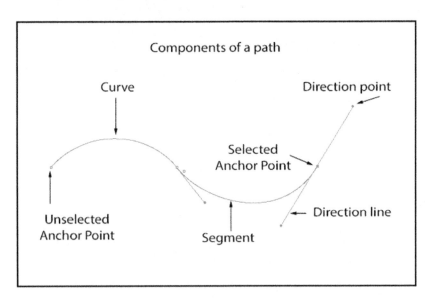

Figure 4-27. *Paths have several components*

Using the Pathfinder Panel, you can modify shapes in relation to each other. The options in the Pathfinder Panel include the following:

- *Combine:* Select two objects, click this option, and the objects unite into a single object.

- *Subtract:* This option subtracts the frontmost objects. When the objects are subtracted, the bottom objects appear as though they were punched out.

- *Intersect:* Where two objects overlap, the Intersect option deletes all of the content around the intersection.

- *Exclude Overlap:* The area where the objects intersect is deleted from the objects.

- *Minus Back:* This item is opposite of Subtract. The backmost object is deleted.

In Figure 4-28, you can see the results of using each of the Pathfinder options.

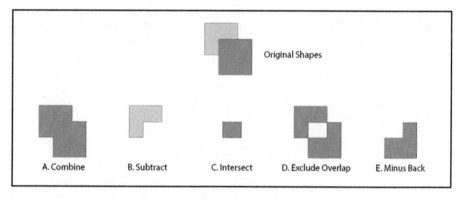

Figure 4-28. *Five options are available for the Pathfinder options*

4.4.3.1   Using the Convert Point Options

The four options that you find in the Pathfinder Panel for Convert Point include the following:

- *Plain:* Select points on a path and click this option to eliminate direction lines.

- *Corner:* By default, direction lines have two halves (or sides). When you move a direction point, both halves/sides of the direction line move. You can divide the direction line so that only one half/side of the line moves independent of the other. Select a point on a curved path and click this tool. The anchor point changes to independent direction lines.

- *Smooth:* Select a corner point (having no direction lines), click this option, and you convert the point to a smooth point with direction lines.

- *Symmetrical:* Changes selected points to smooth points with direction lines.

4.4.4   Using Scripts

There are several scripts that support drawing objects in InDesign. To view the scripts, open the Scripts Panel (Window ➤ Utilities ➤ Scripts). When the Scripts Panel opens, you will find an Application folder. Drill down from Application to Samples to JavaScripts. A number of scripts are available that help you facilitate working with objects.

4.4.4.1   Adding Guides

To execute a script, double-click the script name in the Scripts Panel. Select an object and double-click the script name (AddGuides). The Add Guides dialog box opens. You can add guidelines to an object to determine the center of the object by disabling the checkboxes and only enable Horizontal Center and Vertical Center. Click OK and guidelines are added to the horizontal and vertical center of the selected object, as shown in Figure 4-29.

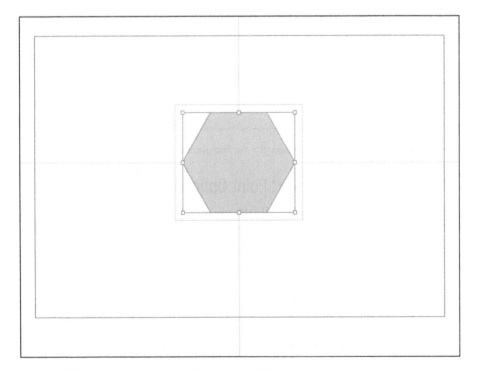

Figure 4-29. *Use the AddGuides script to add guidelines to the center of a selected object*

4.4.4.2   Adding Points

The AddPoints script adds points on a path at the midpoint of objects. Draw a shape and double-click the script name in the Scripts Panel. Anchor points are added between the existing points.

4.4.4.3   Creating Corner Effects

Select a shape and double-click the CornerEffects script. A CornerEffects dialog box opens where you can select any one of the five corner effects. You can set the Offset amount and choose to which corners you want to apply the effect.

4.4.4.4   Using the Neon Effect

Neon is a neat script. You use this effect with strokes. Draw a stroke or an object and double-click the Neon script. The Neon dialog box opens. In the Neon dialog box, you can choose the number of steps for a blend beginning with the start (defined as From), a Stroke Color, a Stroke Weight, and Stroke Tint. You can choose options for the end (To) for Stroke Weight and Stroke Tint, and choose a target layer or create a new layer for the neon effect. Click OK and the neon effect is applied to the stroke(s) of an object or paths. In Figure 4-30, you can see the results for a neon effect applied to an object and stroke.

Figure 4-30.   *Select a stroke or path and run the Neon script to create a neon effect on the stroke*

4.4.4.5   Using Path Effects

The PathEffects script provides you with a number of options to convert shapes—something like Photoshop Filters. Select a shape and double-click the PathEffects script. The PathEffects dialog box opens. You have nine choices for the type of effect that you want to create. In Figure 4-31, you see an example of the nine effects applied to a triangle, square, oval, and polygon.

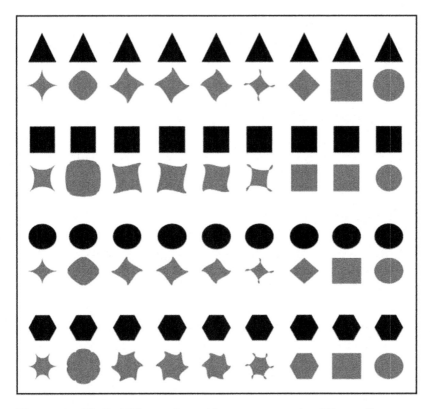

Figure 4-31. *The PathEffects script enables you to create nine different effects on a selected object*

4.5   Duplicating and Aligning Objects

Invariably, after you add an object on a page, you often want to duplicate, rotate, or skew it, and with multiple objects you often want to align or distribute objects. Fortunately, InDesign provides you with many tools and methods for accomplishing all these tasks.

4.5.1   Understanding Essentials for Transformations

Before we delve into creating transformations, there are two important things that you need to know. The first is that using the Alt/⌥ key results in duplicating an action. If you press Alt/⌥ and click and drag an object, you duplicate it. You also duplicate objects when pressing the Alt/⌥ key and clicking one of the transformation tools in the Control Panel. Try to remember that when you use the Alt/⌥ key with many actions applied to InDesign objects, you duplicate the objects.

The second thing that you need to know is that when you transform an object, the transformation is made according to the active reference point. Draw an object on a page, and take a look at the top-left side of the Control Panel. You see a square shape with tiny squares at the center, corners, and midpoints on the sides. These are reference points that you will use when transforming objects. In Figure 4-32, the active reference point is the center. Therefore, if I rotate an object, the rotation is made from the center anchor. If I click the top-left reference point, the rotation is made from the top-left anchor.

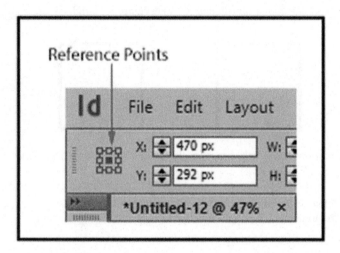

Figure 4-32. *The center square is black, indicating that the active reference point is from the center*

You are not limited to the nine options for choosing a reference point in the Control Panel. When you select a transformation tool in the Tools Panel, click anywhere on a selected object. A tiny dotted circle with four dotted lines 90° apart from each other shows you the reference point. Click again and the icon moves to the new location.

When you apply a transformation to an object, your first order of business is to select the reference point. If you want to duplicate the object while transforming it, press the Alt/⌥ key and click the transformation tool that you want.

4.5.2   Duplicating Objects

There are many ways that you can duplicate items in InDesign. The traditional Cut, Copy, and Paste, Paste in Place, and Paste Into commands are just a few of the ways that you can duplicate items. We know that when you press the Alt/⌥ key and drag an object, you also create a duplicate.

4.5.2.1   Using the Duplicate Command

Notice in the Edit menu that you have a command for Duplicate. If you duplicate
one item, let's say by Alt/⌥ dragging, then select an adjacent object and choose Edit
➤ Duplicate, the second object is duplicated and placed at the same horizontal (or
vertical) plane as the first duplication. In Figure 4-33, on the left, you see an object that I
duplicated using Alt/⌥ and dragging down vertically. When I selected the second object
in the first row and chose Edit ➤ Duplicate, the second item was duplicated and placed at
the same horizontal position as the first duplicated object (see Figure 4-33, right side).

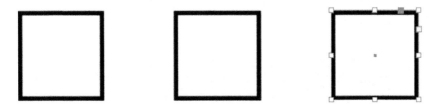

Figure 4-33. *After duplicating an object, select another object and choose Edit ➤ Duplicate*

InDesign remembers the offset value so that you can move to different pages, select
objects, and choose Edit ➤ Duplicate. The duplicate objects are positioned at the same
offset.

4.5.2.2   Using Step and Repeat

To duplicate multiple objects, you might use the Edit ➤ Step and Repeat Command.
Select an object on a page and choose Edit ➤ Step and Repeat. The Step and Repeat
dialog box opens, as shown in Figure 4-34.

In the Step and Repeat dialog box, you can duplicate objects along a column or row,
or you can create a grid with multiple columns and rows. The offset values are easily
determined when you enable the Preview checkbox. As you change offset values, you see
a dynamic preview of the result. When you create the number of duplicates that you want
with the correct offset(s), click OK.

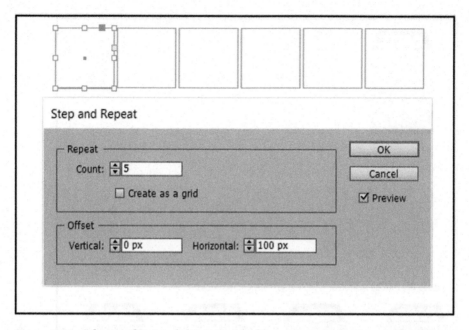

Figure 4-34. *Select an object and choose Step and Repeat to open the Step and Repeat dialog box*

4.5.2.3   Duplicating Using Modifier Keys

Click an object, press Alt/⌥, and click and drag to a new location. Release the Alt/⌥ key but keep the mouse button pressed. With your free hand, strike the Up Arrow key to create copies vertically and press the Right Arrow key to create copies horizontally (see Figure 4-35). You can strike the Up and Right Arrow keys numerous times to create a grid similar to the grid we created when using Step and Repeat.

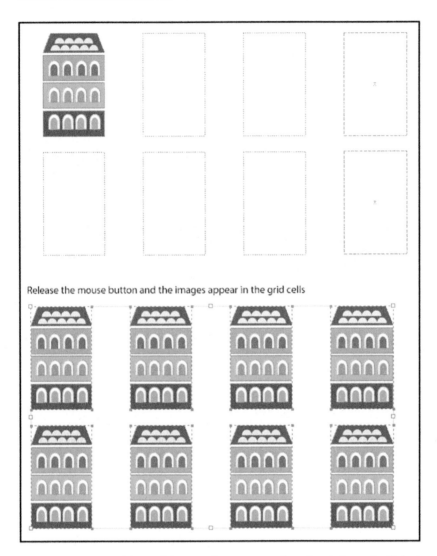

Figure 4-35. *Press Alt/⌥ and drag an object to a new location. Release the Alt/⌥ key and strike the Up and Right Arrow keys*

In InDesign terms, creating multiple objects in a grid like you see in Figure 4-35 is commonly referred to as *gridify*.

4.5.2.4   Duplicating with Precise Measurements

Suppose that you want to duplicate an object or multiple objects and have the duplicates appear 300 pixels below the original object(s). The first thing to do is to set the reference point in the Control Panel—let's say the top-left corner. Then look to the right of the reference point and you will see two text boxes. These are the X and Y Location text boxes.

To move an object down, use the Y Location text box. Move your cursor to the right and unlink the settings by clicking on the Chain link (see Figure 4-36). Type +300 in the Y Location text box. Press the Alt/⌥ key and strike the Enter/Return key. By pressing Alt/⌥, the item is duplicated, as shown in Figure 4-36.

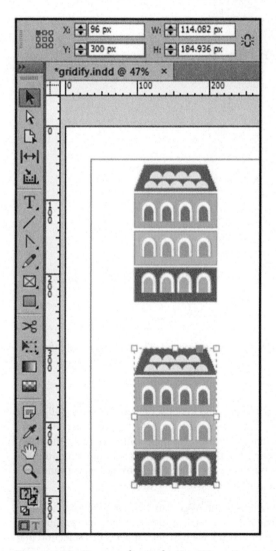

Figure 4-36. *Type a value in the X or Y Location text box and press Alt+Enter/Return*

4.5.3   Aligning and Distributing Objects

When you create multiple objects on a page, quite often you need to align and/or distribute them, especially when you manually add objects without using Step and Repeat or gridifying a group.

To use the Align and Distribute tools, open the Align Panel. Choose Window ➤ Object and Layout ➤ Align, or press Shift+F7 and the Align Panel opens, as shown in Figure 4-37. You can also use the align and distribute options in the Control Panel.

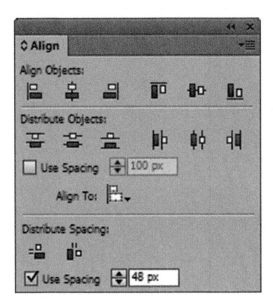

Figure 4-37.   *Choose Window ➤ Object & Layout ➤ Align or press Shift+F7 to open the Align Panel*

▓ **Note**   If you don't see all of the options shown in Figure 4-37, open the Panel menu and choose Show Options.

In the Align Panel, you have two rows at the top. The first row of icons is used for aligning objects. You have options for aligning left, horizontal center, right, top, vertical center, and bottom. The second row of icons is used for distributing objects with essentially the same choices as you find with the first row icons. Distribute objects has an additional option for setting the space between objects. Enable the Use Spacing checkbox and type a value in the text field for the amount of spacing you want between the objects.

One important choice that you need to make in the Align Panel is to tell InDesign what you want to align to. Click the Align To icon to open a drop-down menu. In the menu, you have five different choices. Quite frequently, you'll want to align objects to a selection that is the default. However, there are times that you may want to align to page margins, to a page, or to a spread.

The other choice that you have in the Align To menu is to align to a key object. A key object is determined when you select several objects and then click one more time on one of the objects. The key object appears with a heavy border. The default key object is the topmost, leftmost, bottommost, or rightmost object. Let's say that you have several objects with different vertical positions on a page, as you see in Figure 4-38. If you select all objects and want to align the top edges, the topmost object is the default key object. To instead align all of the objects, however, with the third object, you could click on the third object once more to make it the key object. Then all of the other objects move to the vertical position of the third object.

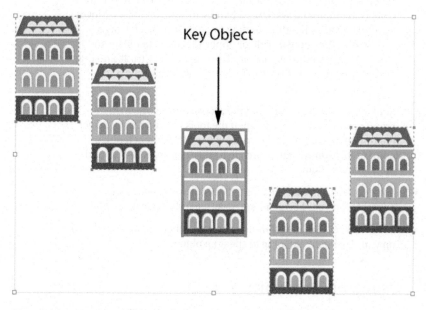

Figure 4-38. *Press Ctrl/⌘ in a selected group of objects to identify the key object*

At the bottom of the Align Panel, you see Distribute Spacing options. Two icons appear here. The left icon is used for vertical spacing, and the right icon is used for horizontal spacing. Enable the Use Spacing checkbox and type a spacing value in the text box.

■ **Note** All text is contained either on paths or within frames. Paths and frames are objects; therefore, you can use the Align options equally on text frames and text on paths.

4.6   Transforming Objects

InDesign provides you with tools and menu commands for transforming objects. You can use the Tools Panel, the Transform Panel, the Control Panel, the Object Transform, and the Object Transform Again commands to transform objects in a number of ways.

4.6.1   Using the Tools Panel

In the Tools Panel, you find four transformation tools that include the following:

- *Free transformation tool (E):* Select the tool or press E on your keyboard. The Free Transformation tool enables you to transform objects in different ways. Drag a handle to scale an object. Move the tool outside a handle and drag to rotate an object. Drag a handle past the opposite side or opposite handle to reflect an object. Drag a handle slightly, and then press the Ctrl/⌘ and drag to shear an object. Press Ctrl/⌘+Alt/⌐ and drag to shear from both sides of an object.

- *Rotate tool (R):* Press and hold the mouse button down on the Free Transformation tool to open the tools pop-up menu. Select the Rotate tool or press R on your keyboard. Set the reference point in the Control Panel and click and drag a rotation around the Reference Point.

- *Scale tool (S):* First set the reference point and then click the tool or press S on your keyboard and drag a handle to scale an object.

- *Shear tool (O):* Set the reference point and click the tool or press O on your keyboard and drag to shear an object.

4.6.2   Using the Transform Panel

Choose Window ➤ Object & Layout ➤ Transform to open the Transform Panel. In the panel, you have a combination of tools and menu commands to handle transformations, as you can see in Figure 4-39.

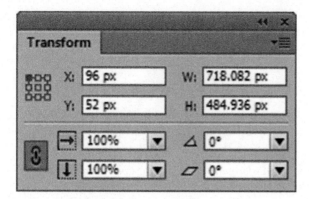

Figure 4-39. Choose Window ➤ Object & layout ➤ Transform to open the Transform Panel

Notice in the Transform Panel that you can set the reference point as well as apply different transformations. The X, Y text boxes are the horizontal and vertical position of the object on a page. You can edit the values to move the object to a different location. The W and H text boxes are used for sizing the object's width and height. The right and down arrow text boxes are used to scale an object by percentage. The last two items are the rotation and scale options by degree.

The menu choices that you have in the top two-thirds are transformations that you can apply using the transformation tools and the Control Panel tools. The bottom section is important for determining how you want to handle stroke and effects scaling. By default, all of the options are enabled.

4.6.3   Using the Control Panel

In the Control Panel, you have much the same options as you find in the Transform Panel. You can scale by percentages, rotate and shear by degree, rotate clockwise and counterclockwise, and reflect objects horizontally and vertically. To the right of the transformation tools in the Control Panel, you see a large P character. By default, the character appears vertically, similar to when you type a character in a text frame. If you apply a transformation, the character mimics the type of transformation. For example, if you reflect an object horizontally, the character is flipped horizontally. To clear all transformations, right-click on the P character in the Control Panel and choose Clear Transformations.

If you want to duplicate an object while transforming it, press the Alt/⌥ key and click the transformation tool in the Control Panel. For example, in Figure 4-40, you can see a triangle in the open document (left side). If you want to duplicate and reflect the triangle so that it appears as shown on the right side of Figure 4-40, press the Alt/⌥ key and click the Flip Horizontal tool. Of course, in this example, I would set my reference point to the middle-right before performing the transformation.

Figure 4-40. *Press Alt/⌥ and click a transformation option in the Control Panel to duplicate and transform together*

4.6.4   Using Menu Commands

InDesign provides you with two menu items that contain commands for working with transformations. The Object ➤ Transform menu contains transformations similar to those found in the Tools Panel and the Transform Panel. Choosing Move, Scale, Rotate, and Shear opens their respective dialog boxes where you can type values for the amount of the transformation type.

When you choose Object ➤ Transform Again, you find four menu items. These menu commands represent some of the real power for making transformations. Selecting an object and rotating it 30° is a nice feature, but it's not such an impressive edit. Duplicating an object and rotating it 10° is also nice, but not so impressive either.

However, what if you want to scale an object, rotate it 30°, and move it a little and you have 15 objects that you want to transform using the same scaling, rotation, and movement? That's where the menu commands come in, and they are quite impressive.

In Figure 4-41, you see the transformations that I applied to the five red objects from the transformation that I performed on the first black object in each row. Instead of duplicating the red objects, I used the Transform Again menu commands. Following is an explanation of how I did it.

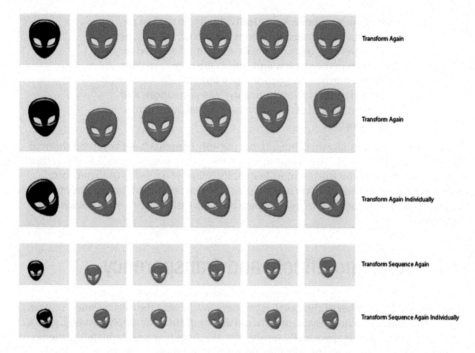

Figure 4-41. *Results of using the Transform Again menu commands*

1. **Transform Again.** In the first row, I pressed Alt/⌥ and dragged the second object to the right. Then I visited the Object ➤ Transform Again ➤ Transform Again menu command. This command duplicates the last transformation on an object.

2. **Transform Again.** In the second row, I applied the same command. However, this time I rotated the black object slightly, selected the five red objects in the second row, and chose Object ➤ Transform Again ➤ Transform Again. Notice that all five red objects rotated as one entity.

3. **Transform Again Individually**. In the third row, I rotated the black object, selected the five red objects, and chose Object ➤ Transform Again ➤ Transform Again Individually. This action transformed the objects and they remained in the same vertical position.

4. **Transform Sequence Again.** In the fourth row, I applied multiple transformations. I scaled the black object, rotated it, and moved it down a bit. I applied the Object ➤ Transform Again ➤ Transform Sequence Again command. Notice the same kind of stair-stepping that you find with Transform Again on the red objects to the right.

5. **Transform Sequence Again Individually.** In the last row, I applied the same transformations for scaling, rotating, and moving the black object in the first column. I selected the five red objects in the last row and chose Object ➤ Transform Again ➤ Transform Sequence Again Individually. This menu command results in duplicating the transformations and movement, and all of the objects are placed at the same vertical position.

Notice in the Transform Again submenu that the only item that has a keyboard shortcut is the Transform Sequence Again command. In most work sessions, you'll find that this command is the one you will use most frequently. When you need to use Transform Sequence Again Individually, you need to use the menu command. You're likely to use this command much less frequently than pressing Ctrl/⌘+Alt/⌥+4 to transform a sequence.

4.7 Applying Effects and Transparency

Another set of feature-rich edits that you can make to objects and imported files in InDesign are the number of choices that you have available in the Effects Panel. You can apply transparency to images and objects and add drop shadows, apply beveling, glows, and feathering to create spectacular results. You also have many of the blending modes that you find in other programs like Illustrator and Photoshop.

You can convert text to outlines and modify anchor points to change the shapes of type, and you can create type masks so that images and objects appear within type characters. You can create compound paths, close paths, and use the Pathfinder options to add, subtract, and join paths. All in all, InDesign provides you with many tools and menu commands that help you create your vision for the artwork that you want in a design piece.

4.7.1 Exploring InDesign Effects

Effects that you add to images, objects, and text, which produce some life in your designs such as drop shadows, 3D effects, glows, and transparency, are equally as important for digital publications as they are for print. In addition to the obvious design characteristics employed with digital publishing documents, effects help you add a little polish to icons and elements that you might use for changing object states, playing media, or branching out to a hyperlink destination.

4.7.2 Using the Effects Panel

To start your journey in learning about and using InDesign effects, you need to become familiar with the Effects Panel. To open the Effects Panel, choose Window ➤ Effects. The Effects Panel opens, as shown in Figure 4-42.

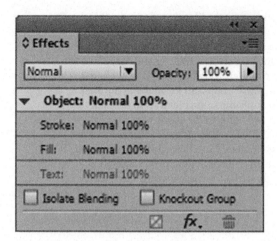

Figure 4-42. *Choose Window ➤ Effects to open the Effects Panel*

In the Effects Panel, you will find the following options:

- *Blend Modes:* Open the drop-down menu where you see Normal. You will find the same blend modes in InDesign as you find in Adobe Illustrator. In Adobe Photoshop, there are some more blend modes, but what you have in InDesign enables you to blend objects in a stacking order in a number of different ways.

- *Opacity:* Move the slider left or type a value in the text box to add transparency to a selected object. This setting acts in the same way as when you use the Object ➤ Effects Transparency command or choose Transparency from the Effects Panel menu.

- *The Target:* The first thing that you need to decide is what are you going to target for applying an effect or transparency. InDesign provides you four choices:

  - *Object:* The Object item and the three items following it permit you to target different areas. Select Object to apply transparency and effects to the entire object.

  - *Stroke:* If you have a frame, you can target the stroke apart from the fill and object and apply effects and transparency to the stroke only.

  - *Fill:* If you have a frame and want to apply an effect or transparency to the fill only, select this item.

  - *Text:* Select a text frame, and you can apply an effect or transparency to all of the text in the frame.

- *Isolate Blending:* When you change the blend mode on an object and blend it with an underlying object—say Multiply to darken the object at the top of the stack—all underlying items in the stack are affected by the blend mode. Presume that you have three items stacked on top of each other. You apply the Multiply blend mode to the topmost item. The blend modes drill down through each item in the stack and apply the same blend to all items. If you want to blend the first two items in the stack, you first need to group them. Then enable the Isolate Blending checkbox. All items below the first two grouped items are unaffected and not blended. In Figure 4-43, you can see the Multiply blend mode applied without (left) and with (right) isolating the blending.

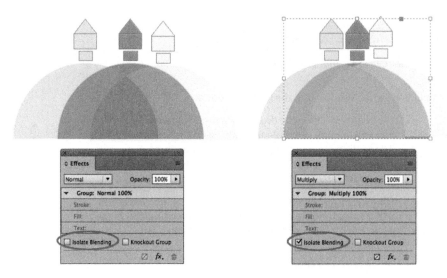

Figure 4-43. *Adding blend modes with and without isolating blending*

- *Knockout Group:* Use this option to knock out opacity and blending attributes of every item in the selected group. In a way, this is like creating a compound path. When you draw two concentric circles, select them, and then choose Compound Path, the center circle becomes transparent—like a doughnut. Knockout group behaves similarly when using transparency and effects.

- *Fx:* Once you apply an effect to an item, you'll notice the *fx* icon appear in the top-right corner of the Effects Panel. When you want to apply the same effect to another object, click and drag the *fx* icon on top of another object. The target object takes on the same formatting created in the Effects Panel for the first object. In a way, it's like using an object style.

- *Effects Panel menu:* Choices in the Effects Panel menu include the following:

  - *Hide Options:* Select this item and the Effects Panel is reduced in size, hiding the Isolate Blending and Knockout Group checkboxes.

  - *Effects:* The submenu lists all of the different effects that you can apply to items (see Figure 4-44). Select any one of the submenu commands, and the Effects window opens, as shown in Figure 4-45.

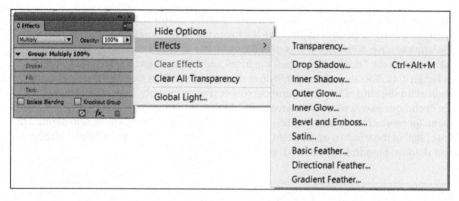

Figure 4-44. *Click one of the Effects submenu items to open the Effects window*

- *Clear Effects:* Clears all effects applied to an item.

- *Clear All Transparency:* Clears all transparency on a selected object.

- *Global Light:* When you select this item, the Global Light dialog box opens. You have two options: Angle and Altitude. The angle setting is the direction of a light source. The Altitude is used to adjust the intensity of the light. When you create an effect and use Global Light in the Effects window, then copy and paste the item in another InDesign document where you have set the Global Light using this dialog box, the pasted object inherits what you have set up in your document. Only use this item when you want the light direction and intensity consistent on all your objects in a layout.

- Buttons at the bottom of the panel include:

- *Clears all effects and makes object opaque:* Click this icon to remove effects and transparency.

- *fx:* Click to open the drop-down menu for Effects choices. This menu is the same as the one that you can access in the Effects Panel menu and the Control Panel menu.

- *Trash:* Select an item and click to clear effects. If any transparency was applied to the item, it remains unaffected.

In a normal workflow, you open the Effects Panel, select the target, and then use either the Panel menu or the drop-down *fx* menu and choose the effect you want.

4.7.3   Using the Effects Window

There are far too many options and switches available to you in the Effects window than I can hope to cover in this chapter. The ten items that you can select in the left pane in the window have different options depending on the item you choose. As an example, take a look at the Effects menu when the Bevel and Emboss item is selected, as shown in Figure 4-45. You see a menu for Style at the top-right side of the window. You make choices for the kind of bevel and emboss that you want to apply. Following that menu is the Technique menu where you have more choices, and then go down to the Direction menu for more choices. You find text boxes for controlling size, softening, and depth. The lower half of the window on the right side offers choices for angle and altitude, highlight and shadow, blending modes, and opacity settings.

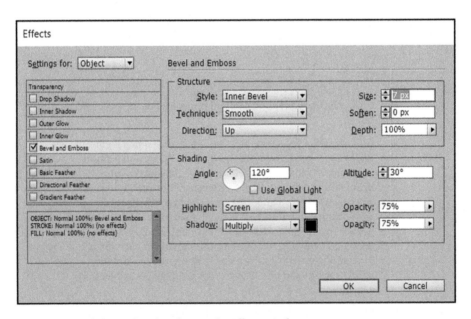

Figure 4-45. *Click Bevel and Emboss in the Effects window*

Click another item in the left column for another type of effect, and the window offers different options. It's mind boggling and somewhat intimidating when you first open the Effects window.

For now, keep in mind that this window is where all of the action happens, and when you want to apply an effect, this is where you set the attributes for the desired effect. We'll explore some of these effects later in this section.

4.7.4   Creating Drop Shadows

When you open the Effects Panel menu and choose Effects, notice in the submenu that the only effect that has a keyboard shortcut is Drop Shadow. Creating drop shadows is by far the most common effect used by InDesign layout artists.

You can apply a drop shadow to any object in your design—text, images, objects, strokes, paths, and so forth. To add a drop shadow, select the object and press Ctrl/⌘+Alt/⌥+M or choose Drop Shadow from the *fx* menu in the Effects Panel.

The Effects window opens with Drop Shadow selected in the left pane. By default, the opacity is set to 75%. I suggested that you reduce the drop shadow opacity to 35–40% when creating drop shadows. I rarely use a drop shadow with 75% opacity. The look you want to accomplish is simple and elegant. Drop shadows are not stars. They're only character actors that help throw the spotlight on the main stars. You add drop shadows to bring a little life to your text or objects as well as dimension.

In Figure 4-46, you can see the settings I used for a drop shadow applied to some text. When the Preview checkbox is enabled, you see a dynamic preview of your adjustments while you make edits in the Effects window.

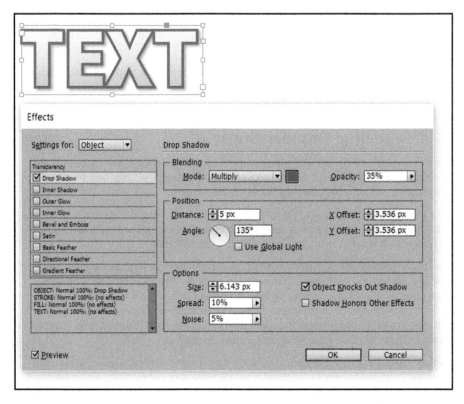

Figure 4-46. *Drop shadow applied to text with the Preview checkbox enabled*

In Figure 4-46, I set the opacity to 35% to lighten up the shadow. The default blending mode for drop shadows is Multiply. I left the blend mode at the default, but I changed the color for the drop shadow by clicking the color swatch adjacent to the Mode menu and chose a blue color from the Swatches Panel.

I set the Size distance to 5 pixels to bring the shadow a little closer to the type, but I set the Spread to 10% to blend the edges out a little further. The Noise setting is something that you should apply to many effects. For print, you might set the noise amount to 1 or 2 pixels. For screen displays, set the Noise to 5 pixels. This adds a little noise in the shadow so that it doesn't look artificial.

For screen displays, you don't need to worry about Object Knocks out Shadow. The second checkbox is used for multiple effects. If you have a drop shadow and a bevel and emboss, for example, you should enable the checkbox for Shadow Honors Other Effects.

4.7.5   Creating Buttons

After Drop Shadow, the next most used effect by InDesign users is Bevel and Emboss. You can find many uses for the Bevel and Emboss effect in InDesign when preparing documents for digital publishing. Among one of the more common uses is creating

130

custom buttons. You might use buttons to set a hyperlink action, as I explain in Chapter 7; initiate an animation, as I explain in Chapter 8; change object states, as I explain in Chapter 6; or create play/pause/stop buttons for media, as I explain in Chapter 10.

4.7.5.1   Adjusting Bevel and Emboss Options

InDesign offers you many default buttons in the Buttons and Forms Panel, but why use the InDesign buttons when you can create some more interesting buttons using InDesign effects?

To create a button with a Bevel and Emboss, select an object or draw an object on a page. Apply a color fill to the object. In my example, I applied a very light gray to an ellipse. Rather than use white, in most cases you should add a little black to white objects. Next open the Effects Panel (Ctrl+Shift+F10) and choose Bevel and Emboss from the *fx* drop-down menu in the Effects Panel.

For my button, I used an Inner Bevel and set the Size to 4 pixels, the Soften amount to 6 pixels, the Technique to Smooth, and I left the Direction at the default Up choice. For the Shading, I wanted the light source to appear from the top, so I set the Angle to 90°.

The Altitude adjustment is like a balance between highlights and shadows. When you raise the value in the Altitude text box to a higher value like 70–80, the shadows lighten up and you get a little shine in the highlight area. I set the Opacity for Highlights and Shadows to 70°, as you can see in Figure 4-47.

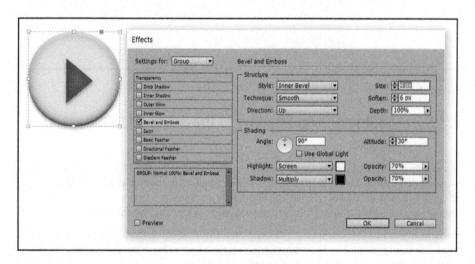

Figure 4-47. *Bevel and Emboss options choices for an ellipse*

4.7.5.2   Adding an Inner Shadow

You're not limited to applying a single effect to an object. After completing the Bevel and Emboss, you can select any item in the Effects left pane and add some more effects. In Figure 4-48, you can see a slight Inner Shadow applied to the same object after adding the Bevel and Emboss effect. I set the Opacity to 17%, set the distance values for Distance to 1 pixel, and set the Size and Choke in the Options area to 7 pixels and 20%, respectively. Choke hardens up the inner shadow so that it appears less feathered and results in a little bit of a ring around the inside of the object.

The final setting in the Inner Shadow Effects pane is the Noise setting. In Figure 4-48, you can see the options I used for the Inner Shadow.

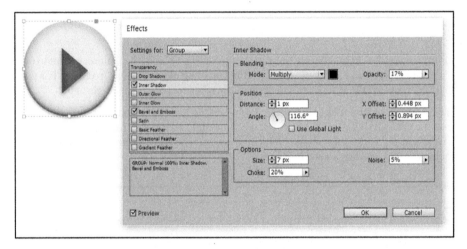

Figure 4-48. *Options used for the Inner Shadow effect*

4.7.5.3   Adding a Drop Shadow to the Bevel and Embossed Object

Good heavens! Where would we be without adding a drop shadow? Designers like to use drop shadows on all kinds of objects. So let's not argue with them and apply yet another effect to our button. However, our drop shadow is going to be a very slight effect—just enough to give a hint of lifting off the page and adding the shadow around the object.

Move from the Inner Shadow effect to Drop Shadow by clicking Drop Shadow in the left pane. I first set the Opacity to 35% to lighten up the shadow from the default 70%. Then I set the Distance and Y Offsets to just 3 pixels.

In the Options area of the Effects Panel, I set the Size to 5 pixels, the Spread to 2%, and added 5% Noise. On the right side of the Drop Shadow Effect, you will find a checkbox for Shadow Honors Other Effects. In this example, enabling the checkbox won't make much difference, but with other effects you may find it necessary. If you see a large square drop shadow on an Ellipse shape for example, you probably need to enable this checkbox. As a matter of rule, I enable it unless it's obviously not necessary.

In Figure 4-49, you can see the settings I used to add a drop shadow with the other effects. Notice that the checkboxes are enabled for all of the effects that you apply to an object.

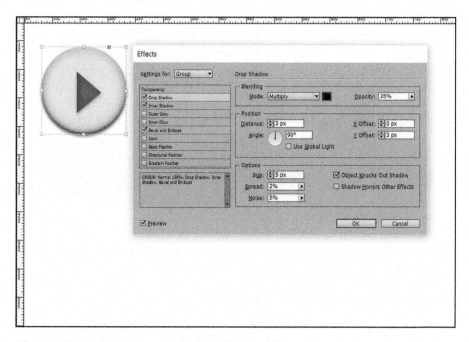

Figure 4-49. *Options settings for the Drop Shadow effect*

Keep in mind that most often there is no right or wrong when applying effects. It comes down to your personal vision for the effect you want to create and how well you feel the effects on an object fit into your overall design. I offered some settings options I used here, but you may have much different tastes. That's okay. It's your design, and you're free to experiment and create effects as you wish.

4.7.5.4 Duplicating Effects

Up to now I created a button with a Bevel and Emboss, Inner Shadow, and Drop Shadow. Let's say that I want to use the button as a Play button for media in my design. I have a right-pointing triangle shape that gives the viewers a clue as to what will happen when they click or tap the button. But I want to apply the same effects to the triangle as I have in the button.

With InDesign, it's a simple task. You don't need to select the triangle and set all of the effects. Just select the button with the effects, and with the Effects Panel open, drag the *fx* item at the top-right corner of the Effects Panel to the triangle (or any other object where you want to duplicate the effects). As you drag the *fx* item to the target object, you'll see the cursor change to a hand icon with a + symbol. When you see the cursor change, release the mouse button and voilá—all of the effects applied to the button are equally applied to the target object.

133

Move the second object to the center of the button and group the objects by selecting both and pressing Ctrl/⌘+G. The graphic shown in Figure 4-50 is now ready to convert to a button. For more information on creating buttons, see Chapter 9.

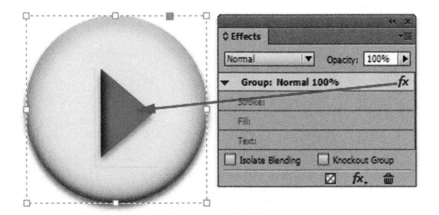

Figure 4-50. *Drag the fx item in the Effects Panel to another object to apply a duplicate effect*

4.7.6   Creating a Double Bevel Effect

One limitation that you have with effects is that you can't apply separate effects to the fill and stroke of text.

Take a look at Figure 4-51. In this example, I want to add a 20-point stroke and have the Bevel and Emboss and Drop Shadow applied to the text and not the stroke. In order to accomplish the effect, I need to have two objects and stack them.

Figure 4-51. *A double Bevel and Emboss effect is obtained when you have two objects in a stack*

CREATING A DOUBLE BEVEL EFFECT

To see how to create such an effect, follow these steps:

1. **Add some text to a text frame on a page**. After creating the text, double-click a handle to bring the frame tight around the text.

2. **Select the text frame, click on "Text" in the Effects Panel, and apply a Bevel and Emboss**. Use options to your liking. In my example, I used an Inner Bevel, selected Chisel Hard, and set the Size to 2. I set the Shading Angle to 90°, the Altitude to 60°, and set the Opacity for Highlight and Shadow to 100%.

3. **Apply a drop shadow.** Again, use the settings you want to use for your drop shadow, but make the shadow appear very subtle. In my example, I used a shadow Opacity of 40%, set the Distance to 5 points, and set the Angle to 90°. I set the Y Offset to 1 point to keep the shadow tight to the text. I set the Size to 2 pixels, the Spread to 7%, and added 5% Noise.

4. **Copy the text with the effects**.

5. **Paste in Place**. Choose Edit Paste in Place to paste the copy directly on top of the copied text.

6. **Add a stroke**. I want a very large stroke on the text. Double-click the text to get an insertion point in the text and press Ctrl/⌘+A to select the text. You want to be certain to select the text and not the frame. Open the Stroke Panel and set the size of the stroke. In my example, I set the stroke size to 20 points.

7. **Add some color to the stroke**. Rather than using a solid paper color for the stroke color, add a bit of black to it. In my example, I added 5% black for the stroke color.

8. **Set the stack order**. The copy with the stroke needs to be behind the beveled and embossed text. Press Ctrl/⌘ and click to select the rearmost object. Right-click to open a context menu and choose Object ➤ Arrange ➤ Bring to Front.

9. **Add some color to the text.** In my example, I applied a gradient to the text.

Since we didn't create outlines from the text, the text is editable. You can edit both objects in the stack and easily change the text.

4.7.7 Knocking Out Text

Using Knockout Group in the Effects Panel is helpful when you want to create a type mask. In Figure 4-52, I have type that knocks out and shows the image behind it through the text—like a type mask.

Figure 4-52. The text knocks out showing the image within the text

KNOCKING OUT TEXT

To accomplish this effect, do the following:

1. **Draw a frame or rectangle over an image**.

2. **Select the frame and click the Type tool inside the frame**. To adjust offsets and alignment, you can choose Object ➤ Text Frame Options and edit the offsets and vertical alignment.

3. **Set the frame color**. You can use a paper fill for the frame or use a 5% black fill.

4. **Change the text color**. Apply the same color you used for the frame to the text. In my example, I used a 5% black fill, so I select the text and apply a 5% black fill to the text.

5. **Select Formatting Effects Container (J)**. In the Swatches Panel, click the T icon adjacent to the color swatches at the top of the panel to set the Formatting effects container or press the J key on your keyboard.

6. **Open the Effects Panel and set the Text Blending mode to Multiply**. In the Effects Panel, you have several objects from which you can choose. At the bottom of the Objects list is Text. Click Text and choose Multiply from the drop-down menu, as shown in Figure 4-53.

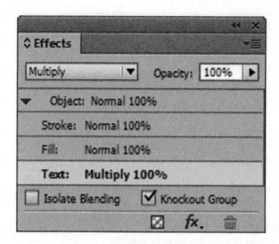

Figure 4-53. *Select the text object, and choose Multiply in the Effects Panel*

7. **Knock out the group**. Click Object in the Effects Panel and enable the Knockout Group checkbox.

Again, the text is editable. You can change the text by setting the Text insertion cursor in the text, pressing Ctrl/⌘+A to select all of the text, and entering new text. The new text retains the Knockout Group effect.

4.7.8   Reflecting Type

You've seen some of those cool type effects like reflective type with gradients. It appears as if the type fades off in a shadow on water, glass, a lawn, or many other backgrounds. Stop envying those who create the cool effects. Now you can add reflective type to your designs, such as the rather simple effect you see in Figure 4-54.

FRUIT MARKET

Figure 4-54. *Type with a reflection*

CREATING A REFLECTIVE TYPE EFFECT

To create a reflective type effect, follow these steps:

1. **Create a text frame and add some type**. Double-click a handle with the Selection tool to bring the frame in close to the type.

2. **Set the reference point**. Click the bottom-middle square in the reference point in the Control Panel.

3. **Reflect a copy of the type**. Press the Alt/⌥ key and click the Flip Vertical tool in the Control Panel.

4. **Check the position of the type**. Zoom in to the type (Ctrl/⌘+the spacebar) and drag around the page to view the type. If the reflected type is not touching the type above, use the Up Arrow key to nudge it so that the type in both frames is touching.

5. **Create a gradient feather**. Click the Gradient Feather tool in the Tools Panel or press Shift+G. Drag from the top of the reflected type down to create the gradient. If you don't like the gradient effect, click and drag again. Repeat the action until the gradient appears as you like it.

6. **Skew the reflected type**. Don't forget to set the reference point in the Control Panel. Set the Control point to the top center. Select the Shear tool and click and drag from the center below the type to the left.

This example is a simple task for reflecting type. You can use the same steps when you want to reflect type on different backgrounds and use different colors for the type.

4.7.9 Creating 3D Arrows

When it comes to 3D objects, InDesign is no match for the 3D effects that you can create in Adobe Illustrator and Adobe Photoshop. However, there are some techniques that you can use to create 3D objects and perspective drawings. All you need is a little know-how and imagination.

3D objects sort of jump out at the viewer. You can call attention to content and button actions in digital publishing documents by adding a 3D object. Take Figure 4-55 as an example. It should be obvious to the viewer of the document that clicking or tapping on the logo and URL to the right of the arrowhead takes you to the company web site. Since the URL specifies a destination, most people would intuitively know that clicking or tapping this area is likely to send the viewer to the hyperlink's destination.

The 3D arrow in Figure 4-55 is an exaggerated clue that a hyperlink exists on the page. Effects like these are little tricks that you can use to easily draw a reader's attention to some kind of interactivity.

Omnimperchil mi, oditassit enis archict oribus ab in ne por as moluptur, simentes ex et latiatus, corepudi berum sintenisit esequatiur, sapel ipsam eum, ommoluptaquo quam et ut porecto volore solorro dolores etur alit laborei cianis vendis sit pario temporere etur, cumquaecto doluptatus ut utem hilique im dunt quatur?

THE FRUIT MARKET
www.fruitmarket.com

Ipicte verchic tionseque quatio maxim simpores et labo. Nam dolesciis moluptat intore mo dolupti di ut dolessum doluptae voluptaeped ullabo.

Dus doluptatiis num veligni minctur restrumet quia incitatquam expere voluptae omnisciust aliquodion corum vollupt asitati nvendi ipsa doluptum quosape rumquam acestrum voloresed maiore, optaspiet iusanis quatur acipsum quiaest, conseque eum idellab oriore et, volut min natus pro est, con ra corepudis estiae.

Figure 4-55. 3D objects can draw a reader's attention to some form of interactivity

CREATING 3D ARROWS

Following are some steps I used to create the 3D arrow:

1. **Create an ellipse**. Use a height of the ellipse similar to what you see in Figure 4-55.

2. **Copy/Paste in Front**. Copy the Ellipse and choose Edit ➤ Paste in Front or press Ctrl/⌘+Alt/⌥+V.

3. **Convert the shape to a rectangle**. Select the pasted copy and choose Object ➤ Convert Shape ➤ Rectangle.

4. **Move the left edge of the rectangle to the midpoint of the ellipse shape by dragging the rectangle to the right**. Use the selection arrow to move the shape. Press the Shift key to constrain the movement horizontally. The left side of the rectangle should be at the midpoint of the underlying ellipse, as shown in Figure 4-56.

Figure 4-56. Move the left edge of the rectangle to the midpoint of the ellipse

5. **Combine the shapes**. Select both shapes and open the Pathfinder Panel (Window ➤ Object & Layout ➤ Pathfinder). Click the Add icon in the Pathfinder Panel.

6. **Copy the object**.

7. **Send the object in view to the back**. At this point, you should have a frame in the document. Send the object behind the frame.

8. **Lock the object or hide it on a layer**. Select the object and choose Object ➤ Lock or press Ctrl/⌘+L. You want to eliminate any chance of selecting the object as you move through a few more steps.

9. **Paste in Place**. The copied object is on the clipboard. Choose Edit ➤ Paste in Place or press Ctrl/⌘+Alt/⌥+V.

10. **Delete the bottom two points on the pasted object**. Click the Direct Selection tool (or press the A key on your keyboard). Click on the object to see the points. Select the lower-right corner point, press the Shift key, and click the lower midpoint. Press the Delete key, and your object should look like that shown in Figure 4-57.

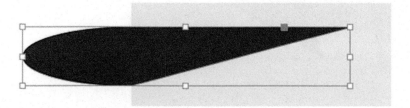

Figure 4-57. *Delete the two bottom points*

11. **Duplicate a copy of the object**. Press the Alt/⌐ key and drag the object up about 50 points.

12. **Select the two left-end points on both shapes with the Direct Selection tool**. Press A on your keyboard to activate the Direct Selection tool and marquee the two left points on the shapes.

13. **Open the Pathfinder Panel and click the Join Path tool**.

14. **Apply a gradient fill to both objects**. Create a little distinction between the objects with the gradient fill so that they show some depth, as you can see in Figure 4-58.

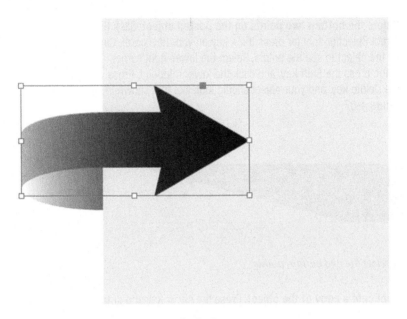

Figure 4-58. Apply a gradient to both objects

15. **Draw the arrowhead**. Draw a square and choose Object ➤ Convert Shape ➤ Triangle. Select the object and click the Rotate 90° Clockwise tool in the Control Panel.

16. **Combine the objects**. Move the arrowhead to the right side of the shape. Select both the triangle and the foreground shape, and click the Add icon in the Pathfinder Panel. To add a little polish to the arrowhead, click the top and lower points and press the Left Arrow a few times to give a little more arrowhead appearance, as you can see in Figure 4-59.

If you need to resize the object, click with the Selection Arrow tool and drag a handle. Don't forget to enable Auto-Fit in the Control Panel if you use Shift+drag.

4.7.10 Punching Out Text Outlines

So far we looked at using live text for several effects. In some cases, you need to convert text to outlines before applying an effect. One example is when you use overlapping frames and you want to knockout text in the background frame. You can't create this kind of effect using live text.

Any text in a document can be converted to outlines, meaning that the text is no longer editable and it becomes a graphic with paths and anchor points. As a rule, you should minimize converting text to outlines, especially when creating reflowable EPUBs. Content providers want the text live so that it can be searched and readers can change the fonts and font sizes in reflowable EPUBs.

Adding some text converted to outlines, such as chapter heads and special effects, will get by the content providers. You need to keep it at a minimum, however, when creating reflowable EPUBs.

In Figure 4-59, you see an effect where converting text to outlines was necessary. The image has a border and the top of the text follows the border color as if a stroke were applied. However, the text outside the image doesn't appear with a stroke.

Figure 4-59. Some text effects require you to first convert the text to outlines

PUNCHING OUT TEXT OUTLINES

Creating an effect similar to Figure 4-59 is quite easy. You just have to pay attention to the proper sequence of edits. Let's take a look at how we create the effect:

1. **Place an image on a page in InDesign**. Press Ctrl/⌘+D to open the Place dialog box and locate the image you want to place. Select it in the Place dialog box and click Open.

2. **Add a stroke to the frame**. This step is important. You must add a stroke to the graphic frame. Open the Stroke Panel and apply a large stroke—something like 6 points.

3. **Add a text frame**. Type text and move the text down with the top portion of the text slightly on top of the stroke.

4. **Convert the text to outlines**. Select the text frame and choose Type ➤ Create Outlines.

5. **Copy the text outline**.

6. **Subtract the front most object (the text outline) from the background (the image).** Select the text and the image and click the subtract icon (second from left) in the Pathfinder Panel.

7. **Paste in Place**.

8. **Choose Edit ➤ Paste in Place (Ctrl/⌘+Alt/⌥+V).**

If you followed the steps precisely, you should see an effect similar to the one shown in Figure 4-59.

4.7.11 Creating a Puzzle Effect

In Photoshop and Photoshop Elements, you have puzzle effects where you can break apart a photo, creating a puzzle effect where each piece in the puzzle can be moved, transformed, and take on various effects.

In InDesign, you can also create a type of puzzle effect. However, you don't have the ability to create puzzle pieces with arbitrary shapes. The puzzle effect that you can create in InDesign results in a square grid. You can then break apart the grid and apply effects. In Figure 4-60, you see the puzzle effect created in an InDesign document.

Figure 4-60. *You can create a puzzle effect directly in InDesign*

CREATING A PUZZLE EFFECT

To create the effect, you need some help from a script. When you use the script, the divisions of a grid are broken apart and you can move and transform the pieces. Follow these steps to create a similar effect:

1. **Place a photo image on a page in InDesign**.

2. **Double-click the MakeGrid script**. Select the image and open the Scripts Panel. Open the Application folder, then the Samples folder, and finally the JavaScript folder. Scroll down to MakeGrid. Double-click the MakeGrid script. The MakeGrid dialog box opens.

3. **Set the grid attributes**. Set the rows and columns to the numbers that you want in your grid. In my example, I use nine rows and five columns. Set the row and column gutters to 0 (zero). Click OK and the grid is created.

4. **Add a drop shadow (optional)**. A drop shadow can make the pieces easily distinguishable. Select all of the pieces, open the Effects Panel, and click Drop Shadow from the *fx* drop-down menu. In the Drop Shadow window, set the distance to 0 and set the size to 3 pixels. Click OK and the grid appears with slight division lines, as shown in Figure 4-61.

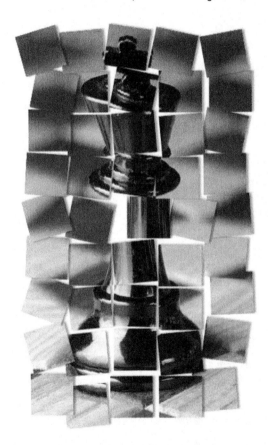

Figure 4-61. Add a drop shadow so you can see the division lines

5. **Move, scale, and/or rotate individual pieces**. Each piece is selectable. Use the Selection arrow to move, scale, and rotate pieces of the puzzle to your liking.

4.7.12   Creating a Retro Look

If you were born after 1983, you probably don't have any Polaroid pictures stored in your attic. If you're an old guy like me, you may have a stack of Polaroid photos along with slides, negatives, and photo prints that one day you hope to scan and get into digital form.

If you can't scan a Polaroid picture, you could use various effects in InDesign to create a Polaroid look using strokes and adding a little black to the strokes—like 5–7%—so the fill looks a little gray. I like to use an original Polaroid photo and scan it. A scanned image picks up some dust and starches that add a little more to the retro look.

In Figure 4-62, you can see a Polaroid photo I had hanging around. I scanned the photo to get the border exactly like the original. There were a few spots on the photo, but I wanted to add a bit more. So I placed a Photoshop file of a coffee stain in the lower-left corner and set the transparency to 40%.

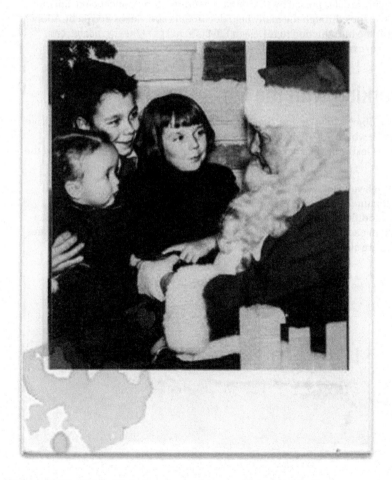

Figure 4-62. *Polaroid photos are great for creating a retro look*

I wanted to add a different photo to the border, so I dug deep into my old photo collection and found a very old photo taken with Santa Claus some years ago. I drew a frame and placed the photo on top of the Polaroid scan and then moved the coffee stain to the top of the stack by choosing Object ➤ Arrange ➤ Bring to Front.

I applied a drop shadow and set the Opacity to 40%, the Distance to 2 pixels, the Angle to 90°, the Size to 5 pixels, the Spread to 7%, and added 5% Noise.

Adding an image like this might be good for a Christmas card design that you want to send to family and friends via Adobe Publish Online. To learn how to use Publish Online, take a look at Chapter 14.

Various effects discussed in this chapter just touch the tip of the iceberg. You have so many options available in the Effects Panel that it's impossible to cover them all here. For more information and to discover the many cool things that you can do with effects in InDesign, search the Internet. To begin, visit the `www.indesignsecrets.com` web site and look over the many articles posted by David Blatner, Anne-Marie Concepcion, and their contributors. Also look through the many help documents and videos posted by Adobe. For starters, visit the introduction to InDesign Effects at `https://helpx.adobe.com/indesign/how-to/create-special-effects.html`.

4.8   Working with the Links Panel

When you place objects in InDesign, the files are linked to a location on your hard drive or another source where the original object is stored. If you move, edit, or delete the source image, InDesign opens an alert dialog box when you open the file containing the links.

In the Links Panel, you will find a list of all of the objects placed in your document. If you view the document in Normal mode with frame edges displayed, the links that are missing or modified display the warning icon or the Missing icon (red circle with a question mark) in each frame where the images were placed. The modified objects and missing objects are also shown in the Links Panel, as you can see in Figure 4-63.

Figure 4-63. Missing and modified links are shown on the document page and the Links Panel

The yellow warning icon indicates that a linked object was modified after you imported it into InDesign. You can easily update the link by clicking the warning icon in the document window or double-clicking the icon in the Links Panel.

The red circle with a question mark indicates that InDesign lost track of the file location. You may have moved the object to another source, another folder, or another location on your hard drive.

To relink a missing file, click the Missing icon in the document window, double-click the Missing icon in the Links Panel, or click the Relink icon (appearing as a chain link) at the bottom of the Links Panel. When you double-click the Missing icon or use one of the other methods for finding a link, the Locate dialog box opens. Navigate to the location where the linked file exists, select it, and click Open.

4.9 Packaging Files

Sometimes you may import a lot of objects into a document, and the objects might be scattered all over your hard drive. It can be an organizational nightmare if you don't add each object to a common folder before placing the objects.

Once you check the Links Panel and you're certain that a document has no missing or modified links, choose File ➤ Package. InDesign opens a summary screen and reports any errors found in your document. If all is okay, click the Package button at the bottom of the Package dialog box.

After you click Package, the next pane is used for printing instructions. If none of the information is helpful to you, click Continue. The last screen is the Package Publication screen. Choose a target location and click Package. InDesign adds your document, all linked assets, and all document fonts to a common folder.

4.10   Summary

As you can see from reading this chapter, InDesign provides you with an abundant set of features and methods for working with objects and images. You learned how to import images, create artwork in InDesign, and apply custom settings for objects and shapes, as well as a variety of methods for displaying artwork.

In the next chapter, we look at working with tables. You will learn how to format table cells and entire tables, use text and images with tables, and add interactivity to tables.

CHAPTER 5

▖ ▖ ▖

Creating Tables

If you poked around the Internet in the early '90s, you saw a lot of tables in Netscape Navigator. Colors were often very bland, using what I call *Netscape Gray* (Red, Green, and Blue, all set to 128 producing a medium-gray color). Web sites weren't as graphically attractive as they are today, and we didn't have CSS (Cascading Style Sheets). But the early versions of HTML did provide us with tags to create tables for displaying tabular data, and with the border=0 tag, web designers could create grid designs. Those early web page designs could use HTML table tags to display tabular data in more concise ways than simply adding text within paragraph tags.

Some people would argue that since the advent of CSS in late 1996, a web designer could eschew using tables in web designs, owing to Div tags and CSS, doing so may have become largely avoidable.

However, when we talk about tables created in InDesign, the artistic flair of the layout artist can reach new levels. The fundamental basis for an object might be a table, but the appearance of the table data can be expressed in so many creative ways that the results don't even look like tables.

To delve into some creative methods for using tables, first you need to understand InDesign table basics. After that, we can explore the many variations and look at going beyond a traditional table design to much more interesting layouts.

In this chapter, I talk about the basics of creating tables and how to format table cells. Then I move on to creative methods that help you produce more dynamic and interesting table designs.

5.1 Understanding the Fundamentals of Tables

One important basic concept that you need to understand is that tables, like text and all other objects, live inside frames. This is good because if you have a table that you want to spread across another page or multiple pages, you can click the outport on the frame, navigate to another page, and click to extend the table.

© Ted Padova 2017
T. Padova, *Adobe InDesign Interactive Digital Publishing*,
DOI 10.1007/978-1-4842-2439-7_5

Just like text frames, you can have overset text within a frame containing a table and you see an overset marker when viewing a document in Normal view. You also have control over corner designs like the graphic objects we looked at in Chapter 4. When you select a frame, click the yellow square and four diamond icons appear at the corners. Move the diamonds together or individually to change the corner options. Press Ctrl/⌘+Alt/⌥ and click a yellow diamond to change the corner effect. (For more on editing corners, see Chapter 4.) Inasmuch as you do have corner controls for tables, you're better off creating a frame behind the table and applying corner effects. If you have table cells with data, the corner effects might interfere with the data.

You can also transform tables by scaling skewing and reflecting. Use the methods described in Chapter 4 to perform a transformation to a table. You can place graphic objects in table cells, format text within cells, and add strokes to table cells. You can anchor objects to individual cells as well as anchoring a table within a text frame.

To anchor a table to a text frame, click the blue square at the top of a frame and drag it to the area that you want in a text frame. Shift+drag to make the object an inline object in the text frame or Alt/⌥+drag to open the Anchored Object Options dialog box.

5.2   Getting a Grip on Table Guidelines

The first thing that you need to do when working with a table is create the table. InDesign provides you with four ways that you can create tables. You can use menu commands, convert existing text to a table, and import data from a spreadsheet or word processing program. Let's look at each method.

CREATING TABLES

1. **Fill the margin guides with a table**. With nothing selected on the page, open the Table menu and choose Create Table. The Create Table dialog box opens, as shown in Figure 5-1. In the Create Table dialog box, you can set the number of rows and columns and indicate whether you want Header and/or Footer rows. If you have a table style (as I explain in Chapter 6), you can choose the style from the Table Style drop-down menu. Click OK and the cursor loads the table gun.

Create Table

Table Dimensions

Body Rows: 4

Columns: 3

Header Rows: 0

Footer Rows: 0

Table Style: [Basic Table] ▼

OK

Cancel

Figure 5-1. Choose Create Table from the Table menu, and the Create Table dialog box opens

2. **Click on the document page**. If you click near the top of a margin guide, the table fills the area between the margin guides, as you can see on the left side of Figure 5-2.

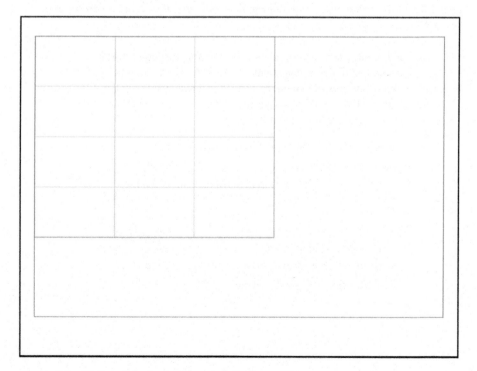

Figure 5-2. Click and drag to set a custom size for a table

153

3. **Specify a size for a new table.** This item is similar to the first way that you can create a table. Click somewhere in a text frame where you want the table to appear. Then choose Table ➤ Insert Table, specify the table attributes in the Create Table dialog box, and click OK.

4. **Convert text to a table**. You can convert text typed or placed in InDesign to a table. Select the text that you want to convert to a table and choose Table ➤ Convert Text to Table. The Convert Text to Table dialog box opens, as shown in Figure 5-3. In this dialog box, you can choose the Column and Row Separators.

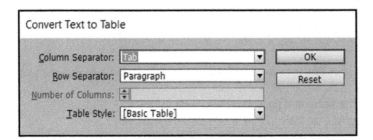

Figure 5-3. *Choose the number of columns and rows and the column separator and click OK*

5. **If you have text separated by commas and carriage returns at the end of each row, choose Comma from the Column Separator drop-down menu**. Leave the Row Separator at the Paragraph default choice. Likewise, if you have text with tabs, choose Tabs for the Column Separator.

6. **Click OK, and InDesign converts the text to a table**.

7. **Import data**. The final method that you can use to create tables in InDesign is to import text from a text document. You can import files saved as text only as well as RTF files, but the data won't be converted as neatly as when importing Microsoft Excel files. You can also import files using the CSV format, but again it won't be as clean as importing an Excel spreadsheet. If you use OpenSource applications like OpenOffice and IMB Lotus Symphony, you need to save the files in an Excel format.

8. **You use the File Place command to import spreadsheet data**. You can choose to handle the data in one of two ways. Import the data as a static block of text, or choose to link the data to the spreadsheet. If you want to link the data so that every time you make an edit in the spreadsheet application, the data are updated in InDesign, you need to adjust a Preference setting.

9. **Press Ctrl/⌘+K to open the InDesign Preferences**. Click File Handling in the left pane. In the right pane, enable the checkbox where you see Create Links When Placing Text and Spreadsheet files, as shown in Figure 5-4. Place the data file and click OK, and the Import Options dialog box opens.

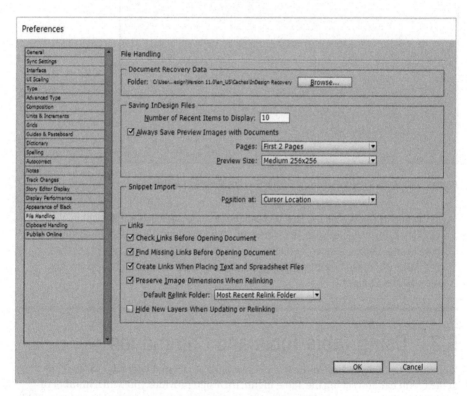

Figure 5-4. *Choose the number of columns and rows and click OK*

In Figure **5-5**, you see the title of the dialog box appearing as Microsoft Excel Import Options and the file name within parentheses. The title of the dialog box changes depending on the file type you choose to import.

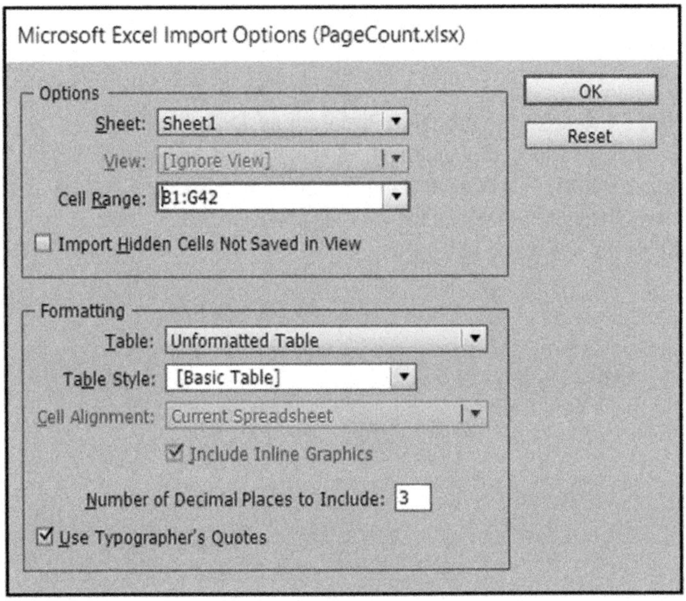

Microsoft Excel Import Options (PageCount.xlsx)

Options
Sheet: Sheet1
View: [Ignore View]
Cell Range: B1:G42
☐ Import Hidden Cells Not Saved in View

OK
Reset

Formatting
Table: Unformatted Table
Table Style: [Basic Table]
Cell Alignment: Current Spreadsheet
☑ Include Inline Graphics
Number of Decimal Places to Include: 3
☑ Use Typographer's Quotes

Figure 5-5. Import options when importing an Excel spreadsheet

In the Import Options dialog box, you can make some choices for the sheet in a workbook, the range of cells, and some formatting options. Click OK, and the table data is imported as a table. If you link a table to the data, you may need to update the link if you make any changes in the original spreadsheet. For more on linking objects, see Chapter 4.

5.3   Using Table Tools and Commands

Your first clue that you have quite a few commands associated with tables is looking at the menu bar and seeing the Table menu. InDesign provides you with a number of commands dedicated to working with tables, and they are neatly tucked away in the Table menu, as shown in Figure 5-6.

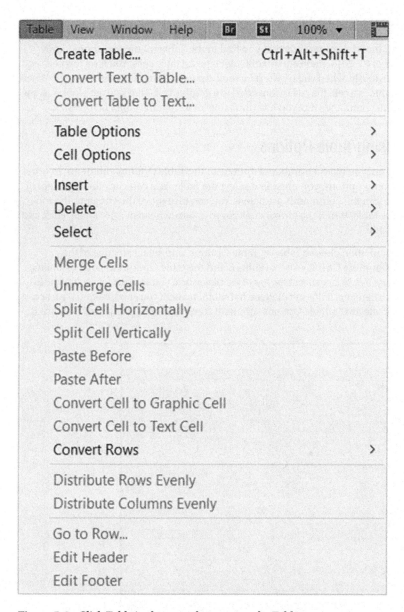

| Table | View | Window | Help | Br | St | 100% ▼ | |

Create Table...   Ctrl+Alt+Shift+T
Convert Text to Table...
Convert Table to Text...

Table Options   >
Cell Options   >

Insert   >
Delete   >
Select   >

Merge Cells
Unmerge Cells
Split Cell Horizontally
Split Cell Vertically
Paste Before
Paste After
Convert Cell to Graphic Cell
Convert Cell to Text Cell
Convert Rows   >

Distribute Rows Evenly
Distribute Columns Evenly

Go to Row...
Edit Header
Edit Footer

Figure 5-6. Click Table in the menu bar to open the Table menu

Like so many other features in InDesign, you also have a number of options in the Control Panel identical to many of the menu commands. Additionally, when you select a table or a cell within a table, you can right-click the mouse button and open a context menu to access a number of table commands easily.

5.3.1   Using the Table Menu

Before we jump into the commands that you find in the Table menu, you should know that as of InDesign CC 2015, there are two different types of table cells. You have text cells and graphic cells. Obviously, when you type text in a cell, the cell is interpreted as a text cell. When you place a graphic in a cell, the cell is converted to a graphic cell. That said, let's look at some of the Table menu commands that you have available for formatting tables in InDesign.

5.3.1.1   Using Table Options

In the Table menu, you have a number of options in the Table Options submenu. In order to use the submenu options, you must first select the table. You can click the Type tool in a cell, and the submenu commands are active. You can also move the cursor to the top-left corner of the table. When the cursor changes to an arrowhead at a 45° angle, click and you select the table.

Use either method, then choose Table ➤ Table Options, and select any one of the submenu items or press Ctrl/⌘+Alt/⌥+Shift+B and the table Options dialog box opens, as shown in Figure 5-7. Notice that at the top of the dialog box, you see tabs for each of the five submenu items. Therefore, it doesn't matter what submenu item you choose—you have access to all of them by selecting a Table Options submenu command or pressing Ctrl/⌘+Shift+B.

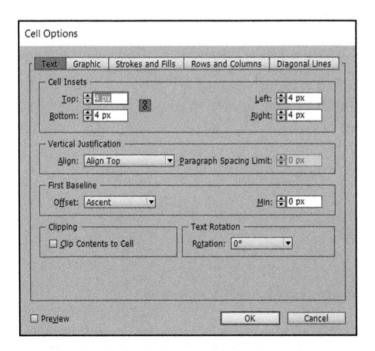

Figure 5-7.   *Press Ctrl/⌘+Shift+B and the Table Options dialog box opens*

There are five tabs in the Table Options dialog box. The default when you choose the
Table Setup submenu command or press Ctrl/⌘+Alt/⌥+Shift+B is the Table Setup tab.

- *Table Setup*: You can change the number of rows and columns
  and add header and footer rows in the Table Dimensions area. For
  a table border, specify the rule weight, color, and type of stroke
  for the border. You can create gaps and use a paper fill (if your
  background is white) so that the design won't look like a table.

  - Leave the Table Spacing at the defaults. If you want space
    before or after a table within a text frame, use Paragraph
    styles, which I I explain in Chapter 6. In the Draw drop-down
    menu, you can choose to show row and column cell strokes
    in the Front.

- *Row Strokes*: The settings in this tab are related to strokes along
  column rows, as shown in Figure 5-8. In the Alternating Pattern
  drop-down menu, you can alternate the stroke pattern (like
  applying different strokes or different colors) for alternating rows.
  InDesign lets you apply the pattern from one to three every other
  rows. If you want to alternate more than three rows, choose Custom.

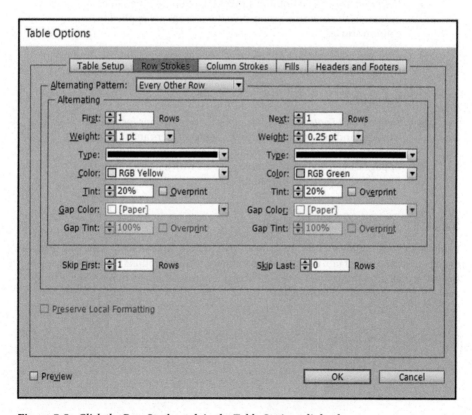

Figure 5-8. *Click the Row Strokes tab in the Table Options dialog box*

- *First/Next*: If you want to alternate more than three rows, type a value in the text boxes and the Alternating Pattern changes to Custom Row. For Type, Color, and Tint, choose from the Stroke styles in the drop-down menus, choose a color for the alternating rows in the Color drop-down menus, and change the color tint values in the Tint text boxes. If you want gaps between the rows other than the default Paper color, choose a color from the drop-down menus.

- *Gap Color/Tint*: These settings apply only to striped, dotted, and dashed strokes. If you have a solid stroke style, the drop-down menu is not active. Choose a color and tint for the gaps between stripes, dashes, and dots.

- *Skip First/Last*: Edit the text boxes for the number of rows that you want to skip for the pattern.

- *Preserve Local Formatting*: Enable the checkbox if you want previously-formatted strokes applied to the table to remain in effect.

- *Column Strokes*: The Column strokes tab offers you the same options as the row Strokes tab, only the settings are applied to column strokes.

- *Fills*: You have similar options for cell fills as you do with row strokes. You can choose alternating patterns, choose colors from drop-down menus, apply a tint to a selected color, and skip first/last rows.

- *Headers and Footers*: In the last tab, you have options for adding a header and/or footer row or rows. Using headers and footers are particularly helpful when you split tables across columns or pages. Each division of a table appears with a header and/or footer if you add them here in this tab.

5.3.1.2   Setting Cell Options

When you choose Table ➤ Cell Options ➤ Text or press Ctrl/⌘+Alt/⌥+B the Cell Options dialog opens at the Text tab. Cell options are similar to Table options with tabs across the top of the dialog, as shown in Figure 5-9. All of the settings that you make in this dialog are applied to the selected table cells.

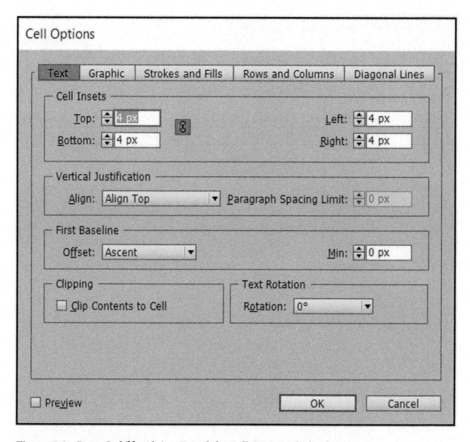

Figure 5-9. *Press Ctrl/⌘+Alt/⌐+B and the Cell Options dialog box opens*

- *Text*: The text tab contains options for text within cells. You can add an offset value for the text, vertically align text, offset the text baseline, clip the contents to a cell, and rotate text.

- *Graphic*: Table cells can be either text cells or graphic cells. Click the Graphic tab, and you can make adjustments for graphic cells such as adjusting the inset values and clipping the contents to a cell.

- *Strokes and Fills*: You can apply strokes and fills to individual cells. The difference between the table strokes is that you can target individual sides of the cell and apply strokes and colors, as you see in Figure 5-10. Click the gridlines at the top of the dialog to deselect or reselect a stroke. The selected strokes are affected when you apply a stroke value or color. Notice that you can also select strokes in tables in the Control Panel.

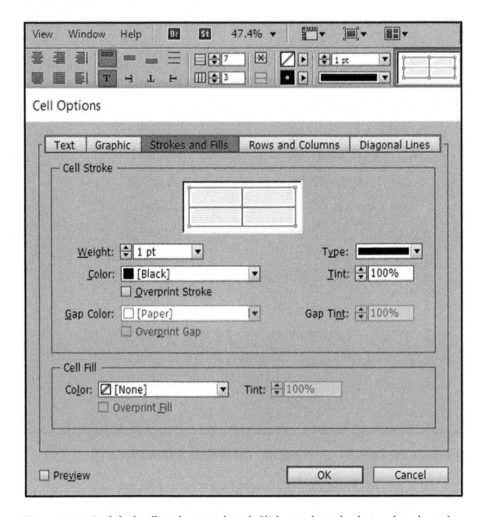

Figure 5-10. By default, all strokes are selected. Click a stroke to deselect and apply stroke weights and colors to the remaining selected strokes

- *Rows and Columns*: If you want a row height set to a fixed value, open the Row Height drop-down menu and choose Exactly.

- *Diagonal Lines*: Click the Diagonal Lines tab, and you can choose from four options: No stroke, 45° angle from to- left to lower-right side of the cell, 45° angle from the bottom-left to the top right of a cell, and two diagonal lines (like an X). You can choose to send the diagonal strokes to the back or have them appear on top of text or an object.

5.3.1.3   Inserting, Deleting, and Selecting Cells

Following Cell Options in the Table menu, you find three menu items for inserting rows and columns; deleting rows, columns, and the table; and selecting cells, rows, and columns, selecting header and footer rows, and selecting the table.

5.3.1.4   Merging Cells/Unmerging Cells

Select cells in a table and choose Table ➤ Merge Cells. The cells are merged into a single cell. If you want to unmerge the cells, select a merged cell and choose Table ➤ Unmerge Cells.

5.3.1.5   Splitting Cells Horizontally/Vertically

You can split individual cells horizontally and/or vertically. When you select a cell and choose either command, the cell(s) are split evenly.

5.3.1.6   Pasting Before/After a Row

These commands relate to rows and columns that you copy to the clipboard. After copying a row or column, choose Paste Before or Paste After a selected row/column.

5.3.1.7   Converting Cells to Graphic and Text Cells

In order to use these commands, you must not have any text/graphic contained in the cell. Select an empty cell and choose to convert a text cell to a graphic cell or a graphic cell to a text cell.

5.3.1.8   Converting Rows

When you choose Table ➤ Convert Rows, you find three options—Convert to a Header Row, Convert to a Body Row (body rows are all the rows between header and footer rows), and Convert to a Footer Row.

5.3.1.9   Distributing Rows/Columns Evenly

Select a range of columns or rows and choose Table ➤ Distribute Rows (or Columns) Evenly. The height of the rows or width of the columns are equally distributed among the selected rows/columns.

163

5.3.1.10 Navigating Rows

Select a table and choose Table ➤ Go to Row. The Go to Row dialog box opens, as shown in Figure 5-11. If your table contains a header and footer, you will find a drop-down menu where you can choose Body, Header, and Footer. Type a value in the text box to the right of the menu to jump to that row. This option is used most often with long tables spread over several pages.

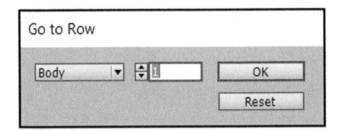

Figure 5-11. *Choose Table ➤ Go to Row to open the Go to Row dialog box*

5.3.1.11 Editing Headers and Footers

The last two menu items in the Table menu are Edit Header and Edit Footer. When you select one of these commands, the leftmost cell of the respective header/footer is selected.

5.3.2 Using the Control Panel

Select one or more cells or select a table, and the Control Panel changes, providing you options for editing rows, columns, and cells. In Figure 5-12, you can see a table selected and the options available in the Control Panel. These options are a subset of the Table menu commands.

Figure 5-12. *Select a table, and the Control Panel displays options for editing tables*

In the Control Panel, you will find the following:

- *Font and font style*: Make choices for the font and font style from the drop-down menus.

- *Font size and leading*: Click the arrow icons or type values in the adjacent text boxes to change font size and leading.

- *Alignment*: Click one of the eight icons to change text alignment in the selected cells.

- *Vertical alignment*: Click one of the four icons for aligning text vertically within cells to the top, center, bottom, or justified.

- *Text rotation*: Click one of the four icons to rotate text to the rotation shown in the icons.

- *Number of rows/columns*: Click the icon to the left of the text boxes to select the respective text in the text box. Click the arrow keys or type a value in the text box.

- *Merge/unmerge cells*: Select two or more cells and click the Merge cells icon to merge the cells. Select a merged cell and click the Unmerge cells icon to unmerge the cells.

- *Stroke color/fills*: Click the right arrowhead to open a drop-down menu showing the colors in the Swatches Panel. Select a color to apply to a cell fill or a stroke.

- *Weight/stroke style*: Edit the text box or choose an option for the stroke weight of the border and cells. Open the Stroke Style drop-down menu and choose a stroke style.

- *Target strokes*: The grid is the same as you find in cell options strokes and fills in Figure 5-10. Click the strokes in the Control Panel that you want to eliminate from options you choose for editing stroke attributes.

- *Cell and stroke styles*: These options relate to styles that you create for cells and tables. For information on how to create and use cell and table styles, see Chapter 6.

- *Column width and row height adjustments*: Choose Exactly from the drop-down menu to set the row height to a fixed value. Select At Least and click the arrows or type text in the text boxes to adjust row and column sizes.

- *Insets*: Edit the text boxes or click the arrowheads to adjust the top, bottom, left, and right cell insets.

5.4   Creating a New Table

The previous section, "Using Table Tools and Commands," is a reference guide that you might want to earmark and refer back to when you want to find the right command or tool to use when creating a table. Now it's time to look at the workflow and actually create a table.

In this exercise, we'll look at getting started on creating and formatting a simple table. In Figure 5-13, you can see a rather simple table created in InDesign. To create a table similar to the one shown in the figure, do the following:

ITEM	PRODUCING COUNTRY	YIELD BUSHELS X1,000
	COSTA RICA	**489,000** Olupta debit acerferro to etur re vellatus eos res aut assit eaque earis sunt ea volum et am coresequos explaccus dites nis remporit, alitas exr, ium sam et faciis res vendebis reptas estinus dolorat accus.
	PHILIPPINES	**512,000** Axim liquaes rere coreped ignam, sinimpo ritiatur adio. Nam hil maximin ratem nit omnis vent, experuptat qui nempori aturio. Et velit exeribus solorio quis dionsequ
	INDIA	**614,000** Nequis eum resto es rendic tem facearum quaeperio qui doluptioris ut poreicium aciis et desae magnis eaquistem conestrumque sequi sum re, exped eossit
	CHINA	**739,000** Ut ipidundio berfero quia cus, ipsaecatum vellectio vendae int est, odiat et maionseditae dolupta tumquodis aut ium re peritatium conseque excersp erepudia

Figure 5-13. *A table created in InDesign*

CREATING A NEW TABLE

1. **Create a new table**. To begin our project, let's create a new table from scratch. Choose Table ➤ Create Table, or press Ctrl/⌘+Alt/⌐+Shift+T. The Create Table dialog box opens.

2. **Specify rows and columns**. For a design similar to Figure 5-13, type 5 for the Body Rows and 3 for the Columns. We won't need a Header row for this simple table, so click OK after specifying the rows and columns.

3. **Set the row height for the first row.** Double-click the table with the Selection arrow and select the first row. Move the cursor to the far left of the first row, and when you see a right-pointing arrow, click. In the Control Panel, set the row height Exactly to 36 pixels (see Figure 5-14).

Figure 5-14. *Table rough setup*

4. **Set the next four row heights to 100 pixels.** Click the left-pointing arrow from the second row to the last row to select them and set the size again Exactly in the Control Panel to 100 pixels (see Figure 5-15).

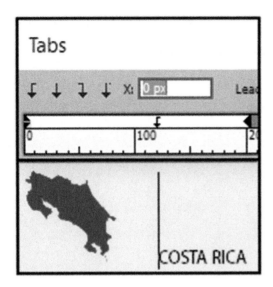

Figure 5-15. *Press Ctrl/⌘+Shift+T to open the Tab ruler*

5. **Set the column widths**. Move the cursor to the top of the table and select the first column. Set the column width to 100 pixels. Select the next two columns and set the width to 220 pixels (see Figure 5-16).

Figure 5-16. *Click the Align button tool in the Control Panel*

6. **Convert cells to graphic cells**. Click the Type tool and click in the second row cell in the left column. Drag down to select the four cells. Choose Table ➤ Convert Cell to Graphic Cell.

7. **Place graphic objects in the graphic cells**. You can use any type of graphic you want—a photo, a drawing, InDesign artwork, and so forth. Choose File ➤ Place and click a graphic cell to place the file in the cell. If you have artwork on a page, copy it and click the graphic cell. Choose Edit ➤ Paste Into. Place graphics in the four rows in the first column.

8. **Add some inline graphics**. In my example, I have another graphic appearing in the second column. Since I have text in the column as well, you can add the graphic as an inline object. Copy a graphic and click the insertion point in a cell. Choose Edit ➤ Paste or press Ctrl/⌘+V.

9. **Set a tab marker in the cells where you have an inline graphic**. Open the Tab ruler by choosing Type ➤ Tabs or press Ctrl/⌘+Shift+T. Set a tab just to the right of the inline graphic, as shown in Figure 5-15. Click the cursor in one of the cells and press Option ➤ Tab on the Mac. On Windows, choose Type ➤ Insert Special Character ➤ Tab. Type some text. In my example, I typed country names.

10. **Set the vertical alignment**. Select the four bottom rows in the second column and click the Align bottom icon in the Control Panel, as shown in Figure 5-16. This aligns the text and the graphic to the bottom of the cells.

11. **Add text to the last column**. In my example, the first line of text in the last column is aligned right. The other lines of text are aligned left. You can set the type attributes in the Control Panel as you would for any type in a text frame. Select the first line of text in the cell and click the Align right icon in the Control Panel. Select the rest of the text in the cell and click the Align left icon in the Control Panel.

12. **Add reversed out type to the first row**. Select the first row by clicking the left arrow on the left side of the first row and click the Foreground color swatch in the Swatches Panel. Click Black for the color. Click the Type tool and click in the first cell in the first row. Set the fill color to Paper in the Swatches Panel and type a head for the first column (see Figure 5-17). Press the Tab key and add type to the second column. Press Tab again and add type for the last column.

ITEM

Figure 5-17. Set the row fill color to Black and set the type color to Paper

13. **Set the type alignment**. Select the first row and click the Align Center tool in the Control Panel. Click the Align Vertical tool in the Control Panel to align the type vertically.

14. **Add alternating row fills**. Click the cursor in a cell, or move the cursor to the top-left corner of the selected table, and click the diagonal arrow to select the table. Choose Table ➤ Table Options ➤ Alternating Fills to open the Table Options dialog and the Fills tab (see Figure 5-18). Choose Every Other Row from the Alternating Pattern drop-down menu. Choose a color for the First and Next items from the drop-down menu and type a Tint value for each. Type 1 in the Skip First text box. Click OK and the table should look similar to the one shown in Figure 5-13.

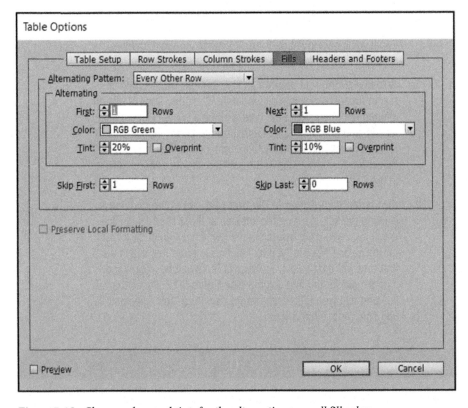

Figure 5-18. *Choose colors and tints for the alternating row cell fill colors*

5.5 Designing Creative Tables

Rather than walk though a bunch of tables showing tabular data and illustrating many of the options available with tables, let's look at some creative ways that you can design tables for inclusion in your digital publishing documents.

You can use many of the features covered in Chapter 3, where I talked about formatting text and applying different type formats to text in table cells. You can also use many of the different techniques for working with graphics that I talked about in Chapter 4.

To make your life much easier, it would be a great advantage for you to use styles—styles for characters, paragraphs, graphics, and tables. But I haven't come to talking about styles yet, which is the topic for Chapter 6. For now, let's look at some techniques for creating some interesting tables. If you need to use repetitive steps when applying edits to multiple cells, look over Chapter 6 and then jump back to this chapter.

5.5.1 Rounding Corners and Anchoring Objects

You can round corners on tables; however, the effects most often won't give you the results that you want. Keep in mind that you deal with two different objects when creating tables—the table and the container frame. If you round corners on the container frame, the table will be offset from the frame. If you try to select the table, you won't find any corner options that you can control. You need to use other methods for creating corner effects.

Anchoring objects is important when creating tables. Look at Figure 5-19. In this table, I have rounded corners and objects in the first column anchored to text frames. In order to have cells with both text and graphics, you need to anchor objects to the cell text fields.

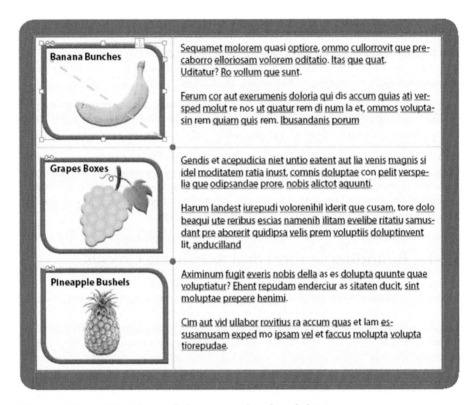

Banana Bunches

Sequamet molorem quasi optiore, ommo cullorrovit que precaborro elloriosam volorem oditatio. Itas que quat. Uditatur? Ro vollum que sunt.

Ferum cor aut exerumenis doloria qui dis accum quias ati versped molut re nos ut quatur rem di num la et, ommos voluptasin rem quiam quis rem. Ibusandanis porum

Grapes Boxes

Gendis et acepudicia niet untio eatent aut lia venis magnis si idel moditatem ratia inust, comnis doluptae con pelit verspelia que odipsandae prore, nobis alictot aquunti.

Harum landest iurepudi volorenihil iderit que cusam, tore dolo beaqui ute reribus escias namenih ilitam evelibe ritatiu samusdant pre aborerit quidipsa velis prem voluptiis doluptinvent lit, anducilland

Pineapple Bushels

Aximinum fugit everis nobis della as es dolupta quunte quae voluptiatur? Ehent repudam enderciur as sitaten ducit, sint moluptae prepere henimi.

Cim aut vid ullabor rovitius ra accum quas et lam essusamusam exped mo ipsam vel et faccus molupta volupta tiorepudae.

Figure 5-19. *A table with rounded corners and anchored objects*

■ **Note**   In order to see the anchor threads, choose View ➤ Extras ➤ Show Text Threads or press Ctrl/⌘+Alt/⌥+Y. You must be in Normal view to see the thread lines.

The rounded corners in Figure 5-19 are applied to a frame. The text frame containing the table was pasted into this frame (`Edit > Paste Into`) to give the appearance that the border for the table contains rounded corners. Since the objects in column 1 were anchored, cutting and pasting the table included all of the elements.

In Figure 5-20, you can see another example of a similar table. The anchored objects are the diamond shapes at the cell intersections. This creates the illusion of beveled corners on the cells.

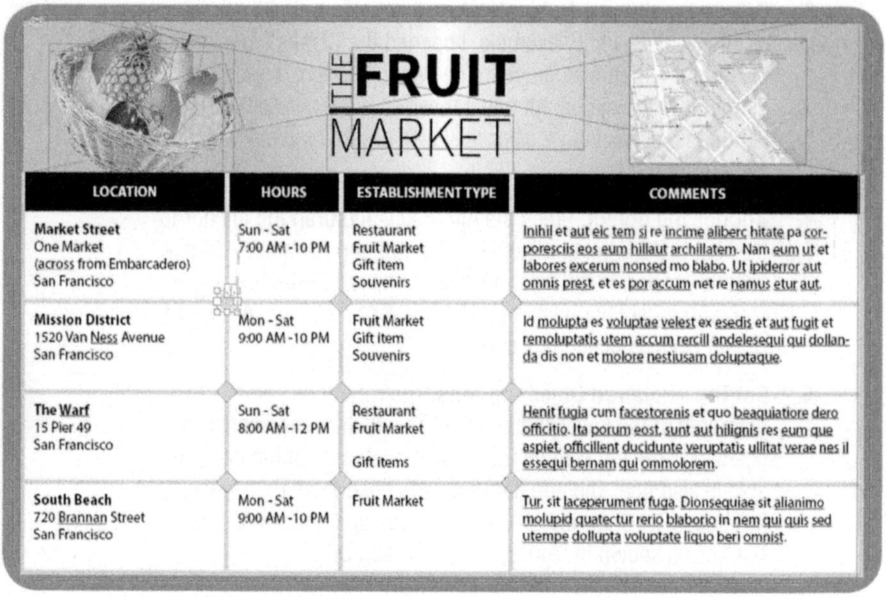
THE FRUIT MARKET
LOCATION
HOURS
ESTABLISHMENT TYPE
COMMENTS
Market Street
One Market
(across from Embarcadero)
San Francisco
Sun - Sat
7:00 AM - 10 PM
Restaurant
Fruit Market
Gift item
Souvenirs
Inihil et aut eic tem si re incime aliberc hitate pa corporesciis eos eum hillaut archillatem. Nam eum ut et labores excerum nonsed mo blabo. Ut ipiderror aut omnis prest, et es por accum net re namus etur aut.
Mission District
1520 Van Ness Avenue
San Francisco
Mon - Sat
9:00 AM - 10 PM
Fruit Market
Gift item
Souvenirs
Id molupta es voluptae velest ex esedis et aut fugit et remoluptatis utem accum rercill andelesequi qui dollanda dis non et molore nestiusam doluptaque.
The Warf
15 Pier 49
San Francisco
Sun - Sat
8:00 AM - 12 PM
Restaurant
Fruit Market
Gift items
Henit fugia cum facestorenis et quo beaquiatiore dero officitio. Ita porum eost, sunt aut hilignis res eum que aspiet, officillent ducidunte veruptatis ullitat verae nes il essequi bernam qui ommolorem.
South Beach
720 Brannan Street
San Francisco
Mon - Sat
9:00 AM - 10 PM
Fruit Market
Tur, sit laceperument fuga. Dionsequiae sit alianimo molupid quatectur rerio blaborio in nem qui quis sed utempe dollupta voluptate liquo beri omnist.

Figure 5-20. *The diamond shapes are anchored objects*

DESIGNING A CREATIVE TABLE

Here's how I created the table.

1. **Create the table.** I created a table with six rows and four columns. I set the size of the top row to 125 pixels, the second row to 33 pixels, and the remaining rows to 75 pixels. This last setting is very important. The rows containing the diamond shapes all need to be the same size, as we'll see later when I talk about duplicating the objects.

2. **Format the table.** I reversed out the type by filling the first row with black and set the type to Paper. I set the internal stroke values to 4 points and applied a color to the strokes below the third row. I set strokes on the reversed-out cells to 4 points and a Paper color. In the initial setup, I added commas for the text in columns 2 and 3. This makes it easy to convert the commas to paragraph returns later after I add the diamond objects.

3. **Create the diamond objects.** You can create a circle, square, or other object. In my example, I opened the Glyphs Panel and looked for a diamond shape in the Wingdings font. I added a diamond to the document and converted the text to an outline. I added no stroke and a color fill. I also created the object to the left side of the table.

4. **Anchor the object.** Press the Alt/‿ key and drag the anchor to the first text frame. In my example, I dragged the anchor to the second column in the first row, just to the left of the text. When you drag an anchor while pressing the Alt/‿ key, the Anchored Object Options dialog box opens.

5. **Set the Anchored Object options.** The reference point defaulted at the lower-left position. This is fine. The anchored position is the left side (in this case the left side of the cell text). This is also fine. The one item that you need to change is the X Relative To. Open the drop-down menu and choose Anchor Marker, as shown in Figure 5-21, and click OK.

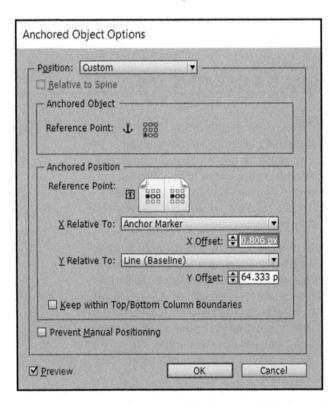

Figure 5-21. *Press the Alt/‿ key while dragging the anchor to the text frame to open the Anchored Object Options dialog box*

6. **Move the object into position.** Drag the object to the first intersection of the row and column strokes.

7. **Create an Object Style.** I've been holding off talking about using style sheets in InDesign because I have an entire chapter devoted to styles and particularly graphic styles. However, we really can't move forward with this design unless you create an Object Style. Open the Window menu and choose Styles ➤ Object Styles. When the panel opens, click the Create new style icon at the bottom of the panel. Click the object and select the new style to be sure that the graphic inherits the style. For more information on creating Object Styles, see Chapter 6.

8. **View the anchor thread.** Choose View ➤ Extras ➤ Show Text Threads or press Ctrl/⌘+Alt/⌥+Y. Be certain that you are in Normal view and not Preview view. If the anchor is properly set in the text field, you should see a dashed blue line from the object to the beginning of the text paragraph in the third row in the second column, as shown in Figure 5-22.

Figure 5-22. *Choose View ➤ Extras ➤ Show Text Threads of press Ctrl/⌘+Alt/⌥+Y to see the text threads*

9. **Cut the object.** Select the anchored object and press Ctrl/⌘+X to cut the object to the clipboard.

10. **Select the cells that you want to change.** Drag the cursor through the cells to which you want to add the anchored objects. In my example, the cells from the third row and second column through the last row and the fourth column are the ones that I want to change.

11. **Open the Find/Change dialog box.** You had a small introduction to searching and replacing with GREP patterns in Chapter 3. You need to use a GREP pattern search and replace to add the objects to all of the row and column intersections. It's very important that all of the row heights are the same size and all of the text insets are the same values for this to work properly.

12. **Choose Edit ➤ Find/Change to open the Find Change dialog box.** Click GREP to open the GREP pane.

13. **Set the GREP Find/Change parameters.** Open the Find What menu (@ symbol with a down-pointing arrow). Choose Locations and select Beginning of Paragraph, as shown in Figure 5-23. This is why we needed to concatenate the sentences and use the commas that we'll later change to carriage returns. You want only single paragraphs in the cells. Return to the menu and choose Wildcards ➤ Any Character. This instructs InDesign to set the anchor position at the beginning of the paragraph, regardless of which character appears first.

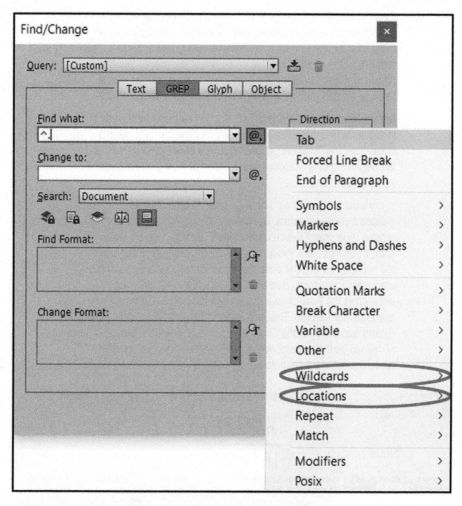

Figure 5-23. *Click the GREP tab and open the Find What menu*

14. **Open the Change To menu.** Choose Other ➤ Clipboard
Contents: Formatted. Since we cut the object with the text
anchor to the clipboard, this option uses the object and anchor
as the replacement. Open the Change To menu again and
choose Found ➤ Found Text. This item ensures that you won't
delete the first character in the paragraph.

15. **Execute the Find/Change GREP search.** Choose Selection in the Search drop-down menu, click Find Next, and click Change to test the search and be sure that everything is working properly. If the change creates an object at the proper location (third row, second column), everything should work fine. Click Change All and your table should be populated with the objects.

16. **Set the paragraph returns.** It should be obvious why I needed to make certain that there weren't any multiple carriage returns in the cells. The Find/Change GREP changes would have stopped at the beginning of each paragraph instead of a single paragraph in the column cells.

    In my example I used a comma (,) with no spaces where I wanted a carriage return. To change the commas to carriage returns, first select the columns where the text appears that you want to change. In my example, the text in columns three below the second row are the ones that have commas where I actually want carriage returns (see Figure 5-24). After selecting the cells, open the Find/Change dialog box (Edit ➤ Find/Change) and click the Text tab. Type a comma in the Find What field. Type a caret and p (^p) in the Change To text box. Click the Change All button, and the replacements should show you paragraphs while the commas are deleted.

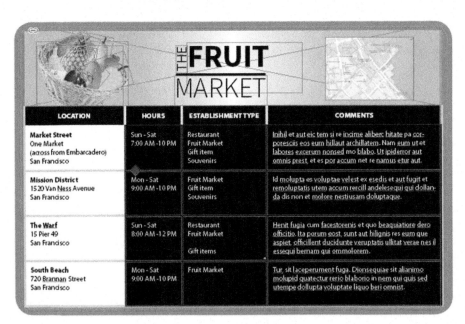

Figure 5-24. Select the cells where you want to replace characters

17. **Add a frame and stroke the edges.** This is the last step because if you add the frame on top of the table, you'll have trouble editing cells and table attributes. It's best to create the frame last or place it on a layer and hide it, or you can send it to the background and lock it (Ctrl/⌘+L) while setting up your table. In my example, I drew a frame around the table, added a 20-point stroke, and set the fill to none. Size the frame so that it slightly overlaps the edges of the table and select it. Choose Object ➤ Arrange ➤ Bring to Front (or press Ctrl/⌘+Shift+]-right bracket key) to position the frame on top of the table.

This sequence seems like a lot of work. Actually, it *is* a lot of work! But once you create a few tables with decorative borders and anchored objects, you should be able to breeze through the steps and be well on your way to creating some interesting table designs.

5.5.2 Using Floating Objects

Sometimes you can't anchor all of the objects in cells. At least it might make you crazy trying to get the cells the right width to anchor objects at the right positions. Rather than trying to fiddle around with setting up anchors, you might find it much easier to use floating objects.

In Figure 5-25, the design is set up as a table. The table has three rows and four columns. Between the rows are white strokes of 20 points. This gives the illusion that the design is not a table but separate frames offset from each other.

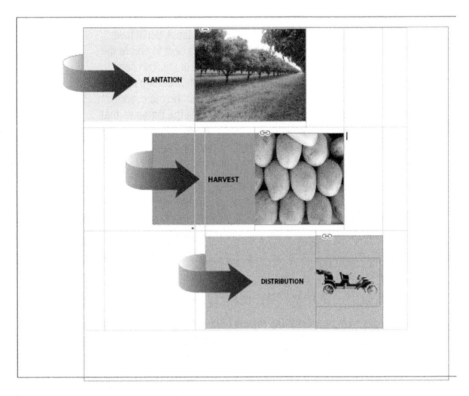

Figure 5-25. *This table has three rows and four columns with large white strokes separating the rows*

One problem that you have with tables is that you can't create a stacking order as you can with multiple objects—at least in the design shown in Figure 5-25. The 3D arrows almost seem to come from behind the cells. In reality, the top portion of the arrows are butted up against the cells—something that we try to avoid in illustration programs. There's always a chance for a tiny space to appear between the elements.

The reason why you can't set up a stacking order with the arrow behind the table is that the cells are constructed with white borders. In the Harvest cell, for example, the cell width is beyond the left side of the arrow because the outside border is set to 20 points. The cell has white borders on the top and the left side. Therefore, you can't send the top portion of the arrow behind the cells, so butting up against the cells is your only choice.

Instead of using anchored objects, I added the elements and positioned them as best I could. After all is finished, you need to group everything. You can use this type of table design in all digital publishing documents, including reflowable EPUBs.

5.5.3   Anchoring Objects in Cell Offsets

In Figure 5-26, you can see a rather simple table where I used cell offsets for the type. The arrowheads are anchored to the text so that the arrowhead shows some ample room to the left of each line of type in the cells.

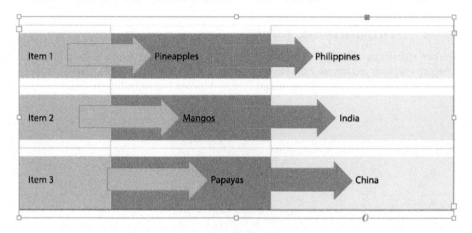

Figure 5-26. *This table has three rows and three columns with the arrowheads anchored to the cells in the second and third columns*

ANCHORING OBJECTS IN CELL OFFSETS

To create this kind of table, I did the following:

1. **Create a table.** In my example, I created a table with three rows and three columns. The horizontal lines are set to 20 points and filled white, which gives the appearance that there are multiple objects even though we only have a single table.

2. **Set the cell insets.** In columns two and three, I set the insets to different values for each row. You can easily change an inset value in the Control Panel and see the results dynamically as you change them.

3. **Create the arrowhead.** I used a Wingding font and found an arrowhead in the Glyphs Panel (Type ➤ Glyphs or Alt/⌥+Shift+F11). I set the type and then converted the type to outlines.

4. **Anchor the arrowheads.** I anchored the arrowheads to the text in each row and column. If you create an Object Style, the task is easier.

5. **Resize the arrowheads.** Since the arrows were converted to outlines, each is now a vector object that you can easily resize. Select the Direct Selection tool and drag the left side of the arrow to the left. This lengthens the arrow.

5.5.4 Transforming Tables

You can transform tables in InDesign using the transformation techniques described in Chapter 4. Before you transform a table, be certain to finalize the table formatting and design. In Figure 5-27, you see the design I created before transforming the table.

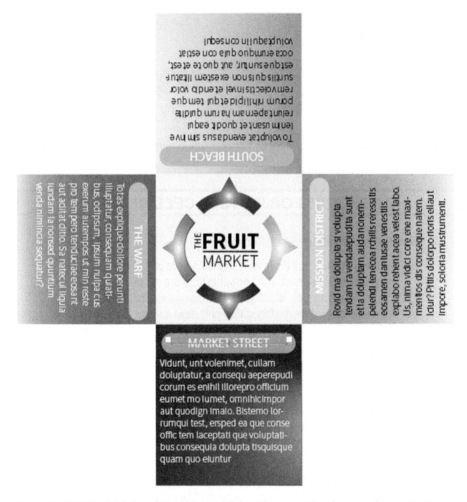

Figure 5-27. *This table has three rows and three columns with inline graphics and objects pasted inside the graphic frame*

If you have objects contained within cells, you have to perform transformations carefully. Grouping objects that are set inline in text cells and objects pasted inside graphic cells can be easily rotated or sheared without problems. However, if you try to scale the table, objects inside the cells won't stay within the cells. You may need to scale the objects individually after the fact and move them into position .

TRANSFORMING TABLES

I created the table shown in Figure 5-27 as follows:

1. **Create the table.** Choose Table ➤ Create Table. When the Create Table dialog box opens, enter the values for the number of columns and rows. In my example, I created a table with three columns and three rows.

2. **Format the cell sizes.** In my table, I set the row and column sizes to 125 pixels in the Control Panel. I chose Exact from the drop-down menu on the right side of the Control Panel and entered 125 in the adjacent text boxes. I selected the table and set the stroke to 0 for all strokes.

3. **Fill the cells.** In my example, I converted the center cell to a graphic cell and pasted a grouped object inside the cell. I added text to the other cells and set the text orientation to the four views that you see in Figure 5-28 using the Control Panel options for text rotations. I added gradient fills to the outside cells and a solid fill in the graphic frame.

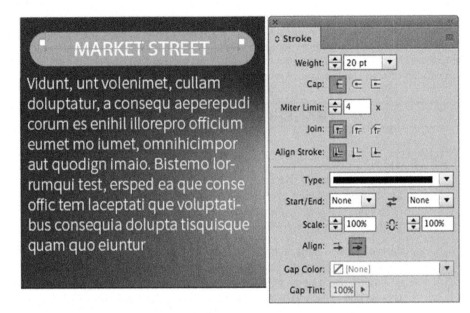

Figure 5-28. Set the stroke to 20 points and use the Type on a Path tool to add type to the path (left). Set the Baseline Shift to -6 points (right).

4. **Add the buttons.** At the top of each text cell is a button. I created a stroke and set type along the path using the Type on a Path tool (Figure 5-28, left). I set the stroke value to 20 points and clicked the Round cap icon in the Stroke Panel. I applied a color to the stroke and set the baseline to -6 points. You can set the baseline in the Control Panel, or press Alt/⌥+Down Arrow to move the baseline shift downward (see Figure 5-29). I then centered the text on the path (Ctrl/⌘+Shift+C) and dragged the end of the stroke horizontally to fit the text. After creating one stroke on a path, I duplicated the stroke three times and applied different type and colors to each one.

5. **Group all objects.** Marquee the table and choose Object ➤ Group to group the objects.

6. **Transform the table.** I rotated the table using the Free Transform tool and sheared the table using the Shear tool. I also scaled the table a bit, but the graphic moved and didn't scale properly. I had to move the object inside the graphic cell and scale it individually. To select the graphic , double-click the table, then double-click the graphic. The final result is shown in Figure 5-29.

Figure 5-29. *The table after rotating, shearing, and scaling*

5.5.5   Creating a Photo Grid

You can place multiple photos in a grid using the File ➤ Place command, and you can add static and live captions using the Object ➤ Captions submenu commands. However, tables provide you with some more freedom over placing photos in a grid. You can easily change the distance between cells from no stroke to huge strokes and apply different colors for the strokes. Working with a table provides you with a lot of freedom and offers you easy methods for managing photos placed in a table.

In Figure 5-30, I created a table with two columns and two rows to show you an example of how you might display a photo grid.

185

Figure 5-30. *A table with photos placed in graphic cells*

One advantage of using a table is that you can easily adjust column widths between cells. If you place multiple photos using File ➤ Place, you can achieve the same results using modifier keys, but that will twist your body extensively. You need to press the Up and Right Arrow keys on your keyboard to determine the grid cells. After you get the columns right, you need to adjust the column width. While still holding the mouse button down, press the Ctrl/⌘ key then the arrow keys. Working through the modifier keys gyrations is a pain compared to using a table.

Something else that I find easier to do with tables is creating multi-state objects within table cells. I cover creating multi-state objects in Chapter 9. For now, recognize that a multi-state object quite often is used to change the state view within the same location on a page. For example, if you want to create a button that advances through a number of photos all within a single table cell, you would create the multi-state object and add a button to advance through the different states.

The way to accomplish setting up the objects is quite simple. Place a photo in a graphic frame in a table cell. Copy the frame and paste it into your document. Duplicate the frame and place another photo in the duplicate frame. You can add as many frames as you like. Align the objects using the Align Panel and select them by dragging the cursor through the group. Open the Object States Panel and create the multi-state object. Cut the object and click the graphic frame in the table. Select the graphic cell, choose Edit ➤ Paste Into, and the object state is pasted into the graphic frame. Then you create a button to advance through the states.

If this sounds a little confusing now, bear with me until you get to Chapter 9. There I explain how to work with multi-state objects thoroughly and how to create buttons that advance through the states.

5.5.6   Magnifying a Cell

You may want to draw a reader's attention to the contents of a particular cell in a table. In Figure 5-31, you see an example of a magnifying glass showing a zoomed view of a map. A technique like this can amplify the contents of a cell and bring the reader's attention to the table cell.

Figure 5-31. A table with photos placed in graphic cells

MAGNIFYING A CELL

To create this design, I did the following:

1. **Create the magnifying glass.** I pressed Alt/⌥+Shift and drew from the center a constrained circle shape. I selected the Scale tool, pressed Alt/⌥, and clicked the circle to open the Scale dialog box. I then sized the circle down 75% and clicked Copy. With two circles on the document page, I selected both and chose Object ➤ Paths ➤ Make Compound Path. I set the stroke to 4 points and chose Black for the stroke color.

2. **For the handle, I drew a rectangle and added rounded corners**. I added a few white strokes to the top-left side of the rectangle and applied a Bevel Emboss to the rectangle. I then grouped the objects and rotated the handle.

3. **Create an ellipse frame.** I selected the Ellipse Frame tool and drew a circle a little larger than the inside of the magnifying glass compound path objects.

4. **Place the photo.** I chose File ➤ Place and placed the original photo.

5. **Paste Into the ellipse frame.** I cut the placed photo to the clipboard and selected the circle frame. I then chose Edit ➤ Paste Into.

6. **Bring the magnifying glass to the front.** I selected the magnifying glass frame and chose Object ➤ Arrange ➤ Bring to Front (Ctrl/⌘+Shift+]).

7. **Size the photo.** I selected the photo and sized it up.

8. **Group and position the object.** I selected the map and magnifying glass elements and grouped them. Then I moved the object to position.

You can use the same technique with table cell frames. When using table cells, first simplify the table by deleting columns and rows outside the area you want to magnify. Try to get the table as small and simple as possible, leaving only the cell(s) you want to size up.

■ **Caution** InDesign has a habit of crashing when you try to cut a table and use the Paste Into command.

When you get the table size right, cut the table and paste into the graphic frame. Size the table cells by pressing Ctrl/⌘+Shift and drag a handle outward. When the size is approximately the size you want, cut the table and paste into the graphic frame.

Selecting the contents of the graphic frame is a little tricky. If you double-click the contents that has a text cell, you get an I-beam cursor in the cell. Once you double-click the cell, press the Esc key on your keyboard. This action will select the cell. Move the cursor to the left and select any adjacent rows and the top to select any adjacent columns. When the table is selected, use the arrow keys on your keyboard to position the contents inside the frame.

■ **Tip**   When you select an object and press an arrow key, the object moves one pixel at a time. To move in larger increments (10 points), press the Shift key and the arrow keys.

5.5.7   Using Table Scripts

Like so many other editing sequences that you can perform using scripts, there are a number of low-cost and free scripts designed to work with tables that you can find on the Internet. One of my favorites is a calendar maker script. This script is very powerful and lets you create calendars for a month, range of months, a year, or range of years, all with a double-click on a script name in the Scripts Panel.

5.5.7.1   Downloading and Installing Scripts

The Adobe InDesign Calendar Wizard was created by Scott Selberg, and you can find the InDesign script at www.scourceforge.net. When you arrive at the home page, type calendar in the search field and you'll be taken to a list of documents, one of which is the Adobe InDesign Calendar Wizard.

You can also find the download by typing InDesign Calendar Script in your web browser search field. Either way you find the download page. When you arrive at the download page, click the Download button.

When the download finishes, unzip the compressed archive. To install the script, open your scripts folder in InDesign. Open the JavaScripts folder and right-click to open a context menu. Choose Reveal in Explorer (Windows) or Reveal in Finder (Macintosh). Copy the scripts you downloaded to the folder that opens when you choose Reveal.

5.5.7.2   Running the Calendar Script

After you install the script, double-click the calendarWizard.js script in the Scripts folder. The Adobe InDesign Calendar Wizard dialog box opens, as shown in Figure 5-32.

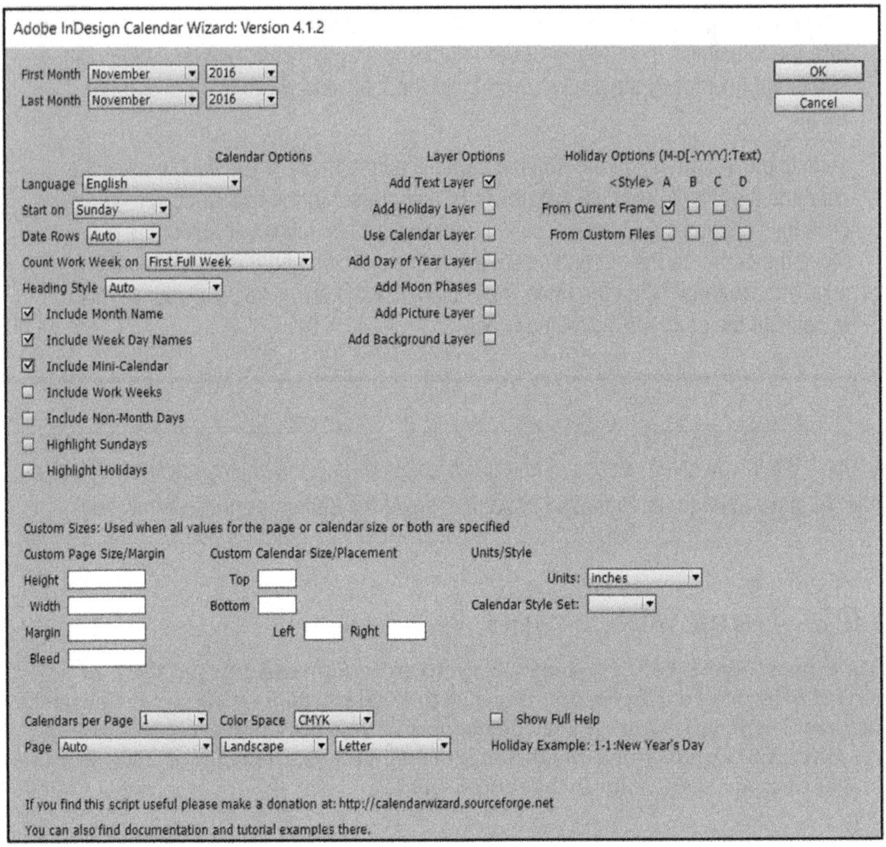

Figure 5-32. *Double-click the calendarWizard.js file in the Scripts Panel to open the calendar wizard*

In this dialog box, you have many choices. You can choose the month range from the drop-down menu in the top-left corner. You can choose the year(s) from menus adjacent to the First Month and Last Month menus. To include holidays in your calendar, enable one of the checkboxes on the right side of the wizard. You can choose to add a mini calendar that appears in the top-right and left corners for the previous and next months. You also have choices for color space and page sizes. Review the options in the wizard, make your choices, and click OK.

The calendar opens as shown in Figure 5-33. This is but one of many scripts that you can find on the Internet to help you work with tables. You can also acquire other scripts that help you become more efficient in other editing tasks.

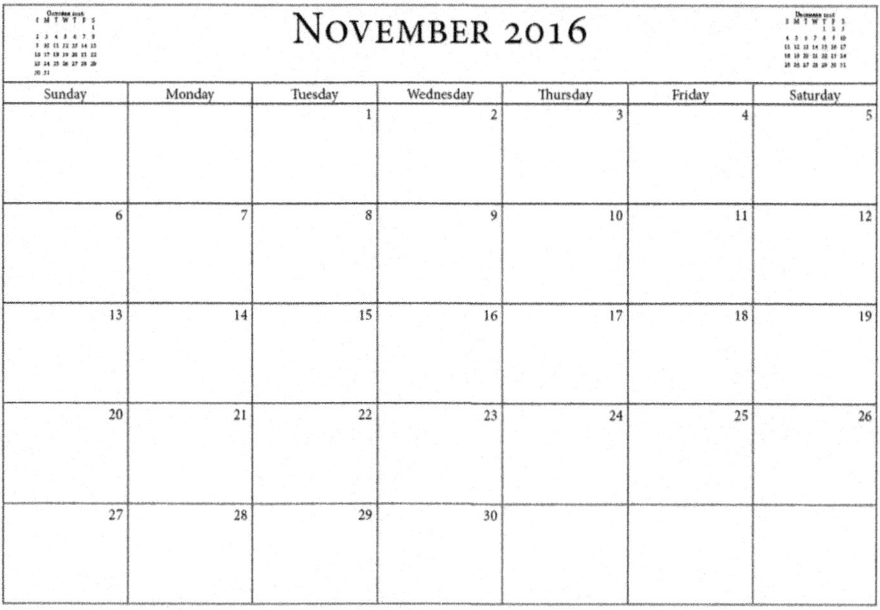

Figure 5-33. *A calendar created with the calendarWizard.js script*

■ **Note**   Many scripts that you can find on the Internet are provided free or at low cost for the download. Many of the developers ask for a donation. If you use a script and find it worthwhile, send the developer some money. $5-10 will mean a lot to those who put in the time to offer you some great tools that can greatly help you in your design sessions.

5.6   Summary

In this chapter, we looked at creating tables. You learned how to format tables and table cells, how to design creative tables, how to transform tables, and how to add some interactivity to your tables. As you can see from reading this chapter, tables in InDesign are much more than grids that contain data. You can be creative and design tables that don't look like traditional tables. We also looked at anchoring objects in tables. Anchoring objects and anchoring tables becomes important when you create reflowable EPUBs, as you'll see in later chapters.

In the next chapter, we continue with working with assets and look at the all-important features related to creating styles for text. Styles are a must when exporting to EPUBs, and the next chapter contains all that you need to know about working with text styles.

■ ■ ■

CHAPTER 6

Creating and Applying Styles

Characters, paragraphs, tables, and objects such as frames and lines can all be assigned styles. Quite simply, a *style* captures all of the attributes that you apply to text, table cells, tables, and objects. Once you create a style, you can apply the style to other text, table cells, tables, or objects throughout your design. This makes the editing process move along much faster and with much more efficiency.

Not only are styles helpful in working faster and becoming more efficient in InDesign, they are absolutely essential when you create reflowable EPUBs. You can get by avoiding styles in other digital publishing documents, but reflowable EPUBs behave differently. You need styles to display your publications accurately.

In this chapter, I cover how to create character, paragraph, table, object, and GREP styles.

6.1   Getting Familiar with Styles

Character, paragraph, and cell styles can be created and applied using either the Control Panel or other respective panels. When you choose Window ➤ Styles, a submenu opens showing you five different style types. When you choose a submenu command, it opens the respective panel. The panels include:

- *Cell Styles*: Cell styles pertain to table cells.

- *Character Styles*: Character styles can be applied to a single character or several words, but they should not be applied to an entire paragraph.

- *Object Styles*: Object styles can be applied to any non-text items, such as images and objects.

- *Paragraph Styles*: Paragraph styles relate to styles that you apply to paragraphs.

- *Table Styles*: Table styles are applied to tables. A best practice is first to create cell styles before you create table styles.

- *GREP Styles*: GREP styles don't have a panel. You create GREP styles in the Paragraph Style Options dialog box.

© Ted Padova 2017
T. Padova, *Adobe InDesign Interactive Digital Publishing*,
DOI 10.1007/978-1-4842-2439-7_6

A style captures the formatting for the given style item. For example, character styles apply to text attributes, cell styles apply to table cell attributes, and so forth.

Cell styles are limited to certain kinds of formatting. You can include colors and borders in cell styles but you cannot include cell widths and row heights in them.

You have two ways to create a style. You can format an item exactly as you want it. For example, if you want to create a character style, you can set the font, font style, leading, text color, baseline shift, and so forth, examine the type to be certain that it appears exactly as you want, and then open the Character Styles Panel and create a new style from the selected text. The new style inherits all of the text attributes and includes them in the style.

The other way that you can create a style is to deselect all type on a page (or objects, cells, or tables) and open the style panel for something like character styles and then click the Create new style icon at the bottom of the panel. All style panels have the Create new style icon at the bottom of the panel. When you click the Create new style panel icon, a dialog box opens where you set attributes for the style.

The easiest way to create a style is to apply formatting to the item you want for the style then click the Create new style icon that captures all of the formatting.

After you create a style, you can apply the style to other items in your layout. For example, if you create a paragraph style for body copy, click inside any paragraph containing body copy and then click the respective style in the Paragraph Styles Panel. All of the text and paragraph formatting in the paragraph that you select takes on the attributes in the style definition.

The real power of using styles is when you want to make changes to various attributes. Suppose that you have subheads with display type throughout a document. You then add another subhead and find out the text doesn't quite fit on a single line. Maybe the point size of the type could be lowered a half-point and the text would fit the column width. For a situation like this, you could easily edit the style, change the font size, and click OK in the Style dialog box. All type using the same style name is updated throughout your document. If you have 1,000 subheads, they would all be changed with one simple edit.

The Styles Panel menus contain more options, and we'll look at some later in this chapter when I cover creating the various style types. For now, just try to understand the value of creating styles, and how they can help your design workflow.

6.2 Creating and Applying Paragraph Styles

Notice that I began by talking about paragraph styles before I addressed character styles. The reason for this is that in your workflow, you want to create paragraph styles first and then go about creating character styles. This is the most normal workflow procedure in InDesign.

Paragraph styles are applied to an entire paragraph. Anything inside the paragraph should not be changed after creating the style. If you need to make changes to text attributes within a paragraph, you need to use a character style. If you do make a change to text within a paragraph style you get an override. You want to avoid overrides, especially when you export your files to EPUB format.

6.2.1   Creating a Paragraph Style

To work with paragraph styles, you need to use the Paragraph Styles Panel. Choose Window ➤ Styles ➤ Paragraph Styles to open the Paragraph Styles Panel, as shown in Figure 6-1.

Figure 6-1. *Choose Window ➤ Styles ➤Paragraph Styles to open the Paragraph Styles Panel*

When you open the panel, you see one style already in the panel. The Basic Paragraph style is an InDesign default. You cannot delete the Basic Paragraph style.

There are two ways that are available to you for creating paragraph styles. For that matter, there are two ways that you can create any other style when using the various styles panels. If you have nothing selected in your document and click the Create new style icon at the bottom of the Paragraph Styles Panel (or open the Paragraph Styles Panel menu and choose New Paragraph Style), the New Paragraph Style dialog box opens. (See Figure 6-2.)

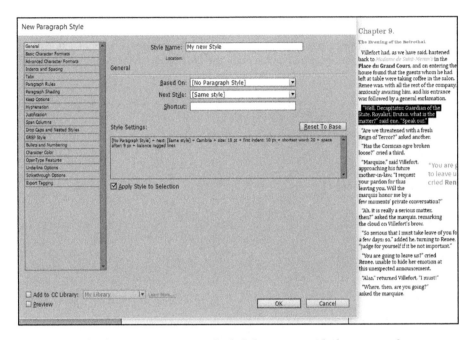

Figure 6-2. *After formatting a paragraph, click the cursor inside the paragraph, press Alt/⌥, and click the Create new style icon in the Paragraph Styles Panel*

At this point, you use the various options to format your paragraph. As shown in Figure 6-2, you have many options for handling text, indents and spacing, character colors, hyphenation, and more.

The other way that you can create a new paragraph style is first to format a paragraph, as you want it including font styles, leading, spacing before and/or after a paragraph, justification, hyphenation, and so on. Get a paragraph to appear exactly as you want it, and then create the paragraph style. I highly recommend this method.

Once you format a paragraph, click the cursor inside the paragraph, press Alt/⌥, and click the Create new style icon or use the Paragraph Styles menu and choose New Paragraph Style. When you use the modifier key, the New Paragraph Style dialog box opens.

The end result is that the new paragraph style captures all of your formatting. In Figure 6-2, you can see the formatting of a paragraph and the New Paragraph Style dialog box to the left of the formatted text. I clicked the text cursor inside the paragraph when I created the new paragraph style. In this paragraph, I changed the font, the font size and leading, added an indent to the first line of text, set the hyphenation to 20 (thus essentially omitting all hyphenation), balanced the ragged lines, and added some space after the paragraph.

Note that in Figure 6-2, the name of the style was changed from the default name— Paragraph Style 1—to Body copy. When you create new styles, it's a good idea to add some descriptive name to the style. Notice also in Figure 6-2 that you see a checkbox in the General Panel for Apply Style to Selection. Check this box and click OK, and the style is created and applied to the paragraph. You also find a checkbox for Add to CC Library.

You will also see a keyboard shortcut appearing in the General Panel. To add keyboard shortcuts to paragraph styles, click in the Shortcut text box in the General Panel and press any combination of Ctrl/⌘+Alt/⌥+Shift+ (a numeric key on your numeric keypad). The keyboard shortcut is displayed in the Paragraph Styles Panel, so it's a nice reminder for the keys that you assign to different styles. When creating body copy, use the same keyboard shortcut each time that you create a body text style. You might choose Ctrl/⌘+1 for all of your body styles so it's easy to remember.

6.2.2 Applying a Paragraph Style

Once you create a paragraph style, you probably want to apply the same style to other paragraphs in your document. To do so, click the cursor and drag through the paragraphs to which you want to apply the same style. If you want to apply the style to all of the paragraphs in a story, press Ctrl/⌘+A to select all of the text within all of the frames that are linked together. When the text is selected, click the paragraph style name in the Paragraph Styles Panel. In Figure 6-3, you can see the Body Copy style applied to all of the text on the page.

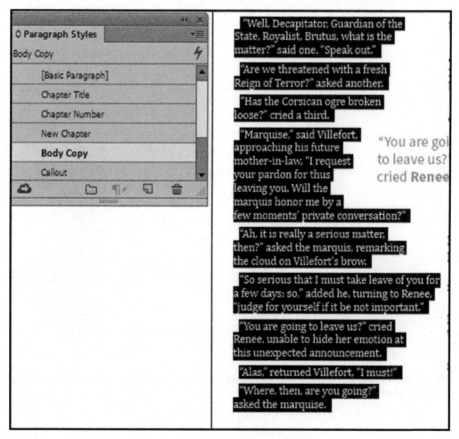

Figure 6-3. *Select multiple paragraphs and click the paragraph style name in the Paragraph Styles Panel to apply the same style to the selected paragraphs*

6.2.3   Modifying a Style

Suppose that you want to change an attribute in a paragraph style. Perhaps you want to change the font, font style, space after a paragraph, the first line indent, or any other paragraph attribute. You can gain access to the Paragraph Style Options dialog box in one of two ways. Double-click the style name or use a context menu by right-clicking the style name in the Paragraph Styles Panel and choosing Edit <style name>.

As a matter of practice, you should always use a context menu. If you have your cursor in a paragraph that is used for a headline, callout, or some other text, and you double-click a style name, the first click applies the style and the second click opens the Paragraph Style Options dialog box. It's very easy to apply a style to the wrong text if you use the double-click method for opening the Paragraph Style Options dialog box. Always right-click and choose Edit <style name> in the Paragraph Styles Panel, and you won't inadvertently assign a paragraph style to the text where you place the cursor.

In Figure 6-4, I edited the Body Copy style. I selected Basic Character Formats and changed the font from Cambria to Minion Pro. When the Preview checkbox is enabled, you can see a dynamic preview of your edits. Notice in Figure 6-4 that all of the text that was defined with the Body Copy text has now changed to Minion Pro.

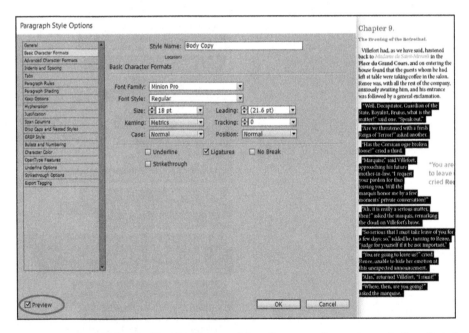

Figure 6-4. Enable the Preview checkbox, and the edits you make are dynamically reflected in the document

6.2.4   Redefining a Style

Suppose that you make a change to text attributes in a document where the text uses a paragraph style. In Figure 6-5, you can see a text paragraph where I changed the font. The text has been defined with the Body Copy style. When I make a change to the text, you find a + symbol adjacent to the style name in the Paragraph Styles Panel. This marker informs you that the paragraph style has an override.

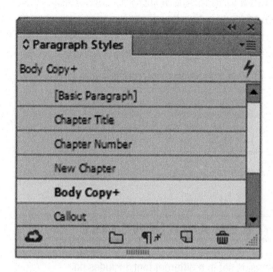

Figure 6-5. *When you edit text attributes directly in a document, the style name appears with a text override, signified by a + symbol adjacent to the style name*

If you want to clear the override and return to the text formatting of the original style, press Alt/⌥ and click the plus symbol. The text returns to the Body Copy style.

Let's say that you want to change the paragraph style to the new formatting attributes that you applied to a paragraph. To change the paragraph style so that it accepts the new text formatting, position the text cursor in the newly-formatted text and then open a context menu on the style name and choose Redefine Style. The paragraph style is modified, and it takes on the attributes of the text around your cursor.

6.2.5   Basing One Style on Another Style

Styles can be set up in parent-child relationships. For example, if you have a Body Copy style and create a new style, you can base the new style on the Body Copy style. All of the attributes that you assign to the new style stay in effect. However if you change other attributes in the Body Style, they are reflected in the new style. To make this clearer, let's inspect Figure 6-6.

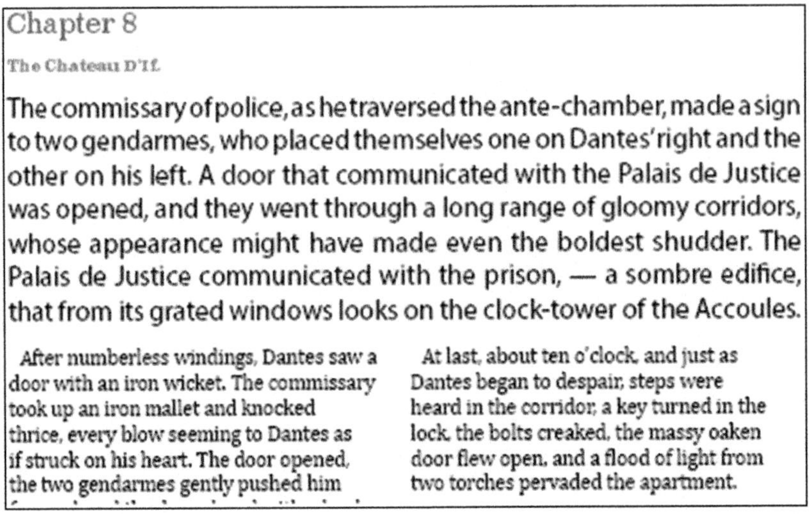

> ## Chapter 8
>
> The Chateau D'If.
>
> The commissary of police, as he traversed the ante-chamber, made a sign to two gendarmes, who placed themselves one on Dantes'right and the other on his left. A door that communicated with the Palais de Justice was opened, and they went through a long range of gloomy corridors, whose appearance might have made even the boldest shudder. The Palais de Justice communicated with the prison, — a sombre edifice, that from its grated windows looks on the clock-tower of the Accoules.
>
> After numberless windings, Dantes saw a door with an iron wicket. The commissary took up an iron mallet and knocked thrice, every blow seeming to Dantes as if struck on his heart. The door opened, the two gendarmes gently pushed him
>
> At last, about ten o'clock, and just as Dantes began to despair, steps were heard in the corridor, a key turned in the lock, the bolts creaked, the massy oaken door flew open, and a flood of light from two torches pervaded the apartment.

Figure 6-6. The text in the document has the first paragraph with different text attributes than the remaining text

BASING ONE STYLE ON ANOTHER STYLE

The lead paragraph spans two columns, is set in a different font, includes no paragraph indent, and the font size is larger than the rest of the text on the page. Let's define a style for the first paragraph.

1. **Create a new style.** Click the cursor in the paragraph, press Alt/⌥, and click the Create new style icon in the Paragraph Styles Panel. The New Paragraph Style dialog box opens. Type a name for the new style. In my example, I use Body 1st Paragraph for the style name.

2. **Set up a Based On style.** Look at the drop-down menus below the style name. The first item is titled Based On, as shown in Figure 6-7. Open this menu, and you will see a list of all of the paragraph styles in the open document. Choose Body Copy, and the style is based on the Body Copy style.

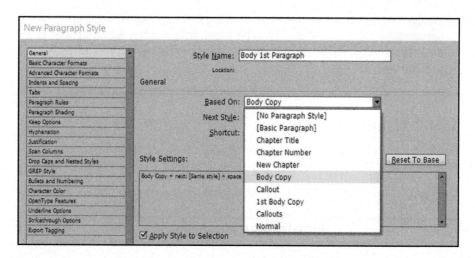

Figure 6-7. Open the Based On drop-down menu and choose Body Copy

3. **Click OK to create the style**.

4. **Edit the Body Copy style**. Right-click on the Body Copy style in the Paragraph Styles Panel and choose Edit Body Copy.

5. **Change the color of the text**. Click Character Color in the left pane and click on a different color in the Character Color menu.

6. **Click OK**. Notice the text on the page. The color was changed in the Body Copy and in the first paragraph. The other attributes for the first paragraph remain intact, as you can see in Figure 6-8.

Chapter 8

The Chateau D'If.

The commissary of police, as he traversed the ante-chamber, made a sign to two gendarmes, who placed themselves one on Dantes' right and the other on his left. A door that communicated with the Palais de Justice was opened, and they went through a long range of gloomy corridors, whose appearance might have made even the boldest shudder. The Palais de Justice communicated with the prison, — a sombre edifice, that from its grated windows looks on the clock-tower of the Accoules.

After numberless windings, Dantes saw a door with an iron wicket. The commissary took up an iron mallet and knocked thrice, every blow seeming to Dantes as if struck on his heart. The door opened, the two gendarmes gently pushed him

At last, about ten o'clock, and just as Dantes began to despair, steps were heard in the corridor; a key turned in the lock, the bolts creaked, the massy oaken door flew open, and a flood of light from two torches pervaded the apartment.

Figure 6-8. Only the color was changed for the text using two different styles

Creating one style based on another provides you with some powerful editing opportunities. You can make changes in the parent style, and they will be reflected in the child paragraph styles without disturbing specific items that you want to retain in the child style.

6.2.6   Using Keep Options

This feature is particularly helpful to people who create reflowable EPUBs. Suppose that you want all chapters to begin at the top of a page, and you want the new chapters on the right-hand page in a two-page layout. Resizing text frames and adding carriage returns won't get the job done. You need to use a feature called Keep Options.

USING KEEP OPTIONS

Follow along with these steps to see how you can place new chapters at the top of the right-side (recto) pages in a two-page layout:

1. **Look over Figure 6-9.** In this figure, you see a right-side page with a new chapter starting at the bottom-right column. The Chapter 9 text is assigned the Chapter Number style. We want to move the chapter number, title, and the text that follows to the top of a right-side page.

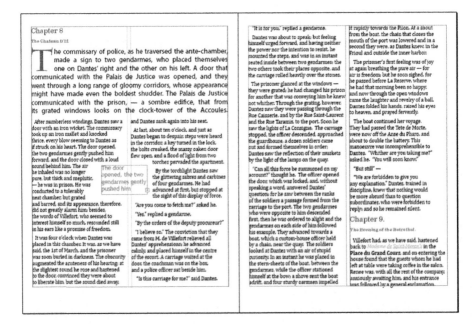

Figure 6-9. *The new chapter is positioned at the bottom-right side of the page*

2. **Create a new paragraph style.** Press the Alt/⌥ key and click the Create a new style icon in the Paragraph Styles Panel.

3. **Name the style.** In my example, I type *New Chapter* for the style name.

4. **Base the style on another style.** In my example, I choose Chapter Number from the Based On drop-down menu in the General Panel.

5. **Open the Keep Options tab.** Click Keep Options in the left pane of the Paragraph Style Options.

6. **Choose On Next Odd Page.** In the Keep Options pane, open the Start Paragraph drop-down menu and choose On Next Odd Page.

7. **Click OK.** The next chapter is now positioned at the top of the odd pages, as shown in Figure 6-10.

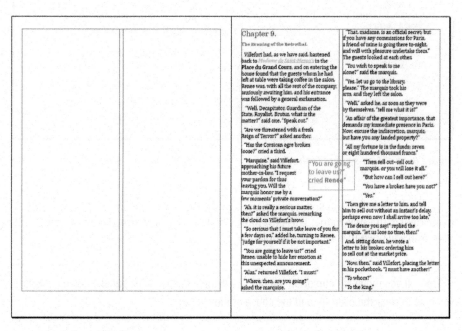

Figure 6-10. *The chapter begins at the top of the next odd page*

6.3   Creating and Applying Character Styles

Character styles are beneficial when you deviate from a paragraph style with some characters within a paragraph. For example, if you create a paragraph style and then decide to change the font style of a word, such as adding bold or italic characters, the paragraph style doesn't account for the new character formatting and you get what is called an override. In Figure 6-11, you can see a paragraph that uses a style. However, the paragraph contains four words with bold italic text while the rest of the paragraph is set without any bold text.

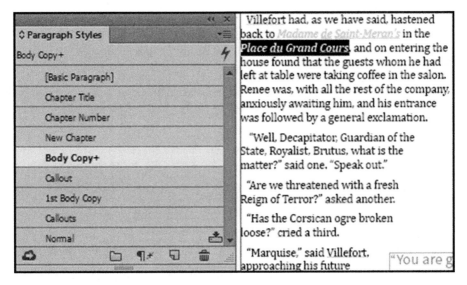

Figure 6-11. *The + symbol to the right of a style name indicates where an override exists in the style*

If you open the Paragraph Styles Panel, you can see the Body Copy style with a + symbol to the right of the style name. This plus indicates that there is an override in the paragraph style. You will need to correct the problem.

■ **Tip**   If you move the cursor on top of the + symbol in any styles panel, a tooltip shows you how to clear the override and the cause of the override.

6.3.1   Creating Character Styles

To create a character style, you follow a similar path as you do when you create paragraph styles. As is the case with paragraph styles, your best approach is to format the text first and then create the style.

CREATING CHARACTER STYLES

To create character styles, do the following:

1. **Create a paragraph style in a paragraph of text**. Apply the style to one or more paragraphs.

2. **Select some text and change the font style to bold**. I want to create a new character style with text that uses a bold font. First select the text and then choose the font style from the Character Control Panel.

3. **Create a new character style for italicized text**. Select text and choose the font style from the Control Panel.

4. **Open the Character Styles Panel**. Open the Character Styles Panel (Window ➤ Styles ➤ Character Styles or press Shift+F11—see Figure 6-12).

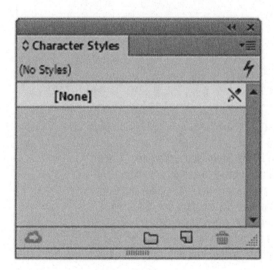

Figure 6-12. Press Shift+F11 to open the Character Styles Panel

5. **Select the bold formatted text**.

6. **Create a new character style**. With the text selected, press the Alt/⌥ key and click the Create new style icon in the Character Styles Panel. When you press the Alt/⌥ key, the New Character Style dialog box opens, as shown in Figure 6-13.

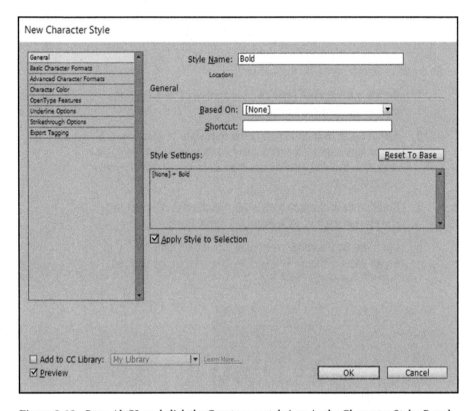

Figure 6-13. *Press Alt/⌐ and click the Create new style icon in the Character Styles Panel*

7. **Type a name for the style in the Style Name text box**. Since you formatted the text, you don't need to assign any other attributes. However, there is one more item that you want to take care of in the New Character Style dialog box. Click the Apply Style to Selection checkbox. When you create a new style, by default the style is not applied to any text. When you click this checkbox, the style is created and it is applied to the selected text. Click OK.

8. **Repeat the same steps for selecting the italicized text and create a new character style**.

9. **Examine the Character Styles Panel**. As you can see in Figure 6-14 on the right, the Character Styles Panel shows you the name of the new styles added to the panel, one of which is the style for bold text. On the left, notice that the Body Copy name in the Paragraph Styles Panel now appears without an override (without a + symbol).

■ **Tip** You can also assign keyboard shortcuts to character styles. When you're in the Character Styles Panel, click the Shortcut text field and type any combination of Ctrl/ Command+Alt/⌥+Shift+ (a Num Pad key). Like paragraph styles shortcuts, the shortcut appears adjacent to the character style name in the Character Styles Panel.

The beauty of using character styles is that a character style doesn't affect any of the other attributes in a paragraph and any paragraph styles that you create. It only affects the formatting for the text you select and use to create the style. Once the character style is created, you can use it with other paragraph styles regardless of the paragraph formatting used. In Figure 6-14, you can see the Bold character style applied to text formatted with a different font and different paragraph style. The only change that appears in the text is the bold style.

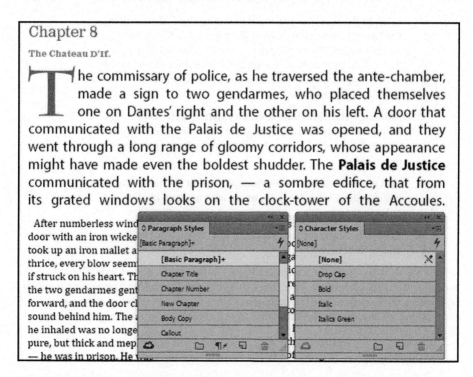

Figure 6-14. *Character styles don't affect any paragraph formatting other than what's defined in the character style*

6.3.2   Redefining Character Styles

Suppose that we have a character style as we do in the Character Styles Panel, the style is then applied to some text, and now you want to make a slight edit by applying a different color to the text. If you select the text and change the color in the Swatches Panel, you see an override—although not in the Character Styles Panel. The override appears in the Paragraph Styles Panel, as shown in Figure 6-13. If you open the Character Styles Panel menu, you see the Redefine Style menu item grayed out.

InDesign sees the override as part of the paragraph style. The reason for this is that when you create a character style and apply an edit, the only thing InDesign handles for the character style is exactly the attribute you change. All other items in the text remain unaffected. Hence, when you apply italicized type to the character style, no information about color is added to the style. That belongs to the paragraph style.

To properly edit a character style, you might do something like the following:

1. **Click in the text that you want to change and Alt/⌥+click the Create a new style icon in the Character Styles Panel.** You could edit the existing character style, but all of the text that you want to italicize would have the color change applied to it. It might be best to create a new style based on the original character style.

2. **Name the style and base it on an existing style.** Type a new name for the style. In my example, I use *Italics Green* for the name of the style. I choose Italics from the Based On drop-down menu.

3. **Edit a text attribute.** In my example, I want to change the text color. I click Character Color in the left pane and click on a color in the panel.

4. **Click OK.** Apply the new style to text that you want italicized and with a color.

In Figure 6-15, you can see the Character Styles Panel with the added style. If you decide to change the color of the text by clicking a different color swatch and open the Character Style menu, the Redefine Style menu item is accessible. Since we changed the color attribute in the Character Style formatting, any changes to what we changed are honored by the Character Styles Panel.

Figure 6-15. *The Character Styles Panel after adding a new character style*

6.3.3   Deleting Styles

If you want to eliminate styles from a document, you should first look over the style definitions. If you have one style based on another and you want to delete the parent style, all of the child styles are going to be affected. Depending on what action you choose to reassign a style, you may get some unexpected results.

If you want to delete a child style, you can apply the style to another style in your panel. For example, suppose that I want to delete the italicized text with a color. Maybe I decide that later I just want the text to be black. I would drag the Italics Green style in the Character Styles panel to the trash icon in the panel. When I do so, I can replace the style with another style that I created and it appears in the Character Styles Panel.

Move a style to the Trash icon in the Character Styles Panel, and the Delete Character Style dialog box opens. From the Replace With drop-down menu, choose a style to replace the first style, as shown in Figure 6-16.

Delete Character Style

⚠   Delete Style Italics Green

and Replace With: [None] ▼

☑ Preserve Formatting

OK   Reset

Figure 6-16. *Drag a style to the Trash icon in the styles panel, and the Delete Character Style dialog box opens*

Select a replacement style and click OK. You can delete styles from other style panels in the same manner.

6.4   Creating Drop Cap and Nested Styles

When you create reflowable EPUBs, they are primarily text documents and rightfully so. Reflowable EPUBs are intended to be read. You can add some interesting icons, illustrations, or even some different text handling to bring the reader into the page. Drop caps are good examples for such an effect. Add a drop cap, change the text color, and it breaks up the page a little and adds some more interest.

If there was one feature that pushed InDesign ahead of QuarkXPress in 1996, it had to be nested styles. Nested styles were introduced in InDesign CS 1, and they were immediately embraced by many people who used QuarkXPress exclusively as their layout program of choice. As you'll see in this section, nested styles provide you with some powerful editing features.

6.4.1   Creating Drop Cap Character Styles

Creating styles for drop caps actually involves using both paragraph and character styles. In the Paragraph Style Options dialog box, you include drop caps as part of your style definition. In the Character Style Options, you assign attributes to the character used in the drop cap and create a character style for the drop cap. Failure to create a character style will result in an override if you edit the font attributes—something like changing the font or the font style.

In the Control Panel paragraph options, you have a setting for applying drop caps. The problem is that if you create a drop cap using the Control Panel, you get an override for the style that you applied to the paragraph, as shown in Figure 6-17. However, starting in the Control Panel isn't a bad idea. You can experiment with the number of lines that you want to use for the drop cap and the font that you want to use. These settings are also available in the Paragraph Style Options dialog box, and with a dynamic preview you can easily see what your drop cap looks like while working in the Paragraph Style Options dialog box. It's a personal choice. I prefer to use the Control Panel, play around with the drop cap and character settings, and then fix the override later.

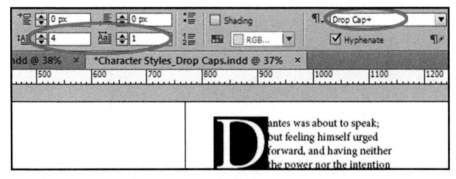

Figure 6-17. *Adding a drop cap in the Control Panel results in an override for the paragraph style assigned to the paragraph*

■ **Tip** To increment the number of lines for a drop cap and the drop cap size by one point in the Control Panel, click the text box adjacent to the Drop Cap tool in the Control Panel and press the Up Arrow key to size up one line. Press Shift plus the Up Arrow key to jump to four lines.

CREATING DROP CAP CHARACTER STYLES

To add a drop cap to a paragraph of text and define a style for the drop cap, follow these steps:

1. **Select the first character in a paragraph and right-click the paragraph style name in the Paragraph Styles Panel**. These steps presume that you have a paragraph style definition for the paragraph to which you want to add the drop cap. In this example, let's go ahead and use the Paragraph Style Options dialog box as our starting point. Right-click the paragraph style name in the Paragraph Styles Panel and choose Edit <style name>.

2. **Click Drop Caps and Nested Styles in the left pane**.

3. **Set the drop cap attributes**. Type the number of lines for the drop cap in the Paragraph Style Options dialog box. In this example, we use one character for the drop cap so leave the Characters text box at the default. Click the Preview checkbox so that you can dynamically see your edits, as shown in Figure 6-18.

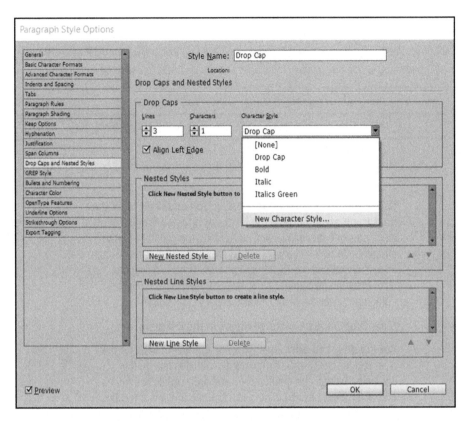

Figure 6-18. *Type a value for the number of lines you want to use for the drop cap*

4. **Create a new character style**. You don't have to leave the Paragraph Style Options dialog box to create a new character style. Open the Character Style drop-down menu in the Paragraph Style Options dialog box and choose New Character Style from the menu, as shown in Figure 6-18.

5. **Set the type attributes.** Type a name for the character style. In my example, I use Drop Cap for the character style name. Set the font and choose a color for it. The disadvantage that you face when creating the character style from the Paragraph Style Options dialog box is that you won't see a dynamic preview of your edits, even if you enable the Preview checkbox. This is the reason why I like to set my drop cap options in the Control Panel first and then take care of the paragraph style override later.

6. **Set the tracking.** One more edit that you need to make in the New Character Style dialog box is to add some tracking to the line of text. By default, InDesign pushes the text to the right side of the drop cap—too close to the text character. You need to add a little breathing room. Click Basic Character Formats and add about 40 in the tracking text box (see Figure 6-19). If your edits need some modification, you can always modify the character style after leaving the Paragraph Style Options dialog box.

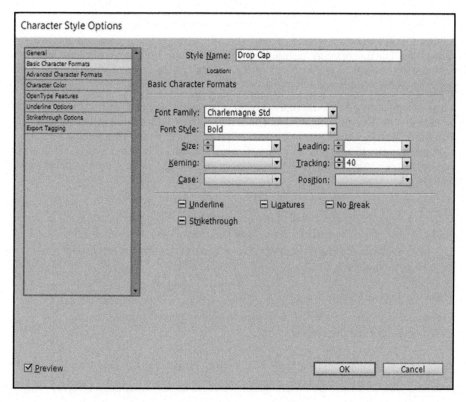

Figure 6-19. Add tracking to the line of text from the Basic Character Formats Panel of the Character Style Options dialog box

7. **New Character Style dialog box.** You return to the Paragraph Style Options dialog box, and the Drop Caps pane displays the character style used for the drop cap as well as a dynamic preview of the results.

When you return to the document page and examine the Paragraph and Character Styles Panels, you see no overrides on the styles.

6.4.2 Creating Nested Styles

As I've stated earlier in this chapter and in the introduction to this book, nested styles were a page layout game changer for Adobe when it they were introduced in InDesign CS 1. When Adobe introduced InDesign, it faced an uphill battle in capturing market share among page layout applications. Enterprises and large publishing houses spent a lot of money installing and updating copies of QuarkXPress, and many firms invested heavily in Quark XTensions (like plugins). Some specialized XTensions cost over $8,500 each! It was a huge challenge for Adobe to sway the corporate world, as well as the independent designers and ad agencies, away from QuarkXPress and to consider Adobe InDesign as their program of choice for page layout.

Adobe needed a wow factor, not as a plugin but something that was hard-coded into the application. The first of many ingenious additions to Adobe InDesign was nested styles. Nested styles made it easier for layout artists creating catalogs, annual reports, product books, and other similar documents to work much more efficiently.

A nested style is, in a way, a number of character styles all bunched up in a single paragraph style. Examine Figure 6-20. The first paragraph is formatted without a style definition. The ISBN text and number are set to 14.5 points, and the text is italicized. The book title appears in bold text, and the text size is 16 points. The author name is italicized, and it also has a 16-point text size. The date is set in 14.5 type, while the parentheses are set in 16-point type.

ISBN-13 978-0553213508: **Count of Monte Cristo** *by Alexandre Dumas* (1844). Set against the turbulent years of the Napoleanic era, Alexandre Dumas's thrilling adventure story is one of the most widely read romantic novels of all time.

ISBN-13-:978-1682040171: The Adventures of Tom Sawyer by Mark Twain (1876). An all-time classic, this is a story that revolves around engrossing childhood stunts and escapades.

ISBN-13-978-1853260209: Jane Eyre by Charlotte Bronte (1847). Jane Eyre is the story of a small, plain faced, intelligent, and passionate English orphan.

Figure 6-20. *The first paragraph has text formatting applied to the paragraph with no style yet defined*

We can capture all of those text attributes and include them in one single paragraph style using InDesign's nested style feature. When you first look at the options for nested styles, it may seem intimidating. However, with a little understanding for how nested styles are created, you will find them easy to build and apply to your digital publishing documents.

6.4.2.1   Using Special Characters

To create a nested style, you need some delimiters. A *delimiter* is a character where you can inform InDesign where a style begins or ends. A colon, a period, a comma, a tab, and so forth can be used as delimiters. Sometimes, however, you may have a space between characters where you want to begin or end a style. Striking the Spacebar on your keyboard won't supply you with a delimiter. You need to insert some special characters.

Choose Type ➤ Insert White Space. In the White Space submenu, you will find several options, as shown in Figure 6-21. Among some of the characters that you might use for delimiters are the following:

Change Case	>	Em Space		Ctrl+Shift+M
Type on a Path	>	En Space		Ctrl+Shift+N
Notes	>	Nonbreaking Space		Ctrl+Alt+X
Track Changes	>	Nonbreaking Space (Fixed Width)		
Insert Footnote		Hair Space		
Document Footnote Options...		Sixth Space		
Hyperlinks & Cross-References	>	Thin Space		Ctrl+Alt+Shift+M
Text Variables	>	Quarter Space		
Bulleted & Numbered Lists	>	Third Space		
Insert Special Character	>	Punctuation Space		
Insert White Space	>	Figure Space		
		Flush Space		

Figure 6-21. Choose Type ➤ Insert White Space to open the White Space submenu

- *En Space:* An en space is the width of an *n* character for the current font. En spaces vary according to the font you use.

- *Em Space:* An em space is the width of an *m* character for the current font. Em spaces also vary according to the font you use.

These two characters should take care of delimiters where you don't have other characters that you can use as a delimiter.

6.4.2.2   Creating Character Styles

You need to create a character style for each set of characters that have different attributes than the body copy in the paragraph. In my example, I created character styles for the ISBN number, the book title, the author name, and the year published. The Character Styles Panel in my example is shown in Figure 6-22.

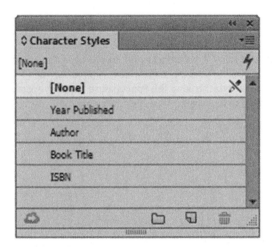

Figure 6-22. *Create character styles for each change in the text attributes*

6.4.2.3 Creating the Nested Style

In this example, I use the text formatted in the first paragraph of Figure 6-18. I also use the character styles, as shown in Figure 6-20.

If you want to use another example to follow along, be certain to format text, create character styles, and insert delimiters for the start and end stops between the character style formats.

CREATING A NESTED STYLE

Follow these steps to create a nested style:

1. **Click the cursor in the paragraph containing the text that you want to format for a nested style**. Press the Alt/⌥ key and click the Create new style icon in the Paragraph Styles Panel. Type a name for the style. In my example, I use *Nested Style* for my style name.

2. **Open the Drop Caps and Nested Styles pane**. Click Drop Caps and Nested Styles in the left pane.

3. **Add a new nested style**. Click the New Nested Style button.

4. **Select a character style from the drop-down menu**. In my example, the ISBN style is the first one that appears in the paragraph. Open the menu and choose ISBN, as shown in Figure 6-23.

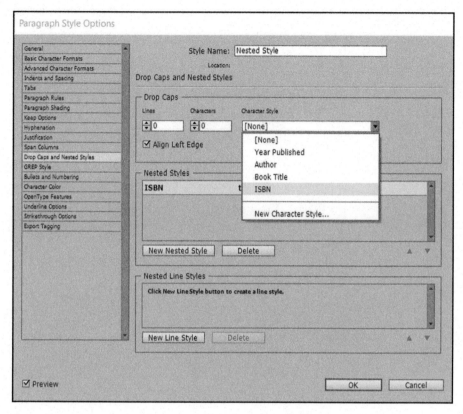

Figure 6-23. *Select a Character Style for the respective text element*

5. **Identify the delimiter.** In my example, the ISBN number ends with a colon. Leave the default through selection at the default, and type a colon (:) in the last field. When you see *Words*, click the cursor and you can type the colon character.

6. **Add a new nested style.** The next item that follows in the paragraph is the book title. Click the New Nested Style button to create another style and open the drop-down menu. Choose Book Title from the menu. Book Title is another character style that I created in my document.

7. **Identify the delimiter.** I added an en space after the book title. Click Words and a drop-down menu opens. Choose En Spaces from the menu, as shown in Figure 6-24.

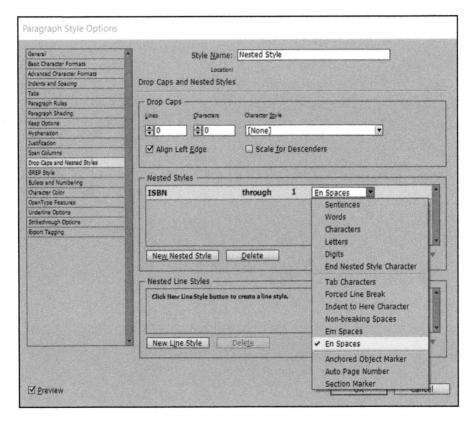

Figure 6-24. Click Words and choose En Spaces from the drop-down menu

8. **Add a new nested style.** Click the New Nested Style button and choose Author in the menu. I added a character style for Author in my example.

9. **Set the delimiter.** Click through to open a drop-down menu, and choose Up To in the menu. We stop the previous character style just before the open parenthesis character. Type an open parenthesis character in the Words text box.

10. **Create a new nested style.** Click the New Nested Style button and choose Year Published in the drop-down menu. Click through to open the drop-down menu and choose Up To. Click Words and type a closed parenthesis character. I added another character style in my example and named it *Year Published*.

11. **Click OK and apply the style.** Click the cursor in another paragraph where you want to use the same nested style. In Figure 6-25, you can see the nested style formatting I used for the remaining paragraphs.

ISBN-13 - 978-0553213508: **Count of Monte Cristo** *by Alexandre Dumas* (1844). Set against the turbulent years of the Napoleanic era, Alexandre Dumas's thrilling adventure story is one of the most widely read romantic novels of all time.

ISBN-13 - 978-1682040171: **The Adventures of Tom Sawyer** *by Mark Twain* (1876). An all-time classic, this is a story that revolves around engrossing childhood stunts and escapades.

ISBN-13-978-1853260209: **Jane Eyre** *by Charlotte Bronte* (1847). Jane Eyre is the story of a small, plain faced, intelligent, and passionate English orphan.

Figure 6-25. *Click the cursor in a paragraph and click the style name in the paragraph panel to apply the style to a paragraph*

6.4.2.4   Creating Nested Line Styles

Suppose that you want to change character attributes for the first few lines in a chapter head for the lead paragraph. For example, adding all caps or small caps to the first few lines of text. If you set up a character style for all or small caps and apply the style to the first two lines of text, as shown in Figure 6-26, everything is fine.

Figure 6-26. *The first two lines of text are small caps*

You can include the character style in a paragraph style and apply the same style to multiple paragraphs throughout your document. The problem, however, is what happens if you apply the style to a paragraph contained in a two-column layout or a three-column layout, or maybe you adjust the size of the text frame larger or smaller?

In Figure 6-27, you see what happens when we resize the text frame to fit a two-column layout. The small caps text in the two-column layout runs through almost five lines of text.

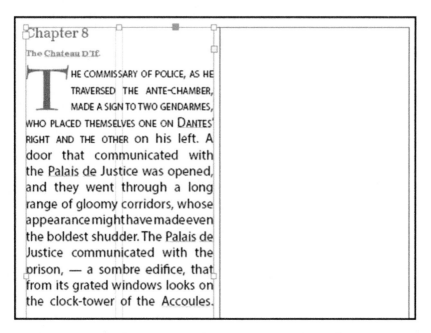

Figure 6-27. *Text confined to a two-column layout shows the small caps spanning more than two rows*

We can overcome this problem by creating a nested line style.

CREATING A NESTED LINE STYLE

To create a nested line style, follow these steps:

1. **Create a character style.** In my example, I create a character style for small caps. You find the Small Caps option in the Basic Character Formats pane in the Case drop-down menu.

2. **Open the Paragraph Style Options.** In my example, the paragraph style name is 1st Body Copy. Right-click the style name in the Paragraph Styles Panel and choose Edit "1st Body Copy."

3. **Open the Drop Caps and Nested Styles pane.** Click Drop Caps and Nested Styles in the left pane.

4. **Create a new nested line style.** Click New Line Style at the bottom of the dialog box and choose the Small Caps character style. Click 1 (for the number of lines) and type 2, as shown in Figure 6-28.

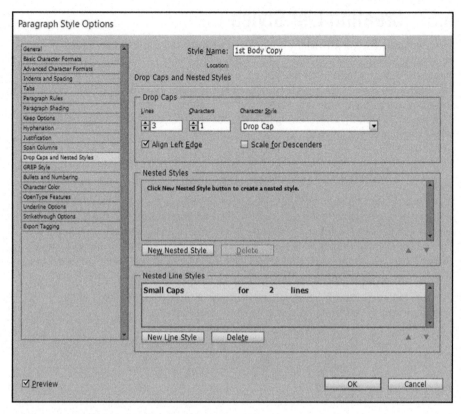

Figure 6-28. *Add a new nested line style*

5. **Click OK and apply the style to a new paragraph.** In Figure 6-29, you see the style applied to two different columns. Notice that the small caps appear only in the first two lines of text in each block of text.

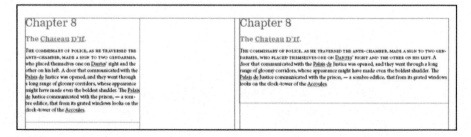

Figure 6-29. *Click in a paragraph and click the paragraph style containing the nested line style*

6.5   Creating List Styles

InDesign provides you with many options for creating lists. You may have created bulleted or number lists and found some editing tasks a little confusing. Maybe you wanted to change a bullet style or right-align numbers. After some frustrating efforts, you may have abandoned creating a list and used the tab ruler to format your lists. I know that some of you may have done this. I know you're out there. I won't tell anyone. It's a secret between us. Hopefully, after reading through this section, you won't have to create these types of workarounds for creating lists.

6.5.1   Creating a Bulleted List Style

When you create a bulleted list, the bullet is not editable in the text frame. Bullets are assigned by clicking the Bulleted List icon in the Paragraph settings in the Control Panel, choosing Bullets and Numbering from the Type menu, clicking the far-right icon in the Control Panel and choosing Bullets and Numbering from the drop-down menu, or by adding a new paragraph style. Lists are all over InDesign, and you have many ways to create them. In this exercise, we'll be working in the Paragraph Styles Panel.

In Figure 6-30, you can see a text frame with no formatting (top) and after adding paragraph styles that formatted a drop cap and a bulleted list.

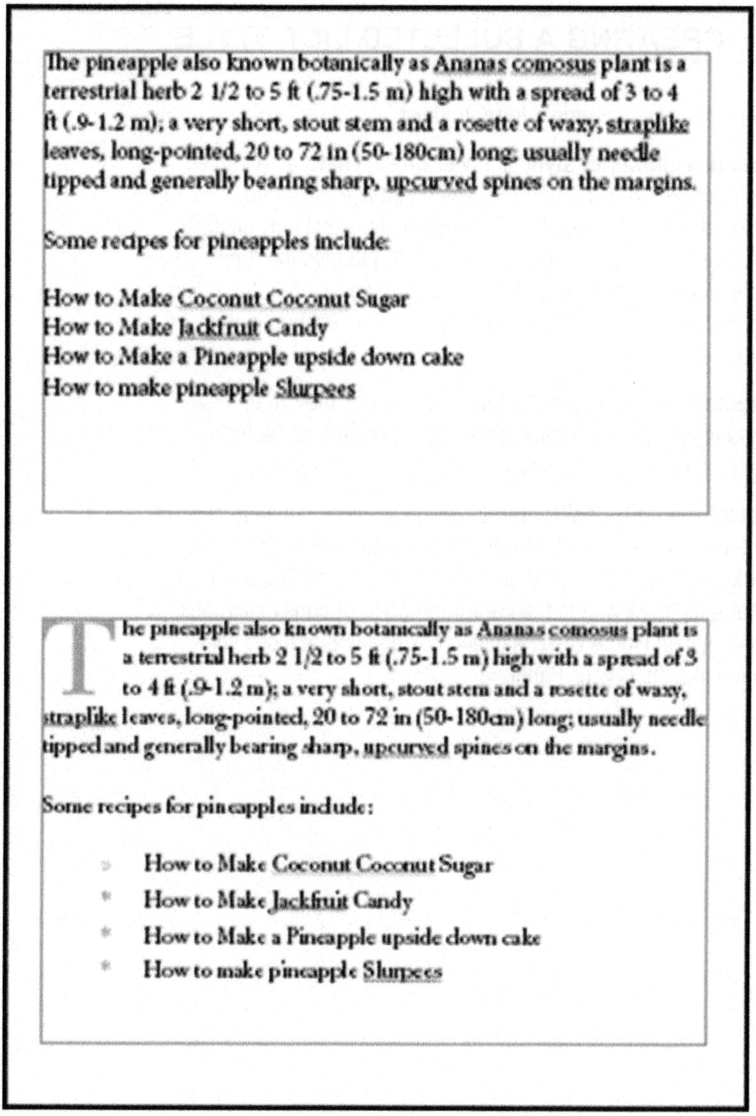

The pineapple also known botanically as Ananas comosus plant is a terrestrial herb 2 1/2 to 5 ft (.75-1.5 m) high with a spread of 3 to 4 ft (.9-1.2 m); a very short, stout stem and a rosette of waxy, straplike leaves, long-pointed, 20 to 72 in (50-180cm) long; usually needle tipped and generally bearing sharp, upcurved spines on the margins.

Some recipes for pineapples include:

How to Make Coconut Coconut Sugar
How to Make Jackfruit Candy
How to Make a Pineapple upside down cake
How to make pineapple Slurpees

The pineapple also known botanically as Ananas comosus plant is a terrestrial herb 2 1/2 to 5 ft (.75-1.5 m) high with a spread of 3 to 4 ft (.9-1.2 m); a very short, stout stem and a rosette of waxy, straplike leaves, long-pointed, 20 to 72 in (50-180cm) long; usually needle tipped and generally bearing sharp, upcurved spines on the margins.

Some recipes for pineapples include:

- How to Make Coconut Coconut Sugar
- How to Make Jackfruit Candy
- How to Make a Pineapple upside down cake
- How to make pineapple Slurpees

Figure 6-30. The formatted text (bottom) contains a paragraph style for a bulleted list

CREATING A BULLETED LIST STYLE

The following is how you create a formatted list:

1. **Create a character style.** In my example, I have a character style for the drop cap and the color. I can use the same character style for the drop cap and the bullets. I only change the color of the drop cap and the tracking to give the drop cap a little distance from the text. The tracking won't affect the bullet characters, and the only thing that you'll see change is the bullet color.

2. **Create a new paragraph style.** Alt/⌥+click the Create new style icon in the Paragraph Styles Panel. Type a name for the style and click Bullets and Numbering in the left panel.

3. **Select the bullet character.** InDesign provides you with a list of different bullet styles. The default is a circle. None of the styles look very good, so we can modify the style by adding a new character. Click Add in the Paragraph Style Options dialog box, as shown in Figure 6-31. A dialog box opens that looks very much like the Glyphs Panel.

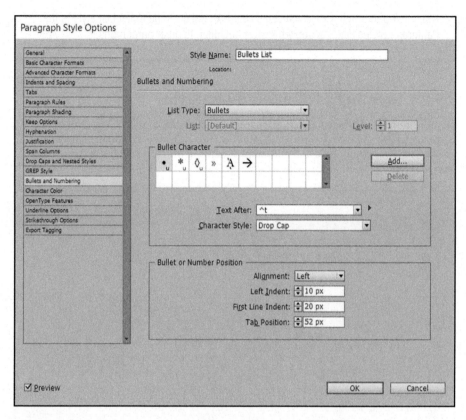

Figure 6-31. *Click Add in the Bullets and Numbering pane in the Paragraph Style Options dialog box*

4. **Choose a font.** In my example, I choose the Wingdings font by opening the Font Family drop-down menu and selecting Wingdings.

5. **Select a character.** Locate the character that you want and double-click or click the Add button and then click OK. You are returned to the Paragraph Style Options dialog box, and the new character appears in the Bullet Character list. Select the character to change the default to your new character.

6. **Adjust the bullet and text position.** In the Bullet or Number Position in the Paragraph Style Options dialog box, you see adjustments for Left, First Line, and Tab Indents. Be sure that Preview is checked and make adjustments to position the bullet and text as you like. When you edit the values, you see a dynamic preview of the results. Click OK. Apply the style to your paragraphs, and you should see a list similar to the one shown in Figure 6-30.

Like other paragraph styles, you can select text and click the Bullet List style in the Paragraph Styles Panel to apply the style definition to other paragraphs.

6.5.2 Creating a Numbered List Style

Creating numbered lists works very similarly to creating bulleted lists. You define a character style if you want to format the numbers in a different style than the list text. Create a new paragraph style and make adjustments in the New Paragraph style dialog box (see Figure 6-32).

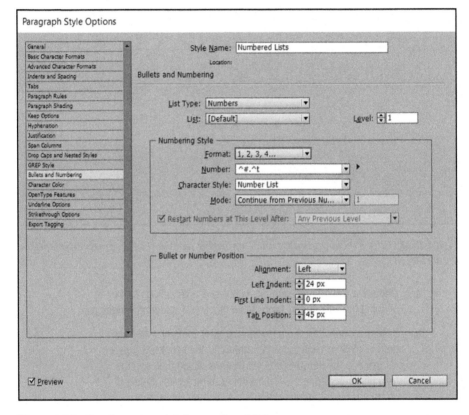

Figure 6-32. *Creating a new style for numbered lists*

As shown in Figure 6-32, Numbers is selected in the List Type. I created a character style for the numbers and chose the Number List character style from the Character Style drop-down menu. This style only changes the color of the numbers. At the bottom of the Paragraph Style Options dialog box, I made adjustments for the position of the numbers. Click OK and the new style is created. You apply the style to lists just as you would do with bullet lists. Select text and click the paragraph style name in the Paragraph Styles Panel.

By default, InDesign creates new numbers each time you apply the same style to a different body of text. If for some reason the numbering continues from the first body of text to a new numbered list, choose Type ➤ Bulleted & Numbered Lists ➤ Restart Numbering.

If you want to convert a numbered list to editable text, select the list and choose Type ➤ Bulleted & Numbered Lists ➤ Convert Bullets and Numbering to Text.

6.5.3   Aligning Numbers

Since you cannot select numbers in a numbered list, there is no way to change the alignment or set a tab for the numbers. You need to return to the Paragraph Style Options dialog box or choose Bullets and Numbering from a menu. If you have a list formatted with numbers and applied a style such as the list shown at the top in Figure 6-33, you can edit the paragraph style (or create a new style) and change the number alignment. At the bottom of Figure 6-33, you see that the Alignment menu command is set to Right and the position options were changed slightly to create the look you see.

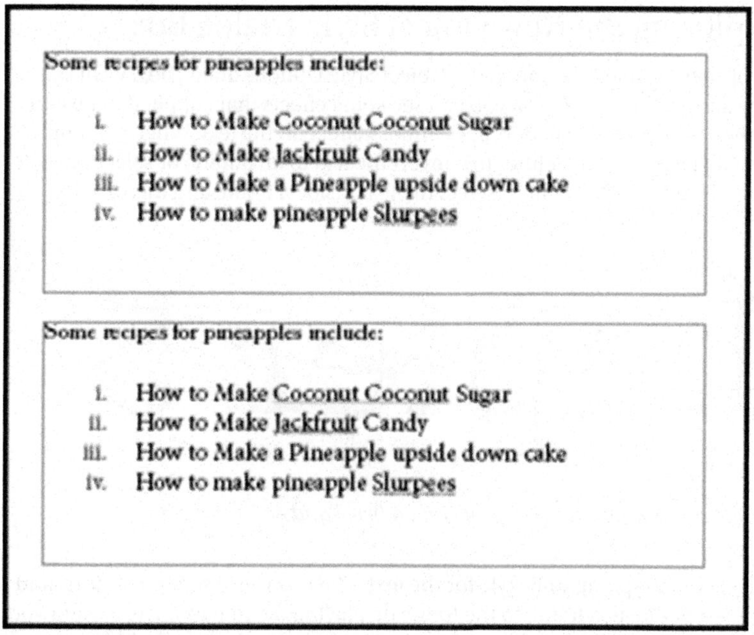

Some recipes for pineapples include:

    i.   How to Make Coconut Coconut Sugar
    ii.   How to Make Jackfruit Candy
    iii. How to Make a Pineapple upside down cake
    iv.   How to make pineapple Slurpees

Some recipes for pineapples include:

    i.   How to Make Coconut Coconut Sugar
    ii.   How to Make Jackfruit Candy
    iii. How to Make a Pineapple upside down cake
    iv.   How to make pineapple Slurpees

Figure 6-33. Numbers aligned right

227

6.6 Working with Object Styles

Every element in your layout is an object. Text lives inside text frames and the frames are objects. Files that you place in InDesign are objects. Anything you draw in InDesign is an object. Strokes are objects. When you change the attributes of an object, you can capture the formatting in an object style. Add a fill and transparency to a text frame, and you can include the fill and transparency in an object style. Apply a text wrap to an object, and you can add the text wrap settings to an object style. Apply any of the effects that I covered in Chapter 4, and you can add the effects attributes to an object style definition. When you create an object style, you set the object style attributes in the New Object Style dialog box. In this dialog box, you will find a huge number of switches and options.

There are very few settings that you cannot apply when creating object styles. Things that you cannot control in an object style include an object's size and position on a page. Some transformations cannot be included in an object style. You cannot modify or create color swatches, create gradients, or create tints of colors. Compared to what you can do with object styles, this list is very short.

6.6.1 Exploring the New Object Style Dialog Box

To display the options available to you in the Object Style Options dialog box, we'll start with something simple. In Figure 6-34, you can see some effects that I applied to text for a chapter number. I used a drop shadow and emboss effect on the text. When you apply effects like these to text, you need either to convert the text to an outline or select the text frame and apply the effects. You cannot select the text inside a frame and then apply an effect.

Figure 6-34. *Text containing a drop shadow and a bevel and emboss effect*

In this example, I create a paragraph style for the text. The text is in a separate frame, and you can anchor a separate text frame to the frame displaying the remaining text. After you set the text attributes and frame location, select the text frame and open the Object Styles Panel. Press Alt/⌥ and click the Create New Style icon to open the Object Style Options dialog box, as shown in Figure 6-35.

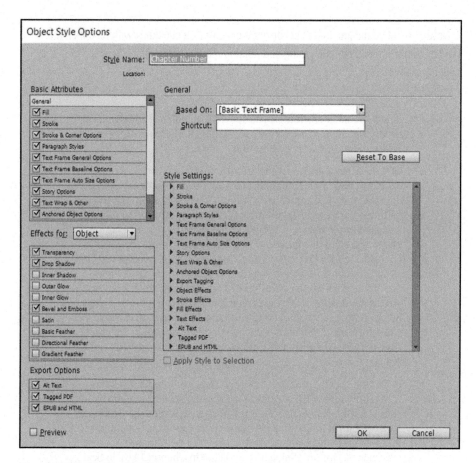

Figure 6-35. *Alt/*⌥*+click the Create new style icon in the Object Styles Panel to open the Object Style Options dialog box*

As you can see, there are many options that you can choose to edit in the Object Style Options dialog box. Your options include the following:

- At the top of the dialog box, you type a name for the style. Notice that you also have a shortcut option. Press any combination of Ctrl/Command+Alt/⌥+Shift + (a Num Pad key to add a keyboard shortcut).

- Along the left side of the dialog box, you have the various options that you can include in your style definition. Notice by default that paragraph styles appear with a horizontal line. This indicates that the option won't be included in the object style definition. Since I added a paragraph style before I opened the Object Style Options dialog box, I want to include my paragraph style in the definition. Click once on the checkbox, and the horizontal line changes to a check mark signifying that the paragraph style will be included in the object style definition.

229

- Below the Basic Attributes, you see a list of effects. I added a drop shadow and bevel and emboss to my object, therefore these items are included in the style definition.

- One thing important to understand is that when you see a checkbox with a horizontal line or no mark in the checkbox, they are essentially the same. Items identified with these marks are not included in the style definition. Let's say that you want to include a single item in the style definition. Text Wrap is a good example. To change all of the options to horizontal lines, press the Alt/⌥ key and click Text Wrap & Other. This action results in the text wrap item being disabled (signified by a horizontal line). Press Alt/⌥ and click again on the Text Wrap item, and all other items are disabled while text wrap is enabled. Essentially, the first click turns off the selected item and a second click turns on the item while turning off the remaining items. When you apply the object style with this definition, the only thing that is applied to an object is a text wrap.

- Below the effects are Export Options. These options are the same as you find in the Object Export Options dialog box you open by choosing Object ➤ Object Export Options. I talk more about Object Export Options in Chapter 12 when I cover exporting documents to reflowable EPUBs. For now, understand that the options are in the Object Style Options dialog box, and later in Chapter 12 we look at why they are important for reflowable EPUBs.

- To the right you see a list of Style Settings. Click the right-pointing arrowheads to drill down to the nested items. This area of the Object Style Options is informational. You can see the settings that are used for every item in the object style definition.

At first glance, the Object Style Options dialog box may be a bit intimidating. It is one of the largest dialog boxes that you will find in InDesign, and it's full of choices. The best way to learn how to use the Object Style Options is to jump in and start creating object styles. That's precisely what we'll do in the next section "Creating and Applying Object Styles."

6.6.2   Creating and Applying Object Styles

You can spend quite a bit of time formatting an object. If you want to apply the same formatting to another object, you have to work through the steps and apply the same formatting to the next object or, in some cases, you can copy a formatted object and replace the contents with new contents. All of this is much more work than you need to do. With object styles, you can let InDesign do much of the work for you.

In Figure 6-36, you see an object frame containing text, an anchored object, and effects applied to the frame. This object is an ideal candidate for an object style.

Figure 6-36. *An object formatted and ready for a new object style*

CREATING OBJECT STYLES

To create an object style for a similar object, do the following:

1. **Format an object.** Just like the way in which we create paragraph and character styles, it's best to start by creating the exact look you want before creating the style. In Figure 6-36, I created an object frame, added some text, and applied a paragraph style. I took two objects, grouped them, and anchored the grouped object to the last line in the text paragraph. I added a drop shadow to the frame and a bevel and emboss. I also added some transparency to the frame.

2. **Create a new object style.** When the object appears precisely as you like, select the object, press the Alt/⌥ key, and click the Create new style icon in the Object Styles Panel. The New Object Style dialog box opens.

3. **Name the new style.** Get in the habit of typing a name first when you create any kind of style. Type a descriptive name in the Style Name text box.

4. **Add a keyboard shortcut.** If this is a style that you will use frequently in a document, add a keyboard shortcut. Like character and paragraph styles, you use the Ctrl/Command, Alt/⌥, Shift modifier keys, and the Num Pad keys on your keyboard. Click the cursor in the Shortcut text box and press Shift and a Num Pad key. In my example, I use Shift+Num 1, as shown in Figure 6-37.

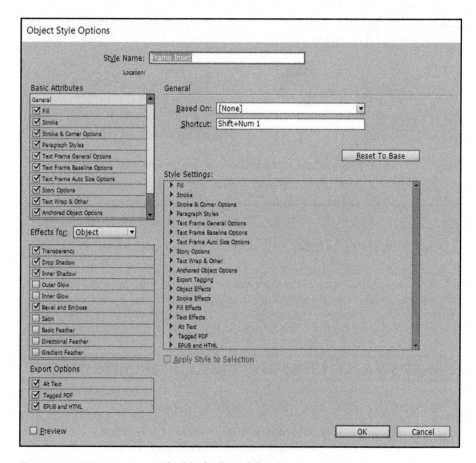

Figure 6-37. *Type a name and add a keyboard shortcut*

5. **Enable paragraph styles**. You need to enable the Paragraph Style item in the Basic Attributes if a paragraph style is used in your formatting. In my example, I use a paragraph style, so I click the checkbox that shows a horizontal line by default and the checkmark appears adjacent to Paragraph Styles. Hence, this option is now turned on.

6. **Click OK.** When you finish editing the Object Style Options, click OK. The new style is then added in the Object Styles Panel.

7. **Apply the style.** Click another object and either click the object style name in the Object Styles Options Panel or press the keyboard shortcut. In Figure 6-38, you see the original frame that I used to capture the style on the left, in the middle a new layout, and on the right the style applied to the new layout

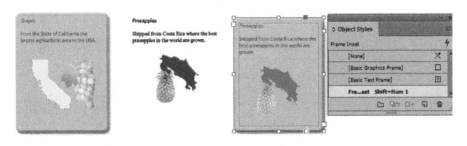

Figure 6-38. *Original frame (left), new layout (middle), after applying the style next, and the Object Styles Panel right showing the keyboard shortcut*

6.6.3   Creating Single Attribute Object Styles

Sometimes you may want to use only a single formatting attribute in your object style definition. Let's say that you want to apply a corner effect that you want on all frames. However, the frames may have other attributes that differ, such as frame fill colors, stroke values, and so forth. When you create an object style, InDesign automatically enables multiple style attributes. You need to turn off everything except the style attribute(s) that you want.

CREATING A STYLE WITH A SINGLE ATTRIBUTE OBJECT

To create a style with a single attribute, follow these steps:

1. **Create a new object style.** You don't need to format an object and then create the object style when editing a single attribute.

2. **Name the style and assign a keyboard shortcut if you use the style frequently**.

3. **Select a single style attribute.** Press the Alt/⌥ key and click the checkbox adjacent to the item you want to edit. Press Alt/⌥ and click a second time to enable the item.

4. **Edit the options for the item.** In my example, I want to use only a corner effect. I want the other attributes for my style to remain neutral or unaffected when I use the style. Click the name of the attribute, and the right pane changes. Click the Stroke & Corner Effects in the left pane. All of the options for the given effect are displayed in the New Object Style dialog box.

In my example, I added a 16-pixel rounded corner to the top-right and bottom-left of an object. The settings are shown in Figure 6-39. Click OK when finished, and the new style is added to the Object Styles Panel.

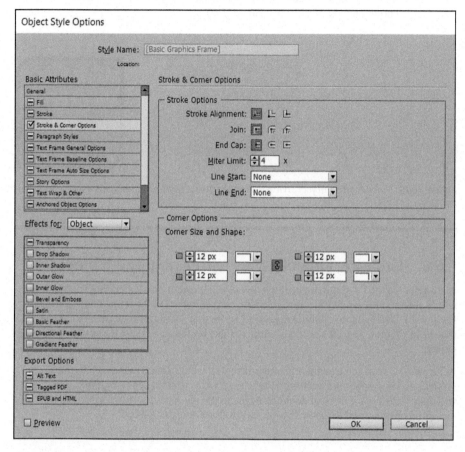

Figure 6-39. *Edit an object attribute directly in the New Object Style dialog box*

■ **Note**   InDesign CC 2017 additionally includes Scale text boxes for beginning and ending arrowheads. If you use a version prior to InDesign CC 2017, your Stroke and Corner Options will appear different than shown in Figure 6-39.

5. **Apply the style.** Click an object and either click the style name or use the keyboard shortcut. In my example, I have three frames assigned different colors and different stroke values. When I apply the object style to each object, the only thing that changes are the corner options, as shown in Figure 6-40.

Figure 6-40. Corner effect object style applied to frames with different colors and stroke values

6.6.4   Creating Object Styles with Anchored Objects

In Chapter 5, I talked about anchoring objects to table cells and stated that you need to use an object style to add objects to multiple cells using a GREP pattern Find/Change. However, I didn't go into creating the object styles that you would use with anchored objects in Chapter 5. At this point, it's time to talk about using object styles with anchored objects.

In Figure 6-41, you see a text frame and images adjacent to each paragraph in the text frame. The images are anchored to the first line of text in each paragraph. To set this document up, we need to anchor a frame to the respective line of text, adjust the anchored options, and assign an object style to the anchored objects.

236

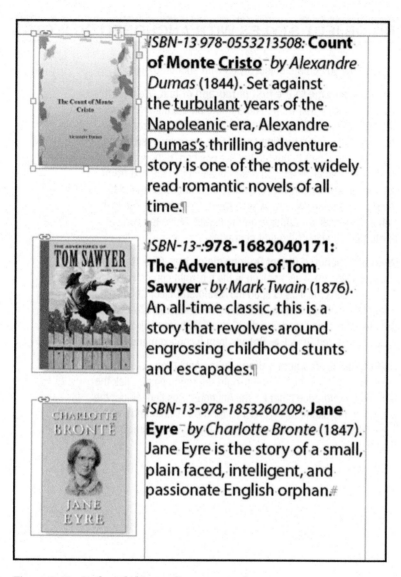

ISBN-13 978-0553213508: **Count of Monte Cristo** *by Alexandre Dumas* (1844). Set against the turbulant years of the Napoleanic era, Alexandre Dumas's thrilling adventure story is one of the most widely read romantic novels of all time.¶

*ISBN-13-:***978-1682040171: The Adventures of Tom Sawyer** *by Mark Twain* (1876). An all-time classic, this is a story that revolves around engrossing childhood stunts and escapades.¶

ISBN-13-978-1853260209: **Jane Eyre** *by Charlotte Bronte* (1847). Jane Eyre is the story of a small, plain faced, intelligent, and passionate English orphan.#

Figure 6-41. *Anchored objects adjacent to text frames*

CREATING OBJECT STYLES WITH ANCHORED OBJECTS

The following is how you create object styles with anchored objects:

1. **Anchor the frame to the first paragraph of text.** We start this sequence with a text frame and a frame on the document page. Click the frame and drag the small blue square to just before the first character in the first line of text. You may need to zoom in on the document to get the anchor position to the left side of the first character. When you drag the anchor to the text frame, you see an arrowhead with a small T character below and to the right of the arrowhead. As you move the cursor to the text frame, a vertical bar appears on the cursor. Move the vertical bar to the left side of the first character.

2. **Open the Anchored Object Options dialog box.** Click the frame, and you see a small anchor icon in the top-right corner. Press Alt/⌥ and click the icon to open the Anchored Object Options dialog box. You can also use the Object ➤ Anchored Object ➤ Options menu command or right-click an anchored object and choose Anchored Object ➤ Options from a context menu.

3. **Adjust anchored object options.** In the Anchored Object Options dialog box, click the top-right reference point. Click the left middle reference point for the Anchored Position. Adjust the offsets. In my example, I typed 110 for the X-Offset and -12 for the Y-Offset, as shown in Figure 6-42. Click OK to dismiss the dialog box.

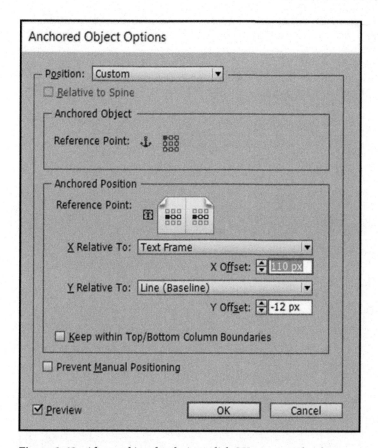

Figure 6-42. After making the choices, click OK to accept the changes

4. **Open the New Object Style dialog box.** Select the anchored object and Alt/⌥ click the Create new style icon in the Object Styles Panel. The New Object Style dialog box opens.

5. **Edit the options in the New Object Style dialog box.** Type a name for the new object style. Click Frame Fitting Options and the right pane changes displaying choices for Frame Fitting Options. Choose Fit Content Proportionately from the fitting menu, as shown in Figure 6-43. Click General and be certain that Apply Style to Selection is enabled. Click OK to create the new style.

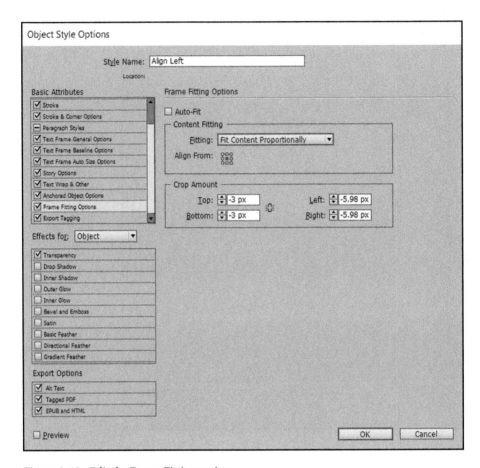

Figure 6-43. Edit the Frame Fitting options

6. **Copy and paste the anchored object.** This document page has only a few paragraphs of text. If we had several pages and needed to add frames to each paragraph, we might use a GREP pattern to search through the document and add the frames to each paragraph automatically. In this example, though, we can just copy and paste a few times.

7. **Click the anchored object, and press Ctrl/⌘+C to copy the object.** Click the cursor just before the first character in the second paragraph and press Ctrl/⌘+V to paste. Insert the cursor before the first character in the third paragraph and press Ctrl/⌘+V to paste again. The final result should look like Figure 6-41.

6.7 Creating Table Cell and Table Styles

When we create paragraph and character styles, we start by creating the paragraph and then the character styles. In essence, we create the whole and then the parts. When working with tables, your workflow is the opposite. We create the parts first and then the whole. In table terms, this means that we create cell styles and then we create table styles.

Creating styles for cells and tables works in a similar manner to creating paragraph and character styles. You first format cells using a number of formatting options, and then you create a cell style. With tables, the workflow is the same. You format a table first using the cell styles, and then you create a table style.

6.7.1 Formatting a Table

When you prepare a table where you want to add cell and table styles, your first step is to format everything in the table and get the appearance exactly as you want it. In Figure 6-44, you see a formatted table. All of the cells are formatted with text attributes, the table has a header and footer row, and the table contains character and paragraph styles. This is your first step in getting a table set up for creating cell and table styles.

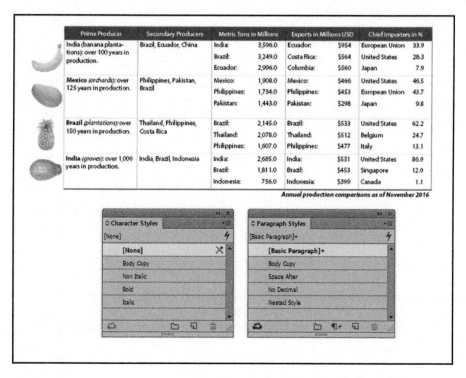

Figure 6-44. *Format a table with all of the table and cell attributes before you create cell and table styles*

Create paragraph styles for the text in cells, and add character styles to be certain that you don't have any overrides in the styles. Do this before you move on to creating cell styles.

6.7.2   Naming Cell Styles

You can name cell styles anything you want, but your job will be much easier if you follow a few fixed naming conventions. In Figure 6-45, you see the Table Style Options dialog box. We'll return to working with this dialog box later in the section "Creating Table Styles." For now, I want to draw your attention to the bottom section of the dialog box in the Cell Styles area. Notice that there are five options for choosing cell styles. You need to create cell styles for the cell formatting that deviate from your body style. In my example, I created five different cell styles and I named the styles Header, Footer, Body, Left Column, and Right Column. When I open the Table Style Options dialog box, there is no confusion about cell styles from which I need to choose the five drop-down menus.

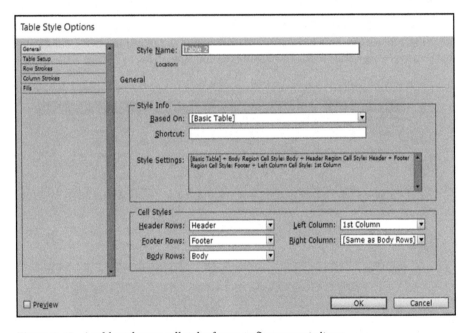

Figure 6-45. *A table style uses cell styles for up to five separate items*

When you create cell styles, keep in mind that you need to choose styles in the Table Style Options dialog box when you create a table style. If you use some different naming conventions, it may be difficult to choose the right style for the respective menu item.

6.7.3 Creating Cell Styles

Cell styles are created similar to the way that you create character and paragraph styles. You first format a cell and then open the Cell Styles Panel (choose Window ➤ Styles ➤ Cell Styles).

Click the cursor in a cell. You don't have to select the cell contents or the cell. Just click the cursor in a cell and then click the Create new style icon at the bottom of the Cell Styles Panel. The Cell Style Options dialog box opens, as shown in Figure 6-46.

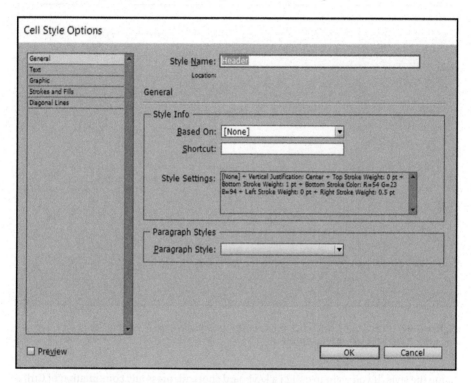

Figure 6-46. *Press Alt/⌥ and click the Create new style icon in the Cell Styles Panel*

Like other styles you create in InDesign, your first task is to provide a name for the style. If you created one style and want to base your next style on the previous style, choose a style name from the Based On drop-down menu. For example, suppose you create a style for the body text and you want to italicize the text in one cell. You would create a new cell style and base it on the Body style. All of the attributes in the Body style are added to your new style and the only addition is the italic text.

If you want to use a keyboard shortcut for a cell style, click in the Shortcut text box and press any combination of Ctrl/⌘+Alt/⌥+Shift+ (a Num Pad key).

Create cell styles for the header, footer, and body text (all of the cells between the header and footer and between the left and right sides of the table).

6.7.4   Creating Table Styles

Before you move on to create a table style, review your work. Be certain that you have used paragraph, character, and cell styles to define formatting in all of the cells. When you're certain that all of the styles have been applied, open the Table Styles Panel (Window ➤ Styles ➤ Table Styles) by clicking the Create new style icon in the Table Styles Panel. The Table Style Options dialog box opens, as shown in Figure 6-47.

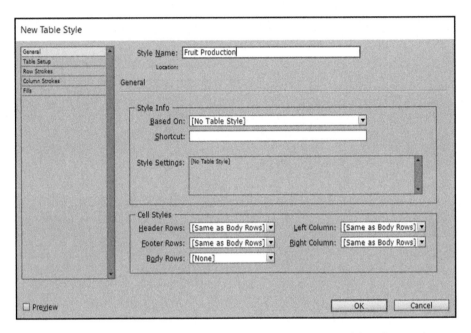

Figure 6-47. *Press Alt/⌥ and click the Create new style icon in the Table Styles Panel to open the Table Style Options dialog box*

Name the style. If you want to assign a keyboard shortcut, press any combination of Ctrl/Command+Alt/⌥+Shift+ (a Num Pad key).

If you want alternating fills for the rows, click Fills in the left pane. Choose a fill color and tint for the first color and another color and tint for the next row. If you have a header and footer, skip the first and last rows. Click OK and the Table Style appears in the Table Styles Panel.

6.7.5   Applying Table Styles

In Figure 6-48, you see an unformatted table. If I want to apply a table style to the new table, I need to select the table. Click in a cell and press Ctrl/⌘+A to Select All or position the cursor over the top-left corner. Wait until the cursor changes to a diagonal arrow and click to select the table.

	Developer	Market Share	Installed Users ~ Millions	Current Version	Year Developed
Photoshop	Adobe Systems	99%	187	CC 2015	1989
InDesign	Adobe Systems	89%	129	CC 2015	1993
Illustrator	Adobe Systems	92%	156	CC 2015	1986
Acrobat	Adobe Systems	84%	92	CC DC	1992
					Status of Adobe Creative Cloud Software

Figure 6-48. *A table with no formatting*

Open the Table Styles Panel and click the table style that you want to apply to the selected table. Unfortunately, table styles are not perfect in InDesign. You always need to do a little cleanup and reformatting. In Figure 6-49, you can see that the top-left cell needs to be cleared of the fill color and the stroke on the right of the body rows needs to be eliminated. Edits like these are frequent when you apply table styles to raw, unformatted tables.

	Developer	Market Share	Installed Users ~ Millions	Current Version	Year Developed
Photoshop	Adobe Systems	99%	187	CC 2015	1989
InDesign	Adobe Systems	89%	129	CC 2015	1993
Illustrator	Adobe Systems	92%	156	CC 2015	1986
Acrobat	Adobe Systems	84%	92	CC DC	1992
					Status of Adobe Creative Cloud Software

Figure 6-49. *After applying a table style to an unformatted table, a little cleanup work is needed*

One little trick I used when formatting my table shown in Figure 6-49 is on the footer row. I merged the cells to the right of the first cell in the row. However, I left the first cell intact in the footer row. Since the left column has left-justified text, having a single row at the footer would justify the text to the left. By keeping a single cell with no stroke and no fill in the footer row, the footer row formatted correctly when I applied the table style. It's not a big issue to reformat the footer row, but eliminating the need for extra cleanup helps you move though a document faster when you have a lot of tables.

6.8   Getting Familiar with GREP

Just seeing the name GREP probably frightens some. When you look at the definition of GREP, which is *G*lobally search with the *RE*gular *E*xpression and *P*rint, it probably adds a little more anxiety. When you learn that GREP is a command-line utility used in UNIX, then you're probably off-the-scale with apprehension. To some degree, your fears are justified if you're a right-brain artist and have little use for coding. Some GREP expressions are very intense and require some knowledge and an ability for coding. However, the upside of using GREP in InDesign is that there are many simple routines that you can easily use in your page layout.

First let's understand a little about what GREP is in InDesign terms. You use GREP patterns to search through a document and replace the pattern with a new pattern, a word, a character, or something else. A *pattern* is something like a date (January 1, 2017). The date here is a pattern. Last, first, middle initial is a pattern for a name. Words beginning with *a q* (or any other character) and ending with a *y* (or any other character) is also a pattern. Just about any combination of characters that you can easily define is what we might consider a pattern.

GREP in InDesign can be used to locate patterns of text and replace the text with other text, change the text formatting, or delete the text. In a practical example, you might want to search for all words contained within parentheses and change the font style to italics. Maybe you want to search for all e-mail addresses and change the color of text or add an underline to the addresses. You might want to delete double spaces or extra carriage returns. All of these examples are easily handled by searching GREP patterns and replacing them with another pattern.

A GREP code can be added in the Find/Change dialog box, and you can create GREP styles in the Paragraph Style Options dialog box. There is no separate panel for GREP styles or expressions.

6.8.1   Understanding Reserved Characters

A GREP expression might appear something like this:

```
(?<=\().+?(?=\))
```

If we type this code in the Find /Change dialog box in the GREP tab, this expression searches for any text inside parentheses, but not including the parentheses. If you change the contents within a parenthetical statement for text or a font, the contents are changed and the parentheses characters remain unchanged.

GREP expressions use reserved characters, meaning that certain characters have a distinct meaning and they are not interpreted by GREP as the specific character. For example, in the expression above, the ? mark, the + symbol, and . (period) characters are reserved characters by GREP. The ? mark is a code used by GREP for something that may or may not be there. The + symbol is for one or more instances (such as one or more characters). The . (period) symbol is a "wildcard" that matches any character.

Let's say that you want to search for a dollar sign and replace it with the mark for another type of currency. The dollar sign is also a reserved character. In GREP terms, it means the end of a paragraph. If you want to search for a plus symbol again, you can't type + in your GREP search because GREP interprets + as one or more instances.

The way to get around the problem when you want to search for characters that have special meanings in GREP is to escape out of the reserved character. You do this by typing a backslash and the character. So for example, if I wanted to search for a dollar sign, I would type \$, searching for a + sign would be \+, and finding a period would be \. You can also escape out of reserved characters by placing them inside brackets [$].

Getting to know many of the special characters helps you understand more about GREP. Moreover, knowing how to escape out of reserved characters can help you debug some of the expressions that you create.

6.8.2   Searching and Finding with GREP

There's so much to discuss when talking about GREP that I can't hope to cover more than a few GREP expressions that can help you with your design projects, especially when you want to export to reflowable EPUBs. The following expressions are not just for creating reflowable EPUBs, but in some cases they are essential for the reflowable EPUB format. Let's take a look at a few expressions that you might want to use frequently.

6.8.2.1   Eliminating Spaces, Characters, and Carriage Returns at the End of Paragraphs

You may be tempted to add a carriage return at the end of a paragraph to provide space between paragraphs, or you may place text created by a client that needs to be included in your design that has double carriage returns. If you export to reflowable EPUB format, the extra carriage returns are ignored in the EPUB format. The only way to add space after a paragraph is to use a paragraph style and adjust the Space After setting in the style definition.

Another thing that can be a real pain is having spaces in your document with a font different than the fonts included in your design. Every time you open the document you see an alert dialog box informing you that a font is missing.

Eliminating extra spaces and carriage returns is a good candidate for a GREP find and change.

PERFORMING A GREP SEARCH AND ELIMINATING CHARACTERS

To perform a GREP search and eliminate the characters, do the following:

1. **Click in a paragraph or a story.** If you want to search the document containing multiple stories, you can skip this step and choose to search the document in the Find/Change dialog box.

2. **Press Ctrl/⌘+F to open the Find/Change dialog box.** Since we're going to type a GREP expression, click the GREP tab in the Find/Change dialog box.

3. **Type the expression in the Find What text box.** In this example, the following expression will find whitespace at the end of a paragraph and delete multiple carriage returns. It's very simple and even the most insecure programmer can easily replicate this expression:

   \s+$

The expression is just four characters—a backslash, a lowercase s used for any whitespace, a + used for one or more instances, and the $ symbol used for the end of paragraph location.

If you forget some reserved characters, InDesign can help you out a little. You won't find all reserved characters in the GREP pane, but there are many common definitions that you can choose by opening the @ menu.

Type just \s+ and leave the $ symbol out of the equation. Open the Find What menu by clicking the @ symbol and scrolling down to Locations. In the submenu, select End of Paragraph, as shown in Figure 6-50. The $ is added to the expression in the Find What text box.

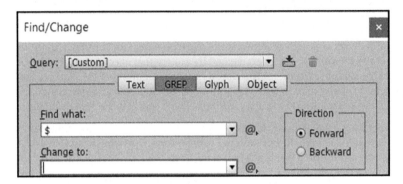

Figure 6-50. Open the Find What menu by clicking the @ symbol and choosing End of Paragraph in the Locations submenu

4. **Leave the Change To text box at the default.** To delete extra spaces at the end of a paragraph and delete multiple paragraphs, you leave the Change To text box empty. InDesign will search and replace the expression with nothing, which is the same as deleting the spaces and carriage returns.

5. **Click Find.** Before you attempt to change all instances, test your expression with a few clicks on the Find button. It's helpful if you show hidden characters by choosing View ➤ Extras ➤ Show Hidden Characters.

6. **When you click Find, you should see a selection in the document for the first found occurrence**. If an alert box appears informing you that nothing was found, click the cursor in the story and click Find again. You can click in a text frame in the document without dismissing the Find/Change dialog box.

7. **Change all.** If everything looks OK when you click the Find button and you're sure that InDesign is finding the expression you want, click Change All. In Figure 6-51, you see a text frame containing the offending text on the left and the corrected on the right after I applied the GREP Find/Change.

Figure 6-51. *After executing Find/Change, the whitespace and extra paragraph returns are eliminated*

6.8.2.2   Formatting Lists

Take a look at Figure 6-52. The number list is a mess. Some tabs were inserted on some lines, while different spaces were applied to other lines. Your lists may not be this messy, but if you acquire text documents from clients, you will find many people still not using a tab ruler properly and formatting lists with spaces. When you resize a text frame, they all go haywire. This document is in need of a GREP fix.

Figure 6-52. *A numbered list with terrible formatting*

FORMATTING LISTS

To clean up the list, I performed the following edits:

1. **Create a character style.** If you want to apply a color to the numbers that's different from the text, you create a character style. In this example, I create a character style and only change the text color.

2. **Create a paragraph style.** Click the Create new style icon in the Paragraph Styles Panel; the Paragraph Style Options dialog box opens. Type a name for the style.

3. **Click Bullets and Numbering in the left pane.** In the right pane, choose the character style for the number's color by opening the Character Style menu and selecting the character style for the numbers. Click OK to create the new paragraph style.

4. **Open the Find/Change dialog box.** Press Ctrl/⌘ to open the Find/Change dialog box and click the GREP tab.

5. **Add a GREP expression in the Find What text box.** What we want to search for is one or more digits at the beginning of each paragraph, followed by a period (or maybe not) if we apply the same expression to lines with no periods after the digits, maybe some spaces or maybe not, followed by anything. To add the expression, the following code performs the search:

```
^\d+\.?\s*(.)
```

In this code, the ^ is used to locate the beginning of the paragraph. The \d is for any digit and the + is for one or more times. The \. is for finding a period and the ? is for maybe a period exists or maybe it doesn't. The \s is for finding spaces that may or may not be there. There is a period at the end of the expression. However, the period appears within parentheses (.). The reason we need to put the period between parentheses is because running the expression will duplicate the number at the beginning of the paragraph. If we add the (.), the number is added but quickly deleted after running Change/Change All.

In the Change To text box, you find $1, as shown in Figure 6-53. This expression picks up the item(s) in parentheses. You want to change the formatting at the bottom of the Find/Change dialog box. Click the magnifying glass, and the Change Format Settings dialog box opens. Select the Paragraph Style in this dialog box and click OK to return to the Find/Change dialog box, as shown in Figure 6-53.

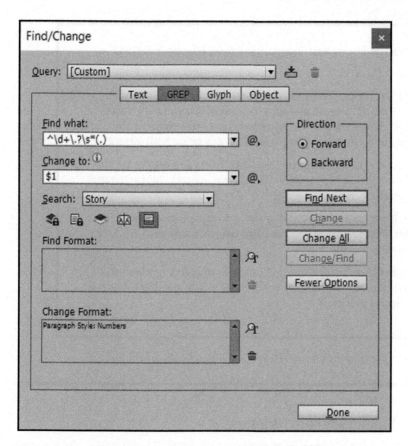

Figure 6-53. *Add Find What, Change To, and Change Format settings*

6. **Click the Find button to be sure that the expression finds the proper pattern and click Change a few times to be certain that the replacement is accurate**. You can always undo the changes if they don't work properly. When you're sure that everything works, click Change All. The new formatted list appears in Figure 6-54.

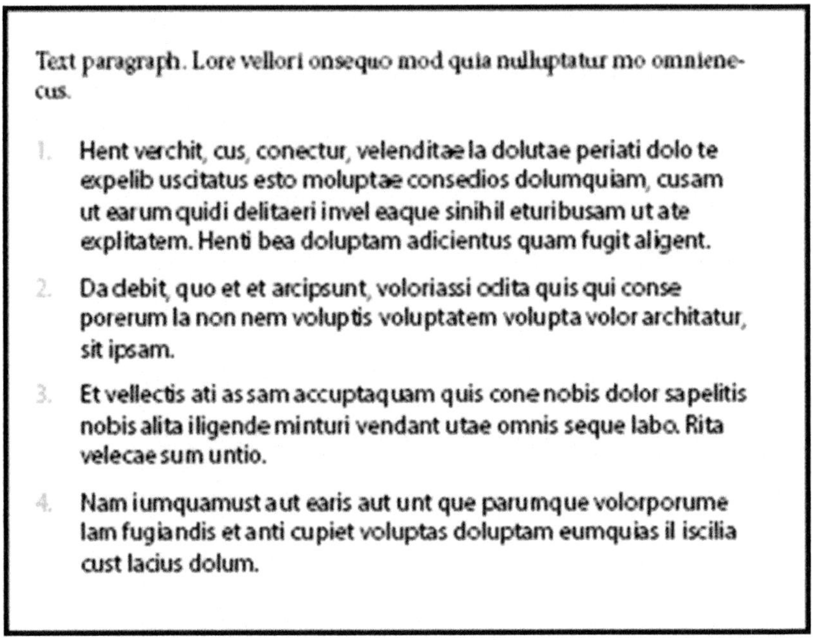

Text paragraph. Lore vellori onsequo mod quia nulluptatur mo omnienecus.

1. Hent verchit, cus, conectur, velenditae la dolutae periati dolo te expelib uscitatus esto moluptae consedios dolumquiam, cusam ut earum quidi delitaeri invel eaque sinihil eturibusam ut ate explitatem. Henti bea doluptam adicientus quam fugit aligent.

2. Da debit, quo et et arcipsunt, voloriassi odita quis qui conse porerum la non nem voluptis voluptatem volupta volor architatur, sit ipsam.

3. Et vellectis ati as sam accuptaquam quis cone nobis dolor sapelitis nobis alita iligende minturi vendant utae omnis seque labo. Rita velecae sum untio.

4. Nam iumquamust aut earis aut unt que parumque volorporume lam fugiandis et anti cupiet voluptas doluptam eumquias il iscilia cust lacius dolum.

Figure 6-54. After running Change All, the formatting for the list changes

6.8.2.3   Saving Presets (Queries)

If you find yourself using a GREP Find/Change expression frequently, you won't want to type the code each time you change some formatting. Fortunately, InDesign provides you with an option to save your queries. Click the Save Query button in the Find/Change dialog box and type a name for the query. Click OK and the query is added to the Query drop-down menu. In my example, I typed Numbered Lists and clicked the Save Query button. The new query is shown in Figure 6-55 along with the code used to change the formatting for numbered lists.

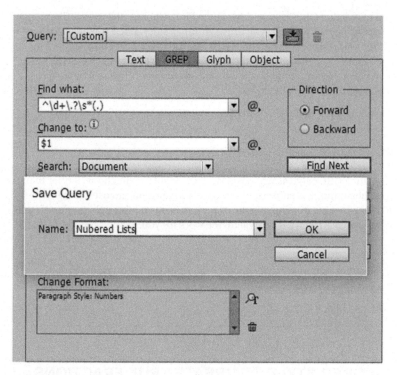

Figure 6-55. *Click Save Query to save the query as a preset*

6.8.3   Creating GREP Styles

As I mentioned earlier in this chapter, there is no GREP panel for creating GREP styles. You can create a GREP style, but that's handled in the Paragraph Style Options dialog box. When you save a query in the Find/Change dialog box, the query is application-specific, meaning that you can use the expression in other InDesign documents. When you create a GREP style, the expression is document specific, meaning that the code is only saved in the document where you create the style. You can open the Paragraph Styles Panel and load a style containing a GREP style in a new document, but that's the only way you can rescue your code.

If you find that you use GREP styles frequently, you can create a master document with Paragraph, Character, Object, Table Cell and Table, and GREP styles. As you work on new documents, load the styles in the respective panels. The nice thing about InDesign is that you can load (style panel menu Load Styles) only the styles that you want from the various panels and make choices for the styles that you import for each panel. This way you won't over clutter your style panels.

So far we looked at creating GREP expressions in the Find/Change dialog box. Changing patterns via Find/Change is fine when you finish editing a story. But if you need to make additional edits for something that was changed using the GREP find and change? You need to rerun the Find/Change again. By adding a GREP style to a paragraph style, any changes that you make in a paragraph are automatically updated. This will be clearer when we look at creating some GREP styles.

Now let's look at a few GREP styles that you can add in the Paragraph Styles Panel.

6.8.3.1   Creating OpenType Fractions

A good candidate for a GREP style is when you want to create true fractions. Rather than trying to set up superscripts and subscript to fudge a fraction, you can use OpenType fonts to create better-looking fractions. Rather than having to run through a series of steps to create a fraction, you can let a GREP style do the work for you.

■ **Note**   OpenType fractions won't work in either reflowable or fixed-layout EPUBs. You can use them with Interactive PDFs. For more information about using fractions in reflowable EPUBs, see Chapter 12.

USING A GREP STYLE TO CREATE TRUE FRACTIONS

To add a GREP style that changes cardinal numbers to fractions, do the following:

1. **Create a paragraph style.** If you want all of the body copy to use the fraction conversion, use the body style or else create a new paragraph style.

2. **Add the GREP expression.** Edit a paragraph style or create a new style. In the Paragraph Style Options dialog box, click GREP style in the left pane. By default, you see a \d+ in the To Text field. At first it appears as though there's nothing that you can do to edit the expression. This dialog box looks like a work in progress. However, you can add code here. Just click the default code and the To Text text box becomes active where you can delete the default expression and type in your own code. To find fractions in the text, type the following code:

   \d+/\d+

   The code is very simple. We look for one or more numbers \ d+ followed by a slash / followed by one or more numbers \d+. That's very easy.

3. **Create a character style.** The next step is to create a character style. You can use a character style properly formatted, or you can create the character style without leaving the Paragraph Style Options dialog box. Click on the line above the expression, and a drop-down menu is available. Scroll to the bottom of the menu and choose New Character Style. The New Character Style dialog box opens.

4. **Format the character style.** Click OpenType Features in the left pane. Click the Fractions checkbox when the OpenType Features pane opens, as shown in Figure 6-56. In my example, I also change the color of the characters and set the font style to bold. This is optional. I only did this so that you can see the screenshot easier in Figure 6-57.

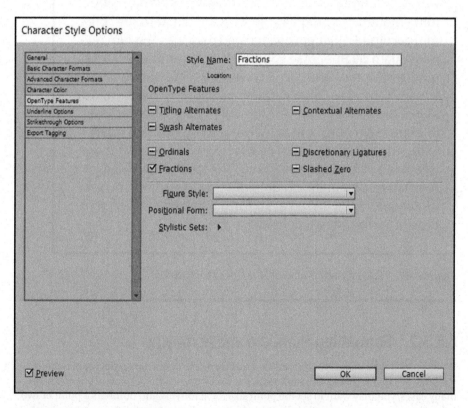

Figure 6-56. Format the character style to use OpenType fractions

5. **Add a name for the style and return to the Paragraph Style Options dialog box.** Type a name in the Style Name text box and click OK to return to the Paragraph Style Options dialog box.

6. **Click OK in the Paragraph Style Options dialog box.** The text is formatted in the text frame(s) where you apply the style, as shown in Figure 6-57. If you type a new fraction in the text frame, the new text is formatted with the Fractions character style.

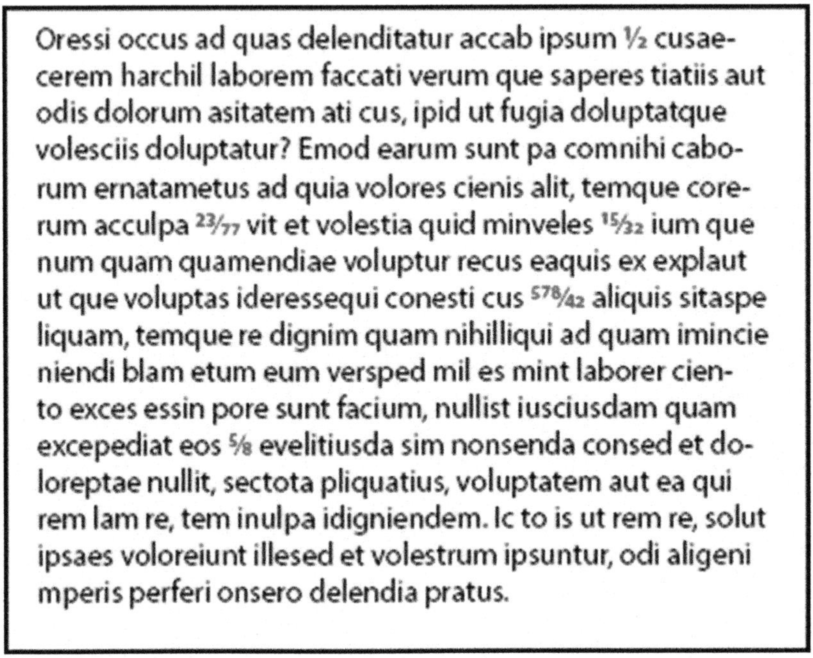

Oressi occus ad quas delenditatur accab ipsum ½ cusae-cerem harchil laborem faccati verum que saperes tiatiis aut odis dolorum asitatem ati cus, ipid ut fugia doluptatque volesciis doluptatur? Emod earum sunt pa comnihi cabo-rum ernatametus ad quia volores cienis alit, temque core-rum acculpa $^{23}/_{77}$ vit et volestia quid minveles $^{15}/_{32}$ ium que num quam quamendiae voluptur recus eaquis ex explaut ut que voluptas ideressequi conesti cus $^{578}/_{42}$ aliquis sitaspe liquam, temque re dignim quam nihilliqui ad quam imincie niendi blam etum eum versped mil es mint laborer cien-to exces essin pore sunt facium, nullist iusciusdam quam excepediat eos $^{5}/_{8}$ evelitiusda sim nonsenda consed et do-loreptae nullit, sectota pliquatius, voluptatem aut ea qui rem lam re, tem inulpa idigniendem. Ic to is ut rem re, solut ipsaes voloreiunt illesed et volestrum ipsuntur, odi aligeni mperis perferi onsero delendia pratus.

Figure 6-57. Text in the text frame uses the OpenType fractions

6.8.3.2 Formatting Numbers and Acronyms

When you set type and use acronyms and numbers, the characters often seem to be too large at a quick glance. Depending on the font you use, they can blare out at you. In many cases, you may want to set the point size for acronyms and numbers a point or two lower than the point size used in the Basic Character Formats definition in a paragraph style. In the top part of Figure 6-58, you see several acronyms and numbers in the paragraph. The acronyms and numbers clearly appear larger than the body copy. This is a good candidate for a GREP style, where you can lower the point size on the type for the acronyms and the numbers.

The NASA Mars mission photos are now playing in IMAX theaters. NASA officials are very excited to bring you the most recent images of the red planet. Beginning FY 2018 NASA's powerful Space Launch System rocket will enable the proving ground missions to text new capabilities. Future missions like the Mars 2020 rover will demonstrate new technologies that can help astronauts survive on Mars.

The NASA Mars mission photos are now playing in IMAX theaters. NASA officials are very excited to bring you the most recent images of the red planet. Beginning FY 2018 NASA's powerful Space Launch System rocket will enable the proving ground missions to text new capabilities. Future missions like the Mars 2020 rover will demonstrate new technologies that can help astronauts survive on Mars.

Figure 6-58. Acronyms and numbers often appear larger than the font size in a paragraph

LOWERING THE POINT SIZE ON THE TYPE FOR NUMBERS AND ACRONYMS

To lower the point size, do the following:

1. **Set up a paragraph style for the text**. In my example, I use a Body style.

2. **Edit the paragraph style.** Right-click the paragraph style and choose Edit Body (or whatever name you use for your paragraph style).

3. **Open the GREP Styles.** Click GREP Styles in the left pane to open the GREP Styles Panel.

4. **Add a character style.** The default expression \d+ will work for the numbers. Click Apply Style and scroll down to New Character Style.

5. **Set the font size.** In the New Character Style Options dialog box, click Basic Character Formats.

6. **Reduce the point size for the type.** In my example, I have the point size for the type set to 22 points. I lower the font size to 20 points and click OK to return to the Paragraph Style Options dialog box.

7. **Add another GREP Style.** Click the New GREP Style button and a new set appears below the first GREP style.

8. **Type the expression.** Click the To Text field and type the following code:

\u\u+

This expression searches for uppercase characters \u and is repeated to avoid selecting words with cap and lowercase.

9. **Add a character style.** The same character style used for the numbers can be used for the acronyms. Open the Apply Style menu and choose the character style you created for the number expression. Click OK; the final result is shown at the bottom of Figure 6-58.

As you can see, you can layer GREP styles in the Paragraph Style Options dialog box. If you have some routines for which it is difficult to write a complete expression, you can try to break them down and write several GREP styles.

There are many GREP patterns, and the codes are available in blog posts and web sites. Search the Internet and you may find some patterns that you can copy and use in your documents.

6.9 Summary

We covered a lot of territory in this chapter. You learned how to work with character and paragraph styles, object styles, table and cell styles, and GREP styles. Styles are critical for EPUBs, and they make your layout work so much easier in InDesign. You can appreciate styles when you need to modify a document or edit a document created by coworkers or other users. The more you know about styles, the faster you can work through any InDesign assignment.

This chapter ends our review of some of the basics and essentials for working in InDesign. From Chapter 7 forward, we look at interactivity. We begin the next chapter by first understanding hyperlinks.

PART III

Adding Interactivity

CHAPTER 7

■ ■ ■

Creating Hyperlinks

If you've poked around the Internet, you certainly know about hyperlinks. Every time you've clicked an HREF tag (associated with a button or text) and it sent you to a new location, you've experienced a hyperlink destination.

Hyperlinks have two parts: the source and the destination. In InDesign, your source can be text, text frames, images, objects, interactive elements, and object frames. The destinations for hyperlinks can be a URL, launching the default e-mail application, a page within a document, an anchor contained within a document, and links to external documents.

As you can see, there's much more to InDesign hyperlinks than simply opening up web pages. In this chapter, I cover how to create hyperlinks from various sources and how to set them up for various destinations.

■ **Caution** As I discuss in Chapter 15, you should avoid creating hyperlinks in InDesign when you export to Interactive PDF documents. Use Acrobat's tools for all hyperlink creation in PDF files.

7.1 Understanding Some Basics for Hyperlinks

InDesign hyperlinks can link to URLs, external files, e-mail clients, pages within a document, text anchors, and shared destinations. A *shared destination* is shared by two or more sources. When the destinations are shared, they appear in a hierarchy in the Hyperlinks Panel and nested below a folder. When not shared, each destination is listed separately in the panel.

7.1.1 Getting Familiar with the Hyperlinks Panel

Hyperlinks in your InDesign document all appear in the Hyperlinks Panel, as shown in Figure 7-1. To open the panel, choose Window ➤ Interactive ➤ Hyperlinks. This panel includes a number of options for working with hyperlinks.

© Ted Padova 2017
T. Padova, *Adobe InDesign Interactive Digital Publishing*,
DOI 10.1007/978-1-4842-2439-7_7

Figure 7-1. Choose Window ➤ Interactive ➤ Hyperlinks to open the Hyperlinks Panel

- URL: When you click an object (text, text frame, image, object, rectangle frame, shape, and so on), the URL text field becomes active. To link to an external URL, type the URL address in the text box.

- *Name:* You will see two icons adjacent on the right of Name. The first is the Page icon. Each hyperlink is contained in the panel with an icon indicating the type of hyperlink. Adjacent to the icon is a number that corresponds to the page number where the hyperlink exists. If you click the number, InDesign jumps to the page and selects the source.

- Each hyperlink is also color-coded. A green circle indicates that the URL is valid. A red circle indicates that the URL is invalid. Clicking the valid icons takes you to the destinations.

- *Refresh URL Status:* Click this button to refresh the list.

- *Create new hyperlink:* Something must be selected in the document for this icon to be active. When text or an object is selected, click the icon to create a new hyperlink.

- *Trash icon:* To delete a hyperlink, click the one that you want to delete in the Name list and click the Trash icon.

The Hyperlinks Panel has an extensive number of menu commands, as shown in Figure 7-2. To open the menu, click the top-right corner in the Hyperlinks Panel. The menu opens, and the options include the following:

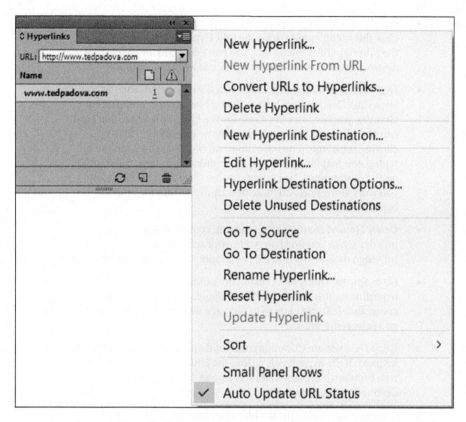

Figure 7-2. *Open the Hyperlinks Panel menu to access the hyperlink options*

- *New Hyperlink:* Click this menu item to create a new hyperlink. Its behavior is the same as clicking the Create new hyperlink icon at the bottom of the Hyperlinks Panel.

- *New Hyperlink from URL:* If you select a URL in text in the document, clicking this menu item creates a new hyperlink to the URL.

- *Convert URLs to Hyperlinks:* Use this item with caution. InDesign doesn't distinguish between valid URLs and non-valid URLs. If you have text appearing like *realize.It*, InDesign will create a URL. Any text where there is no space between the end of a sentence followed by a period and the next word with no space are treated as URLs in InDesign.

- *Delete Hyperlink:* The result of using this command is identical to using the Trash icon in the Hyperlinks Panel.

- *New Hyperlink Destination:* Click the menu item, and a dialog box opens where you can choose a destination for a page, text anchor, or URL.

- *Edit Hyperlink:* Select a hyperlink in the Hyperlinks Panel and click this menu item to open the Edit Hyperlink dialog box. In the Edit Hyperlink dialog box, you can edit a URL or change the destination, choose character styles, and edit PDF options.

- *Hyperlink Destination Options:* Click the menu item and the Hyperlink Destination Options dialog box opens. Among other changes, you can alter the name for the hyperlink. (Note that you can also change a hyperlink name in the Hyperlinks Panel by clicking the name, pausing a moment, clicking again, and then typing new text for the name). Hyperlink names have no effect on the destinations. You might rename the hyperlink names as you work along and add more descriptive names for what the hyperlink does.

- *Delete Unused Destinations:* Using this command is a good practice when you finish up your work and are ready to publish. InDesign deletes any unused destinations in the document.

- *Go to Source:* This is like clicking the number to the right of the hyperlink names in the Hyperlinks Panel. When you select the command, InDesign jumps to the page where the source is found and selects the source.

- *Go to Destination:* Click this command and the hyperlink action is invoked. If the hyperlink is a URL, the URL opens in your default web browser. If the destination is a page, InDesign jumps to the destination page, and so on.

- *Rename Hyperlink:* This is a bit redundant since you have two other methods for renaming hyperlinks. When you click the menu item, a simple dialog box opens where you can type a new name.

- *Reset Hyperlink:* Suppose that you have a hyperlink where the source is some text. Then later you realize that you want the hyperlink to use a different source. You select the new source, and then select the hyperlink in the Hyperlinks Panel and choose Reset Hyperlink. The new source uses the hyperlink destination that was established from the original source.

- *Update Hyperlink:* Use this menu item when you link to external documents (something like a PDF file). If you change the file name or location, select the hyperlink in the Hyperlinks Panel and click Update Hyperlink.

- *Sort:* By default, you can't move the hyperlinks around in the Hyperlinks Panel. However, if you choose Sort ➤ Manually in the menu, you can drag items up or down in the list. The other sort options include By Name and By Type, where you can sort the list by the name of the hyperlinks and you can sort by type of destination.

- *Small Panel Rows:* When you select this command, the type in the list gets smaller so that you can see a longer list in the panel.

- *Auto Update URL Status:* By default, this item is checked. If you work offline, you might uncheck the item and then enable it when you're back online. InDesign updates URL status automatically when enabled and provides you real-time feedback on valid and non-valid URLs.

7.1.2   Using Hyperlink Styles

When you create your first hyperlink in an InDesign document, you may not be immediately aware of it, but InDesign creates a Character Style for you. (For more on Character Styles, see Chapter 6.)

Open the Character Styles Panel (Window ➤ Style ➤ Character Styles). The Character Styles Panel opens. If you want to change the attributes for the style, right-click the Hyperlink style in the Character Styles Panel and choose Edit Hyperlink (where Hyperlink in this case is the name of the Character Style). The Character Style Options dialog box opens, as shown in Figure 7-3, where you can make changes to the font, font size, leading, color of the text, and more. I provide a thorough explanation of using the Character Style Options dialog box in Chapter 6.

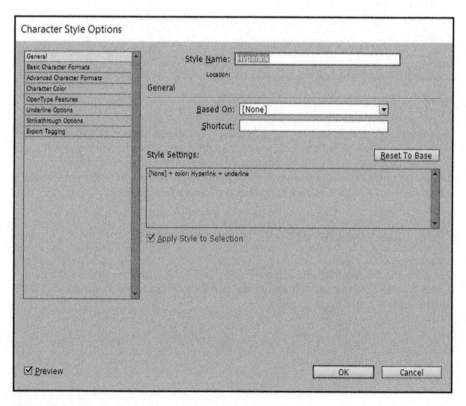

Figure 7-3. *When you create your first hyperlink, InDesign automatically creates a Character Style*

7.1.3   Editing Hyperlinks

If you want to edit a hyperlink to change a destination, URL, character style, or PDF appearance, select the hyperlink in the Hyperlinks Panel and choose Edit Hyperlink in the Hyperlinks Panel menu. The Edit Hyperlink dialog box opens, as shown in Figure 7-4.

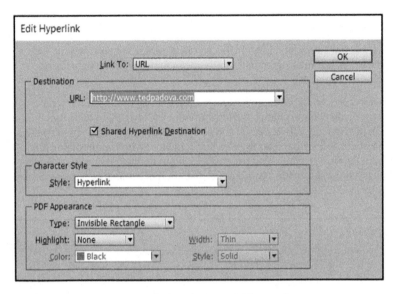

Figure 7-4. *Click Edit Hyperlink in the Hyperlinks Panel menu*

One thing that you might look for in the Edit Hyperlink dialog box is the checkbox for Shared Hyperlink Destination. If the box is unchecked and you have a long list of hyperlinks all using the same destination, you might want to edit them and check this checkbox. The hyperlinks will nest in a folder in the Hyperlinks Panel and make it easier to manage them if your document contains many different hyperlinks.

7.1.4   Editing Hyperlink Destinations

Click Hyperlink Destination Options in the Hyperlinks Panel menu to open the Hyperlink Destination Options dialog box, as shown in Figure 7-5. All of the hyperlink destinations in your document are listed in the Destination menu. As you add new destinations, they are dynamically added to the menu.

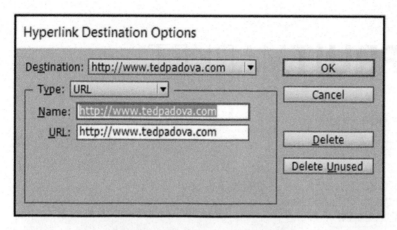

Figure 7-5. *Click Hyperlink Destination Options in the Hyperlinks Panel menu*

In this dialog box, you can change the destination type, change the hyperlink name, and change the URL if the destination is a URL.

7.2   Linking to URLs

As you can see, InDesign provides you with a very elaborate set of features and commands that work with hyperlinks. Now that you have become familiar with the dialog boxes and the Hyperlinks Panel, it's time to create some hyperlinks in a document.

CREATING A HYPERLINK

To create a hyperlink that opens a URL, do the following:

1. **Select some text, an object, image, or drag open a Rectangle Frame**. In my example, I select some text, as shown in Figure 7-6. If you have several text frames that you want to use, select them and group them (Ctrl/⌘+G).

Figure 7-6. Select text or several text frames grouped and open the Hyperlinks Panel

2. **Select the grouped items, and open the Hyperlinks Panel**. Click the Create new hyperlink icon. Add the URL for the hyperlink in the URL text box and press Enter/Return.

3. **Examine the Hyperlinks Panel**. In the event that you mistyped the URL, InDesign will report back to you any URL that is not valid by changing the circle icon to red. Verify that the circle appears green.

4. **Rename the hyperlink**. By default, the hyperlink name is derived from the URL address. If you have a long URL, it might be best to change the name to a shorter descriptive name. Click once on the name in the Hyperlinks Panel, pause a moment, and click again. When the text is selected, type a new name. Alternately, you can choose Rename Hyperlink in the Hyperlinks Panel.

5. **Check the link destination**. Click the green circle in the Hyperlinks Panel. If the URL takes you to where you expect to go, the URL is working properly. If you get an unexpected result, review the URL in the Hyperlinks Panel.

7.3   Linking to E-Mail Clients

When you link to an e-mail client, a new message is created in your default e-mail client. You can control the target e-mail address, the subject line, and even the contents of the e-mail. Everything begins in the Hyperlinks Panel, where you create a new hyperlink to an e-mail address.

You may have a document where you want feedback from readers of your content, want to share additional information that appears in a file link, or have any other way for your readers to communicate with you. Creating an e-mail hyperlink is rather simple. When it gets to adding a longer line of text in the Hyperlink text box, things get a bit more complicated.

7.3.1   Creating an E-Mail Hyperlink

To start things off, first we'll look at creating a rather simple e-mail hyperlink.

CREATING AN E-MAIL HYPERLINK

To create your first e-mail hyperlink, follow these steps:

1. **Select an object, text, or other item in the document, and click the Create new hyperlink icon in the Hyperlinks Panel.** The new Hyperlink dialog box opens.

2. **Choose Email from the Link To menu.** Type a valid e-mail address in the Address field. Type a subject line (optional), as shown in Figure 7-7. Click OK.

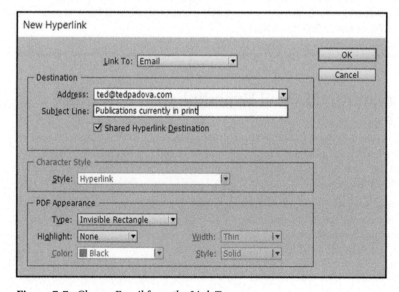

Figure 7-7. *Choose Email from the Link To menu*

3. **Notice the URL in the Hyperlinks Panel**. You see some code along with the e-mail address (See Figure 7-8).

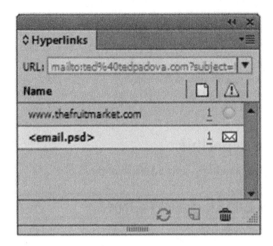

Figure 7-8. *The Hyperlinks Panel after adding an e-mail link*

4. **Click the E-mail image in the Hyperlinks Panel to test the address**. You should see a new message window open in your default e-mail client. If all works well, you completed the e-mail link task.

This e-mail link was a simple task. To explore more options with e-mail links, you can add a description in the message field, create a link to an external file, and add it all to the URL name in the Hyperlinks Panel.

7.3.2   Creating an E-Mail Hyperlink with a Message

The line for typing a URL link is very small in InDesign and there's no alternative for adding URL information. Even the dialog boxes that permit you to edit a URL have only a single line for a text box. If you have a long URL and you need to edit the information, it's not a bad idea to create the text on the InDesign pasteboard and copy and paste the text into the URL text line.

In Figure 7-9, you see text on the InDesign pasteboard. The text contains a hyperlink where a PDF document can be downloaded. I added some carriage returns to help ease the writing and make it more sensible. After writing the code, you need to remove the carriage returns, which then results in a single line of text.

For a list of current publications send me an email. You can also search amazon.com or perform a Google search to find publications that are now in print.

Figure 7-9. Type the information for the e-mail content on the InDesign pasteboard

You're not done yet. You need to remove all of the spaces, and they need to be replaced with %20. You may have seen web addresses appear like this since spaces are not allowed in URL address lines.

■ **Note**   Spaces are not allowed in URL lines. %20 is an ASCII encoded value for a space in a URL string

---

Rather than polish this up manually, you can use a script to take care of the formatting for you. This script comes from Keith Gilbert at www.gilbertconsulting.com. I loaded Keith's script and ran it on the text on the pasteboard. The result is shown in Figure 7-10.

Figure 7-10. After running Keith Gilbert's Replace Spaces with Entity script, all of the spaces were replaced with the proper code

> ■ **Note** Keith Gilbert is an author, conference speaker, and consultant with specializations in InDesign and Adobe DPS. His web site (`www.gilbertconsulting.com`) hosts a wealth of information on digital publishing and some nifty InDesign scripts that he has written. His two sets of scripts (Digital publishing pack 1 and Digital publishing pack 2) are great tools for those working with DPS and digital publications, and I highly recommend that you take a look at these.

After running the script, copy the text and paste it into the URL text field.

7.4 Linking to Pages

You might want to create some cross-references in a file for readers to branch out to read content related to a given subject or create a contents page that links to chapters.

LINKING TO PAGES

Linking to pages is easy using the Hyperlinks Panel:

1. **To link to a page in a document, open the Hyperlinks Panel and select a source.** This could be text or a graphic. Click the Create new hyperlink button in the Hyperlinks Panel. The New Hyperlink Destination dialog box opens, as shown in Figure 7-11.

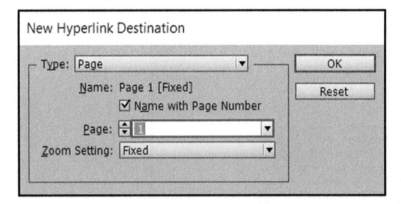

Figure 7-11. Select Page and choose the page number

2. **Select Page in the Link To menu and choose the page number in the Page menu**. All of the pages in your document are listed in this menu. Click OK to create the hyperlink.

Another type of page navigation is linking to anchors. (See more about creating anchors in Chapters 4 and 12.)

LINKING TO ANCHORS

To link to anchors, do the following:

1. **Click the type tool in a text frame or select text within a frame and open the Hyperlinks Panel**.

2. **Open the Hyperlinks menu and choose New Hyperlink Destination**. The New Hyperlink Destination dialog box opens.

3. **Choose Text Anchor from the Type menu and type a name for the text anchor (see Figure 7-12)**. The default name is Anchor 1 followed by Anchor 2, Anchor 3, and so forth. For additional anchors, you add to the document. It's best to name the anchor with a descriptive name, especially when you have many anchors in your document.

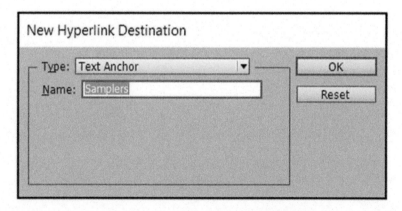

Figure 7-12. To create an anchor as a destination, click the cursor or select text and choose Text Anchor in the New Hyperlink Destination dialog box

So far we created the destination, but we haven't yet identified the source.

4. **Create a frame, select an object, or select text for the source**.

5. **In the Hyperlinks Panel, click the Create new hyperlink button**.

6. **When the New Hyperlink dialog box opens, select Anchor in the Link To menu and choose the anchor name in the Text Anchor menu**.

When you create a hyperlink to a text anchor, the hyperlink is displayed in the Hyperlinks Panel with the anchor symbol. You can easily check the hyperlink by clicking the anchor symbol in the Hyperlinks Panel. If you set up the link up correctly, InDesign jumps to the page where the link destination is found.

7.5 Summary

In this chapter, we begin our journey into creating interactive elements in InDesign. Hyperlinks provide only one of the many methods for adding interactivity to your documents.

We start off easy in this chapter with some simple tasks. Things get more complicated when we look at other interactive features, such as animations, as you will see in the next chapter.

CHAPTER 8

■ ■ ■

Working with Animations

Adobe InDesign is not an animation tool. You can find many more opportunities to create animations with Adobe Animate CC and Adobe After Effects. However, you do have an impressive set of features within Adobe InDesign that enable you to create a variety of animations.

Animations from InDesign can be exported to fixed layout EPUBs, Interactive PDFs (with a workaround—but only on desktop computers), and Adobe Publish online. Animations are not supported in reflowable EPUBs and DPS/AEMM documents.

In this chapter, we explore creating animations and setting them up to play in the documents that support animations. I cover using animation presets, setting duration and speed, using motion paths, and using animations with multi-state objects. I also offer a few project ideas and walk you through the steps required to create similar designs.

8.1 Understanding the Animation Panel

Actually, you have two panels to use when creating InDesign animations: the Animation Panel and the Timing Panel. In this section, I talk about using the Animation Panel and later in the section "Reordering Animations in the Timing Panel," I cover using that panel for duration, speed, and linking animations to play together.

When you work on animating text and objects in InDesign, you should open both panels. They work together to help you produce the animations that you add to your documents. You'll also use the Layers Panel frequently, so it's best to set up your work environment to easily access the three panels.

8.1.1 Using Animation Presets

Create a new document in InDesign and create an object (rectangle, ellipse, or polygon). Select the object and open the Animation Panel, as shown in Figure 8-1. The Animation Panel contains 48 presets that control five basic animation settings, which include: Motion Paths, Easing (speed and duration), Rotation, Scale, and Opacity. In the panel, you have many choices for setting attributes for animations. Your choices include the following:

© Ted Padova 2017
T. Padova, *Adobe InDesign Interactive Digital Publishing*,
DOI 10.1007/978-1-4842-2439-7_8

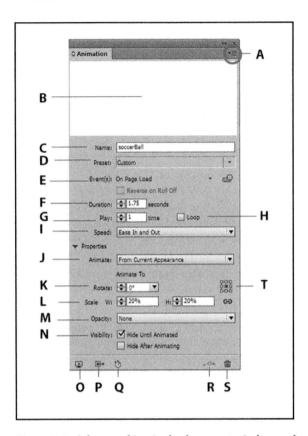

Figure 8-1. *Select an object in the document window and open the Animation Panel*

A.   *Animation Panel Menu*: Click the icon in the top-right corner of the panel to open the menu. At the top, you will find Save. After making various choices in the panel, you can save your settings as a preset.

B.   *Preview*: The top portion of the animation shows you a proxy preview for the animation that you select from the Preset menu.

C.   *Name*: The name is derived from the Layers Panel. You should name objects and text frames in the Layers Panel when creating animations. Or, if you change the object name here, the name changes in the Layers Panel.

D. *Preset*: The Preset menu provides you with a long list of different animations. When you select an animation from the Preset menu, the preview window at the top of the Animation Panel displays a proxy view of the animation.

E. *Events*: Notice the down-pointing arrowhead adjacent to the text. Click the arrowhead to open a menu where you can select the event trigger. By default, the event trigger is set to On Page Load, which means that when the page is viewed the animation will play.

   To the right of the menu is an icon. Click this icon to create a button that will trigger the event.

F. *Duration*: In the text box you can set the minimum acceptable value of .125, which speeds up the animation, or set it to 60 seconds, which slows it down.

G. *Play*: Make choices for the number of times that you want the animation played by entering a value between 1 and 99.

H. *Loop*: Check the box to loop the animation to play over and over again.

I. *Speed*: In the Speed menu, you have choices for From Preset, None, Ease In, Ease Out, and Ease In and Out. Easing accelerates the animation. When you choose Ease In, the animation appears slowly at first and then accelerates. Ease Out is just the opposite. Ease In and Out begins slowly, accelerates, and then finishes up slowly.

J. *Animate*: The Animate menu contains three options:

   - *From Current Appearance*: If you animate a ball that scales down, the From appearance begins with the size of the ball when you place it in InDesign. As the animation progresses, the ball is scaled down.

   - *To Current Appearance*: The animation is run from an appearance to the current appearance. For example, if you start with a small ball and the ball appears large on the page, you scale the ball from the smaller object to the current larger appearance.

   - *To Current Location*: If you bounce a ball, the animation ends at the current location for where the ball appears in the design.

K. *Rotation*: Rotation rotates an object up to 7,200°.

L. *Scale*: Scaling sizes an object up or down. The largest size available to you is 7,200%.

M. *Opacity*: You have only two choices for opacity. Fade In and Fade Out. The range is 0% to 100% (or 100% to 0%).

N. *Visibility*: You can choose to hide the animation until it plays, and you can hide the animation after it finishes animating by enabling the respective checkboxes.

O. *Preview*: Click the icon in the lower-left corner of the panel to preview the animation in the EPUB Interactivity panel. Press Alt/⌥ and click to preview the animation in the SWF Preview Panel.

P. *Animation Proxy*: The icon to the right of the Preview icon is very helpful. When you click the icon, a square gray box appears as a proxy to show you the beginning or end point of the animation.

Q. *Timing Panel*: Click the next icon to the right of the Animation Proxy to open the Timing Panel.

R. *Convert to Motion Path*: On the bottom-right side of the panel, you find Convert to Motion Path. Any line that you draw in a document, either straight or a Bézier curve, can be used as a motion path. When you select an object and a path and then click this icon, the stroke weight of the path disappears and the object is animated along the path.

S. *Remove Animation*: Select an object assigned an animation and click the trash icon. This action removes the animation (your object still remains in the document window).

T. *Point of Origin*: Click on one of the nine points for the axis or point of origin. For example, if you want to rotate an object from the center, click the center square.

The second item in the Animation Panel menu is Manage Presets. Select this option, and a window opens where all the presets are listed. You can delete custom presets, duplicate a preset, load a preset file, and save the presets to a new file. InDesign default presets cannot be deleted.

The remaining items in the Animation Panel menu are the same as those discussed in this list with the exception of Preview Selection SWF. You can select an object and preview just that object's animation in the SWF preview window.

8.1.2 Creating Animations

Now that we know about all of the switches and toggles in the Animation Panel, let's have a little fun creating a few simple animations.

CREATING ANIMATIONS

1. **Create a new document in InDesign.** Use one of the EPUB page sizes. In my example, I'll set the Intent to Mobile, the Page Size to iPad, and the orientation to landscape.

2. **Choose File ➤ Place and place an object on the page.** If you want a background graphic, place the background and then the object. The object can be an image or illustration. We'll make this animation from a preset to fly in from left, so move the object to the right of center on the page (see Figure 8-2).

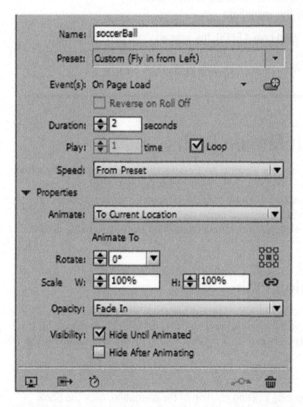

Figure 8-2. With an object selected, set the attributes for the animation in the Animation Panel

3. **Select the object and open the Animation Panel**.

4. **Set the animation attributes in the Animation Panel**. Open the Preset menu, choose Fly in from Left, and type 2 for the Duration. In the Animate Properties, choose To Current Location from the menu, set the Opacity to Fade In, and check the Hide Until Animated checkbox. The settings should appear as you see in Figure 8-2.

5. **Preview the animation**. Click the Preview Spread: EPUB icon in the Animation Panel (lower-left corner in the panel). In some cases, you may need to click the Play button (the right-pointing triangle) in the bottom-left corner of the EPUB Interactivity Preview Panel to play the animation.

When you export the file to a fixed layout EPUB, the animation plays on page load. This is the default setup in the Timing Panel. What you see is a brief animation from 0% opacity and the object moving right and fading in to 100% opacity.

8.2 Working with Motion Paths

Most of the animation presets use motion paths. A *motion path* is the length and direction of an animation. When you choose a preset in the Animation Panel, InDesign creates the path for you. You can edit a motion path by making it longer or shorter, change the direction of the path, add points to a path, and move the individual points to create up, down, left, and right directions. Also, you can create custom motion paths using the Pen tool or the Pencil tool.

8.2.1 Editing a Motion Path

Using the previous example, let's take a look at the animation. When you select the object, you see a horizontal line with an arrowhead on the right side. This is a motion path line and the arrowhead tells you what direction the object moves when viewing the animation.

■ **Tip**   If you want to see the precise starting position of the animation, click the Show animation proxy icon (second from left at the bottom of the panel). The proxy displays a gray square where an animation begins or ends along a path.

Suppose that you want to increase the distance of the motion path. Click the Selection tool (or press V) in the Tools Panel and click on the path. After selecting the path, move the end point to lengthen (or shorten) the path.

Suppose that you want a little bounce on the ball (in this example, I use a soccer ball) as it moves right. Let's take a look at how we'll accomplish this.

ADDING POINTS TO A MOTION PATH

1. **Create a path with the Pen tool.**

2. **With the path selected, select the Add Anchor Point Tool in the Tools Panel** (click and hold the mouse button down on the Pen tool and select the Add Anchor Point tool from the menu or press the = key).

3. **Click on the path to add an anchor point as shown in Figure 8-3.**

4. **Choose the Convert Direction Point tool** (also in the Pen tool submenu) **and drag a point to create a Bézier curve.**

5. **Use the Direct Selection tool** (white tipped arrowhead in the Tools Panel) **to move the point to a location that you want the animation to follow.**

6. **Move to another location and follow the same sequence**.

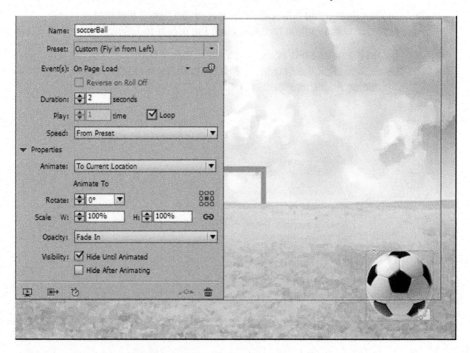

Figure 8-3. *With the Add Anchor Point tool, click on the path to add a point*

When you preview the animation, you see the object move up and down according to where you move the points on the path.

8.2.2   Creating Custom Motion Paths

When you use the presets in the Animation Panel, InDesign creates a motion path for you. You don't have to rely on the motion path directions that InDesign provides you. You can create any path using either the Pen tool or the Pencil tool and draw a path.

CREATING A CUSTOM MOTION PATH

Follow these steps to create a custom motion path:

1. **Create a new document in InDesign**.

2. **Use one of the EPUB page sizes**. In my example, I use an iPad and set the orientation to landscape.

3. **Choose File ➤ Place and place an object on the page**.

4. **If you want a background graphic, place the background and then the object**. The object can be an image or illustration.

5. **Draw a path using either the Pen tool or the Pencil tool that represents the motion that you want the object to follow**.

6. **Select the path, Shift-click the object to select both items, and click the Convert to Motion Path button in the Animation Panel**, as shown in Figure 8-4.

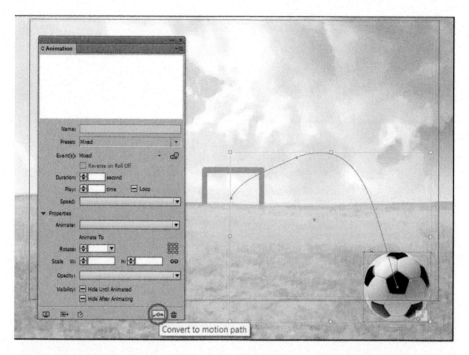

Figure 8-4. *Select the object and path and click the Convert to motion path button in the Animation Panel*

7. **The object will now follow the custom motion path when animated.**

8. **In the Animation Panel, select Ease In and Out from the Speed menu.**

9. **We'll add a little flair to the animation.** In my example, the soccer ball will start slowly, increase speed at the top of the arc, and slow down as it hits the goal.

10. **Adjust the scale.**

11. **For this example, scale the object down to 20%.** As the ball animates and moves farther away from view, the size of the ball scales down to a smaller size.

12. **Preview the animation by clicking the Preview Spread: EPUB button in the Animation Panel.**

The final frame in the animation shows the object sized down at the end of the path (see Figure 8-5).

Figure 8-5. *The end of the animation displays the soccer ball scaled down*

8.3   Showing and Hiding Animations

You can show/hide and initiate play on any kind of animation. What's more, you can show/hide any object (text, images, illustrations, video, and so forth). The single ingredient that you need to perform such actions is a button.

Your life will be so much easier in InDesign if you organize elements and name them with descriptive names. In Figure 8-6, you see a layout with three buttons. I want to click a button and assign an action to initiate an animation and show the item being animated.

Figure 8-6. *Layout with three buttons*

Several things need to be accomplished to obtain the result I want. First I need to place objects on different layers. I have a layer for my first three buttons and a separate layer for the objects that I want to animate. When all of the objects are animated, you see the result in Figure 8-7. The three text frames in the figure are also buttons. I use button actions to hide the current view and return to the default view.

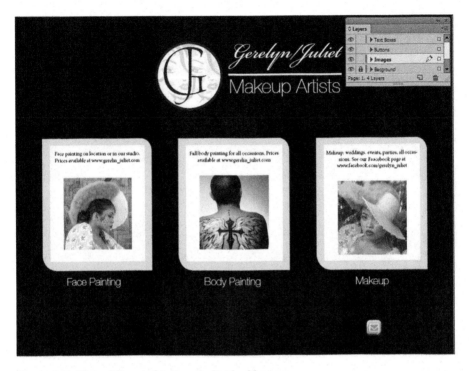

Figure 8-7. Place different objects on individual layers

Let's walk through some steps to see how we add buttons to trigger animations.

FLYING IN ELEMENTS ON BUTTON CLICKS

1. The first step in setting up the file is to create the animations. Each of the three text frames is set to fly-in from the bottom. **Drag the first text frame down below the page edge.**

2. **Open the Animation Panel. Select the Fly in from Bottom preset.** By default, animations are triggered on a page load.

3. **Open the down arrow for Events and uncheck On Page Load.**

4. **Set the Duration to 1.5 seconds, choose Fade In, and check Hide Until Animated.**

5. The motion path is much shorter than you need. **Click the path and move the bottom point down to the preferred animation starting point, as shown in Figure 8-8.**

    Repeat the same steps for the remaining two text frames.

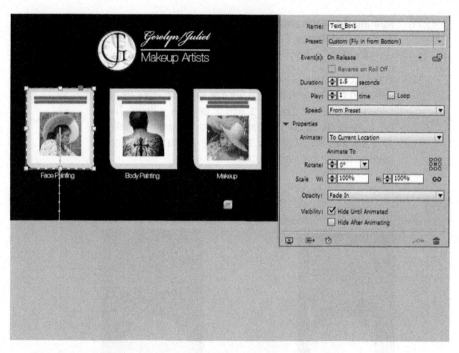

Figure 8-8. *Assign the animation and lengthen the motion path*

6. **Open the Buttons and Forms Panel, select the first frame, and Choose Button from the Type drop-down menu.** At this point, we just create the buttons. Later we'll assign actions to them. Convert each of the three frames to buttons.

7. **Open the Layers Panel and hide the text boxes.** You now have access to the default buttons.

8. **Convert the three circles on this layer to buttons.** At this point, you have all the buttons you'll need and can now assign actions to them.

9. **Click the first circular button and click the + icon in the Buttons and Forms Panel.**

10. **Add Animation from the drop-down menu and choose the item that you want to animate.** In my example, I named the text frame buttons Text_Btn1, Text_Btn2, and Text_Btn3. This naming convention makes it easy for me to tell what item and in what location I want to assign the actions. The first circular button is set to run the animation on the Text_Btn1 item, the second circular button runs the animation on Text_Btn2, and so forth.

287

11. **Add another action. Click the + icon and choose Show/Hide Buttons and Forms.** The choices you make here will affect the visibility of the buttons.

12. The Text_Btn2 and Text_Btn3 items are set to hidden as indicated by the slash through the eye icon. The other items that I need to set up are the Btn_1, Btn_2, and Btn_3 items. There are three circles shown on the current layer. I want to make sure that they are all in view. In Figure 8-9, you can see the settings for the first circle button.

Figure 8-9. *Settings for the first circle button*

13. **Repeat the same steps for the other two circle buttons.**

14. **Next, open the Layers Panel and show the text frames.** We made these frames buttons too. Now let's assign actions to the buttons. All three of the buttons on this layer are set to hide all of the text frames. When a user clicks a button on the first layer, the text frame comes into view. When the user clicks a text frame, the view returns to the default view.

15. **Add an action to each button.** Click the + icon and choose Show/Hide Buttons and Forms. The choices you make here will affect the visibility of the text frame buttons.

16. **For each text frame button, set the visibility for that button to an eye icon with a slash through it, meaning that it should be hidden.** Then specify an "x" for each of the other buttons, meaning that the visibility of those buttons should remain as they are.

In Figure 8-10, you can see the settings that I used to hide the text frames.

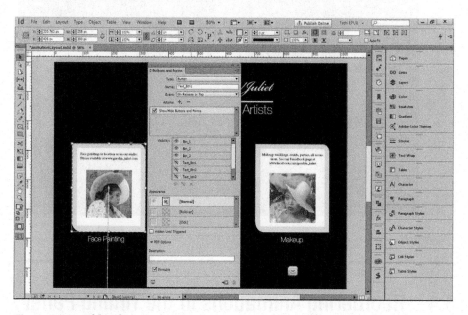

Figure 8-10. *Add a Show/Hide Buttons and Forms action and hide all the text boxes*

17. **After you finish, preview the final result.** Actually, you should preview several times during your editing session. Before you preview, however, open the Layers Panel and make sure that all of the layers are turned on.

18. **Choose Window ➤ Interactive ➤ EPUB Interactivity Preview. Click each of the buttons.**

You should see a text frame appear after clicking a button, and the frame should disappear after clicking it again. In Figure 8-11, you see the preview after I clicked the third button.

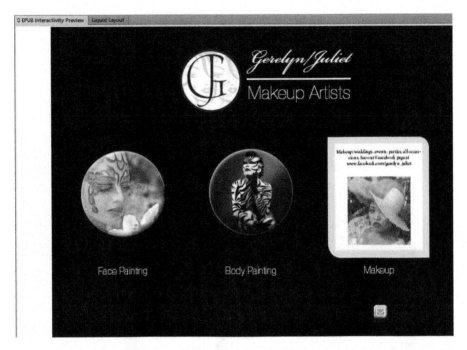

Figure 8-11. Test the results in the EPUB Interactivity Preview Panel

8.4   Reordering Animations in the Timing Panel

If you want to change the order of the animations, open the Timing Panel. As shown in Figure 8-12, you see the list of animation items in the panel. If you want to reorder the animations, just click and drag an animation to a new location. For example, the objects fade in beginning at the right side of the basket. We want to have the banana fade in first, followed by the papaya, then the pineapple, and so on.

Figure 8-12. *Animations are displayed in the Timing Panel*

To set the banana to appear first, click `banana.ai` in the Timing Panel and move it up to the top of the stack. Next, click and drag the `pineapple.ai` animation and move it up to sit below the `banana.ai` animation, as shown in Figure 8-12.

8.4.1   Linking Animations

Sometimes you may want an animation to play at the same time as another animation. Using the fruit basket as an example, suppose that we want all of the fruit in the basket to fade in at the same time. You handle this action in the Timing Panel.

Click the animations that you want to link together so that they play at the same time. To select items in the Timing Panel in contiguous order, click one animation and press the Shift key to select the last animation. All animations between the first and last are selected. To select items in noncontiguous order, click an animation and then press Ctrl/⌘-click.

After selecting the animations that you want to play at the same time, click the Play Together button in the Timing Panel (see Figure 8-12). The Play Together button is second from right at the bottom of the panel.

8.4.2   Delaying an Animation Play

By default, animations are set to play on a page load, meaning that when you open the animation in a viewer, the animation begins to play. If you want to delay the play, enter a value in the Delay text box. You can enter a value between .001 and 60 seconds.

8.5   Auto-Scrolling Text

Adobe DPS (Digital Publishing Solution) documents contain scrollable frames where the viewer can tap the frame and scroll the text within a frame. This is a marvelous feature in DPS documents. You can create designs where large bodies of copy don't handicap the page design. Designers have always struggled with clients who want to have more text on a page than is practical for a nice layout.

Unfortunately, as of this writing, scrollable frames are not supported with fixed layout EPUBs, Interactive PDFs, and Publish Online (Preview) documents. You can, however, animate a body of text so that it appears as though the text is scrolling in the document. In this example, I use a table but you can also use a text frame to create the same effect. In Figure 8-13, you see the final result of a table that was animated to fly in from the bottom of the page.

Figure 8-13. *A table was animated to scroll in from the bottom of the page*

Note the gradient at the bottom of the page. The gradient fades to transparency. To create the gradient, draw a rectangle or frame and choose Object ➤ Effects ➤ Gradient Feather. You can also open the Effects menu by clicking on the Effects icon (*fx*) in the Control Panel.

Adding the gradient feather makes the animation appear as though the table is changing opacity as it travels up on the page. The table needs to appear below the gradient in the layer stack for the effect to animate properly. In Figure 8-14, you can see the Layers Panel where the table is positioned below the gradient.

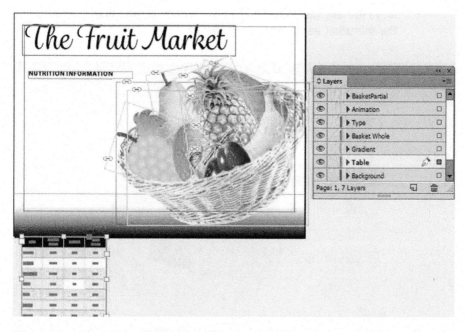

Figure 8-14. *The animated object should appear below the gradient feather in the Layers Panel*

CREATING SCROLLING TEXT ANIMATIONS

To create a similar animation, follow these steps:

1. **Create a gradient feather on a rectangle or frame set to 90°.**

2. **Place a text frame or table at the edge of the page boundary.**
   In my example, the animation is set to fly in from the bottom. Therefore, I placed the table below the page on the pasteboard. Be certain that the text frame (or table) appears below the gradient in the Layers Panel, as shown in Figure 8-14.

3. **Apply the animation**.

4. **Open the Animation Panel and choose the animation preset for where you want the animation to fly in from**. In my example, I use Fly-In from Bottom. Choose To Current Location in the Animate menu. For Opacity, choose None. Check Hide until Animated and set the duration to 6 seconds.

5. **Adjust the location**.

6. **Move the text frame/table to the final position at the end of the animation, as shown in Figure 8-15**.

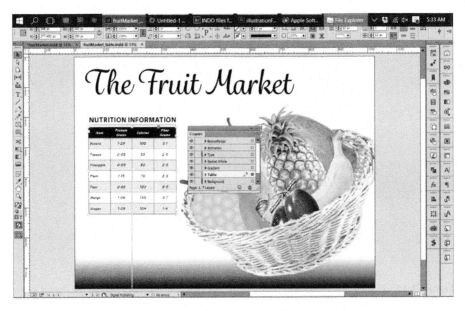

Figure 8-15. *Move the object to the final location*

7. **Adjust the motion path**.

8. **Click the beginning of the motion path (see Figure 8-15) and move it to the page edge**. Make sure that the animation starts at the page edge and moves to the current location.

9. **Review the Timing Panel**.

10. **Notice the Timing Panel in this example (see Figure 8-16)**. I linked all of the fruit to fade in together. The group appears first in the Timing Panel. After the fruit fades in, the text/table animates.

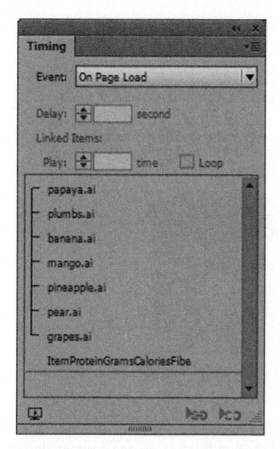

Figure 8-16. *The animation order is displayed in the Timing Panel*

11.   **Preview the animation**. Click the Preview Spread: EPUB button in the Timing Panel to preview the animation.

8.6   Using Sound with Animations

Animations come alive when you add sound. Sound files need to be saved as .mp3. If you have audio files in .wav or .aiff formats, you can use Adobe Media Encoder to convert the audio to .mp3 format.

If you need to obtain audio files, you can find a number of free downloads at www.Freesound.org. Browse the extensive Freesound library, and you'll find a vast number of different sound effects.

Once you have an audio file and an animation, you're ready to add sound to your animation project. Audio files are imported in InDesign like any other asset. Choose File ➤ Place and place the sound file. By default, the sound file will display a poster graphic in Layout view in InDesign. When you view the file in the EPUB Interactivity Preview window, or export the document, you find a controller bar at the bottom of the sound file. If the size of poster image is small in your layout, the controller bar may be hard to view and subsequently use.

If you intend to use buttons to control the play, you can size the audio file import small (such as one-pixel by one-pixel) to get it out of the way. Also, you add sound files to separate layers, as shown in Figure 8-17.

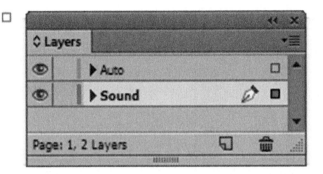

Figure 8-17. *If you can't place an audio file behind a filled object, set the audio frame size to 1 px by 1 px*

8.6.1   Setting Media Properties

After placing an audio file, open the Media Panel. By default, you see a speaker icon in the preview area. If you have None selected for the poster image, the audio icon will not be displayed in the audio frame.

The only setting that you need to make here is to check the box for Play on Page Load. You can use a button to trigger a sound event, but if you don't use a button, check this box.

8.6.2   Syncing Audio and Animations

If you want an audio file to play along with an animation, you need to sync them in the Timing Panel. Open the Timing Panel and select an animation that you want to sync with the audio file. Shift-click to select the audio file and click the Play Together button at the bottom of the panel.

8.7   Using Animations with Multi-State Objects

Sometimes you may have several different animations that you want to play on button events. You may have several different objects and text frames that you want to animate based on the reader clicking a button. The problem is that the only items that you see animate when you click a button is the first item or group in the layer stack. To solve this problem, you can use a multi-state object (MSO) and assign various buttons to display different states in the MSO. We'll review MSOs in greater detail in Chapter 9.

Examine Figure 8-18. You see the end result of two animations played on a state in an MSO. The maps at the bottom of the page are buttons. When the user clicks a button, the large map changes, the text on the right flies in from the left, and the callout box in the center zooms in using the Grow animation.

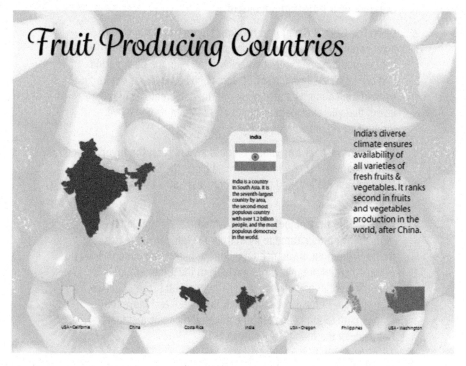

Figure 8-18. *A final MSO state viewed after the animations*

To construct a similar design, you need to follow a sequence of steps. First you must use the Layers Panel to help simplify your work, and each layer should have a descriptive name. You'll easily get lost of you don't use the Layers Panel wisely.

The large map of the left side of the window is a placed object. The other two objects are animated. You first create the animations and preview each one to be certain that it animates properly. After completing the animations, group the objects. In my example, I have seven groups. Once each set is grouped, you create a multi-state object. The buttons at the bottom trigger the respective object state. Sounds easy, right? To see how the project is set up, follow these steps.

CREATING A MULTI-STATE OBJECT

1. **Create a new InDesign document**.

2. **Open the Layers Panel and rename Layer 1 to Background**. If you want any background image or headline text in your design, add the objects to the background. Hide the background and create a new layer. In my design, I use seven layers where each of the countries/states appears. You can create all of the layers that you anticipate using, or create them as you move forward laying out your design.

3. **Name a new layer and place objects and text on the layer**. In my example, I start with California. I place the large map of California on the left, add a callout box, and add a text frame with text.

4. **Animate the first object**. We start with the text frame on the right. We want this frame to fly in from the left. Move the text frame to the right. If you need a guideline here to match up all of the other text frames, drag one in from the left ruler. Open the Animation Panel and choose the Fly In from Left preset. Set the Animation to Current Location. Click the object and move the motion path to the left so that the animation begins just to the right side of the map (See Figure 8-19).

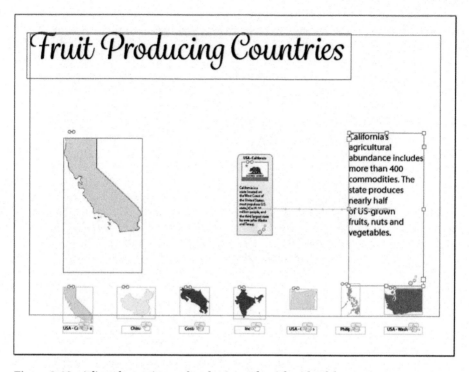

Figure 8-19. *Adjust the motion path to begin on the right side of the map*

5. **Animate the second object**. In my example, the middle object
   animates with the Grow preset. We set the amount to 150%.
   You may need to play with the amount a little depending on how
   small the object is when you place it. Continually preview the
   animation until it appears as you like.

6. **Set a button event**. In my example, I have small maps
   and text at the bottom of the page. Select one object and
   the corresponding text and group them (Object ➤Group or
   Ctrl/⌘+G). With the grouped object selected, open the Buttons
   and Forms Panel and create a new button. (Click the New
   Button icon or choose Button from the Type menu.) Click the
   + icon to add an event. Choose the event from the Animation
   menu. Click the + icon again and choose the second animation
   from the Animation menu (see Figure 8-20).

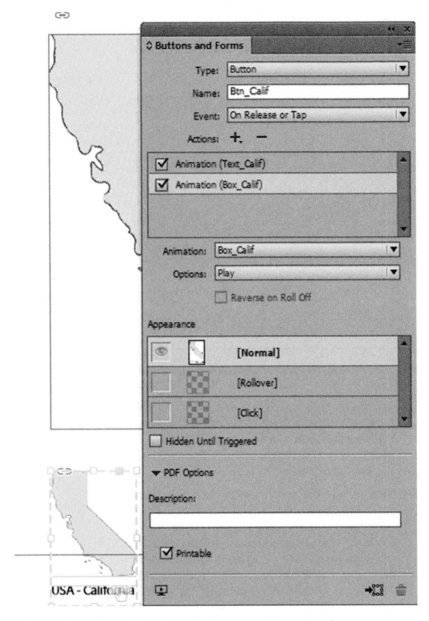

Figure 8-20. *Add the animations in the Buttons and Forms Panel*

7. **Review the Timing Panel**. With the button selected, open the Timing Panel and verify that the animations play in the order you want. If you need to change the order, click and drag the animations up or down in the Timing Panel.

8. **Preview the animation**. Click the Preview icon in the Animation Panel. Click the Play button to play the animation. If it doesn't display the animations properly, you need to return to the objects and double-check the animations.

9. **Group the items**. Select all of the items that you want to appear in a given state when you create the MSO and group them (Ctrl/⌘+G).

10. **Rename the group in the Layers Panel**. By default, InDesign places grouped items on a new layer and adds the layer name as *group*. Change the name to a descriptive one as you work on the animation groups. In my example, I rename the layer as *California*.

11. **Follow the same steps to create additional animation groups**. Be certain to preview the animations each time that you finish a group.

At this point, you would create a new multi-state object.

I cover multi-state objects thoroughly in Chapter 9. To give you an idea for where we're going with this project, I created an MSO from the grouped objects and animations. You can see the different object states in Figure 8-21. The button actions at the bottom of the layout are assigned triggers to view different states in the MSO. We'll get to the how-to's in Chapter 9. For now, be aware that you can create MSOs with different states containing content and animations and view the different states by clicking buttons.

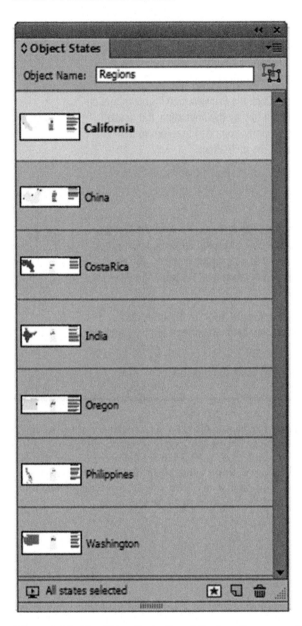

Figure 8-21. *The Object States Panel displays the names of each state from names assigned in the Layers Panel*

The MSOs and animations can be viewed in fixed layout eReaders and Adobe Publish Online (Preview). For Interactive PDF documents, you need to create a workaround. For more on animations and Interactive PDFs, see Chapter 15.

8.8   Exploring Some Project Ideas

There are a ton of projects that you can create with animations. To get your creative juices flowing, I'll discuss a few here. The rest is up to you. Just let your mind think *out of the box* and you'll find many new and interesting ways to use InDesign's animation features.

8.8.1   Animating a Logo

Digital publications have an advantage over print in many ways when you add interactivity, videos, sounds, and animations. The printed piece needs an eye-catching graphic or outrageous headline to bring the readers into the document or a story. When you create publications, you should try to think of ways to bring the readers into the content. Make it interesting, make it dynamic, and offer some element of surprise. These methods guarantee grabbing a reader's attention for more than a split second.

One eye-catching method for digital publishing documents is to add a movie file or animation on the opening page. Rather than using a simple title, you can make the cover page interesting and create a rather cool effect.

In Figure 8-22, there's a cover page for a business document. This could be an annual report, financial report, five-year plan, or any other such business document. The cover page shown in the figure contains several animations that include the following:

Figure 8-22. *Cover page for a business document containing animations*

- *Vertical line*: The vertical lines that you see in the figure are two lines that draw from the center.

- *Animated text*: The first line of text appears a character at a time. The word *THE* flies in from the top after the first line of text appears. The word MARKET fades in.

- *Animated logo*: The logo to the left of the vertical lines rotates to the current appearance.

ANIMATING A LOGO

To create a similar design, follow these steps:

1. **Create a new InDesign document**. Use the settings for output on the device(s) on which you want to view the document. In my example, I use an iPad. In the Layers Panel, name the default layer Background and apply a color to a rectangle frame. If you want the background to be white, you don't need to fill a rectangle shape or frame.

2. **Draw two vertical lines**.

3. **Draw a frame over each line and fill the frames with the same color as the background**.

4. **Animate the lines**. Select the top frame over the top line and open the Animation Panel. Select Appear from the Preset menu. Choose From Current Appearance from the Animate menu and click the top-center square in the Reference Point icon below the Animate menu and to the right of the Rotate menu, as shown in Figure 8-23. Edit the H text box and type zero (0). For Opacity, choose None from the menu. Repeat the steps for the second frame, hiding the bottom line, but click the bottom-center square in the Reference Point icon.

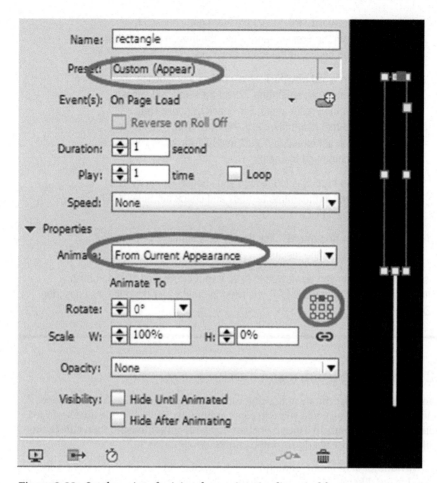

Figure 8-23. Set the point of origin when animating lines and frames

5. **Set the Timing Panel to animate the lines together**. Open the Timing Panel and select both animations. Click the Play Together icon.

6. **Animate the word FRUIT**. The text is made up of individual text frames—one for each character. Select all of the characters (in the order that you want them animated) and open the Animation Panel. Choose Appear from the Preset menu. Set the Duration to .125 seconds and check Hide Until Animated.

■ **Note**   Animations play, by default, in the order you select them.

7. **Animate the word THE**. Select the word and choose Fly In From Top from the Preset menu. Move the motion path so that the animation begins at the top of the page.

8. **Animate the word MARKET**. This word simply fades in after the characters finish animating. Select the word and choose Fade In from the Preset menu. For Opacity, choose Fade Out from the menu commands. We know that this seems to contradict the animation, but trust me, this works as you would expect the animation to appear.

9. **Animate the logo**. Select the logo and choose Rotate ➤ 180 CW. Type 720° in the Rotate text box and check the Hide Until Animated checkbox.

10. **Preview the document**. Click the Preview icon in the Animation Panel to preview the results.

This kind of animation can be viewed in fixed layout EPUBs and Adobe Publish Online (Preview). For Interactive PDF, you need to create a workaround, as I describe in Chapter 15.

8.8.2   Creating Business Charts

You can make static charts interesting using various designs. Business charts, however, are much more interesting when you add some animation. You can guide the viewer to key points by showing parts of a graph or chart first with animation and then fade in the remaining parts or choose to add secondary animations.

There are a number of different animations that you can add to charts. You can explode pie charts having different slices and move them in or out, animate columns that move up from the baseline, animate lines in a graph, and more.

In this example, I use a simple graph chart to demonstrate some of the possibilities. In Figure 8-24, you see the end result after a chart completes the animation. In this chart, we animate the lines and fade in the plot points. Beginning with the bottom row, each line appears to be drawn, the second plot point then appears, and the line continues to the last plot point. Next, the middle line animates in the same manner with the top line animating last.

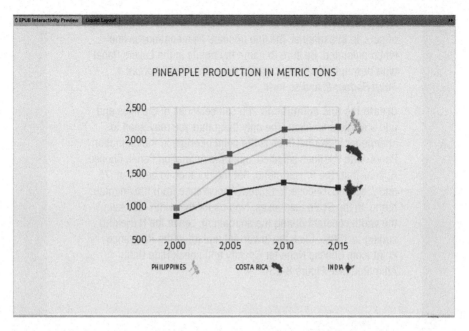

Figure 8-24. *A graph shown after the animation finishes*

CREATING AN ANIMATED CHART

To create a similar animated chart, do the following:

1. **In a new InDesign document, add elements for the graph grid and text, and then all other non-animated content.**

2. **After placing the background elements, lock the Background layer and create a new layer for the animation.**

3. **Draw the lines.** The primary thing to understand about animated lines is that you must first draw a horizontal line. You cannot draw a diagonal line and animate it along a path like the one you see in Figure 8-24. After drawing a horizontal line, use the Rotate tool to rotate the line. When the line is properly rotated, you can use the Direct Selection tool to move the points, making the line shorter or longer as needed. Continue drawing several lines in the same manner and position them similar to what you see in Figure 8-24. Be certain to name the lines in the Layers Panel with descriptive names. I used layer names such as *Line Bottom 1, Line Bottom 2,* and so on, for the bottom lines.

4. **Add points**. I added points above the lines to hide any slight offsets. In this manner, the line appears as a continuous line when animated. Be sure to name the points in the Layers Panel with descriptive names. I named the points *Point Bottom 1*, *Point Bottom 2*, and so forth.

5. **Create the line animations**. You can select all of the lines and add a single animation. The only thing that you may need to change for individual lines is the point of origin in the Animation Panel. With the lines selected, open the Animation Panel. Choose Appear from the Preset menu. Set the duration to between .75 and 1 second. Choose To Current Appearance from the Animate menu. In the Scale text boxes, type 0% for the width (this keeps the width constant during the animation). Leave the H (Height) setting to 100%. Click the lower-left square in the Reference Point icon. Choose None for Opacity and check Hide Until Animated (see Figure 8-25).

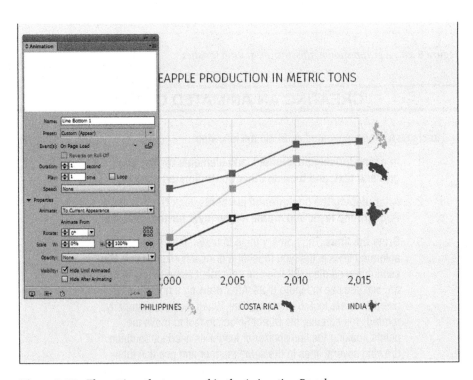

Figure 8-25. *The settings that you need in the Animation Panel*

6. **Change points of origin**. In my example, the last line in the bottom and middle groups need an adjustment for the point of origin. Select both lines and click the top-left corner Reference Point icon in the Animation Panel. Be sure to review all of the settings. When you make an adjustment in the Animation Panel, some of the other items may change.

7. **Animate the points**. Select all of the points and choose Appear from the Preset menu in the Animation Panel. Set the duration to .25, the Opacity to None, and check Hide Until Animated.

8. **Set the timing for the lines and points**. Open the Timing Panel. Select the line and point that belong together. The names are derived from the Layers Panel. If you name the layers with descriptive names, this task is made much easier. This is because, as you can see in Figure 8-17, the Timing Panel displays the descriptive names. You need to link the items that you see in Figure 8-17. Beginning at the top of the panel, the second line in the bottom row is linked with the second point in the bottom row. When the animation plays, the point appears as the second line begins to draw.

9. **Preview the final design**. When the animation appears to work as you designed it, you're ready to distribute it for viewing in fixed layout EPUBs and Adobe Publish Online (Preview). If you want to include such a chart in an Interactive PDF, you need a workaround, as I discuss in Chapter 15.

8.9 Summary

There are a huge number of animation presets available to you in InDesign. I covered only a few in this chapter. Nonetheless, the settings work similarly for all of the presets. You want to pay attention to the options in the Animation Panel and understand the settings. Play with several presets and create some of your own animations for practice.

In the next chapter, we leave animations and explore the world of multi-state objects or MSOs. You'll find many great uses for MSOs in your documents, and the next chapter explains in detail how to create and work with them.

CHAPTER 9

■ ■ ■

Changing Object Views with Multi-State Objects

Multi-state objects, or MSOs as they are commonly referred to, add a wealth of opportunity with interactive publications. MSOs can be used with fixed layout EPUBs and Adobe Publish Online (Preview). You can export a document with MSOs to Interactive PDF files with a workaround, but unfortunately they only work on desktop computers. As of this writing, I haven't found a PDF reader that supports MSOs in PDF files.

You can use MSOs to view slideshows, change views for text, images, and objects within an open page. You can play animations within different states, as I discuss in Chapter 8, and you can nest MSOs inside other MSOs.

Using multi-state objects opens up a huge opportunity for digital publications that you can't replicate with printed documents. The extent to which you can use MSOs is limited only by your imagination.

9.1 Using the Object States Panel

To begin our discussion on MSOs, let's start by looking at the Object States Panel where all of the action happens. If you haven't set up your workspace for Interactive documents, choose Window ➤ Interactive ➤ Object States. If the panel is in your workspace, click the Object States Panel. By default, the panel opens with nothing available except creating a new MSO. When you create a new MSO, the panel displays information related to the MSO contents, as shown in Figure 9-1.

© Ted Padova 2017
T. Padova, *Adobe InDesign Interactive Digital Publishing*,
DOI 10.1007/978-1-4842-2439-7_9

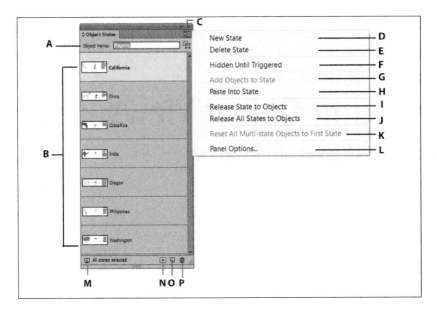

Figure 9-1. *Choose Window* ➤ *Interactive* ➤ *Object States to open the Object States Panel*

In the Object States Panel, once you create a new MSO, you find the following options:

A. *Object Name*: By default, the Object name is Multi-State 1 when you first add a new MSO to a document. Even if you have only one MSO in your document, you should type a descriptive name in this text box. Get into the habit of naming the Object Name and the State names to make it easier when you revisit the document or you assign button actions.

B. *States*: In the list below the Object Name are the states with thumbnail images in an MSO. When you click a state, the state is shown in the document window. You can easily select a state and then edit the contents of the respective state in the document by double-clicking the state in the document window. By default, the state names are *State 1, State 2, State 3*, and so forth. To rename a state, click once, pause a moment, and then click again. Type a new name for the state. You should add descriptive names for all the states in an MSO.

312

C. *Object States Menu*: Click the icon in the top-right corner of the Object States Panel, and the Object States menu opens. Here you have several menu choices that include the following:

D. *New State*: Click New State to create a new MSO or to duplicate the selected state in an existing MSO.

E. *Delete State*: Select a state in the panel and click to delete the respective state from the MSO.

F. *Hidden Until Triggered*: Click this item if you want the MSO hidden when the document is opened. When you click a button assigned to view a state, the state opens in the document.

G. *Add Objects to State*: Select a state and then Shift-click on a page object that isn't in the state. Then, when you choose this command, the object will be added to the state.

H. *Paste Into State*: If you copy an object and want to paste it into an MSO, click this item to paste what's contained on the clipboard into the MSO current state in view.

I. *Release State to Objects*: When you click this item in the menu, the selected state is extracted from the MSO but the remaining states are still contained in the MSO. The difference between this menu command and the Delete State command is that the extracted state remains in the document while the Delete State is like cutting the state and removes it from the document.

J. *Release All States to Objects*: This command is helpful when you want to start over, perhaps to make several edits and then return to create the MSO. When you select the command, the MSO is deleted from the document but the contents all remain.

K. *Reset All Multi-State Objects to First State*: If you have a state other than the first state selected, this command resets the default view to open the first state when viewed in the document.

L. *Panel Options*: By default, the thumbnail images are set to display the smallest thumbnail view. If you click Panel Options, a pop-up menu opens where you can choose to change the thumbnails to larger views.

M. *Preview Spread*: Click this button to preview the document in the EPUB Interactivity Preview Panel. Press Alt/⌥ and click to preview in the SWF Preview Panel.

N. *Paste Copied Objects Into Selected State*: This button is helpful when you want to create nested MSOs. You can paste an MSO inside a given state, change the state view, and paste another MSO inside the second state and so forth. Nesting MSOs involves a little trickery, which I explain in the section "Creating Nested MSOs."

O. *Create New State*: Click this button to create an MSO from selected objects in the document or to duplicate the selected state in an existing MSO. When you click the button, it results in the same action as when you click the New State menu command.

P. *Delete Selected State*: Click a state, then click the Trash icon, and the state is deleted from the MSO. Using the Trash icon results in the same action as when you choose Delete State from the menu.

9.2   Creating a Multi-State Object

To create a new multi-state object, you must have objects selected on a page. The objects can be images, objects, text frames, or a combination of them. Once images/objects and/or text frames are selected, click the Convert selection to multi-state object icon at the bottom-right of the Object States Panel, or open the Object States Panel menu and click New State.

When you create an MSO, the Object States Panel names the MSO as *Multi-State 1* if it's the first MSO you create in a document. The next MSO you create is named *Multi-State 2*, and so forth.

Below the object name you see a separate state for each object that you selected when you created the MSO. If you have the objects on layers with layer names, the state names inherit the layer names. If the objects were placed in InDesign on the same layer, you will see the different states named *State 1*, *State 2*, and so on, as you can see in Figure 9-2.

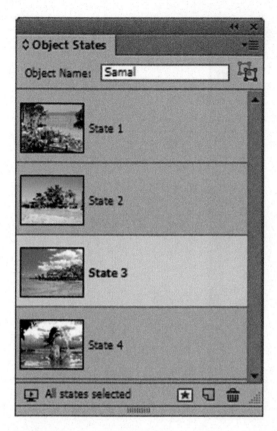

Figure 9-2. *An MSO uses default names if you haven't placed objects on layers with layer names*

Your first order of business is to add some descriptive names for the object name and the different state names. This will make your job much easier if you want to trigger state views with button events.

Typically, the first item in the MSO is selected, which becomes the default view of the MSO. In reality, an MSO is like working with layers. You can hide one layer (or state) and the next layer (or state) comes into view. If you click a state in the Object States Panel, that state becomes the default view. In Figure 9-3, I added names for the object name and the different states. I also selected Sunset. If we close the Object States Panel, the Sunset state becomes the default view.

To edit a name for the states, click the state once, pause a moment, and click again. The state name is selected, and you can type a new name.

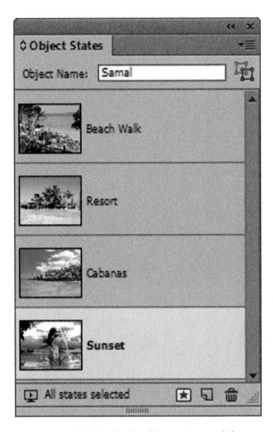

Figure 9-3. MSO with the object name and the state names edited.

If you want to scale the MSO, you first need to select the MSO. When you select an MSO, you see a dashed line appearing at the bounding box. You can select the MSO by clicking and dragging around or through the MSO with the Selection tool, or by clicking the edge of the bounding box until you see a dashed line. Once the MSO is selected, you scale it in the same way that you scale any graphic; that is, press the Ctrl/⌘+Shift keys and drag a corner handle.

CREATING A NEW MSO

To create a new MSO, follow these steps:

1. **Import some images, use several text frames, or use a combination of both in an InDesign document**.

2. **Align the objects (optional)**.

3. **Open the Align Panel (Window ➤ Object & Layout ➤ Align)**. Objects don't have to be aligned, but if you have several objects of the same size, it may appear better on the page if they are aligned. Select all of the objects and click the Align horizontal centers or Align left edges icon. Click again on the Align vertical centers or Align top edges icon.

■ **Note** If you want to align several objects within a single state, you must group the objects.

---

4. **Create a new multi-state object**. Drag the Selection tool around the objects to select all objects and open the Object States Panel. Click the Convert selection to multi-state object button or open the Object States Panel menu and choose New State.

5. **Name the MSO and name each state**. The default name for the MSO is *Multi-state 1*. Type a more descriptive name in the Object Name text box. You should see *State 1, State 2*, and so on if the objects were not placed on separate layers. To change the state names, click once on the name, pause a moment, and then click again. Type a new name for each state. In Figure 9-4, you see the MSO I created with the names added for the object name and the state names.

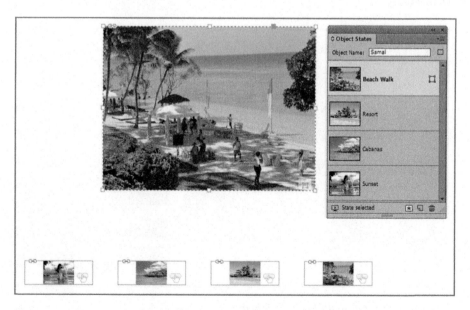

Figure 9-4. Type a name for the object name and rename each state name

6. **Set the default view**. The first item in the stack is typically selected and it becomes the default view when the MSO is viewed on a page. To change the view to another state, click on the state that you want to appear as the default view.

■ **Note**   When you click a state in the Object States Panel, there is no OK button to confirm the action. You just click and the state becomes the default.

9.3   Editing MSOs

In Figure 9-1, you see a number of options for editing MSOs. I provided a brief explanation for each menu command, but now we want to explore some of these options in more detail. As you work with MSOs, you'll want to remove a state, add a state, edit the contents of a state, and add some empty content so that one state in the MSO appears empty. Let's begin by looking at these tasks in greater depth.

9.3.1   Deleting States

In Figure 9-5, you can see an MSO and the last state that's selected in the Object States Panel. Corresponding to the Object States Panel, you also see the state in view in the document.

Figure 9-5. Last state in the MSO is selected

If you want to remove the bottom state, there are two ways to handle removing a state. It's important for you to understand both options and what they do for you. If you click the trash icon in the panel or open the Object States menu and choose Delete, or you right-click on the state and choose Delete, the state is permanently deleted from the MSO and the object is also deleted from your document. Unless you press Ctrl/⌘+Z to undo the action, you won't be able to get it back. That's fine if you're absolutely certain that you want to eliminate the state/object from your document.

The other method for removing a state is to select the state and choose Release State to Objects in the Object States Panel menu, or right-click the state and choose Release *state name* to Objects, where *state name* is the name of the object state. When you use this method, the state is removed from the MSO but the state converts back to an object and remains in the document. Therefore, the first method completely deletes the state from your document, and the second method removes the state but keeps the content in your document.

■ **Tip** If you're not certain if you want to delete a state/object from your document and you want to keep it around for a while just in case you may want to reuse it, create a new layer and name it something like Not Used. Move the released state object to the layer and hide the layer in the Layers Panel. The object remains in your document, but it's hidden from the layout. You can always go to the layer and move the object to another layer in view.

9.3.2   Releasing States to Objects

We know what happens when we select a state and choose Release State to Objects in the Object States Panel. The state is converted to an object, and it remains in the document. Suppose that you want to start over. Let's say that you have a lot of work that you want to do to edit objects within an MSO, and you want to add new states and perhaps delete some other states.

The way that you start over is to convert all of the states back to objects. To do this, select the MSO and choose Release All States to Objects in the Object States menu. The states are converted to objects and appear on top of each other in the same position as when you created the MSO. In Figure 9-6, you see an MSO on the left and after releasing all states to objects on the right.

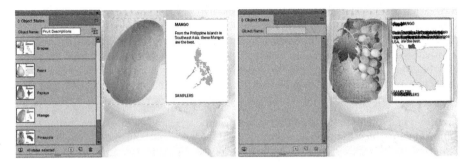

Figure 9-6. *Select an MSO and choose Release All States to Objects*

From here you can move the objects around, make your edits, add new objects to an MSO, and delete objects. When finished editing, simply select all of the objects and click the Convert selection to multi-state object button or choose New State in the Object States Panel menu.

9.3.3   Adding New States

Suppose that you're working on a layout and you created an MSO. Later on, you realize you have another state that you want to add to the MSO. This might be another state with more content, or perhaps you want to set the default view to a blank view so that the content appears only when a user clicks a button.

Let's use the empty state as an example here. With an MSO in view, draw a frame with no stroke and no fill on top of an MSO. The frame can be small, and it doesn't need to occupy the entire bounding area of the MSO.

Select both the MSO and the frame and click the Convert selection to multi-state object button in the Object States Panel, or open the menu and choose New State. The frame is added as a new state to the MSO. You can add new states to an MSO repeatedly using this method.

■ **Note**   When you select objects and look at the button at the bottom of the Object States Panel, the tooltip reads *Convert selection to multi-state object.* When you add a new state to an existing MSO, the tool icon changes to a blank page with a + symbol in the lower-left corner and the tooltip appears as *Add objects to visible state.*

If you create a blank empty state and you want to have it appear as your default view, drag the state in the Object States Panel to the top of the stack and select it, as shown in Figure 9-7. When a user opens the document, nothing appears where you added the MSO. If you assign buttons to view different states, each state is viewed on button clicks.

320

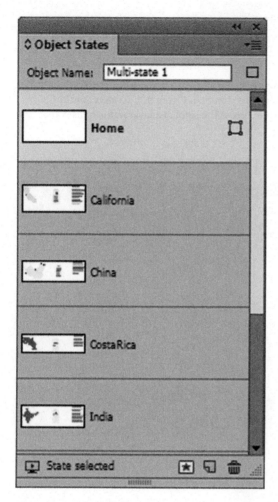

Figure 9-7. The default state is empty, and it appears at the top of the stack

9.3.4 Selecting Content in States

Assume for a moment that you have a number of different objects on a given state and you want to delete the objects or modify their appearances. When you click on an MSO, you select the MSO. Double-click and you select an object within the currently selected state in the MSO. If you have multiple objects in a given state and you press Shift and click again, you have two objects selected. If you press Shift and click again, the first two objects are deselected and the third object is selected. InDesign doesn't permit you to select more than two objects in a given state using Shift-click.

Let's say that you have a number of pins on a map and you want to change the appearance of the pins or resize them. The best way to select objects is in the Layers Panel. This means, of course, that you need to have well-organized layers and the layers should be named with descriptive names.

Open the Layers Panel and click the box to the far right of a layer name, or press Alt/‑⌥ and click the layer name to select the item, as shown in Figure 9-8. To select multiple objects, press the Shift key as you click the box to the right of a layer name or as you Alt/‑⌥-click on the layer name.

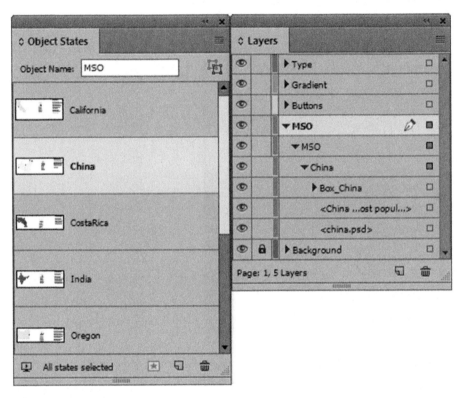

Figure 9-8. Click the box to the far right of a layer name in the Layers Panel to select the object

■ **Note** When you press Alt/‑⌥ and click a layer name, you select all of the content on the target layer. If you need to select individual objects on a layer, twirl down in the Layers Panel to view the individual objects and Shift-click the individual objects, or press Alt/‑⌥ and click on each object name.

9.3.5   Pasting Content Into an MSO

This task is something that you will use often, especially when creating nested MSOs, as I explain a little later in the section "Creating Nested MSOs." If you copy an object or a text frame, open the Object States Panel, and select a given state, you click the Paste copied objects into selected state button in the bottom-right side of the Object States Panel, as shown in Figure 9-9.

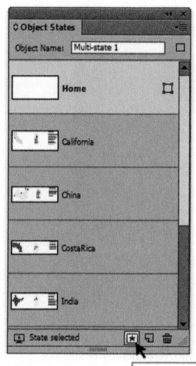

Paste copied objects into selected state

Figure 9-9. *Click the Paste copied objects into selected state to paste whatever is on the clipboard into the state*

Using this method is fine when you have a single object that you want to paste into a state. View the state in the document and place the object at the location where you want the object to appear in the state. Choose Edit ➤ Cut and cut the object to the clipboard. Select the state in the Object States Panel and click the button to paste the object.

Where you can experience problems, however, is when you have multiple objects that you want to paste into a state. If you place the objects at the location that you want to appear in the state and use the same method for cutting and clicking the Paste copied objects into selected state, the end result is that the pasted objects won't appear at the location that you expect.

323

In order to add multiple objects in an exact location, you need to use a different approach:

- Move the objects to where you want them to appear, but don't copy or cut them.

- With the objects selected, press the Shift key and click the MSO (be sure that you see a dashed line at the bounding box when you select the MSO), as shown in Figure 9-10.

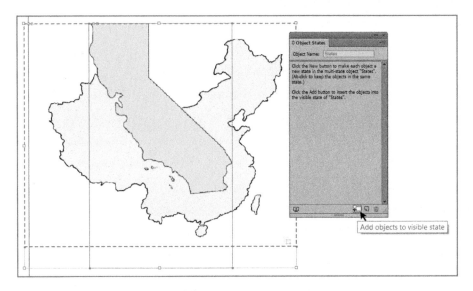

Figure 9-10. *Select the objects and the MSO*

- When all of the objects including the MSO and the target state are in view in the Object States Panel, move your cursor over the button in the Object States Panel. Notice that the tooltip now reads *Add objects to visible state.*

- Click the button and the objects are added to the state selected in the Object States Panel.

This method is particularly helpful when you want to add buttons to the individual states. The buttons are only active when the given state is in view.

9.4   Creating Buttons to Change State Views

An MSO isn't worth much unless you can change the view to see other states in the stack. To change views, you can create a single button that scrolls through each state, or you can create separate buttons to view respective individual states. For example, suppose that you want to set up something like a slideshow. You can create one button that advances each state when the reader clicks or taps on a single button. You can also use thumbnail images of photos and convert each one to a button. When the reader clicks or taps a button, the respective large photo of the thumbnail is placed in view.

The choice you make for displaying different states on button clicks is handled in the Buttons and Forms Panel. When you select an object and open the Buttons and Forms Panel, click the Convert to Button icon (lower-right corner of the panel) or choose Button from the Type menu. You then click the + icon in the Buttons and Forms Panel to open a menu with several choices, as shown in Figure 9-11.

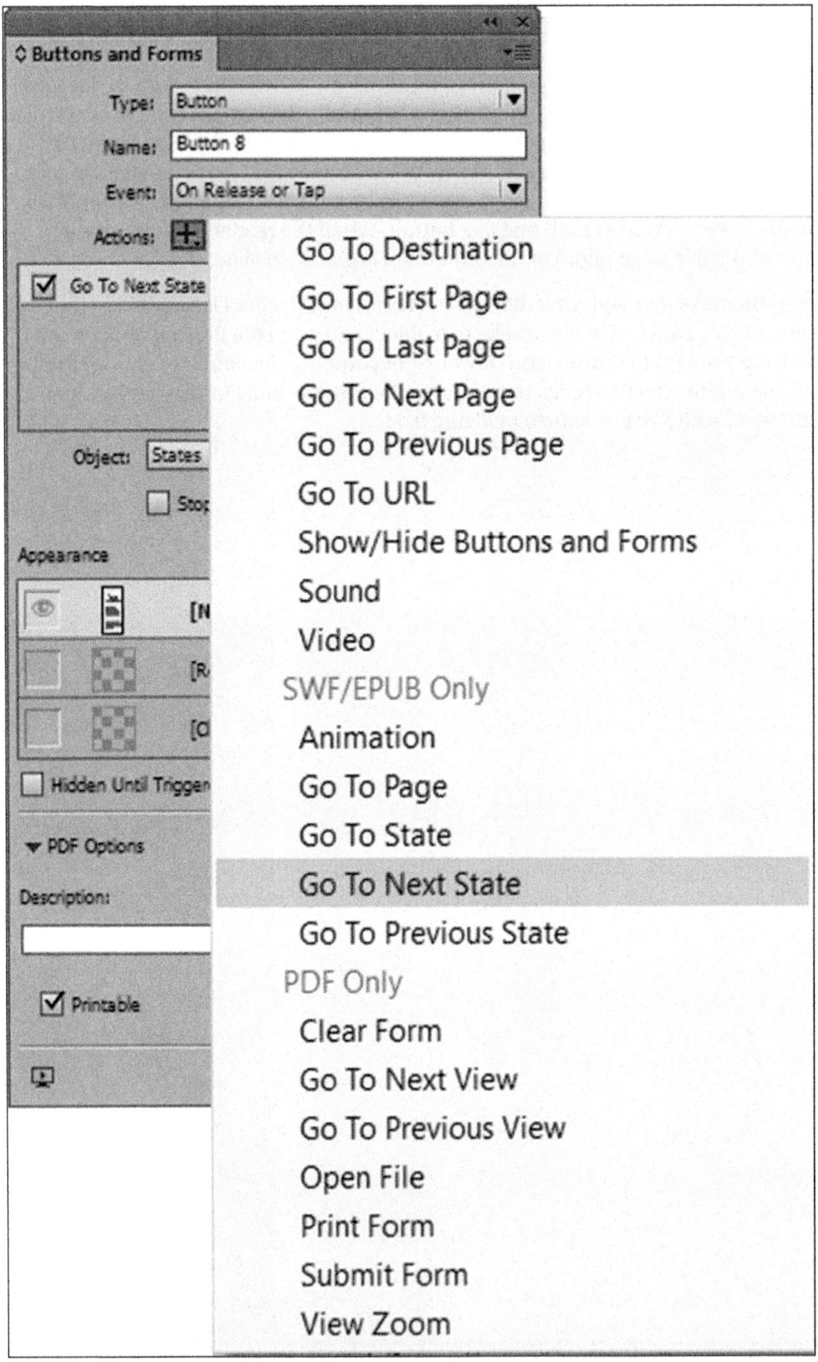

Figure 9-11. *Click the + icon to open the Actions menu*

Choices you make for MSOs are Go To Next/Previous State or Go to State. If you choose Go To Next State, the reader clicks or taps on a button to view the next state. Click/tap again and the following state opens and so forth. In this manner, only a single button is needed to advance the state views. If you choose Go To State, the action displays the state assigned to a specific button. This behavior is intended for use with multiple buttons, each assigned different state views.

CREATING BUTTONS ASSIGNED SEPARATE STATES

To create buttons that are assigned separate states, follow these steps:

1. **Create an MSO**.

2. **Follow the steps in the earlier section "Creating a Multi-State Object" to add an MSO to a page in InDesign**. Create icons or text that you want to use as buttons to view individual states. Convert the first object to a button. In my example, I use the slices of the Apple on the left side of the document shown in Figure 9-12 as buttons. Select the first object and open the Buttons and Forms Panel. Choose Button from the Type menu (or click the Convert to Button icon at the bottom of the panel). Type a name for the button.

Figure 9-12. *Create separate objects or text that you want to use as buttons*

3. **Set the button action**.

4. **Click the + icon to open the Actions menu and choose Go to State**. If you want a single button to scroll through the different states, choose Go to Next State.

5. **Choose the object and state**. By default, if you have only one MSO contained on your spread, the MSO appears by name in the Object menu. When you use separate buttons to open different states, you need to target the respective state in the State menu. In my example, the object name is Fruit Descriptions and the top button shows the first state named *Grapes*. The second button is set to open the next state named *Pears*, and so on. Each state is selected in the State menu. The State menu is active only if you use the Go to State action. If you choose Go to Next State, you can't select different states in the State menu. InDesign just assumes that you want to scroll through the different states.

6. **Complete the rest of the button assignments**. Once again, if you have several buttons used to view different states, follow the same steps (Steps 3 through 5) for the remaining buttons. If you have a single button set to Go to Next State that you want to use to scroll through the different states, your work is finished in the Buttons and Forms Panel and you're ready to preview.

7. **Preview the document**. Click the Preview Spread icon at the bottom-left corner of the Buttons and Forms Panel. In the EPUB Interactivity Preview window, click the button(s) to make sure that it/they work properly.

9.5   Creating Nested MSOs

Suppose that you have an MSO that has states for a European tour. You have images and maybe text showing various places in Italy, France, England, and Germany. When you click the button for Italy, an image and text appear (or whatever content you have in the state). Suppose that you want to show some of the sites you visited, but just those that are in Italy. You create a second MSO with images and descriptions for the Coliseum, the Pantheon, the Leaning Tower of Pisa, the Vatican Museum, and so forth. In this scenario, you would have one set of buttons to select the different countries and another set of buttons to scroll through content respective to a single country.

9.5.1   Pasting One MSO Inside Another MSO

Inasmuch as the section title implies that you can paste one MSO inside another MSO, you don't have access to the Edit ➤ Paste Into command when working with MSOs. You need to use other methods for pasting MSOs inside MSOs.

In this example, we need to nest the MSOs so that various sites within the individual countries can be viewed by clicking buttons that advance to the next state. Using the example I discussed in the preceding section ("Creating Buttons to Change State Views"), we'll use the same MSO and create a second MSO for the different fruit instead of using countries.

NESTING MULTI-STATE OBJECTS

To nest MSOs, you need to employ a little trickery. Here's how you do it:

1. **Create an MSO in an InDesign document**. For this example, we use the first MSO created in the section "Creating Buttons to Change State Views."

2. **Create content for the second MSO**. If you have background elements on the page, use the Layers Panel and hide the background. Create a new layer for the second MSO content. Add objects, text, or both and group each one. Create additional content to use in a new MSO. Align the objects using the Align Panel.

3. **Create the second MSO**. Select the objects and choose New State from the Object States Panel menu, or click the Convert selection to multi-state object icon in the panel. At this point, you may think that you can just cut the second MSO, select the state where you want it to appear, and choose Paste Into from the Edit menu. Unfortunately, Paste Into isn't active when you cut or copy an MSO.

4. **Anchor the MSO to an empty text frame**. You should open the Object States Panel and select the state you want to use for the second MSO. Position the second MSO in the location where you want to have it appear within the first MSO. Create a text frame—just a small frame with no stroke, no fill, and no text. Click the second MSO and drag from the anchor point to the empty text frame, as shown in Figure 9-13.

Figure 9-13. *Anchor the second MSO to an empty text frame*

5. **Cut the text frame**.

6. **Select the text frame and choose Edit ➤ Cut or press Ctrl/⌘+X**. When you cut the text frame, the MSO is also cut and both are placed on the clipboard.

7. **Paste the clipboard contents into a selected state**.

8. **Instead of using the Edit ➤ Paste Into command, you click the Paste copied objects into selected state button in the Object States Panel** (see Figure 9-14). Just be certain that the state you want to paste into is selected in the Object States Panel.

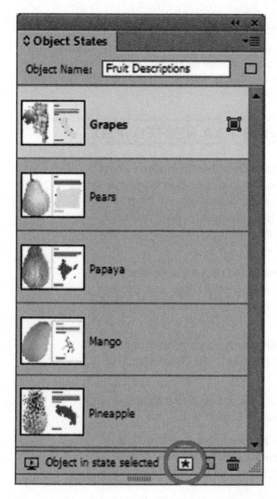

Figure 9-14. *Click Paste copied objects into selected state*

9. **Add buttons to view the different states in the second MSO.** Create a new layer at the top of the layer stack. Draw frames for the next and previous view buttons. If you have artwork on the states in the MSO to show the direction of the button click, for example left and right arrows, you can create frames with no stroke and no fill and convert them to buttons. If you don't have artwork on the states, create or import a graphic and convert it to a button.

10. **Repeat the same steps (Steps 2 through 7) to add MSOs and anchor them to different states in the first MSO.**

9.5.2   Adding Buttons to Nested MSOs

Once you create a nested MSO, the next step is to add buttons that change state views for the second MSO. You can create Go to Next State and Go to Previous State buttons, or you can create a single button that goes to the next state. In this regard, the MSO cycles through the states in a loop.

ADDING BUTTONS TO A NESTED MSO

1. **The first step is to create buttons, but don't worry about adding any events to the buttons.** You'll need to address the actions after you finish adding the buttons to the MSO. To get the buttons into a given state, you need to position the buttons where you want them to be the active zone and choose Edit ➤ Cut.

2. **Open the Object States Panel and click the state where you want to add the buttons.** If you have multiple states and want to add a Go Next and Go Previous button, you need to add them to every state.

3. **With the buttons on the clipboard, click the Paste copied objects into selected state button in the Object States Panel.**

4. **Click the next state in the pane and paste the objects using the same button in the Object States Panel.**

5. **After you paste all of the buttons into the various states, you need to assign the button actions.** For every button, you need to add the Go to Next State or Go to Previous State action, depending on the button.

You can see my example in Figure 9-14. The default view shows a map of California on the right. On the word *Samplers* is a button that opens the nested MSO. On the nested MSO, we have invisible buttons occupying the entire state so that when the users click or tap, they see the next state. In this example, when the user clicks on the Map of California, the right side changes to Robotic Farming, as shown in Figure 9-15.

Figure 9-15. *Appearance when the nested MSO is in view on the right side of the MSO and you advance to the next state*

9.6 Showing/Hiding Object States

Up to this point, you know how to create MSOs and trigger events with buttons. You now know how to go to a given object state and you know how to go to the next state in an MSO. What you've accomplished up to this point, though, has been showing an object state on a button event, but you haven't hidden object states when you click another button. To make this a little clearer, examine Figure 9-16.

Figure 9-16. *The windows in the design are buttons*

When you click a button, a figure appears in the respective window. Continue clicking buttons, and each window displays an image, as shown in Figure 9-17.

Figure 9-17. *As the user clicks each button, images appear in the windows*

In this particular design, it might be best if we set up the file to show only a single image in a respective window. As the user clicks one button, the last image in view is hidden while the new image appears. In this manner, only a single image is in view as the user interacts with the document.

CREATING A STATE WHERE ONLY A SINGLE STATE IS VISIBLE

To create an effect where only a single state is visible on a page, do the following:

1. **Set the file up properly. For this kind of document, it's best to use layers**. In this example, I have one layer for empty windows, one layer for occupied windows, and a background layer with the rest of the artwork.

2. **Draw an empty frame (no stroke and no fill) off to the side of the images**.

3. **Select the frame and images**. (See Figure 9-18.)

Figure 9-18. *Select the empty frame and the images*

4. **Create an MSO**.

5. **Name the different states**. In this example, I use numbers beginning at the top from 1-9, as shown in Figure 9-19. Name the empty state *Empty*, *Home*, or something easily recognizable as the empty state.

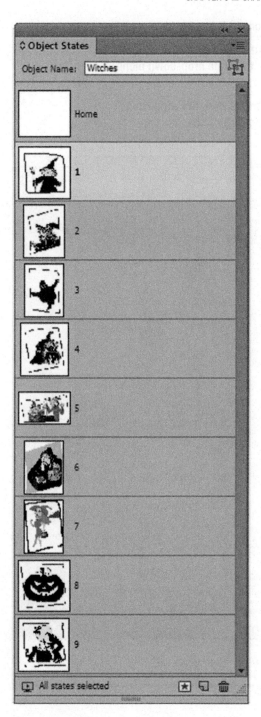

Figure 9-19. Object states named

6.   **Select each window and convert it to a button**.

7.   **Beginning with the first button, set the button action to Go to State and choose 1 from the State drop-down menu**, as shown in Figure 9-20.

8.   **Continue converting the remaining empty windows to buttons and set the action to Go To State**.

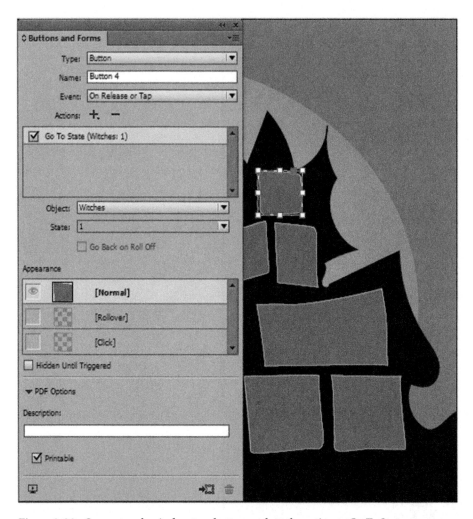

Figure 9-20. *Convert each window to a button and set the action to Go To State*

When the user clicks a button, the image below the button appears. When the user clicks a second button, the first image is hidden while the new image comes into view.

9.7 Summary

In this chapter, we looked at multi-state objects. You learned how to create MSOs and edit them in terms of adding, changing, and deleting specific states, how to add blank states, and how to set the default state. You also learned how to nest MSOs, anchor MSOs to text frames, and paste inside a state.

There's much to learn about working with MSOs. Once you become familiar with creating and setting attributes of MSOs, you'll find many uses that can be applied to fixed layout EPUBs and Publish Online documents.

In the next chapter, you learn how to include rich media (video and sound) in InDesign documents.

CHAPTER 10

■ ■ ■

Using Rich Media

You might think that using audio and video is a simple task because InDesign can import audio and video easily. However, when it comes to digital publishing there's really quite a bit to learn if you're not a video specialist.

You need to become familiar with using the proper media formats, how to crop away those ugly black bars on videos, add poster frames to videos, compress video to the smallest possible sizes, add video masks, and more. In this chapter, I cover how to prepare your media and offer some tips for producing the best results for exporting to various formats.

10.1 Preparing Media

It would be nice if you could just shoot video with a smartphone or camcorder, download the file to your computer, place it InDesign, and export it to a format that you want to use for your digital publishing documents. The reality, however, is that after shooting video, you have some work to do before you can place files in InDesign.

10.1.1 Using Proper Media Formats

To keep this simple, there are two file formats that you should use when preparing media. These file formats include the following:

- *Audio*: There's only one choice to make when using audio files in your publications. You must save the files in .mp3 format. If you have .aiff, .wav, or other format, you need to convert the audio to .mp3.

- *Video*: InDesign supports Flash FLV, F4V, and SWF formats. Apple users, however, won't be able to view the content on their iOS devices. The best format that you can use, which is available to all devices that support viewing video files, is MP4 or M4V with H.264 encoding.

© Ted Padova 2017
T. Padova, *Adobe InDesign Interactive Digital Publishing*,
DOI 10.1007/978-1-4842-2439-7_10

If you have media files, you can convert most audio and video formats to the acceptable formats using Adobe Creative Cloud applications. For audio files, you can convert files using either Adobe Audition or Adobe Media Encoder. For more information on using Media Encoder, see the section, "Using Adobe Media Encoder," later in this chapter. If you're not a Creative Cloud subscriber, you can find some free audio converter applications and some with nominal prices by searching the Internet.

Converting video is best handled with Adobe Media Encoder. However, you need to be a Creative Cloud Subscriber to use Media Encoder. Like audio converters, you can also find a number of different video conversion applications by searching the Internet.

■ **Note**   Use only .MP3 for audio files and MP4 or M4V formats with H.264 encoding for video files.

10.1.2   Rotating Video

You may have video files taken with a smartphone, and the video may have been shot in a portrait mode. When you preview the video, it appears rotated. You can easily fix this problem using Adobe Photoshop.

- *Open a video in Photoshop*: Understand that video is a collection of different frames. If you attempt to make some adjustments— such as painting on a frame—the adjustment is applied only to the respective frame. You can crop a frame, and the crop is honored on all subsequent frames. In some cases, though, you might want to use Smart Objects to ensure that all of your edits are applied to all frames.

- *Convert the video layer to a Smart Object*: When you make Photoshop adjustments to video, you need to convert the video to a Smart Object. To do so, right-click the video file in the Layers Panel and choose Convert to Smart Object, as shown in Figure 10-1.

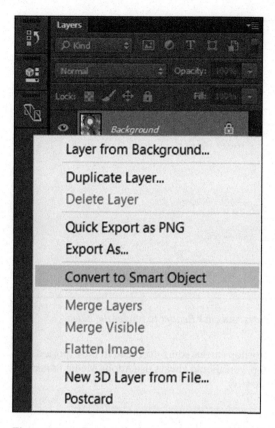

Figure 10-1. *Convert the layer to a Smart Object*

- *Transform the video layer*: At this point, you can use Photoshop's transformation tools to rotate the video. Choose Image ➤ Rotation and then choose either 90° clockwise or 90° counterclockwise depending on the rotation you need.

- *Render the video*: After completing the editing, choose File ➤ Export ➤ Render Video. In the Render Video dialog box, choose the format and size for the video, as shown in Figure 10-2, and click Render.

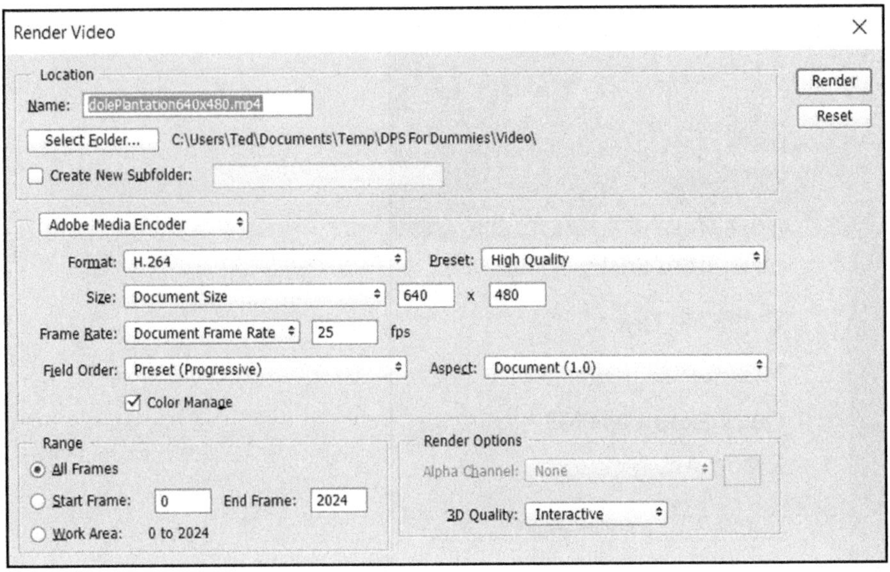

Figure 10-2. Set the video export attributes and click Render to render the video

Be aware that video rendered from Photoshop carries some overhead in the exported file. After exporting the video from Photoshop, you should always use Adobe Media Encoder to compress the video and reduce the file size.

10.1.3   Editing Video

Suppose that you want to edit video for brightness, color correction, and contrast, or maybe you want to convert the video from RGB color to grayscale and apply a sepia tone. Your best solution for editing the video for these kinds of adjustments is using Adobe Photoshop. Programs like Adobe Premiere and Adobe After Effects can help you produce some stunning results, but that requires some intense learning of new applications. If you're a Photoshop user, then you can easily make most of the adjustments that you want directly in Photoshop.

When you open a video in Photoshop, you must convert the layer to a Smart Object, as I discussed in the preceding section, "Rotating Video." For brightness and contrast adjustments, color correction, and even converting video to grayscale, your best solution is to use the Camera Raw filter. Once the video is converted to a Smart Object, choose Filter ➤ Camera Raw Filter. The Camera Raw filter opens, as shown in Figure 10-3.

Figure 10-3. *After converting the video layer to a Smart Object, open the Camera Raw filter*

If you haven't used the Camera Raw Filter previously, the first time you open it the dialog box may seem quite intimidating. However, there are only a few adjustments that you need to address in this window. These adjustments include:

- *Temperature*: You move the temperature left or right to make the video appear cooler or warmer. In some cases, there is no right or wrong here. You simply want to get the video to represent your vision for how you want the video to appear. In other cases, you may find a video that definitely needs to be warmed up or cooled down. Use this slider to make your adjustment.

- *Exposure*: You may have a video clip that was shot at dusk or in the evening that needs to be brightened up a little, or you may have a video that is overexposed and needs to be darkened a little. Move the Exposure slider left and right to adjust exposure.

- *Contrast*: To boost the contrast, move the slider to the right slightly. To reduce contrast, move it to the left. Be careful to not add or decrease contrast too much.

- *Highlights and Shadows*: I group these two adjustments together because just about every image or video clip needs an adjustment to highlights and shadows. Highlights might be something like cloud formations that appear as the lightest areas of the video clip. Shadows might be trees on a landscape where detail is lost in the shadow areas. Move the highlights slider to the left to increase detail in the light areas and move the Shadows slider to the right to bring out more detail in the dark areas.

■ **Note**   The measure between the lightest and darkest areas of a photo or video clip is referred to as *dynamic range*. The best DSLRs and video camcorders out there have f-stop ranges of about 10 f-stops. The human eye has a dynamic range of about 18 f-stops. Therefore, all digital equipment capturing stills and video clips will cut off the lightest and darkest areas of the media. By using the Highlight/Shadow adjustments, you can regain a little lost data that typically will improve your media files.

- *Clarity, Vibrance, and Saturation*: Move the sliders to the right to pump up the midtones, vibrance, and saturation. The advantage of digital publishing over print is what you see is what you get (WYSIWYG). Make the adjustments that look good to you on screen. You will see similar results on all of the devices on which you view your work.

- To convert an RGB video clip to grayscale, just move the saturation slider to the far left to desaturate the color.

APPLYING A SEPIA TONE

To apply a sepia tone, click the Tone Curve icon in the top right after desaturating the clip.

1. **Click on the Point Curve tab and choose Red from the Channel menu.**

2. **Click on the middle of the diagonal line and type** 141 **in the Output text box.**

3. **Choose Green from the Channel menu and click a point in the middle of the line.**

4. **Type** 131 **in the Output text box.**

5. **Choose Blue from the Channel menu and click a point in the middle of the line.** Type 119 in the Output text box. (See Figure 10-4.)

Figure 10-4. *Make adjustments to each Channel in the Tone Curve tab*

These adjustments provide you with a starting point for creating a sepia tone effect on the video. You can adjust the tone curve points to deepen the sepia effect or lighten it up.

After you complete adjustments in the Camera Raw converter, click OK and then choose File ➤ Export ➤ Render to video.

10.1.4   Cropping Video

Those awful black bars appear at the sides, top, and bottom of your videos. How do you get rid of them? You can use one of two ways to crop a video:

1. **Open the video in Photoshop.** Use the Crop tool to crop the video and export the video file using File ➤ Export ➤ Render to Video.

2. **You can also crop out any unwanted sidebars on a video in InDesign.** Move the frame handles containing the video to crop the video. If you crop using this method, you may lose the controller and need to have buttons in your layout that play, pause, and stop a video.

347

If losing the controller is okay for you, choose File ➤ Place and import a video clip. Move the bounding box to crop off the edges, as shown in Figure 10-5. Cropping video only works for fixed layout EPUBs, supported on both iBooks and Adobe Digital Editions, and when you export to Adobe Publish Online (Preview). With Interactive PDF files, you won't see the cropped areas honored in PDF documents if you crop the video in InDesign. You need to crop videos in Photoshop in order to eliminate the cropped area in Interactive PDF documents.

Figure 10-5. *Cropping a video in InDesign*

10.1.5   Moving the Controller

If you convert animations and animated tables to video files, as I will explain in Chapter 12, you may want to move the controller down a bit so that the bottom row of data is not obscured by the video controller. You can move the controller down in reflowable EPUBs but the view is only honored on desktop eReaders. Device eReaders show the controller on top of the video. To learn how to move the controller below a video, see Chapter 12.

10.2   Using Adobe Media Encoder

Since users will be downloading your publications, you need to keep the file sizes down to prevent long download times. You may be in an area where you have a 4G connection, and your download rates may be running at over 40 MBPS. However some who view your work may live in third-world countries or even rural areas of the United States where dial-up connections are still being used. In both of these situations, the bandwidth is narrow and connection speeds are infinitely slower than what you may be used to. Therefore, as a rule of thumb, try to keep your video files less than 10MB per minute and use only short clips in your publications.

10.2.1   Choosing a Preset

When you open the Adobe Media Encoder, you see a screen that looks a little overwhelming. That's because there are a huge number of presets that permit you to export to many different devices of various sizes, and assorted quality controls such as HD, Standard, and so forth.

The first step in using the Media Encoder is to import a video. You can either click the + icon just below the word *Queue* or simply drag a video clip to the Queue pane.

Once the media is loaded in the Media Encoder, you can choose a preset by clicking the down-pointing arrow adjacent to the default preset choice, as shown in Figure 10-6. Choose a preset that you want to use for the exported video.

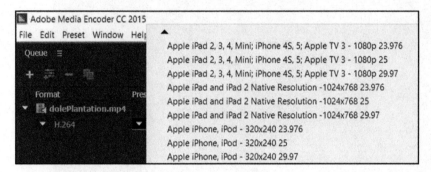

Figure 10-6.   *Choose a preset from the Preset menu*

On the left side of the Media Encoder window, you will see the Preset Browser. If you select a preset and right-click on the name, you can open the preset settings by choosing Preset Settings in the pop-up menu. There's one adjustment I tend to make to a preset. If you scroll the Preset Settings window, you find bit rate settings toward the bottom of the window. You might try lowering the value for the Target Bitrate and the Maximum Bitrate. Start out with values of 0.59 for each, as shown in Figure 10-7. Ultimately, you need to test results to be certain that the rendered video meets the quality standard you want.

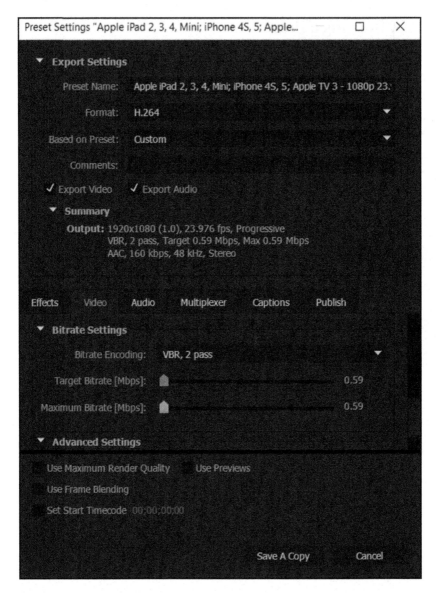

Figure 10-7. Right-click a preset in the Preset Browser and choose Preset Settings to open settings for a selected preset

Be careful with bit rate adjustments. If you lower the amount too much, you'll see mottling in the video and the overall quality is likely to be unsatisfactory.

After choosing a preset and making any other adjustments, click the green right-pointing arrow at the top right side of the Queue pane. Media Encoder displays a progress bar as the video is rendered.

10.2.2   Saving a Preset

If you make a change to a preset such as changing the bit rate, you may want to save the settings as a new preset. This way, you won't need to open the Preset Settings window and make changes every time that you want to use the same settings.

To create a new preset, make your adjustments in the Preset Settings window (shown in Figure 10-7) and type a descriptive name for your new preset. You might use part of the default name but add some text at the end of the name so that you can easily identify it in the long list of presets. In my example, I used the *Apple TV, iPad, iPhone, 3G and Newer – 360 Widescreen 29.5* preset and renamed it *Apple iPad 360 Wide 0.5 Bitrate*. You must first address naming your new preset. If you choose Save a Copy before changing the name, you won't be able to go back and edit the name.

After changing a new preset name, click Save a Copy. You won't see much happen here but a copy is saved and it now appears at the very top of the presets in the left pane. Import a video and open the preset list. You should see your new preset appear at the top of the menu.

Just to give you an idea for the file compression that I was able to achieve, my original media clip was 104MB after making an adjustment to the Apple iPad 360P Widescreen 23.9 preset. After using the default preset, I reduced the file size to 9.0MB. After using the adjusted preset where I lowered the bit rates, the file size was reduced to 6.5MB. I was able to reduce the video 2.5MB lower than the default preset. This is a huge amount when you think about people downloading your digital publications.

10.3   Controlling Media with the Media Panel

After preparing your video, you'll find the next steps for including a video in your digital publication to be far less painful and a little more fun.

You import video in InDesign just like you import any other content. Choose File ➤ Place, select a video, and click OK. You can also import video from the Media Panel. Open the Media Panel ➤ Window ➤ Interactive ➤ Media. When the Media Panel is open, click the Place a Video or Audio File button in the lower-right corner.

10.3.1   Using the Media Panel

When you import a video and open the Media Panel, you see all of the options available for you to adjust how a media clip is played, as shown in Figure 10-8.

Figure 10-8. *When you import a video, you have a number of options to choose from in the Media Panel*

Let's take a look at all of the options that you have available to you when using the Media Panel:

- *Options:* Click the Play on Page Load checkbox if you want the media to play when the page comes into view. You can also initiate a play from a button or have the user click directly on the video frame. If you use a button or want the user to click the video frame, don't enable the Play on Page Load checkbox. The other option that you have is to loop a media file (play over and over again). As indicated in the Media Panel, looping media does not work with Interactive PDF files.

▩ **Note**   Play on Page Load doesn't work on devices. Apple disabled playing video on page loads to protect users who are charged by carriers for bandwidth usage back in iOS 6. On most devices and with most eReaders, you need to tap a video or a controller to play the video.

- *Poster:* A poster image is the default view of the media clip. The Poster image can be derived from a video frame. You can choose None for no image, Standard, in which case you get an ugly video icon, and From Image. If you choose From Image, a dialog box opens where you can locate and import an image file.

  In most cases, you'll want to use a video frame by choosing From Current Frame. Use the slider just below the preview area in the Media Panel and move it around until you find a frame that you want to use as the poster image. The poster image will appear as soon as the page is loaded in a viewer. When you locate the frame, click the circle icon adjacent to the right of the Poster menu. You can also locate a frame, open the menu and choose From Current Frame, which will also use the current frame in view as the poster image.

- *Controller:* You have an abundant number of choices for a controller skin. The skins are media controllers that appear at the bottom of the media clip. If you choose something simple, like SkinOverPlay, the controller has a single button—a Play button and a Resume button. Remember that if you crop a video in InDesign, you lose the controller. When exporting to Publish Online and EPUBs, the web browsers and eReaders use their own controllers. Settings here apply only to Interactive PDFs.

- *Show Controller on Rollover:* If you use a controller, then you should check this box. When the user mouse's over or taps the media, the controller appears. Moving the mouse away or tapping outside the video frame dismisses the controller.

- *Navigation Points:* You can add markers to a media clip that will send the user to a location on a button click. Click the + icon to add a marker on the current frame in view. Scroll through the clip and add another marker to the respective location.

353

- *Preview Spread*: You can preview the spread in either the EPUB Interactivity Preview Panel or the SWF Preview Panel by clicking the button in the lower-left corner of the Media Panel. For a SWF Preview, press Alt/⌥ and click the EPUB Interactivity Preview icon in the Media Panel.

- *Place a Video from a URL*: If you have a large media clip that's impractical to include in your publication, you can have the media stream from a web site. Click this button where you type the URL for the file location.

- *Set Options for Exporting Interactive PDF*: The choice you have in the dialog box that opens is to use a floating window in Adobe Reader or Acrobat when the publication is an Interactive PDF document. Be certain not to use this option if you have SWF files. The floating window will be all over the page in the PDF viewer, and you can't move it to a desired location.

- *Place Video or Audio File*: Use this button to import media.

■ **Note**   You can import audio files as well as the video files saved in MP3 format.

10.3.2   Controlling Navigation Points with Buttons

Navigation points enable readers of your documents to jump to different sections in media clips. Users typically click a button assigned to a navigation point.

CONTROLLING NAVIGATION POINTS WITH BUTTONS

To see how to accomplish this task, do the following:

1. **Add navigation points to a media clip after importing into InDesign**. See Figure 10-8 to help you add navigation points.

2. **Create buttons on the layout aside the media clip**. The objects can be text frames, images, or both text and image. If you use text and an icon or image, group the items. With the object selected, open the Buttons and Forms Panel and choose Button from the menu.

3. **Assign the first button to a Navigation Point**. In the Buttons and Forms Panel, click the + icon to add a new action.

4. **Choose Video from the menu and choose the video clip you want to use**. If you have only one video on a page, InDesign defaults to the current video.

5. **In the Options menu, choose Play from Navigation Point**. In the Point menu, choose the navigation point that you want to associate with the button, as shown in Figure 10-9.

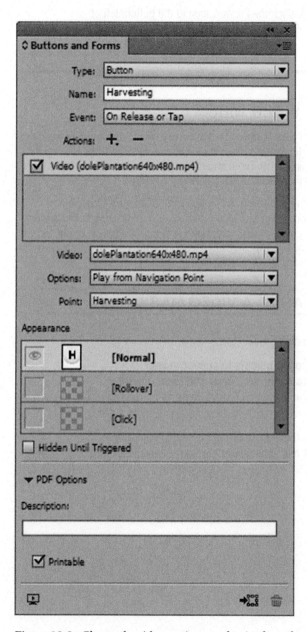

Figure 10-9. *Choose the video, options, and point from the respective menus*

6. **Repeat the same steps (Steps 2–3) to add similar events to different buttons**. Remember you must select a new button and add the actions to the second, third, and so on buttons.

7. **Preview the spread**. Click the Preview icon at the bottom left of the Buttons and Forms Panel to preview in the EPUB Interactivity Preview Panel.

10.4   Creating a Video Mask

Maybe you want a frame around your video or perhaps a company logo appearing on top of the video. You can add such elements by creating a video mask. One thing to keep in mind is that interactive elements such as video should be placed on their own layer. This is not essential, but it will make your work much easier in InDesign.

Another thing that you want to keep in mind is that you don't want any extra objects placed on the same layer as when you create a compound path or MSO. If you accidently select another object when you create a compound path or MSO, things get really whacked out. Just keep it clean by placing different objects on different layers and lock the layers as you assemble your spread.

CREATING A VIDEO MASK

To see how to create a video mask, follow these steps:

1. **If you want background objects to appear in your design, add them to the bottom layer and name the layer** Background. Lock the background, and create two new layers. Name one layer Video and the other layer MSO or similar names.

2. **Place the mask on the MSO layer**. In my example, I use a border frame with a map inset inside the frame, as you can see in Figure 10-10.

Figure 10-10. *Add the mask and place it on a separate layer*

3. **Select all of the objects for the mask and choose Object ➤ Paths ➤ Make Compound Path**. Making a compound path is like creating a donut where you can see through the center. In my example, the border and map can be filled and the rest of the object is transparent.

4. **Color the path**. This is optional. If you want a color fill, select the path and apply a color from the Color and Swatches Panel. (Just select the object and click the color in the panel that you want to apply.)

5. **Create a multi-state object**. This is an important step. If you don't create an MSO, you won't be able to move the mask above the video.

6. **Import a video on the Video layer**. Lock all of the other layers and select the Video layer. Then choose File ➤ Place and import the video.

7. **Adjust the order in the Layers Panel**. If the mask is below the video, you need to move the Mask layer so that it appears above the video in the layer stack.

8. **Set the video to play on page load**. Select the video and open the Media Panel. Check the box for Play on Page Load.

9. **Preview the results**. Click the Preview icon in the Media Panel. If all of the steps were properly performed, you should see the video play behind the mask. In Figure 10-11, you see the results of our example.

Figure 10-11. *When you play the video, it appears behind the mask*

If your mask covers the bottom portion of the video, you can't access any of the Controller Skins. If you want users to be able to play, pause, and stop a video, you can add buttons to perform these actions. Create a button and open the Buttons and Forms Panel. Click the + icon and choose Video from the Actions menu. If you have only one video in your design, the default video shows up in the Video menu. In the Options menu, choose Play or another choice for how you want to handle the video. Create multiple buttons for different options such as Pause, Stop, and so on.

10.5 Adding Multi-State Objects

If you read Chapter 9, you are aware of the power built into InDesign to use multi-state objects. Those wonderful software engineers at Adobe Systems provided InDesign users with spectacular tools that enable you to create marvelous interactive documents.

When it comes to rich media, you can use MSOs to show/hide videos. This provides you with more real estate on a spread where content can be in view for the reader, and with the click of a button what appears like a pop-up video opens. The reader views the video, dismisses it, and returns to the spread.

In Figure 10-12, we have such a document. The text and graphics at the bottom of the page appears with *Watch the Video* text and a button over the text.

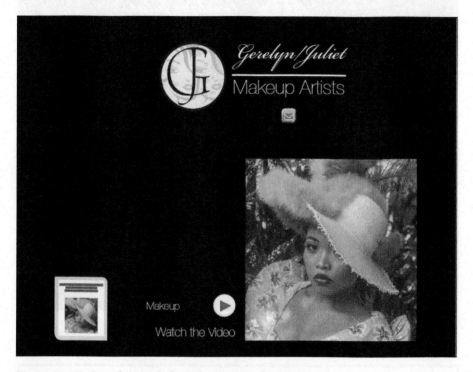

Figure 10-12. *Over the Watch the Video text is a play button*

When the reader clicks the button, a video opens. In Figure 10-13, you can see the result of clicking the button. The MSO has an empty frame and a frame with a transparent black rectangle. Inside the rectangle is the video.

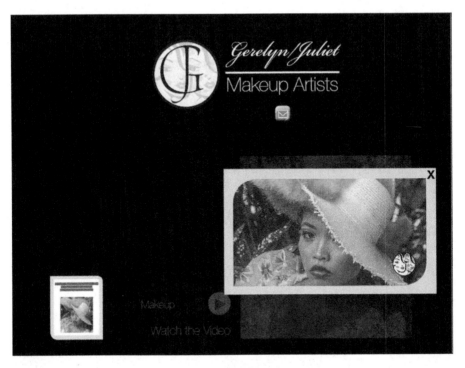

Figure 10-13. *When the reader clicks the button, the second state in the MSO opens*

ADDING MSOS

The way you set this up is as follows:

1. **Create two frames and fill one black**.

2. **Apply some transparency to the black frame**. Use the Object ➤ Effects ➤ Transparency command and adjust the transparency of the black rectangle. The other frame has no fill and no stroke. When the document opens, the Empty State is in view, hiding the black rectangle and the video.

3. **Create an MSO of the two rectangles and name them in the Object States Panel.** Select the two objects, open the Object States Panel, and click the Create new state button or choose New State from the Object States Panel menu.

4. **Draw a text frame with the video state in view.** In the Object States Panel, select the video state. Draw a small text frame on the video state.

5. **Anchor the video to the text frame.** Drag the video anchor to the text frame. To learn more about nesting MSOs, refer to Chapter 9.

6. **Cut the text frame. In this case, the video is cut too.**

7. **Paste the text frame and video into the video state.** In the Object States Panel, you click Paste copied objects into selected state. Just be certain that you have the right state selected in the Object States Panel. In this example, the video state is selected.

8. **Create a button appearing from the top of the MSO to just above the *Watch the Video* text.** So far, everything is set up right. However, we need something for the reader to return to the spread after watching the video. This is where we hide the video. In the top-right corner of the Video mask is a close box. We'll use this item as our close button.

9. **Set the button action.** In the Buttons and Forms Panel, choose Go to State and select the Empty State. When the reader clicks the button, the video and transparent frame disappear.

You could use an icon or text for the reader to click to hide the video state, but this entire process is a little complicated and I wanted to make it as easy as possible for you.

10.6 Summary

In this chapter, we looked at importing video into InDesign and setting various attributes for video play. We looked at working with MSOs and creating video masks.

Up to this point, you learned the many ways to add interactivity to InDesign documents. You can preview the results in InDesign using the EPUB Interactivity Preview Panel, but the ultimate use for your interactive documents is when viewing these files on various devices.

In the next chapter, we look at various ways to upload files to viewing devices.

PART IV

Publishing Documents

CHAPTER 11

■ ■ ■

Uploading and Downloading Files

Digital publishing documents come in a variety of formats, can be seen using many different types of viewers, and are accessible on several different devices. Some viewers can open the files you copy directly to desktop computers, laptops, and Android devices. Apple's closed ecosystem prevents you from copying files directly from your computer to an iOS device unless you use a third-party application. Thus, after creating your masterpiece, the next questions are "How do I get my files on a device?" and "How do I add the file to my app?"

When you launch an application from a device (particularly on desktops and laptops), most applications enable you to open files using a File ➤ Open command locally on your device. When you use tablets and mobile devices, you use either a Wi-Fi connection or enable the tablet or mobile device's apps to access files from a location on the device.

There are many different file-sharing utilities that you can use and a number of different methods for getting your files onto a device and recognized by a viewer. I won't cover all of the options in this chapter, rather I'll address a few of the more popular methods for accessing files with a number of different apps.

In Chapter 12, I talk about previewing EPUB files in various eBook readers. Before you can preview a file, though, you need to know how to the get files onto a device in order to view them. In this chapter, I talk about exchanging files between computers and devices.

11.1 Transferring Files from Computers to Devices

Preparing files for digital publications is typically handled on your desktop or laptop computer. After you assemble the content, you need to send the file to the device application that is likely to view your content.

Depending on the computer OS you use (Windows or Mac OS X), there are some peculiarities and differences for uploading files to devices.

© Ted Padova 2017
T. Padova, *Adobe InDesign Interactive Digital Publishing*,
DOI 10.1007/978-1-4842-2439-7_11

11.1.1   Transferring Files from Non-iOS Devices

File transfers from your Windows computer to devices is relatively easy. Almost all of the devices that you can plug in via the computer's USB port open a menu where you make some choices about how you would like to handle the files. Much like plugging in a USB flash drive, you can view the contents of the device. Folders are visible, and it's just a matter of dragging and dropping files from the computer to the device. The same method applies to Android devices, Kobo eReaders, Amazon Kindles, Sony eReaders, and Barnes and Noble Nooks.

The more complicated step is knowing in which folder to place a file so that an app can view it. You may have locations on your tablet for Books, eBooks, Downloads, Digital Editions, Amazon, Kindle, Kobo, and so on. Some eReaders can access just about all of the potential locations where files are stored, while other eReaders want a specific directory location. You may need to open the reader you'd like to check out and look for a button to Import Files. Test if you can import from a number of different folders and copy files from your tablet to a given app. Poke around, and eventually you'll figure out the proper location for storing your documents for each eReader app.

11.1.2   Transferring Files to iOS Devices

You have a few options for getting files from your computer to an iOS device.

11.1.2.1   Using Apple iTunes

Apple has made a number of changes to iTunes in version 12, and you may find that trying to get EPUBs and PDF files into iBooks to be a nightmare if you are running the most recent version of iTunes. No longer do you have a Books tab in iTunes, and no longer do you have a left column displaying your iOS device. You can't sync books as you used to do with earlier versions of iTunes. Even when you add EPUBs and PDF files to iBooks on your computer, you'll likely experience problems seeing the books on your device's iBooks app. It's really quite frustrating.

Rather than spending a lot of time trying to figure out the mess, I suggest you bypass iTunes and use Dropbox, as I explain later in this chapter in the section, "Using Dropbox."

11.2   Using Android File Transfer

Android File Transfer was developed by Google to provide Macintosh users with a method for connecting Android devices to Macintosh computers. You can download the free application from https://www.android.com/filetransfer/.

After installing Android File Transfer, you hook up an Android device to your Mac via a USB cable and launch the application. This application is helpful when you need to test documents that you create in InDesign running on a Macintosh and you want to copy the files to an Android device. Once connected to your computer, you have access to files and folders, as shown in Figure 11-1. You can drag and drop documents to your Android device (up to a 4GB maximum).

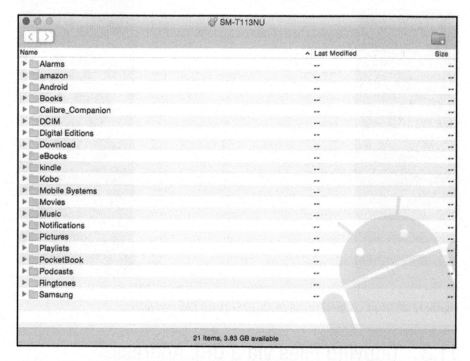

Figure 11-1. Android File Transfer gives you access to files and folders on your Macintosh

11.2.1   Using iExplorer

Apple's closed ecosystem prevents you from accessing files and folders on an iOS device. In order to see the folders where you want to copy files from your computer to your iOS device, you need a third-party application. iExplorer from Macroplant does the job. You can download a free demo from www.macroplant.com. If you want to continue using the program, it will cost you $35 U.S. for a license.

After downloading and installing iExplorer, connect your iOS device to your Macintosh and launch iExplorer. As you can see in Figure 11-2, you have access to the iOS device's files and folders. You can delete files and drag and drop files from your computer to folders on the iOS device.

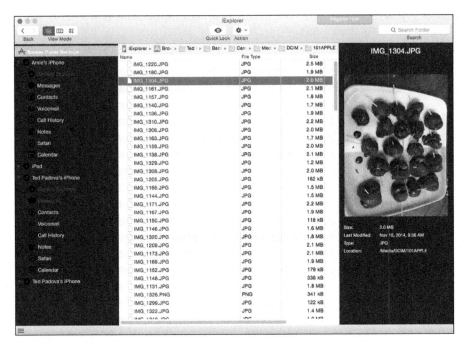

Figure 11-2. iExplorer gives you access to iOS devices files and folders

11.3   Copying Files via a URL Address

Quite common to PDF viewers running on tablets and smartphones is transferring files via a web browser. Interestingly enough, most third-party PDF viewers use this method while Adobe's own Adobe Acrobat Reader does not support transferring files via a Web browser. With Adobe Acrobat Reader on a tablet or smartphone, you need to access a PDF file hosted on a web site via Document Cloud, iCloud, Google Drive, or Dropbox.

If you use a third-party PDF viewer, you may see a Wi-Fi icon in the app, such as the one shown for GoodReader in Figure 11-3. You are offered two methods for accessing your computer via a URL.

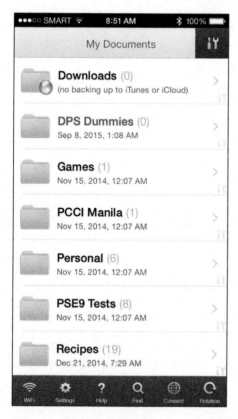

Figure 11-3. *PDF viewers often provide a Wi-Fi transfer option to get your PDF files from the computer to an iOS device*

Tap the Wi-Fi icon, and a Help screen opens where information is provided for the method to connect your iOS device to your computer. As shown in Figure 11-4, you can type an IP address in your computer's web browser, or you can access a Bonjour-address.

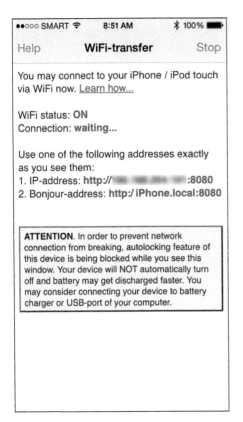

Figure 11-4. *A help screen provides information on how to connect your iOS device with your computer*

Notice that both methods inform you that you need to type an address followed by a : 8080. This is common for all apps permitting you to use an address for transferring files.

If we use a web browser, then you open it on your computer and type the URL provided in the app Help screen. If you use the Bonjour-address, go to the Mac desktop, then to the Finder view, and press ⌘+K or choose Go ➤ Connect to Computer. When using the Bonjour-address, you don't need to worry about working in another application like a web browser. Once you type the address into the Connect to Server dialog box, a window opens displaying the location of the PDF viewer files, as shown in Figure 11-5.

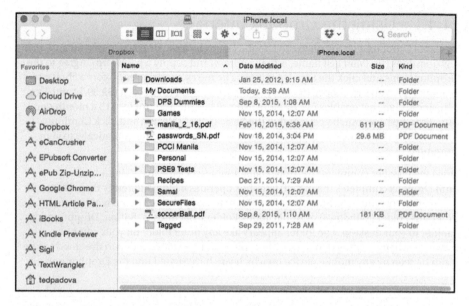

Figure 11-5. *Using the Bonjour-address connection, a new window opens displaying files for the app used to make the connection*

You also find the folder mounted on your hard drive. Therefore, if you have several files that you want to add and/or edit, this method makes it much easier to add files, update files, and delete files.

The window that you see is like any other folder. Simply drag and drop files to the mounted drive to add them to your iOS device. You can also delete files and rename them. You can organize files by creating new folders and nesting files within folders. Keep in mind that you must have the Wi-Fi Transfer screen (shown in Figure 11-5) open when making changes.

11.4   Using Dropbox

Dropbox is a cloud storage application that lets you share files on all of your devices. You can install Dropbox on each device—computers, tablets, and mobile devices. There are a number of options available to you when choosing a cloud storage program, such as Apple's iCloud, Microsoft's OneDrive, JustCloud, ZipCloud, and more. Of all the options available for cloud storage, I think Dropbox is the best all-around service, and it's free to download from www.dropbox.com.

To sync files between your computer and other devices, you need to download and install Dropbox on your computer. You also need to install Dropbox on all of the devices that you use to transfer files between the devices. Dropbox is available for iOS, Android, Mac OS X, and Windows.

11.4.1   Using the Dropbox Interface

To install Dropbox, you log on to the Dropbox web site (www.dropbox.com) and answer a few questions (first and last name, e-mail address, and supply a password). Agree to the Dropbox terms and click the Sign Up button. The next screen you see offers a choice of account type. You can choose the Basic (free) account, a Pro account ($9.99/month), or a Business plan that enables five or more users to use the account for $15 a month per user. For a free account, be certain that the Basic item is selected and click Continue. After clicking Continue, the application installer is downloaded automatically to your computer.

Once the installer completes the download, double-click the installer and wait until Dropbox completes the install. Dropbox operates a little differently than other applications on your computer. You don't launch the application from within your Programs Folder (Windows) or Applications Folder (Macintosh). Rather, Dropbox adds a folder to your desktop. The folder appears like any other folder on your computer. However, when you drag and drop a file to the folder, the file is added to the cloud where it can be seen by any mobile device on which you have signed into the Dropbox app.

■ **Tip**   For Macintosh users, you can add the Dropbox folder to your list of favorites in a folder view. Drag the folder to the list on the left side of an open folder. When Dropbox appears as a favorite, you can drag files to the item or click to open the Dropbox folder, as shown in Figure 11-6.

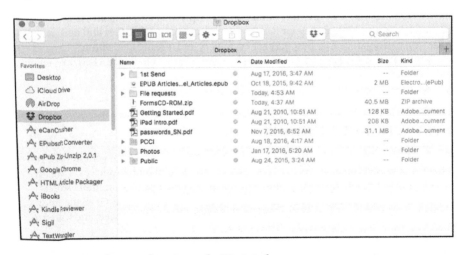

Figure 11-6. *Dropbox as a favorite on the Macintosh*

In order to upload files from your local computer, you need to log on to your Dropbox account. When you log on with a web browser, you see in the center of the screen files stored in your Dropbox cloud storage, as shown in Figure 11-7. To the left are links to several items that include:

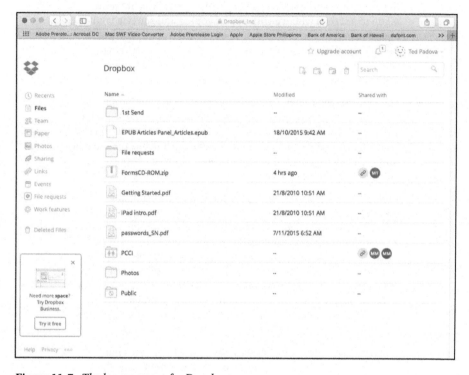

Figure 11-7. *The log-on screen for Dropbox*

- *Recents:* Recent files list.

- *Files:* Click Files, and the screen is refreshed showing you the files under the name column.

- *Team:* Collaboration with others.

- *Paper:* Real-time editing with team members.

- *Photos:* Click this link, and you open a slideshow displaying photos you uploaded to your Dropbox account.

- *Sharing:* When you click Sharing, the screen changes and you find a button to click for sharing files. You can have several sharing folders for your account. When you click the button, the Share a Folder dialog box opens. You can choose to share a new folder or add more people to a shared folder. Make a choice and click the Next button in the Share a Folder dialog box. You are then taken to a screen where a URL can be copied and sent via your e-mail client, or you can choose to let Dropbox send an e-mail. Recipients of the e-mail can access the files that you add to the shared folder; even users who don't have Dropbox accounts can access the files.

- You can also right-click on the files appearing in your Dropbox folder on your computer and choose Share Dropbox Link. When you choose the menu command, a link is copied to the clipboard. You can open your e-mail client and paste the link in a new e-mail message. Once again, the recipient doesn't need a Dropbox account to access the files.

- *Links:* This is similar to sharing. When you share a link, the recipient of the link can click to view the contents and elect to download the linked file(s). On your desktop computer, right-click a file in your desktop Dropbox folder and choose Share Dropbox Link. The link URL is copied to the clipboard, and you can paste it into an e-mail message. On the web site, hover your mouse cursor over a file name and click the Share button that appears. A pop-up window opens. Enter the e-mail address of the recipient(s) and click Send. All of the files that you have linked appear in the Links column.

- *Events:* Click Events and you see a timeline of all of the changes that you made in your Dropbox account, such as sharing files, uploading files, a list of other computers and devices that linked to your account, and so forth.

- *File Requests:* Click File Requests and you can send a request for a user to send you files. You can add a title for a message and specify a folder where another user sends the files. Click the Next button and a URL link appears. You can copy the link and paste it into a new e-mail message or supply an e-mail address of the one from which you're requesting a file and Dropbox will e-mail for you.

- *Work Features:* Admin services and file recovery.

When you install Dropbox, you get an account page on the Dropbox web site and a local folder on your hard drive. You can add files and folders to your local folder, and files are automatically uploaded to Dropbox. You can see all of the files on all other mobile devices where you install the Dropbox app, but the list represents just aliases (links) to the original files. This is particularly helpful on tablets and smartphones, since you're not using a lot of disk space for files that you may not use. Tap a link and the file is downloaded to the device.

■ **Note**   Keep in mind that on desktop and laptop computers, any files in the Dropbox folders are actually downloaded to each computer. This is different than the behavior on tablets and smartphones, where files appear listed but are not downloaded until you manually instruct an app to perform a download.

11.4.2   Loading Files on Devices

To follow along in this section, you need to download Dropbox and install it on your computer. Log on to www.dropbox.com and follow the steps to provide your name (first and last), e-mail address, and password. Check the box to agree to terms and conditions and click Next. Click Basic for the free account and click Continue. The application installer begins a download. Double-click the Installer to add the application to your computer.

On a device (tablet or smartphone), log on to the device's store. For iOS devices, tap the App Store icon to log on to Apple's App Store. Search for Dropbox and install the application. On Android devices, tap the Play Store icon and search for Dropbox. Tap Install when the Dropbox page opens.

Copy some files from your computer to the Dropbox folder. (When you install Dropbox, a folder is added to your computer.) Open the folder and drag some files to the folder. Using this method actually moves the files from your computer to your Dropbox folder. You can also right-click on a file on Windows and choose Move to Dropbox.

If you want to add a copy of files to the Dropbox folder, press Option on a Mac when you drag files to the folder. On Windows, right-click a file and choose Send To ➤ Dropbox. On both Mac and Windows, you can also copy the file and paste it into the Dropbox folder.

Launch Dropbox on one of your devices. The files that you added to Dropbox on your computer are listed in Dropbox on your device. You can copy a number of different file types to Dropbox, such as Microsoft Office files, plain text files, photos, PDFs, EPUBs, and so forth. When you tap one of the files, you will see a preview of the document in Dropbox. The file has not yet been downloaded to your device. Dropbox simply opens a preview of the document so that you can easily check through various files and locate the one you want to use.

Since our interest is primarily focused on EPUBs and PDFs, let's look at how you get files from Dropbox to a device viewer.

11.4.2.1   Adding EPUB Files to Devices

On Android devices, when you tap an EPUB file on your device in Dropbox, a pop-up screen displays the apps that you can use to view your document. The file extension should be .epub. To view the EPUB in one of the apps, tap the file name in the Dropbox window. Tap Always to permanently open EPUBs in a given viewer or tap Just Once to view the EPUB one time in the viewer (see Figure 11-8). When you tap again on an EPUB, you make the choice for Always or Just Once again.

Figure 11-8. *Tap the viewer that you want to use with the downloaded file*

■ **Note**   The list you see on a device only shows you the contents of files residing in the Dropbox folder in the cloud. The files are stored in the cloud (on the Dropbox server). Files in Dropbox are downloaded to your device only when you add them to a viewing app or tap the file to add it to your device. This keeps your device free from a lot of file storage, which you may not want on the device.

On the Macintosh, I also use Dropbox to add files rather than using iTunes. If you use iTunes prior to version 12 to add a book, iTunes needs to sync your library. All of the books in your library are re-synced. If you have a lot of books, syncing the library can take some time. If you need to review updates several times, you'll lose a lot of time waiting for iTunes to complete the task of syncing the library.

With Dropbox on an iOS device, you can open the EPUB file in iBooks or any other EPUB reader that you have on the device. Tap the file name in Dropbox on an iOS device, and the file is downloaded to the device. The first screen that you see may or may not have a preview. If you see a screen with no preview, as seen in Figure 11-9, don't be alarmed; the file is still there.

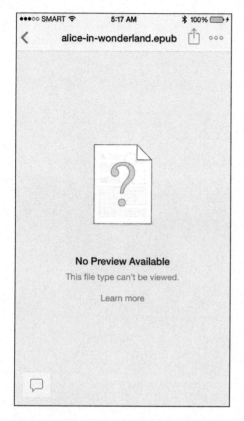

Figure 11-9. Tap the file name in the Dropbox app, and the file opens in Dropbox

Tap the share icon in the top-right corner, and Dropbox opens a screen similar to what you see in Figure 11-10. You can share the file, or you can open the file in an app. Tap the Open In button to choose an app for viewing the file.

Figure 11-10. *Tap the file name in the Dropbox app, and the file opens in Dropbox*

After tapping Open In, the screen changes and displays all of the apps on your device that can view the EPUB. If you want to view the file in iBooks, tap Open in iBooks, as shown in Figure 11-11, or choose another app for previewing the document. Using this method for adding EPUBs to an iOS device is much faster than using iTunes.

Figure 11-11. *Tap the app that you want to use to view the EPUB*

For more information on viewing EPUB documents on devices, see Chapter 13.

11.4.2.2   Adding PDF Files to Devices

You can use Dropbox to open a PDF file on a mobile device. Locate the file in the Dropbox app, and tap the down-pointing arrowhead to open a menu, as shown in Figure 11-12. In the menu, you have a number of options. The one that you want is Open With. Tap Open With, and the screen changes to display all of the PDF viewers that you have installed on your device.

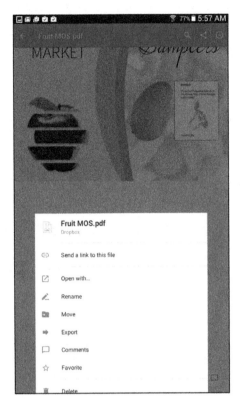

Figure 11-12. *Tap the top-right icon to open a menu*

A number of eBook readers support viewing PDF files, as shown in Figure 11-13. Your best option is to view PDFs in Adobe Acrobat Reader or use a third-party viewer, however, such as GoodReader. Tap the viewer you want to use, and the file opens in the target viewer.

Figure 11-13. *Tap the PDF viewer you want to use and the file opens in the viewer*

If you want to open a PDF in iBooks on the iPhone or iPad, follow the same steps to open a PDF file in Dropbox, choose Open In, and select iBooks. The file opens in iBooks, and it's added to your iBooks bookshelf.

11.5 Summary

This brief chapter discussed moving files from your computers to various devices. We looked at copying files via USB devices and Apple iTunes, and we looked at copying files to PDF viewers and eReaders.

In order to copy files, you first need a file on your hard drive to copy. In the next chapter, we begin a journey through exporting content from Adobe InDesign to various formats. Our first format covers exports to reflowable EPUBs.

■ ■ ■

CHAPTER 12

Creating Reflowable EPUBs

When it comes to EPUBs, there are two types: reflowable and fixed layout. Reflowable EPUBs are commonly used for long text documents, such as novels and lengthy reading material. Fixed layout EPUBs are documents that appear similar to PDF files. The layout and organization of type and objects for the most part mimic the layout design.

When it comes to interactivity, reflowable EPUBs are much more limiting than fixed layout EPUBs. You cannot use buttons to change events in reflowable EPUBs, and you cannot directly view animations in reflowable EPUBs. These types of interactivity are available in fixed layout EPUBs.

Reflowable EPUBs are not completely limited to static content, however. You can import audio and video files, and you can create hyperlinks that work fine in reflowable EPUBs. You can also add some animation, which is a bit clunky, using a little workaround.

This chapter is all about creating reflowable EPUBs. It showcases many of the best practices and considerations that you need to make to create EPUBs that meet common EPUB standards. In Chapter 13, we will look at creating fixed layout EPUBs.

12.1   Understanding Reflowable EPUBs

EPUBs are almost exclusively viewed on devices such as tablets and smartphones. Nonetheless, you can view reflowable EPUBs on desktop computers as well. To view an EPUB, you need an application that can open an EPUB file (something like story.epub, where the file extension is a recognized EPUB format) on your device, commonly known as an eReader. There are a number of different eReaders that you can acquire for iOS, Android, and Linux operating systems as well as for desktop computers.

Most eReaders have built-in tools for sizing type and changing fonts. As type is sized up or sized down, a reflowable EPUB reflows the content so that it conforms to the page size in view on a device—hence, the word *reflowable*.

All eReaders look for a file with an .epub extension. When a file has an extension of .epub, it can be opened in eReaders—if the contents were created as an EPUB file. The .epub file itself is nothing more than a compressed .zip archive containing XHTML files. In essence, EPUBs are like web sites where you can navigate through web pages with a swipe of your hand on a device.

© Ted Padova 2017
T. Padova, *Adobe InDesign Interactive Digital Publishing*,
DOI 10.1007/978-1-4842-2439-7_12

Knowing what an EPUB is helps you understand some things about formatting text. You need to adhere to standards used by HTML and use tags, divs, CSS, and related HTML coding. Fortunately, InDesign handles writing the HTML, CSS, and it almost always produces a valid EPUB that can be viewed on just about any device with any kind of eReader.

12.2   Formatting for Reflowable EPUBs

Since EPUBs are a collection of HTML files, you need to account for some design considerations when exporting to an EPUB format. Failure to format and organize content properly can lead to some bizarre and unexpected consequences. The layout you preview in InDesign may appear quite different in an eReader. Examine Figure 12-1. This is a layout in preview mode in Adobe InDesign.

Chapter 8

The Chateau D'If.

The commissary of police, as he traversed the ante-chamber, madea sign to two gendarmes, who placed themselves one on Dantes' right and the other on his left. A door that communicated with the **Palaisde Justice** was opened, and they went through a long range of gloomy corridors, whose appearance might have made even the boldest shudder. The *Palais de Justice* communicated with the prison, — a sombre edifice, that from its grated windows looks on the clock-tower of the Accoules. After numberless windings, Dantes saw a door with an iron wicket. The com-

missary took up an iron mallet and knocked thrice, every blow seeming to Dantes as if struck onhis heart.

The door opened, the two gendarmes gently pushed him forward, and the door closed with a loud sound behind him. The airhe inhaled was no longer pure, but thick and mephitic, — he was in prison. He was conducted to a tolerably neat chamber, but grated and barred, and its appearance, therefore, did not greatly alarmhim; besides, the words of Villefort, who seemed to interest himself so much, resounded still in his ears like a promise offreedom. It was four o'clock when Dantes was placed in this chamber. It was, as we have said, the 1st of March, and the prisoner was soon buried in darkness. The obscurity augmented the acuteness of his hearing; at the slightest sound he rose and hastened to the door, convinced they were about to liberate him,but the sound died away, and Dantes sank again into his seat. Atlast, about ten o'clock, and just as Dantes began to despair, steps were heard in the corridor, a key turned in the lock, the bolts creaked, the massy oaken door flew open, and a flood of light from two torches pervaded the apartment. By the torchlight Dantes sawthe glittering sabres and carbines of four gendarmes. He had advanced at first, but stopped at the sight of this display of force. "

Figure 12-1. *Layout in Preview mode in Adobe InDesign*

When you export this file and view it in an eReader on a desktop computer, you may see something like Figure 12-2. At the top of the page, you see the photo image followed by the frame containing color. Since the text color for the chapter number and title were set to paper, the text doesn't appear and it's not set inside the frame.

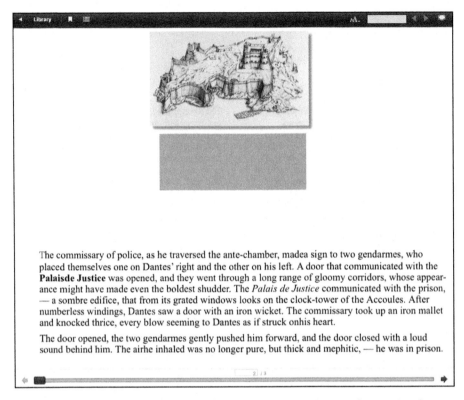

Figure 12-2. *The same InDesign layout as shown in Figure 12-1 viewed in an eReader*

As I mentioned in several earlier chapters, you need to use styles for everything when creating reflowable EPUBs. You also need to adjust the reading order so that graphics and text appear in the order that you want them. In short, there's quite a bit of formatting that you need to control in InDesign before you export to an EPUB format.

12.2.1   Formatting Text for Reflowable EPUBs

In InDesign, you can easily move text frames around, add carriage returns to add space between paragraphs, add drop caps, add columns and margins to text frames, add line indents, and add text wraps to graphics. You don't need to create styles (although you should) to get a layout to appear as you want it.

When it comes to EPUBs, however, you need to pay attention to every detail when formatting text, and some formatting tasks that you will perform in InDesign do not translate to the EPUB format. For example, setting up multi-column pages will not translate to an EPUB format. Moving text frames apart from each other to create whitespace will not be honored in the EPUB, nor will adding multiple tabs and carriage returns.

Understanding Text Formatting Guidelines

Here are some guidelines that you need to follow when preparing a document for export to EPUB:

- *Add styles for paragraphs and text*: I've said many times, each and every paragraph and any overrides need to be converted to styles. If you add bold, italicized, or colored text, you need to create character styles.

- *Add styles for drop caps*: When you create drop caps, you need to add a character style that defines the formatting for the drop cap character(s).

- *Adding whitespace*: In HTML, you need a <break> tag to force a carriage return or hard break between paragraphs. When creating EPUBs, you need to use styles and add space before and/or after to add space between paragraphs.

- *Aligning text*: Include text alignment in paragraph styles. Don't align text in the Control Panel without defining a style.

- *Anchoring objects and images*: You cannot use floating objects if you want the objects to appear on the same pages and in the same locations in your layout. You need to anchor objects to text if you want objects included next to the text. If you do not anchor objects, all the objects are shown at the end of the text. For example, if you have a book with one story spanning several pages, the images and objects appear at the end of the story. As a matter of practice, anchor objects either with a custom setting or above line. Don't use inline anchoring. For more information on how to anchor objects in text, see the section "Formatting Graphics" later in this chapter.

- *Fix all overrides*: Use the Redefine Style setting in the Styles Panels to redefine a style and use character styles when formatting characters within a paragraph style.

- *Fonts*: Try to use Typekit fonts when embedding fonts. These fonts can be embedded without any permissions. With all other fonts, always check for permissions to embed the fonts. OpenType fractions are not supported.

- *Lists*: In HTML, you have ordered and unordered lists that are defined by tags. In InDesign, you need styles for each list that you create.

- *Page breaks*: If you want a chapter page or a section to start at the top of a page, you need to adjust the Keep Options in the Paragraph Style Options dialog box. Choose an option in the Start Paragraph drop-down menu in the Keep Options tab in the Paragraph Styles Options dialog box.

- *Rules*: You can add rules above and below text. If you do use rules, you need to use a paragraph style and add rules in the Paragraph Style Options dialog box. Do not draw rules on a page between paragraphs.

- *Text wraps*: You can create text wraps and export to EPUB, but you need to follow the same rule as when using objects and images. After setting the text wrap options, you need to anchor the object to the text at the location where you want it to be positioned.

Cleaning Up a Layout

You can use the Find/Change dialog box and search for formatted text overrides and change them to character styles.

CLEANING UP A LAYOUT

The following is a procedure for how you can search for a font style and change the formatting to a character style:

1. **Choose Edit ➤ Find/Change to open the Find/Change dialog box**.

2. **Click Text to open the Text tab and click in the Find Format box**. The Find Format Settings dialog box opens.

3. **Click Basic Character Options and choose Bold from the Font Style drop-down menu**. Click OK to return to the Find/ Change dialog box. You can choose any format in the dialog box. For example, suppose that you want to search for a Bold font.

4. **Choose a character style**. Click the Change Format box, and the Change Format Settings dialog box opens. Choose a style from the Character Style drop-down menu. If you don't have a style, choose New Character Style from the menu and create a new character style. Click OK and you return to the Find/Change dialog box.

5. **Click Find and click Change.** Test the Find/Change criteria and click the Find button once, as shown in Figure 12-3. Text should be highlighted for the first occurrence of bold text in a paragraph. Click Change and observe the results. The bold font should be changed to a new format (plain text, text with a color, italicized, and so on—whatever you defined in the character style).

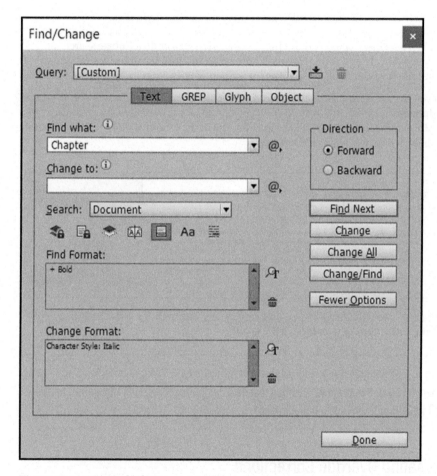

Figure 12-3. *Use Find/Change to search for and change formatting*

6. **Change All.** When everything looks like it's working properly, click Change All to change the text in your document globally.

> **Note** You can make changes in All Documents, the current open Document, a Story, and To End of Story in the Search drop-down menu.

Finding Overrides

You can download a marvelous InDesign script from the Internet called FindChangeLocalFormatting by Mark Autret. Log on to http://www.indiscripts.com/post/2010/05/show-local-formatting-in-indesign-cs4 or do a Google search for Find Change Local Formatting. Download the script and install it in the Scripts folder. For more information about installing scripts, see Chapter 6.

When you run this script, all overrides in your document are marked with a nonprinting strikethrough, as shown in Figure 12-4. As you eliminate the overrides, the strikethrough marks are eliminated. This script can save you a lot of time if you acquire text from your client and need to do a lot of cleanup work.

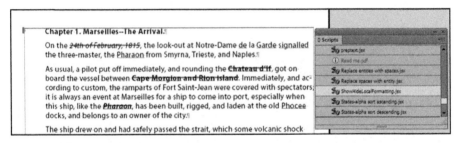

Figure 12-4. *Open the Scripts Panel and double-click the FindChangeLocalFormatting script to see strikethroughs on text with overrides*

> **Note** This script is needed for all users of InDesign CC 2015.2 and earlier. If you have InDesign CC 2015.3 and above, you can use the Toggle Style Overrides Highlighter feature found in the Paragraph Styles Panel menu.

Automating Override Corrections

Computers are supposed to make life easier and magically perform tasks for us without having to make changes manually ourselves, right? Wouldn't it be nice if we could just click a button and all text overrides could be converted to different character styles? Well, when it comes to InDesign, some magical things can indeed happen.

Again, this magic comes in the form of a script. The script is PerfectPrepText written by Theunis DeJong (aka *jongware*), and you can find it at my favorite InDesign resource, *InDesignSecrets.com* (www.indesignsecrets.com/downloads/PerfectPrepText.zip).

Download and install the script. This is one of many helpful tools that David Blatner and Anne-Marie Concepcion provide to the InDesign community on their www.indesignsecrets. com web site.

After installing the script, double-click on preptext and all of the local overrides are converted to character formats. In Figure 12-5, you see the Character Styles Panel with two character styles. I didn't create the character styles. The preptext.jsx found local overrides, created new character styles, and applied the styles to the overrides.

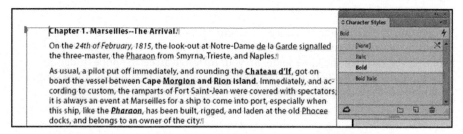

Figure 12-5. *New character styles were added to the Character Styles Panel using the preptext.jsx script*

New scripts are continuously created by developers, many of whom don't ask for any money or ask for a nominal donation. To discover the latest and greatest in InDesign tools, log on to InDesignSecrets (www.indesignsecrets.com) routinely. If you find a script that helps you and the developer asks for a small donation, be sure to send in a few dollars. It means a lot for developers to be able to collect some money for their hard work, and it keeps them motivated to create more scripts that are useful for the entire InDesign user community.

12.2.2   Formatting Graphics

In Chapter 6, I talked about using the Object Styles Panel. When you add some effects to an object, you need to create an object style. Something like a drop shadow or bevel and emboss effect won't appear in some EPUBs unless you define and use a style with the objects.

You also need to anchor objects in the text so that the objects don't show up on the last page of the EPUB.

Following are some considerations that you need to make when using graphics in EPUBs.

Preparing Images

Reflowable EPUBs are intended to be read. People view EPUBs on devices and read novels, books, reports, and so forth using a variety of applications that display EPUBs. When you create EPUBs, you want to capture the largest market available and make your documents accessible to as many people as you can. One significant minority group that devours books is people with visual challenges. People who cannot see text on a computer or device often use screen readers or text-to-speech software to read aloud text files to them.

Screen readers work marvelously with computer files, but they need a little of your help to make the documents fully accessible. When it comes to images, you need to add a tag to image files. The tags are Alt (alternative) tags where you provide a text description of an image. You may have images with names like img_001.jpg, DCIM677.tiff, photo1.psd, or some other file name. When the screen reader encounters an image without an Alt tag, the exact name of the file is read aloud. This is obviously confusing to people using screen readers.

You can add Alt tags to images either in a photo editing application, Adobe Bridge, or directly in InDesign. Basically, these programs are the best two choices. This is purely your call. You can view the Links folder for your InDesign assets in Adobe Bridge and add a description field in the IPTC Core Description, as shown in Figure 12-6. Add a short description of the image. For example, *image of the company logo in red and green.*

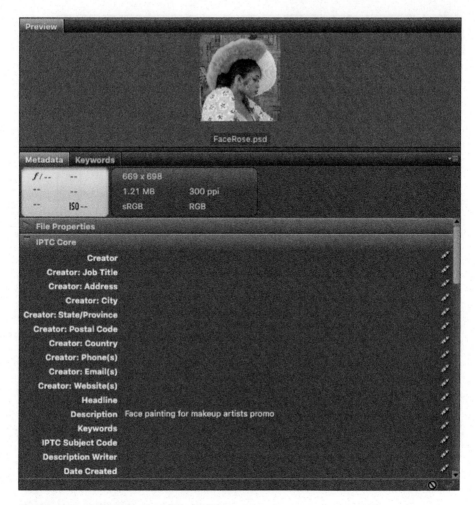

Figure 12-6. *Add Alt tags in Adobe Bridge*

Before you place images in InDesign, use Adobe Bridge to add all of the Alt tags. Be sure to use the same field in the IPTC Core data area. The data are saved automatically from Adobe Bridge as XMP data.

The other way that you can add Alt tags to images is in InDesign. You select an image and choose Object ➤ Object Export Options. When the Object Export Options dialog box opens, the Alt Text tab is in view by default. You can choose to add custom text or import XMP data with descriptions by choosing a menu item from the Alt Text Source menu. If you choose Custom, you can type the text that you want for the Alt tag, as shown in Figure 12-7.

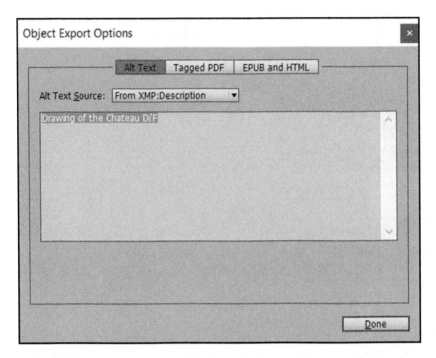

Figure 12-7. *Choose Custom from the Alt Text Source and type a description*

There's a trade-off with the particular method you use. If you add descriptions in Bridge, you can quickly add the data for the Alt tags. If you add Alt tags in InDesign, you have to open the Object Export Options dialog box each time that you place an image. The advantage that you have when adding Alt tags in InDesign is that you can use descriptions in the context of the page layout. In Bridge, the images are the same; however, in some cases, the context in which the images are used may influence your descriptions.

This is a personal choice. I prefer adding descriptions in Adobe Bridge. That method seems to work much faster. If you do add descriptions in Bridge, then don't use the Object Export Options dialog box to import the XMP data. There's a better way to import the data from Bridge, using object styles.

Using Object Styles

If you have a handful of images, six or fewer, you can get by without using object styles. But if you use a dozen or more images in an EPUB, you will do well to create object styles for your images. In some cases, it's a necessity while in other cases it just helps you speed up your workflow.

A couple of things that you want to set up in an object style include `Alt` tags (if you use Adobe Bridge to add `Alt` tags) and Anchored Object Position. Create a new object style and click Alt Text in the left pane. From the Alt Text Source drop-down menu, choose From XMP Description, as shown in Figure 12-8. If you add `Alt` tags to the Description field in the IPTC Core data in Bridge, the descriptions for all of your images are handled in the object style. To verify that the description made it through, open the Object Export Options dialog box and check the Alt Text tab. You should see the description imported from the XMP data.

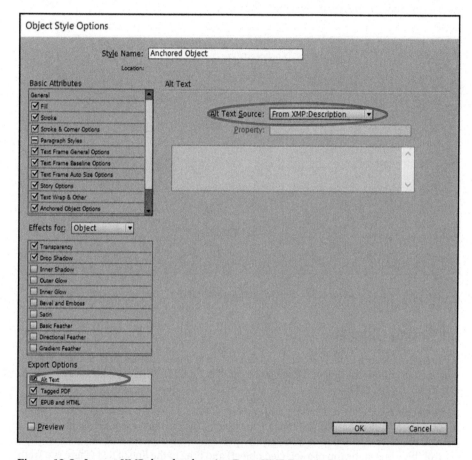

Figure 12-8. *Import XMP data by choosing From XMP Description*

The other important setting for an object style is the position of anchored objects. If you have several object positions using Above Line and others using an alignment to the spine, you might create two styles based on the style you use for `Alt` tags. Deselect all of the options and just choose the Anchored Object Options you want for a given position for your images, but base the style in the General Panel on the style name you use for the `Alt` text.

To create a style for an anchored object, Alt/⌥+click the Create new style icon in the Object Styles Panel. Base the style on the Alt Text style, and deselect all of the other options in the panel. Click Anchored Object Options in the left pane.

When anchoring objects for EPUBs, don't use Inline as a matter of practice. You should choose Above Line, as shown in Figure 12-9. Here you can set the space before and after and choose an alignment option. If you choose Custom from the Position drop-down menu, you can choose alignment relative to the spine and adjust offsets. When the Preview checkbox is enabled, you can see the position of the object in the layout for either choice you make in the Anchored Object Options.

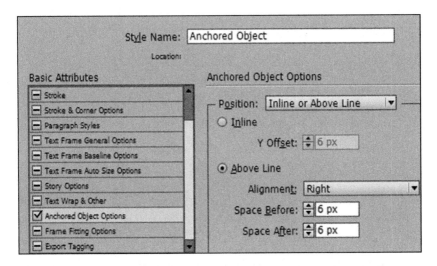

Figure 12-9. *Choose Above Line and adjust the Space Before and Space After settings*

Anchoring Objects

If you have a column of text and you want an object to appear somewhere within the text, you need to anchor the object. Floating objects, if not anchored to the text, always appear at the end of your EPUB.

Some people try adding line breaks and carriage returns to get the right space for adding inline objects in text frames. You can cut an object, click the cursor in a text frame, and paste to create an inline object. You can also press the Shift key and drag the anchor control (blue box at the top of a selected object) and drag to the line of text where you want to anchor the object. Using inline objects can be cumbersome to position on a page, and they can sometimes produce unexpected results with some eReaders. Your solution and a best practice is to use an Above Line option in the Anchored Object Options dialog box.

To anchor an object, click and drag the anchor control (blue box on a selected object frame) to the location where you want the object to appear in the text. Immediately you'll notice that the object doesn't move, and you don't see a preview for where the object is placed. Not to worry, we can fix the problem.

After anchoring an object, you can modify the location in one of two ways. Select an anchored object and choose Object ➤ Anchored Object ➤ Options to open the Anchored Object Options dialog box, or you can use an object style as I discussed earlier in the section, "Using Object Styles." If you have several objects, then creating an object style is your best option.

Earlier in Figure 12-9, you saw the options for anchored object positions in the Object Style Options dialog box. Be sure to enable the Preview checkbox to view adjustments in your document as you make them in the Object Style Options dialog box.

Grouping Objects

If you add text to a frame, the text and frame color appear fine in an EPUB. You may see some slight differences between eReaders, but most often the attributes you assign to frames, such as insets, are honored in the EPUB.

If for some reason you have a text frame over a geometric shape, you need to group the objects (Object ➤ Group or Ctrl/⌘+G) and then anchor them.

Wrapping Text

You can wrap text in EPUBs, but the wraps that you add to an object can only be applied to rectangular objects. You can't use circles and ellipses using the Text Wrap Panel or when using Float Left and Float Right.

WRAPPING AN OBJECT

Following is a description for how you wrap an object in InDesign for export to a reflowable EPUB:

1. **Add a carriage return before the paragraph where you want to anchor the object.** If you anchor an object at the beginning of a paragraph, you can experience problems with the first line of text not wrapping properly and the object hides part of the first line.

2. **Anchor the object.** Drag the blue square at the top of a selected object to the text frame at the location where you want the object to appear. When the object is anchored, you see an anchor icon, as shown in Figure 12-10.

3. **Open the Text Wrap Panel.** Open the Text Wrap Panel (Window ➤ Text Wrap or press Ctrl/⌘+Alt/⌥+W).

4. **Apply a text wrap to the object.** Select the object and move it into position. Click the Wrap Around bounding box icon (second from left) in the Text Wrap Panel. Adjust the offsets by typing values in the Offset text boxes. As you make adjustments, you see the results on the document page, as shown in Figure 12-10.

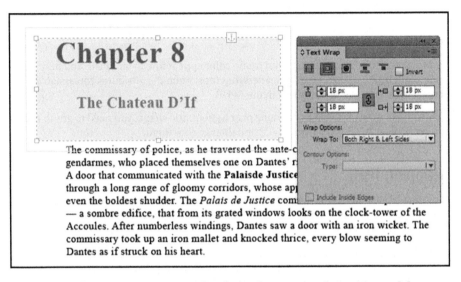

Figure 12-10. View the text Wrap Panel aside the object to view the position and the text wrap offsets

5. **Create an object style.** Select the object, press Alt/⌥, and click the Create New Style in the Object Style Panel.

6. **Set the attributes for the anchored object.** In the Object Style Options dialog box, click Anchored Objects in the left pane. From the Position drop-down menu, be certain that Custom is selected, as shown in Figure 12-11. (You don't want Inline as your choice for the Position.) Since you applied the text wrap before creating the style, the new object style captured the text wrap settings. Click OK to dismiss the Object Style Options dialog box.

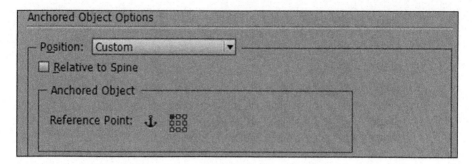

Figure 12-11. *Group separate objects, and anchor the single object to a text frame*

7. **Open the Object Export Options dialog box.** Select the object, and choose Object ➤ Object Export Options to open the Object Export Options dialog box. Click the EPUB and HTML tab in the Object Export Options dialog box.

8. **Adjust the Object Export Options.** Enable Custom Layout and choose Float Left (or Float Right if the object is on the right side of the text frame), as shown in Figure 12-12.

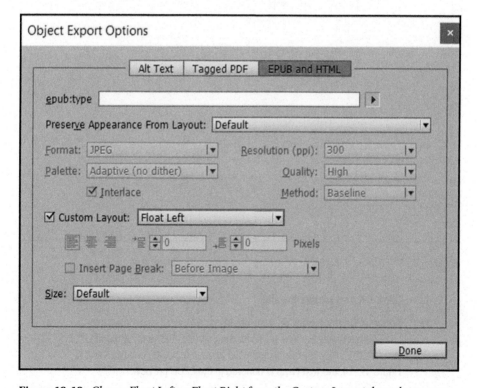

Figure 12-12. *Choose Float Left or Float Right from the Custom Layout drop-down menu*

9. **Export to EPUB.** Choose File ➤ Export or press Ctrl/⌘+E. Choose EPUB (Reflowable) for the file format and click Save. The EPUB – Reflowable Layout Export Options dialog box opens, as shown in Figure 12-13.

10. **Adjust the object settings.** Click Object in the left pane in the EPUB – Reflowable Layout Export Options dialog box. Be certain the first checkbox is enabled, as you see in Figure 12-13, and the CSS Size option is set to Relative to Text Flow.

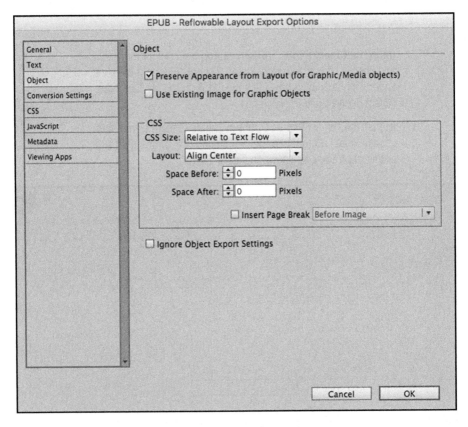

Figure 12-13. *Choose Relative to Text Flow from the CSS Size menu*

11. **Click OK and export the file.**

12. **Preview the document on your desktop computer.** In my example, I use Adobe Digital Editions (ADE) for the preview. After adding the file to my ADE Library, double-click the file to open it. As you can see in Figure 12-14, the Text Wrap is honored in the EPUB preview.

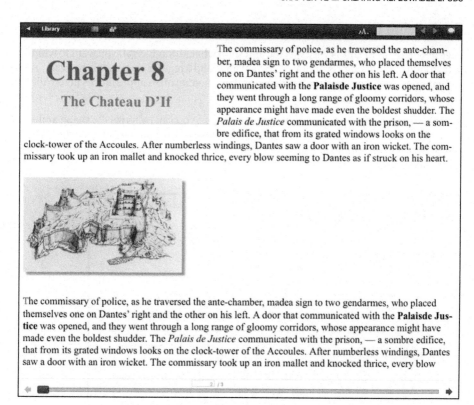

Figure 12-14. The EPUB is viewed in Adobe Digital Editions

If you want to wrap text around an object in the middle of a paragraph, you follow similar steps as you would with objects wrapped at the beginning of a paragraph, but with a few exceptions. First you don't use a carriage return inside the paragraph. Anchor the object inside the paragraph and move the object to position. The page view in InDesign should approximate the view that you want in your EPUB.

Also, don't use Float Left or Float Right in the Object Export Options. From the Custom Layout drop-down menu, choose Alignment and Spacing. Export to EPUB (Reflowable).

■ **Note**   This book covers creating content in Adobe InDesign CC 2015. If you use an earlier version of InDesign, the procedure for setting up text wraps is very different.

Rasterizing Objects

Page geometry in EPUBs is very specific and somewhat unforgiving. If you want to wrap text around circular objects or draw diagonal lines and irregular shapes, the objects appear in the EPUB as rectangular shapes or they often result in appearances unlike the view you have in InDesign.

In order to finesse the appearance of irregular shapes, you can rasterize the shape and then apply text wraps or have the shapes appear as they do in your layout. In Figure 12-15, you see a text wrap around an elliptical shape. In order to produce this effect, you need to rasterize the frame.

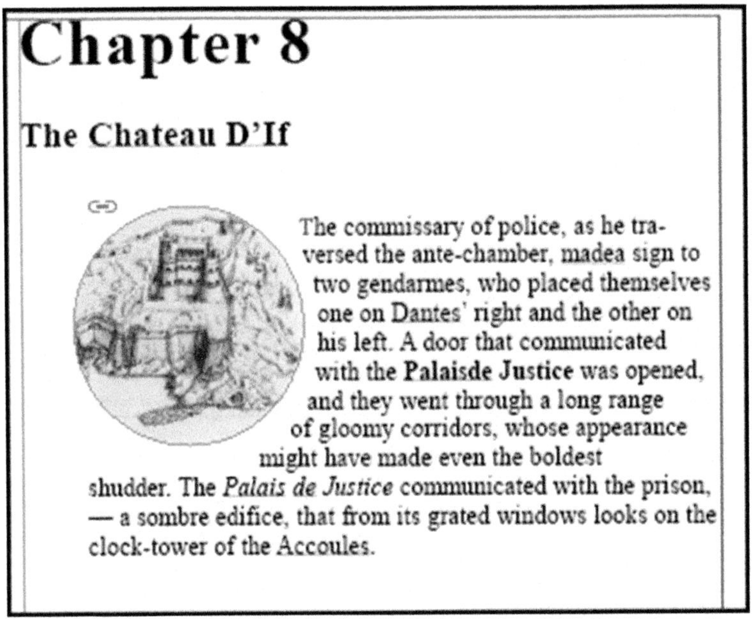

Figure 12-15. *Text wrapped around an elliptical frame*

To rasterize an object or text, open the Object Export Options dialog box (Object ➤ Object Export Options). From the Preserve Appearance From Layout drop-down menu, choose Rasterize Container and click OK (see Figure 12-16). Apply the other settings that you use with text wraps and export to EPUB.

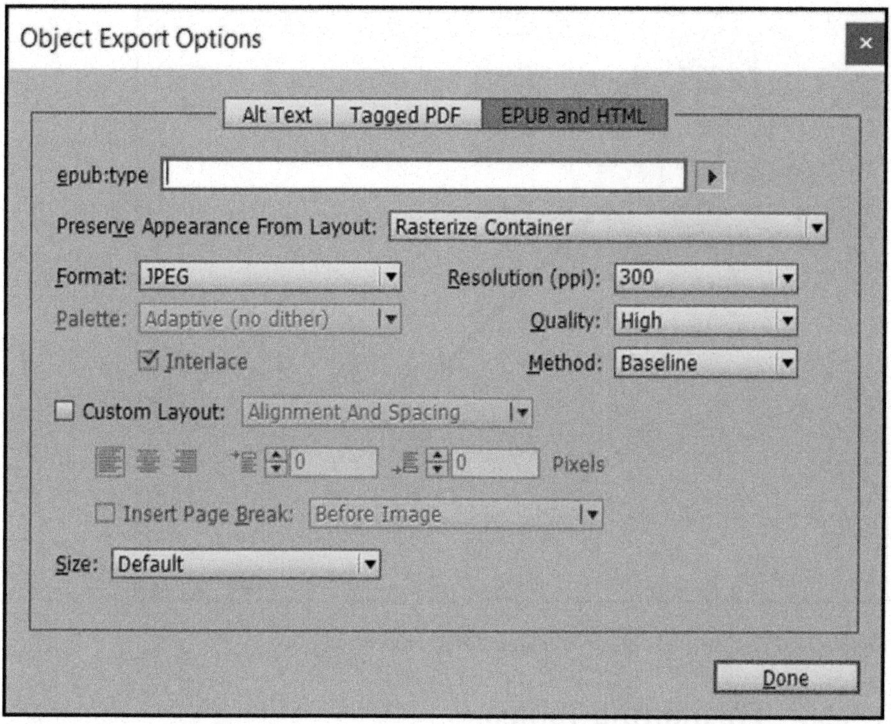

Figure 12-16. *Choose Rasterize Container in the Object Export Options dialog box*

Strokes that you add to a layout that are not straight (horizontally or vertically) also need to be rasterized. If you use a pull quote inside a non-rectangular frame, you also need to rasterize the object. When you do rasterize text, the text is no longer *live text*. It's an object and therefore cannot be sized or searched in the EPUB.

If you group several objects, the grouped object has a rectangular bounding box and therefore you don't need to rasterize the objects. In Figure 12-17, you see a diagonal stroke. If the stroke was a separate item, you would have to rasterize it. However, when the stroke is grouped with the two shapes, the objects appear the same in the EPUB as they appear in the InDesign layout.

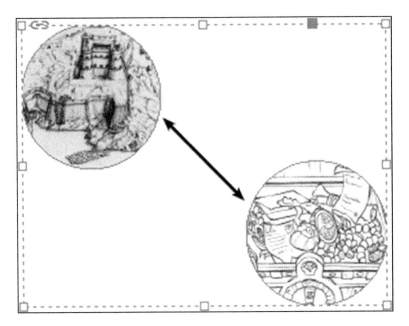

Figure 12-17. *Grouped objects don't need to be rasterized*

12.2.3   Formatting Tables

If you apply all of the options for cell styles covered in Chapter 6, adding tables to a reflowable EPUB is very simple. You don't need to apply any special handling for introducing tables in your documents.

Before InDesign 2015, you couldn't export tables with alternating fills. You also had problems with text offsets in cells. In InDesign 2015, you simply create cell styles from the cells as they are viewed in your layout and export to EPUB. In many readers, you can export to EPUB without using cell styles, but other readers have a problem with tables—particularly with cell text offsets. As a matter of practice, you should always create cell styles. Table styles are not necessary for EPUB viewing, but they are helpful if you have a lot of tables in your document.

In Figure 12-18, you see a table formatted with no cell styles shown in Apple iBooks. InDesign does quite well without any cell styles. Table formatting is preserved quite well in many EPUB readers without using any styles.

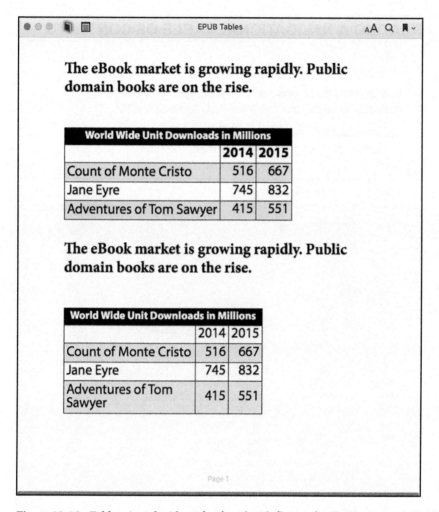

Figure 12-18. *Tables viewed without (top) and with (bottom) cell styles in Apple iBooks*

12.3   Creating a Navigational Table of Contents

One thing that you need to do with all EPUBs is to create a Table of Contents (TOC) style. You don't need to add a TOC to your EPUBs, but you do need to create the TOC style. Virtually all eReaders have a TOC. If you don't create a TOC style, the only thing that shows up in the Table of Contents is the name of your file. If you create a TOC style, then the built-in TOC displays a list of chapters/articles in your document based on the styles you apply to the TOC style.

CREATING A NAVIGATIONAL TABLE OF CONTENTS

To create a navigational TOC in an EPUB, use the following steps:

1. **Create paragraph styles.** Add paragraph styles for chapters, subheads, or other items that you want to appear in the TOC.

2. **Choose Layout ➤ Table of Contents Styles.** The Table of Contents Styles dialog box opens (see Figure 12-19).

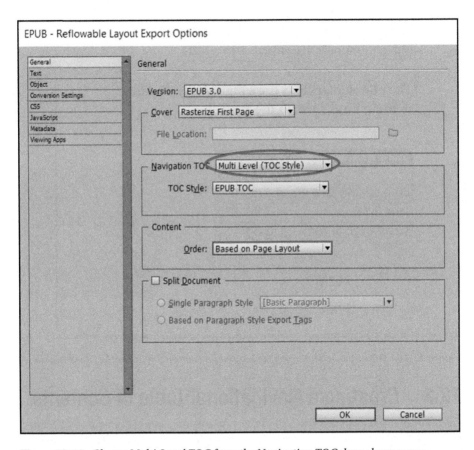

Figure 12-19. Choose Multi-Level TOC from the Navigation TOC drop-down menu

3. **Create a new TOC.** Click New in the Table of Contents Styles dialog box. The Edit Table of Contents dialog box opens.

4. **Set the paragraph style to the styles that you want included in the TOC.** In Figure 12-19, the TOC Style text box shows the name of the style. In this example, I used EPUB TOC as the style name. A list of all of the paragraph styles in the document appears on the right side of the pane. Click the style(s) that you intend to use for the TOC list. Below the Other Styles list are additional items.

5. **Click OK to dismiss the Edit Table of Contents Styles dialog box. Click OK again to dismiss the Table of Contents Styles dialog box**. At this point, the cursor is not loaded and you aren't placing a TOC in the document. We just defined the style here. If you want to include a page with a TOC as a separate page inside your EPUB, you can open the Layout menu and choose Table of Contents. The Table of Contents dialog box opens. If everything is set the way you want it, click OK and the cursor is loaded with a text gun. You can place the text on a page, and the table of contents is generated. For most reflowable EPUBs, it's not necessary to include a table of contents page since readers are likely to use the eReader's built-in TOC.

6. **Export to EPUB.** Choose File ➤ Export (Ctrl/⌘+E), and choose EPUB (Reflowable) for the format.

7. **Edit the general settings.** In the General Panel, choose Multi-Level (TOC Style) from the Navigation TOC drop-down menu. Open the TOC Style menu and choose the name of the style that you added in Step 4, as shown in Figure 12-19.

8. **Click OK to export the file as an EPUB**.

9. **Preview the document**. In Figure 12-20, you see a preview of the EPUB in Adobe Digital Editions with the TOC list expanded. Each item in the list is a hyperlink that sends the viewer to the respective chapter.

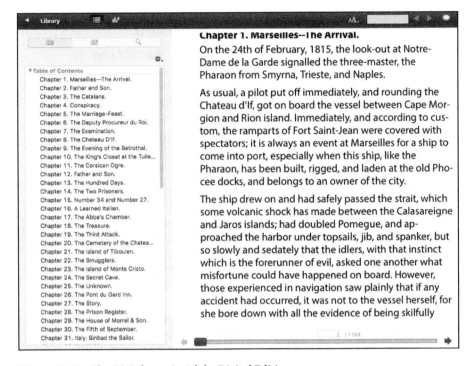

Figure 12-20. The TOC shown in Adobe Digital Editions

12.4 Exporting to the Reflowable EPUB Format

After formatting text with paragraph and character styles, adding cell styles (if using a table), and adding object styles, there are a few other tasks that you need to understand. First you need to set up the order of the InDesign layout in terms of what elements appear first, next, and so on. After you set up the order of the elements, you then need to control all of the options for exporting the EPUB.

12.4.1 Using the Articles Panel

When you export to EPUB, InDesign looks at the page geometry and exports in an order from left to right and top to bottom. You can mess around with a layout and move text frames and objects around so that they export in an order you want, but quite often satisfactory results are difficult to achieve. You have two options for exporting the order of elements in InDesign: (1) using the page layout order and (2) using the Articles Panel.

Prior to InDesign's addition of the Articles Panel and back in the days of the EPUB 1.0 format, getting any kind of reasonable EPUB exported from InDesign was a challenge and required quite a bit of manual work. When the Articles Panel was introduced in InDesign CS5.5, the entire world of eBook publishing changed. Layout artists and book publishers found InDesign CS5.5 a true blessing for creating eBooks without the burdensome tasks of fidgeting with the layout order.

Exporting EPUBs Using Page Layout Order

In Figure 12-21 you see a layout in InDesign. At the top of the page, the book title appears with the text justified right. The chapter number and the chapter title appear below the title. Next a text frame appears, followed by an image, another text frame, and an image. What you see in Figure 12-22 is a document preview, but the page layout order is quite different.

THE COUNT OF MONTE CRISTO

Chapter 8
The Chateau D'If

The commissary of police, as he traversed the ante-chamber, made a sign to two gendarmes, who placed themselves one on Dantes' right and the other on his left. A door that communicated with the **Palais de Justice** was opened, and they went through a long range of gloomy corridors, whose appearance might have made even the boldest shudder. The *Palais de Justice* communicated with the prison, — a sombre edifice, that from its grated windows looks on the clock-tower of the Accoules. After numberless windings, Dantes saw a door with an iron wicket. The commissary took up an iron mallet and knocked thrice, every blow seeming to Dantes as if struck on his heart.

The commissary of police, as he traversed the ante-chamber, made a sign to two gendarmes, who placed themselves one on Dantes' right and the other on his left. A door that communicated with the **Palais de Justice** was opened, and they went through a long range of gloomy corridors, whose appearance might have made even the boldest shudder. The *Palais de Justice* communicated with the prison, — a sombre edifice, that from its grated windows looks on the clock-tower of the Accoules. After numberless windings, Dantes saw a door with an iron wicket. The commissary took up an iron mallet and knocked thrice, every blow seeming to Dantes as if struck on his heart.

Figure 12-21. *Page layout order of a document*

The page layout order is based on page geometry from left to right and top to bottom. The leftmost object on the page is the image in the center of the page. The body copy is the next order of objects, followed by chapter number, and then chapter title. The book title is next, followed by the graphic at the bottom of the page.

If you export to EPUB and you choose the default, Based on Page Layout, in the General Panel under the Order drop-down menu, the EPUB follows the page layout order. When you hand off the EPUB to a device, the document may look like Figure 12-22. In this example, the first page shows the image that was placed at the far left in the layout, followed by text, and then the last page (shown right) displays the chapter number and title.

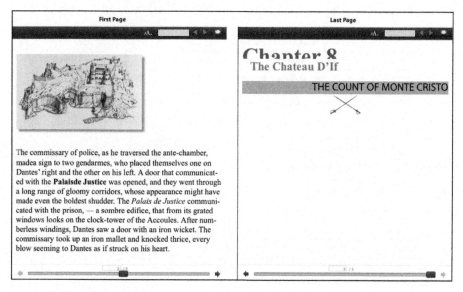

Figure 12-22. *EPUB export using Page Layout order*

Exporting Using the Articles Panel

If the elements in your EPUBs are not ordered properly, the fix is quite simple.

EXPORTING USING THE ARTICLES PANEL

Use the Articles Panel to arrange text and objects in the order that you want them to appear by following some simple steps:

1. **Open the Articles Panel.** Choose Window ➤ Articles.

2. **Add elements to the Articles Panel.** You can press Ctrl/⌘ and click the + icon in the Articles Panel, or you can drag and drop elements to the panel. Pressing Ctrl/⌘ adds all of the elements as articles in the Articles Panel.

3. **Order the elements.** Click and drag articles up/down to reorder them. In Figure 12-23, you can see the Articles Panel populated with the elements on the document page in the order that I want exported.

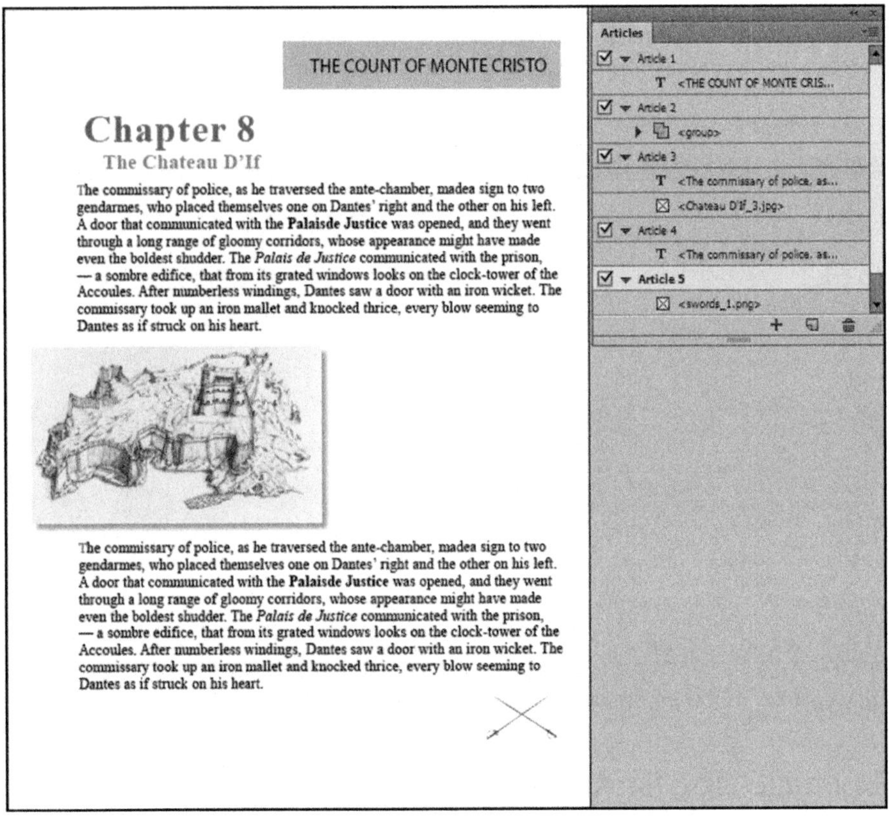

Figure 12-23. Drag and drop elements to the Articles Panel

4. **Export to EPUB.** Choose File ➤ Export or press Ctrl/⌘+E and export to EPUB (Reflowable). The EPUB – Reflowable Layout Export Options dialog box opens.

5. **Export the order based on the Articles Panel.** Choose Same as Articles Panel, as shown in Figure 12-24, and click OK.

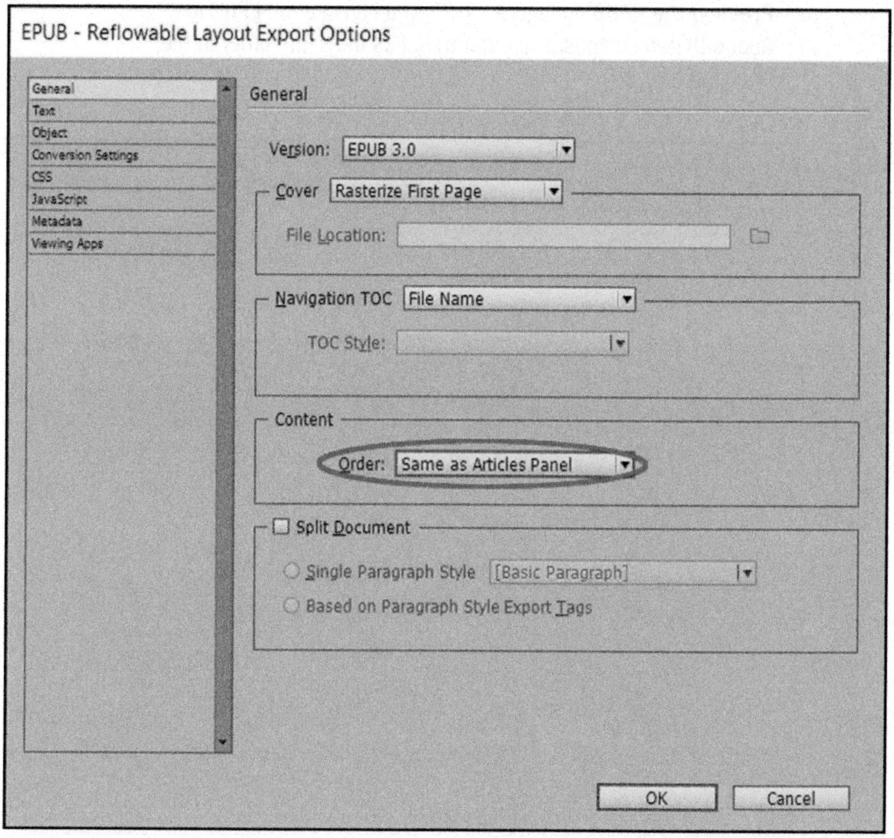

Figure 12-24. *Choose Same as Articles Panel*

6. **Preview the EPUB.** In Figure 12-25, you can see the EPUB in Adobe Digital Editions. The order matches the same order in the InDesign file.

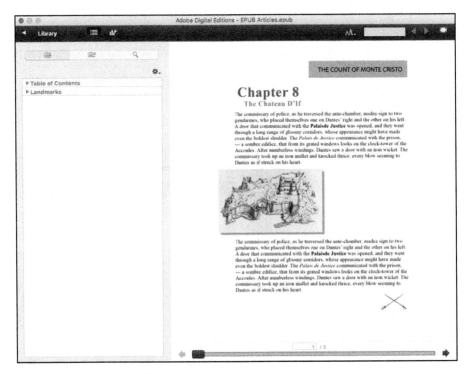

Figure 12-25. *The result of exporting to EPUB using the Same as Articles Panel on an iPad*

12.4.2   Controlling Export Options

Throughout this chapter, I made references to the EPUB – Reflowable Layout Export Options and the Object Export Options. Proper settings you make in these dialog boxes determine whether your publication meets EPUB standards and become valid documents that can be hosted on content provider sites.

It's worth a little time to look over all of the settings that you can make for document and object exports.

Using General Export Options

When you choose File ➤ Export and choose the EPUB (Reflowable) format, the EPUB – Reflowable Layout Export Options dialog box opens. You will find eight categories on the left side of the dialog box. The default is the General options, as shown in Figure 12-26.

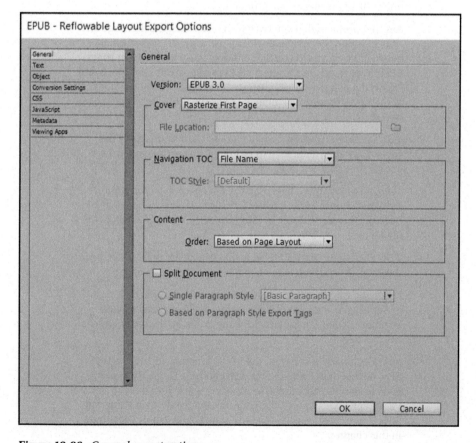

Figure 12-26. *General export options*

Adjustments that you can make in the General Panel include the following:

- *Version*: Choose either 2.01 or 3.0 for the EPUB version. One reason why you might choose version 2.01 is for some older eReaders that don't support the EPUB 3.0/3.01 format. Many of the popular eReaders have been updated to accept EPUB version 3.0, but if you find a given eReader not displaying your document properly, you might try exporting the 2.01 format.

- *Cover*: From the drop-down menu, you have three options: None, Rasterize First Page, and Choose Image. Some content providers require a separate image for the cover. If that's the case, choose None. As a matter of practice, you might add a cover to your EPUBs and rasterize the first page. If the cover image appears pixelated or degraded, use Choose Image. When rasterizing the first page, be sure to group all objects. If you have a background and a text frame over the background, the text won't show up unless all of the objects are grouped.

  Another problem that you have with rasterizing the first page for a cover is that the cover may not fill the page, or it may be split between two pages. If you find either of these problems in your EPUB export, create a single page the same size as your EPUB and export the page as a JPEG file from InDesign. Use Choose Image in the Cover drop-down menu and use the JPEG file as your cover image.

- *File Location*: Active only when you use Choose Image for the cover. Click the Folder icon to locate the image that you want to use for the cover.

- *Navigation TOC*: As a best practice, always create a Navigation TOC and choose Multi-Level (TOC Style). If you choose File Name from the menu, the Table of Contents in the eReader displays the file name.

- *TOC Style*: Choose the TOC style that you create in InDesign from the drop-down menu when using Multi-Level (TOC Style).

- *Content:* From the Order menu, choose Based on Page Layout or Same as Articles Panel. You rarely would use Same as XML Structure. If you use the Articles Panel to set up the order, choose Articles Panel.

- *Split Document*: If you want the EPUB split into separate HTML files, enable this checkbox. You can choose a Single Paragraph Style to split the document, or you can choose Based on Paragraph Style Export Tags. For more information on Paragraph Style Export Tags, see the section, "Using Style Export Tags," later in this chapter.

Using Text Export Options

Click Text in the EPUB – Reflowable Layout Export Options dialog box, and the right pane changes, as shown in Figure 12-27.

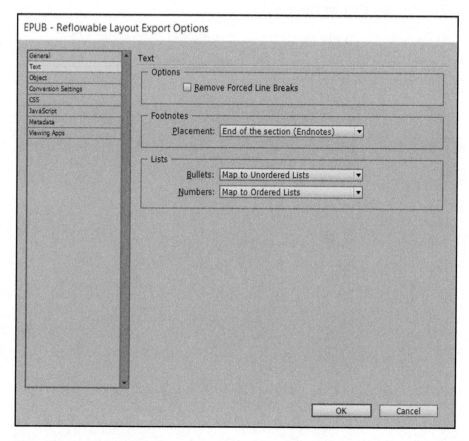

Figure 12-27. Text export options

- *Remove Forced Line Brakes*: Enable the checkbox to remove forced line brakes. Forced line breaks work in EPUBs, but they are often undesirable. When viewed on narrow screens or with large type, forced line breaks (or soft returns) can be a mess. If you don't manually remove line breaks in a document, you can have InDesign remove them for you by enabling the checkbox.

- *Footnotes*: Choose where you want footnotes to appear if you use them. You can choose to display footnotes at the end of a section, after a paragraph, or inside a pop-up (supported only in the EPUB 3.0 format).

- *Lists*: From the menus, you can choose to map bulleted and numbered lists to unordered and ordered HTML tags respectively, or you can choose to convert lists to text.

Using Object Export Options

Click Object in the left pane, and the right pane changes, as shown in Figure 12-28.

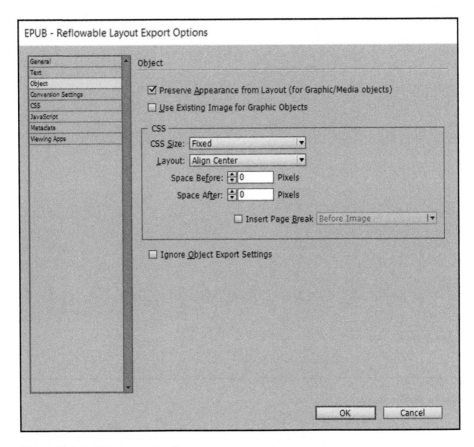

Figure 12-28. *Object export options*

- *Object*: You have two options. The first option is Preserve Appearance from Layout for Graphic/Media Objects. This is the default that you will use for most of your imported images and objects. If you resize an object, crop it, apply effects, or change it in any way, you want to enable this checkbox.

The second option is Use Existing Image for Graphic Objects. You use this option if you have the images prepared for optimization in a program like Photoshop, and the images are placed at 100%. No changes are made to the images and no effects are applied.

- *CSS Size*: In the CSS area, adjustments you make here are written to a CSS file that accompanies the HTML files when the EPUB is packaged (exported as an EPUB file). For CSS Size, you have two options. The first option is Fixed. If you choose this item from the drop-down menu, images and objects remain at a fixed size according to the relative size in your layout.

  If you choose Resize to Text Flow, images are sized as text is reflowed in a document. For example, if an image occupies 50% of the horizontal width in a text frame, as text is sized up or down in an eReader, the image is resized and remains at 50% of the size relative to the text. As a matter of practice, you should choose this option as it optimizes performance on multiple devices, such as tablets and smartphones.

- *Layout*: Choose an alignment from the drop-down menu for Left, Center, and Right. If you want space before or after images and objects, edit the Space Before and Space After text boxes.

- *Insert Page Break*: Enable this checkbox if you want a page break Before, After, or Before and After your images.

- *Ignore Object Export Settings*: Check this box if you want to ignore settings applied to individual objects in the Object Export Options dialog box.

Using Conversion Settings

Click Conversion Settings in the left pane and the right pane changes, as shown in Figure 12-29.

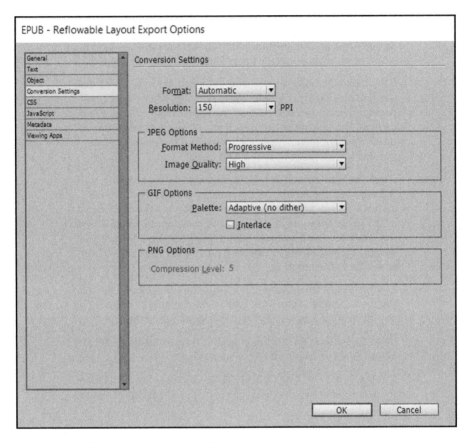

Figure 12-29. *Conversion Settings Panel*

- *Format*: Options in the drop-down menu include Automatic, JPEG, GIF, and PNG. Choose Automatic to let InDesign determine the best conversions for the file formats. If you choose another option, all images are converted to the selected format.

- *Resolution*: Choices from the drop-down menu include 72, 96, 150, and 300 ppi. Inasmuch as newer screen technologies like Apple's retina devices support higher resolutions, the best trade-off that you can make between quality and file size for image resolution is 150ppi. Use this setting as your default.

- *Image Quality:* Options are available for JPEG and GIF when you use the Automatic method for the conversions. Choose High for the JPEG Image quality and leave the Format Method at Progressive. For GIF images, choose Adaptive (no dither). The only time you might include GIF images is when you have images with large areas of a given color or limited numbers of colors in the image. Don't save files as GIF if they are continuous tone images (such as photographs).

Using CSS Options

You can add CSS style sheets and custom CSS code in the CSS panel.

Using JavaScript Options

JavaScripts can only be added to EPUB exports in the 3.0 format. You need to choose EPUB 3.0 in the General Panel, and the JavaScript options are accessible. JavaScript code is written in a text editor (do not use Microsoft Word for writing scripts). You save the JavaScript file as text with a `.js` extension. InDesign won't recognize a text file without the `.js` extension. You click the Add JavaScript File button, and the file is listed in the JavaScript Panel.

Using Metadata Options

Click Metadata in the left pane and the right pane changes, providing you with several text boxes for adding metadata. Many online content hosts require you to add metadata to your EPUBs. Be sure to complete the data fields in this dialog box before finalizing your EPUB.

Using Viewing Apps Options

Click Viewing Apps in the left pane and the right pane changes, providing you with options for adding a viewing app to preview your exported file and choosing the viewer that you want. Click the Add Application button and locate a viewer on your hard drive. Select the new viewer and enable the checkbox adjacent to the viewer name. When you export to EPUB, the document opens in the selected viewer application.

12.5   Using Style Export Tags

When you export to EPUB, InDesign creates CSS files from the character and paragraph styles used in your document. You don't need to know anything about writing code for HTML and CSS. InDesign handles all the work for you.

InDesign does a great job of creating HTML and CSS files, but it falls a little short when mapping styles to HTML tags. If you know something about writing HTML code, you might want to map styles to different HTML tags. The reason why you want to map styles to tags is because the world of EPUBs and eReaders is a moving target. New apps are being introduced frequently, and as developers take advantage of the EPUB 3.0 format they may require some compliance with HTML5 and CSS3 standards.

To map paragraph styles to tags, you use the Paragraph Style Options. Create a new paragraph style or edit an existing paragraph style and click Export Tagging in the left pane. Let's say that you have a document with chapters using a paragraph style for chapters, subheads using another paragraph style, and a level 2 subhead assigned another style. In the Export Tagging options, you might tag the chapter heads with an HTML h1 tag, the subheads with an h2 tag, and the level 2 subheads with an h3 tag. In the Export Tagging options in the Paragraph Style Options dialog box, you choose the heading tags from the Tag drop-down menu, as shown in Figure 12-30.

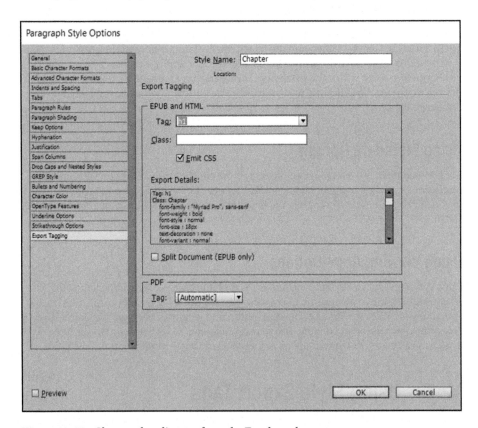

Figure 12-30. Choose a heading tag from the Tag drop-down menu

Notice that the Tag drop-down menu is very limited. If you have other tags, such as an ordered list (ol), a table row (tr), block quote (blockquote), and so forth, you can type in the Tag text box where you see Automatic appear by default.

To edit multiple tags in your document, you can use the Edit All Export Tags dialog box. Open either the Character Styles Panel menu or the Paragraph Styles Panel menu and choose Edit All Export Tags. The Edit All Export Tags dialog box opens.

The tag column in the Edit All Export Tags dialog box is editable. Click on Automatic or on a tag in the column, and a drop-down menu opens, as shown in Figure 12-31. You can also edit the items in the Tag column by clicking to select the text box and typing a new tag name.

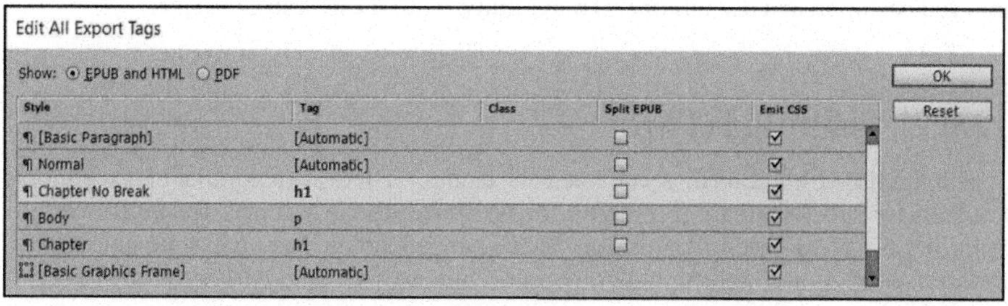

Edit All Export Tags					
Show: ⊙ EPUB and HTML ○ PDF					OK
Style	Tag	Class	Split EPUB	Emit CSS	Reset
¶ [Basic Paragraph]	[Automatic]		☐	☑	
¶ Normal	[Automatic]		☐	☑	
¶ Chapter No Break	h1		☐	☑	
¶ Body	p		☐	☑	
¶ Chapter	h1		☐	☑	
☐ [Basic Graphics Frame]	[Automatic]			☑	

Figure 12-31. *Open the Character or Paragraph Styles Panel menu and choose Edit All Export Tags to open the Edit All Export Tags dialog box*

12.6   Editing the Contents of an EPUB

As I've said many times, EPUB files are nothing more than an HTML file or multiple HTML files along with CSS files, all packaged together in a zipped archive. You can open the contents of the .zip archive, edit the HTML and CSS, and repackage the files back to a .zip archive.

12.6.1   Decompressing Zipped Archives

When you create an EPUB file, the file extension is .epub. You can change the extension to .zip and unzip the archive using a number of tools. On Windows, be certain that you can see the file extension. If you just add a .zip extension to a file name, it won't be converted to a .zip file. First open the File Explorer (Windows 10), select a file, and click the View tab in the ribbon. Enable the File Name Extensions checkbox (right side) of the ribbon.

When you see your EPUBs with an .epub extension, rename the extension to .zip. Then right-click the file and choose Extract All from the context menu.

On the Macintosh, rename the .epub files to the file name plus .zip for the extension. MacOS will unzip any .zip file by just double-clicking on the .zip file. You can download an AppleScript called ePub_Zip_Unzip from https://code.google.com/p/ epub-applescripts/downloads/detail?name=ePub%20Zip%20Unzip%202.0.1.app. zip&can=2&q=. You can also use StuffIt Expander to unzip files on the Mac if you have it installed. Or you can just search the Internet for ePub Zip, click on the ePub_Zip_Unzip link, and you arrive at the download page.

The best utility for both Windows and the Macintosh is *eCanCrusher*. You can download the free application from http://www.docdataflow.com. Drag an EPUB file to eCanCrusher, and the file expands showing you a folder with the same name as your EPUB. Inside the folder are two folders and a single file. After editing the HTML and/or CSS files, drag the root folder on top of eCanCrusher to convert back to EPUB. You don't need to worry about changing file extensions when using this utility.

All of the files that you need to edit are contained in the OEBPS folder. Open that folder, and you see a list of XHTML files and a CSS folder with CSS files. These are the two items that you can open in a text editor and make edits to the HTML and CSS code.

12.6.2 Editing HTML

To edit the HTML and CSS files, you need a text editor. There are a number of text editors available for free download. You can use *TextWrangler* on the Mac and *NotePad++* on Windows as well as *Dreamweaver*. You can also download the free open source program *Brackets*, which is available for both Mac and Windows. Download *Brackets* from http://brackets.io.

In Figure 12-32, you see the code shown in Brackets on Windows. To edit the HTML or a CSS file, you need to have some knowledge of HTML coding. You can begin by making some minor changes in the code, but be careful and be certain that you know how to make changes.

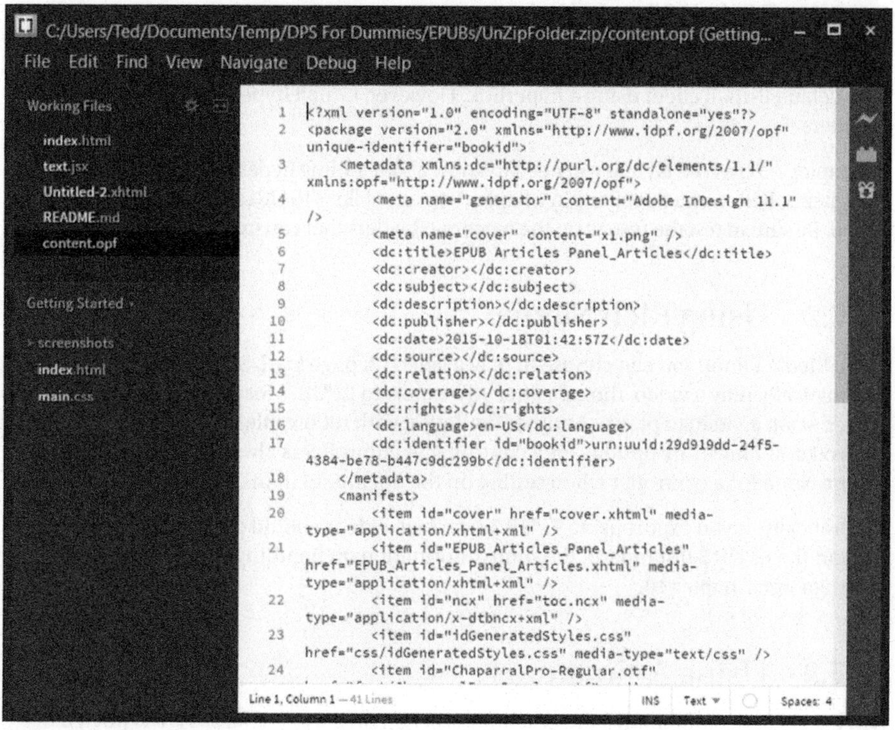

Figure 12-32. HTML code viewed in Brackets

Offering instructions on HTML coding is beyond the scope of this book. Just be aware of the fact that you can access the code, make changes, and convert back to an EPUB.

After making edits in the HTML code, compress the root folder of the extracted EPUB using eCanCrusher, WinZip, Stuffit Zip, or other utility that you use for compressing files. After the folder compresses, change the file extension name from .zip to .epub, and you're good to go. If you use eCanCrusher, you don't need to change the file extension.

12.7   Using Interactivity in Reflowable EPUBs

Adding interactive elements in reflowable EPUBs is quite limited and rightfully so. Reflowable EPUBs are typically long text documents such as novels, reports, essays, and so forth. This doesn't mean that some kinds of interactivity can't offer people consuming the content a little more appeal.

You can't use buttons and multi-state objects in reflowable EPUBs. You're limited to hyperlinks and rich media. You might want to show a video on the opening page in an EPUB, add some narration, or add some links to other resources.

12.7.1 Using Hyperlinks

You can link to a URL and a destination in your EPUBs. In some eReaders, you can open your default e-mail client using a hyperlink. However, e-mail hyperlinks don't work in all eReaders.

In Chapter 7, I covered all that you need to know about adding hyperlinks in InDesign documents. Follow the directions in Chapter 7 to create links to URLs, text anchors, and e-mail. Be sure to test the results on the types of eReaders that you expect your viewers to use.

12.7.2 Using Rich Media

In the Media Panel, you can choose to play a video on page load. Some eReaders won't automatically play a video, though, after you export to EPUB. Most eReaders require the viewer to tap a video to play it. Another limitation with reflowable EPUBs and video is that you don't have any options for a controller. A controller is always present even if you choose None for a controller when setting up the document in InDesign.

Theoretically, if you export using EPUB 3.0 format, videos should play in all eReaders that support the EPUB 3.0 standard. For more information on handling audio and video in InDesign, see Chapter 10.

12.7.3 Using Animations

When you create animations, the animations are created as SWF files. SWF is not a file format that you want to use for EPUBs, especially since SWF is not supported on Apple iOS devices.

However, you can get animations to play in EPUBs using a workaround. In Figure 12-33, you see a layout in InDesign previewed in the EPUB Interactivity Preview Panel. The table contains animations. The black bars on top of the graph move up revealing the columns. Also notice that the graph has a watermark. I'll address that a little later.

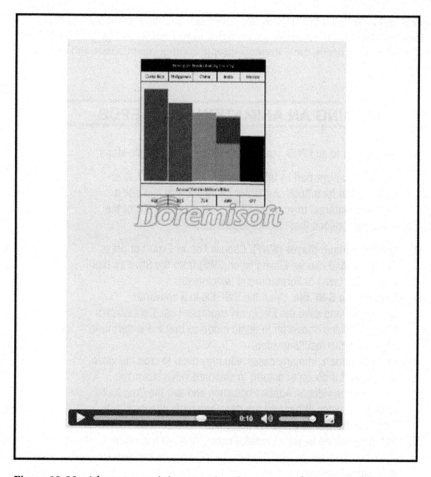

Figure 12-33. *A layout containing an animation converted to a movie file*

The way that you add animations to a reflowable EPUB is by converting the SWF file to a video file. Buttons and multi-state objects won't work, but InDesign animations can be used.

Converting SWF to a Video Format

To convert SWF to video files you have two options. You can use a video converter or you can use a screen recorder to capture video. There are a number of different SWF to Video converters available, and they all cost you money for the applications. Be aware though that very few actually convert SWF to Video, even though the developers claim that they do.

I've searched for SWF to Video converters for some time, and the one I found to be the most reliable is Doremisoft's *SWF to Video Converter* (Windows) and *Mac SWF Video Converter* (Macintosh). You can download the software from www.doremisoft.net. The cost of the converter as of this writing is $99 US. You can download the software and run it in demo mode. The resulting video file contains a watermark, as you can see in Figure 12-33. If the application serves your needs, the watermark disappears after you purchase and register the product.

ADDING AN ANIMATION TO AN EPUB

To add an animation to an EPUB, you need to follow a few simple steps.

1. **Create an animation in InDesign on a blank page.** A lead-in animation for a book or chapter can work well and add a little more interest to your publication. You can use any of the animation options that I discussed in Chapter 8.

2. **Export to Flash player (SWF).** Choose File ➤ Export or press Ctrl/⌘+E, and choose Flash Player (SWF) from the Save as Type menu (Windows) or Format menu (Macintosh).

3. **Convert the SWF file.** Open the SWF file in a converter application and save the file. In my example, I use Doremisoft's Mac SWF Video Converter in demo mode so that the watermark appears in the resulting video.

4. **Crop the video.** In many cases, you may need to crop the video, especially if it doesn't conform to standard video sizes. You can open the video in Adobe Photoshop and use the Crop tool to crop the video. When you are done cropping, choose File ➤ Export ➤ Render to Video in Photoshop.

5. **Place the video in your layout.** Press Ctrl/⌘+D and place the video in InDesign. See Chapter 10 for more information on working with video.

6. **Export to EPUB (reflowable).** Follow the same procedure discussed many times in this chapter for exporting to video.

7. **Preview the EPUB file.** Open the file in an eReader and tap the video to play it. In Figure 12-34, you see an animation in the middle of the play in Adobe Digital Editions. The bars move horizontally left to right.

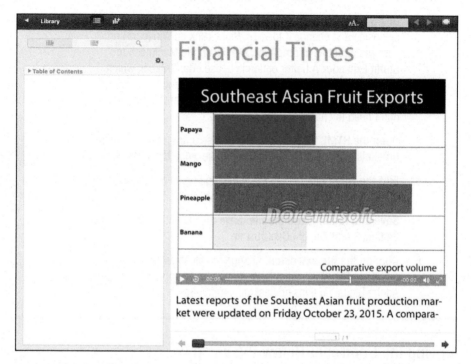

Figure 12-34. *An animation converted to video playing in Adobe Digital Editions*

Autoplaying Videos

You can set up the animation to autoplay, but it only works on desktop eReaders. Autoplaying videos won't work on device eReaders. To set up autoplay for Apple iBooks and Adobe Digital Editions on desktop computers, you need to edit the HTML file containing the video tag.

```
AUTOPLAYING A VIDEO
```

To make the edits for autoplaying on desktop eReaders:

1. **Unzip the EPUB document.** Select the file with the `.epub` extension and change it to `.zip`. Right-click on Windows and choose Extract All or drag the `.zip` file on the Macintosh to Stuffit Expander. A better option is to use eCanCrusher, which you can find as a free download for Windows and Macintosh from `http://www.docdataflow.com`. With eCanCrusher, you don't need to change the file extension.

2. **Open the HTML file in a text editor.** Use a program like Adobe Brackets and open the file containing the video tag in Brackets.

3. **Edit the video tag.** Locate the video tag beginning with `<video id =...` and insert `autoplay = "autoplay"`.

4. **Save and recompress the file.** Save the file and zip it up using WinZip, Stuffit Zip, or eCanCrusher.

5. **Change the file extension.** Change the file extension from `.zip` to `.epub`. The EPUB video file will autoplay in Apple iBooks and Adobe Digital Editions on desktop computers.

Moving the Controller Below the Video

If you look at the Media Panel in InDesign and open the Controller menu, you see a number of controller skins from which you can choose. All of the controllers position the controller over the media. When the controller is visible, it obscures the content in the video. It's not a major problem since the controller automatically hides after a few seconds. However, it can be a little annoying, and you may want to move the controller below the video for some videos playing animations. You can do this for EPUBs shown on computers only. This workaround is not supported on device eReaders.

```
MOVING THE CONTROLLER BELOW THE VIDEO
```

To move the controller below a video on a desktop eReader, do the following:

1. **Decompress the EPUB.** Use WinZip, Stuffit Zip, or eCanCrusher to unzip the EPUB archive.

2. **Open the OEBPS folder and the CSS folder inside the OEBPS folder.**

3. **Open the CSS file.** If you have several CSS files, you need to do a little search for the `idContainer` class.

4. **Edit the CSS file.** You should see an `idContainer` section followed by a `div`. The height of the image should be the same for each item. Locate the height in the `div` and change the value larger than the default value (see Figure 12-35). You may need to test it a few times to be certain that the controller is just below the animation.

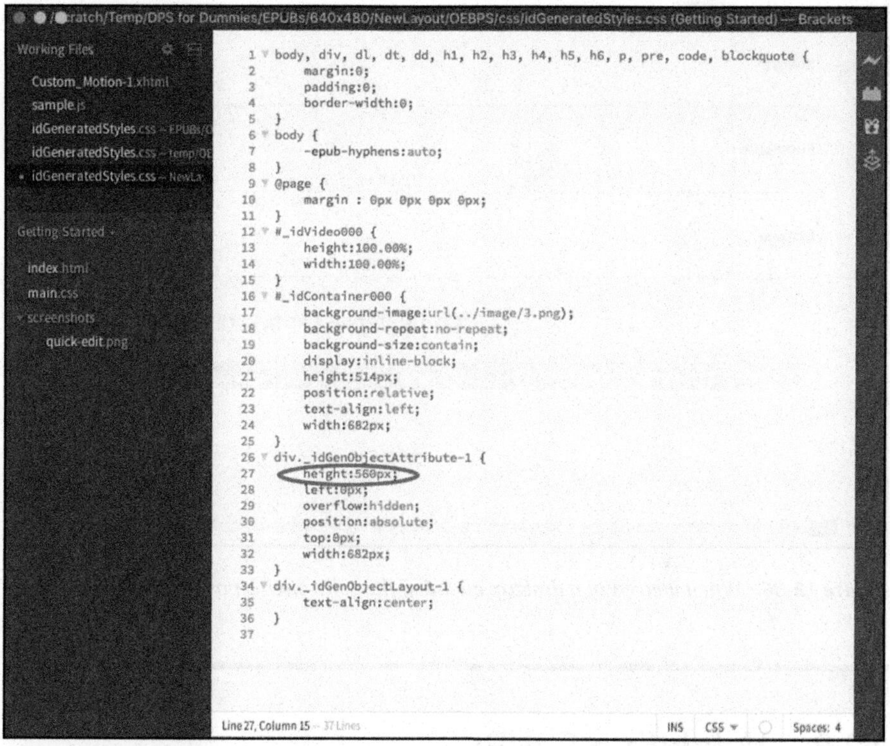

Figure 12-35. *Edit the height value in the div tag*

5. **Save and recompress.** Save the file and use WinZip, Stuffit, or eCanCrusher to convert back to EPUB format.

6. **Open the file in a desktop eReader.** The controller is moved below the video, as you can see in Figure 12-36.

Figure 12-36. *When viewed in a desktop eReader, the controller is positioned below the video*

12.8 Validating EPUBs

If you expand a zipped EPUB, make some edits, and recompress back to EPUB, you definitely need to validate the EPUB with an EPUB checker. As a best practice, you should validate all of your EPUBs before hosting them online.

You can download some free EPUB checkers, which you can run locally on your computer, and you can also find online services where you upload an EPUB and use the online checker.

You can find an EPUB checker app at www.pagina-online.de. This site is based in Germany, and the web pages are in German. Scroll down the page to find the English version if you're an English speaker. You can download versions for Windows and Macintosh. You can also find a nice EPUB checker at https://github.com/IDPF/ epubcheck/releases. When you download either of the EPUB checkers, they're command-driven utilities.

If you're not comfortable using the Run command on a Windows or Mac terminal, you can use an EPUB checker as an online service. Log on to www.validator.idpf.org and upload a file to the EPUB Validator web page. After the upload finishes, you see a report of any problems found in your EPUB, or you may find validation with no reported problems.

■ **Note**   The www.idpf.org (International Digital Publishing Forum) web site is a great source of information for EPUB authors and enthusiasts. There you'll find articles, news, announcements, EPUB standards, and more. Periodically review postings on this site to learn more about EPUB publishing.

There are other commercial applications and online services for validating EPUBs that you can find. Just do a Google search for EPUB validators.

12.9   Viewing EPUBs on Devices

In Chapter 11, I talked about uploading files from your computer to devices. In most cases, the best method I've found is using Dropbox. If you have a USB connection from your computer to an Android device, you can copy publications to devices, but in most cases Dropbox works best. When you use Dropbox, you can choose the type of viewer that you want to open your publication.

There are a number of different viewers available for opening EPUBs. When you host a publication with a content provider, you want to make your publications accessible to as many eReaders as possible. Therefore, you should plan on opening EPUBs on a variety of devices.

12.9.1   Using Apple iBooks

Files copied to Dropbox are aliases and aren't downloaded to a device until you view the publication. On an iPad or iPhone, open Dropbox and tap a document in the files list. The file displayed in your Dropbox list is then downloaded to your device. Tap the Share button at the top of the screen, as shown in Figure 12-37.

Figure 12-37. Tap the AirDrop Share button

Below the first line of icons, you will find the Open In button. Tap this button, and the screen displays the applications that can display your publication, as shown in Figure 12-38. Tap the Copy to iBooks button, and the publication opens in Apple iBooks.

Figure 12-38. Tap Copy to iBooks to view the publication in iBooks

12.9.2   Working with Kindle KF8 Format

The lion's share of the eBook market is hosted by Amazon.com. If you want to sell eBooks, you can't overlook Amazon. Earlier Kindle eReaders used the Amazon proprietary MOBI format. Today Kindle devices use what Amazon calls the KF8 format. One thing that's a bit confusing is that when you export a file for Kindle, the file extension still appears as .mobi. Don't worry though, if you use updated Kindle tools for creating an EPUB that can be read on Kindle viewers, the files are created in KF8 format.

To convert an EPUB to KF8 (MOBI), download and install the Kindle Previewer. You can download the Kindle Previewer from http://www.amazon.com/gp/feature.html?docId=1000765261 or Google search for Kindle Previewer.

You also need to download KindleGen from http://www.amazon.com/gp/feature.html?docId=1000765211 or Google search for KindleGen and follow the links to the download page. When you open a file in Kindle Previewer, the file is converted by KindleGen and saved with a .mobi extension, but it is converted to KF8 if you use a recent version the Kindle Previewer.

After installing Kindle Previewer, launch the application and you arrive at a welcome screen. The welcome screen has a number of links to help documents hosted by Amazon, as you can see in the Help section. Click the Open Book button to open an EPUB in the Previewer. The list of files supported include MOBI, EPUB, HTML, and OFP. The reason that you see MOBI as a supported format is that you can convert older .mobi files to the new KF8 format.

As of this writing, the Kindle Previewer is in beta for the Kindle Previewer 3 application. Kindle Previewer 3 does a great job in converting EPUBs to KF8 format. In Figure 12-39, you see a preview of an EPUB and the Preferences dialog box for the Kindle Previewer 3 application.

Figure 12-39. *An EPUB converted using the Kindle Previewer 3*

Right-click the file on your desktop and choose Open With from the context menu. If the Kindle eReader is installed on your computer, the Kindle app is shown as the default viewer.

To send an eBook to a device and view it on a Kindle eReader or a Kindle viewer app on a device, use the Send to Kindle application, which you can download from Amazon.com at http://www.amazon.com/gp/sendtokindle/pc. Launch the Send to Kindle app and drag and drop an EPUB file to the screen.

12.9.3 Using Dedicated EPUB Readers

There are a number of software applications and dedicated eReaders available. Most often you can download desktop versions for various eReaders and apps. Kobo readers are popular in Canada and Europe. You can download a Kobo viewer for your desktop computer from https://store.kobobooks.com.

Various device eReader apps are available for download. You can acquire Stanza or Calibre as eReaders for desktop and device eReaders and a host of other applications. You might download a few to test your EPUBs and verify that they work properly in several eReaders.

The world of eReaders and digital publishing is continually changing. Search the Internet regularly for trends, popular applications, and developments in the EPUB format.

12.10   Marketing EPUBs

If you want to sell EPUBs, you need an online host. The most popular hosts are Amazon for Kindle eReaders and Apple for iOS devices. For the widest range of potential buyers for your EPUBs, you need to consider both content hosts.

Before you do anything, even create an EPUB, you need to review the provider's requirements thoroughly for the books that they sell. You need to know what can and what cannot be included in your EPUBs, certain formatting rules, and a long list of other requirements.

12.10.1   Distributing via Amazon

Major content providers like Amazon and Apple require you to follow standards specified in their publishing guidelines. For Amazon, you can find publishing guidelines and help information at www.kdp.amazon.com.

You must create an account with Amazon. If you have an account you use for purchasing items, you can use the same account logon and password. If you don't have an account, you need to sign up for a new account. If you want to keep an existing account separate from an account used for publishing, you can create a second account.

Unfortunately, there's no link from the KDP web pages to KF8 web pages. In order to review guidelines and help information regarding the KF8 format, navigate to http://www.amazon.com/gp/feature.html?docId=1000729511, or simply type KF8 in a Google search window. The first link that you see in Google is a link to the KF8 Format page, as shown in Figure 12-40.

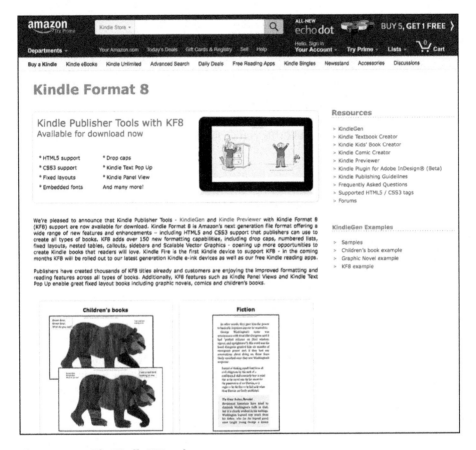

Figure 12-40. *The Kindle KF8 web page*

Along the right side of the web page, you find links to a number of help pages. Among those is a link to Kindle Publishing Guidelines. When you click the link, a PDF document opens. The document has 91 pages and is full of information regarding Amazon's standards and requirements for making books available to Kindle devices. Be sure to review the document thoroughly before you create an EPUB for distribution on Amazon.com.

Notice on the KF8 web page that you see a link to an Adobe InDesign plugin. Don't bother downloading the plugin. It's been in beta forever, and it only supports InDesign up to CS6. InDesign CC is not supported.

To distribute books through Amazon, you need to review the steps outlined in the Kindle Direct Publishing web pages. Type Kindle Direct Publishing in your web browser to search for the link to the Amazon web page. The first hit you see is a link to where Amazon details information about uploading eBooks for publishing on Amazon.com.

12.10.2 Distributing via Apple iTunes

Apple also has publishing guidelines that you need to follow to host books in the Apple iTunes store. Again you need to sign up for an account with Apple at http://developer. apple.com. Creating an account is free, and you first need to create the account before you can proceed to find information about publishing with iTunes.

After creating an account, log on to www.itunesconnect.apple.com. Click the Resources and Help button on the iTunes Connect web page and you will find guides and help information. Click the iBooks Store Formatting Guidelines and the iBooks Publisher User Guide links. Review these documents thoroughly before creating EPUBs that you intend to distribute via Apple iTunes. On Apple's web site, you will find all of the information that you need for formatting publications and uploading to Apple.

When you first log on to Apple's iTunes Connect web page, in addition to the Resources and Help button, you will also find buttons for My Books and Sales and Trends. Apple makes it easy for you to track your publication's sales on the Sales and Trends web page, as shown in Figure 12-41, where you see a list of your publications on the My Books web page.

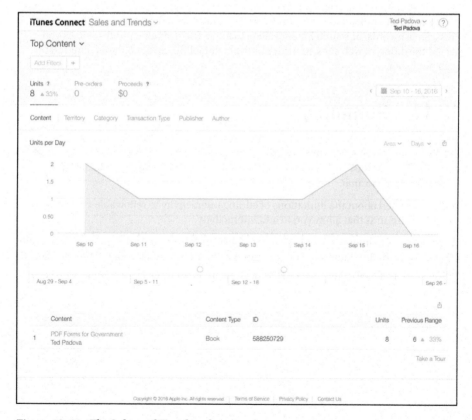

Figure 12-41. *The Sales and Trends web page*

Under each book title, you see drop-down menus for the number of stores carrying your books according to country and the number of stores not carrying your books according to country. A book I have posted on Apple shows 51 stores carrying the book and 1 store not carrying the book. When I click on the Not in 1 Store button, the drop-down menu shows that the book is not available in China.

After you post a book on Apple iTunes, be certain to visit the iTunes Connect web site regularly. You can check the progress of your sales and the number of stores by country carrying the book.

12.10.3   Using Other eResellers

You may want to distribute your books to other sources beyond Amazon and Apple. Once you create a valid EPUB, most of your work is done. Some differences among eResellers might be whether or not to include a cover as a separate file, add a preface and/or acknowledgement page, acquire an ISBN number or whether the host acquires the ISBN number, whether or not paragraph styles need HTML tags, and so on.

Each eReseller has help pages on their web sites for what you need to do to prepare your work and how to upload the content. To explore other eResellers, search for Kobo, Nook Press, Smashwords, or search for eResellers to find a list of smaller publishers. As you peruse the different web sites, look for publisher guidelines and standards required by each publisher.

12.11   Summary

This chapter was all about reflowable EPUBs. You learned how to create reflowable EPUBs, some best practices for properly creating EPUBs, how to open an EPUB archive and view the contents, and various considerations when exporting from InDesign to reflowable EPUB format.

You also learned about the limitations of adding interactivity to reflowable EPUBs and some workarounds that allow you to add interactivity.

When it comes to interactive EPUBs, reflowable EPUBs are very limiting. The chains come off when you add interactivity to documents and export to fixed layout EPUBs. In the next chapter, you learn about all of the benefits for creating fixed layout EPUBs.

■ ■ ■

CHAPTER 13

Creating Fixed Layout EPUBs

In Chapter 12, I talked about reflowable EPUBs. If you read the chapter, you certainly are aware that creating reflowable EPUBs requires a lot of work. You need to export to EPUB continually, review the results, and invariably return to InDesign to make corrections and modifications in the publication. Then you must export again and review the results. What you see on the computer screen, in terms of the layout and design, is often not what you see in an eReader.

Fixed layout EPUBs are quite different. A fixed layout EPUB is very similar to a PDF file exported from InDesign. The layout and construction is typically preserved in the final export, and all of the interactivity you add to a document is supported in fixed layout EPUBs.

Reflowable EPUBs have been around since InDesign CS 4. Fixed layout EPUBs are relatively new. They were introduced as an export option in InDesign CS 6. As a newer file format, you'll find some limitations with eReaders and the tools that support viewing the content on devices. The market is growing; however, and what I talk about in regard to viewing fixed layout EPUBs on devices is likely to change as developers scurry around and offer more support for the format.

13.1 Understanding Reflowable versus Fixed Layout EPUBs

When it comes to creating documents that you export to fixed layout EPUBs, you will find many advantages and some disadvantages over working with reflowable EPUBs. Advantages of fixed layout EPUBs include the following:

- *Easy to create*: Just about all of the design aspects for creating a document in InDesign can easily be exported intact to a fixed layout EPUB. You don't need to anchor objects; you can place text over images, add transparency, format text and graphics as you want them to appear in the final layout, and about 99.9 percent of the time InDesign exports to a valid fixed layout EPUB.

© Ted Padova 2017
T. Padova, *Adobe InDesign Interactive Digital Publishing*,
DOI 10.1007/978-1-4842-2439-7_13

- *Maintains design integrity*: The WYSIWIG view that you see on-screen is captured in the fixed layout EPUB. Text wraps, drop caps, nested styles, and so forth all appear exactly as you would see them in exported PDF documents.

- *Open standard*: Whereas PDFs are based on PostScript and the code is not editable, a fixed layout EPUB is an open standard, and the underlying code is completely accessible just like it is with reflowable EPUBs.

- *Interactivity support*: All of the interactivity that you add to an InDesign document, including hyperlinks and cross references, bookmarks, multi-state objects, animations, buttons and events, audio, and video are supported in fixed layout EPUBs.

- *Creative freedom*: You find the same creative freedom for fixed layout EPUBs as you do with files for print and export to PDF. Design your documents at will, and you don't need to struggle with tools to get the final result to appear as you like in the eReader.

Of course with every advantage you gain by choosing one format over another, you're likely to find some disadvantages. A single format can't capture all of the attributes of its counterpart. Disadvantages that you will find with fixed layout EPUBs include the following:

- *No reflow to fit small devices*: Pages sizes can conform to small devices like smartphones, but the text remains proportional to the page size and won't size up or down like you find with reflowable EPUBs.

- *Fewer devices support viewing fixed layout EPUBs*: With reflowable EPUBs, you have a number of eReaders that can be installed on tablets and mobile phones for viewing EPUBs. However, for fixed layout EPUBs, the number of applications supporting them is much more limited. (For a list of supported devices, see the section, "Viewing EPUBs on Devices," in Chapter 12.)

- *Fonts must be embedded*: In a way, you might think that this is an advantage. However, embedding fonts in a document that you intend to distribute requires you to do some research as to whether you can legally embed fonts. You must conform to the licensing agreements of font foundries and thoroughly investigate your right to include a font in a document. With reflowable EPUBs, you have a choice as to whether or not to embed fonts. Fixed layout EPUBs don't offer a choice, and InDesign automatically embeds fonts. (For more on embedding fonts and licensing them, see the section, "Working with Fonts," later in this chapter).

- *Creating accessible layouts is more challenging*: If you want to create accessible fixed layout EPUBs, you need to do much more work than when creating reflowable EPUBs. Alt tags in images won't work in fixed layout EPUBs. You need to edit the CSS and modify designs to include captions for images and objects for screen readers that aren't CSS-aware.

- *Not completely supported by Kindle*: As of this writing, you can convert fixed layout EPUBs to Kindle KF8/MOBI formats, but you won't get all of the interactivity supported by other eReaders. Amazon is continually updating their KF8/MOBI format, so you may eventually see this change for more interactive support with Kindle devices.

13.1.1   Examining the Anatomy of Fixed Layout EPUBs

As I mentioned in Chapter 12, you can convert an `.epub` file to a `.zip` file and unzip the contents to gain access to the HTML. You can do the same for fixed layout EPUBs. In a reflowable EPUB, you may have one or several HTML files and the files are based on articles in the InDesign document. With fixed layout EPUBs, every page is an HTML file. In Figure 13-1, you see the HTML files from a reflowable EPUB on the left and the HTML files for a fixed layout EPUB on the right.

Figure 13-1. *HTML files in the OEBPS folder for a reflowable EPUB (left) and a fixed layout EPUB (right)*

When you examine the HTML in one of the fixed layout files, you see an extraordinary number of tags for the text. Each word in the HTML is tagged with a separate class and an absolute position, as shown in Figure 13-2.

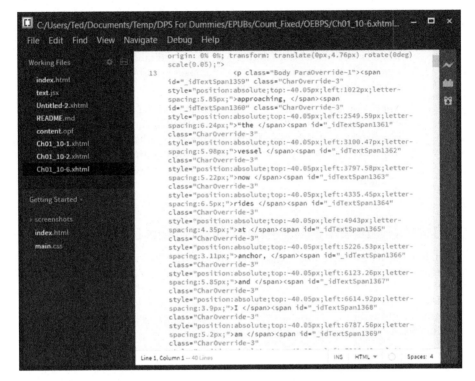

Figure 13-2. *Each word in a fixed layout EPUB is tagged with a separate class and an absolute position*

As you look over the HTML in a fixed layout EPUB, you'll notice that it's virtually impossible to write code for text in the document. You can make edits to the HTML, but InDesign is near perfect at exporting to fixed layout and you don't need to worry about making any edits in the HTML.

13.1.2   Designing for Genre-Specific Books

When you are planning on which format to use for a book, you might consider the recommendations listed in Table 13-1. The table lists books that might benefit from fixed layout EPUBs and those that might benefit from creating reflowable EPUBs. In many cases, PDF files work well. If you choose an EPUB format, however, you might consider the format that works best for the type of document you deploy.

Table 13-1. *Fixed Layout versus Reflowable EPUBs*

Fixed Layout EPUBs	Reflowable EPUBs
Brochures	Essays
Children's Books	Novels
Comic Books	Poetry Books
Cookbooks	Professional Journals/Articles
Graphic Novels	Reference Books
Photo Essays	Trade Books
Travel Guides	User Manuals
Tutorials	White Papers
Text Books	

Table 13-1 is simply a basic guideline for the kinds of books that may lend themselves to using one EPUB format over another. You may find some book genres to overlap, such as textbooks without graphics for reflowable EPUBs, user manuals that may include animations for fixed layout, and poetry books with graphics and narrations more suited for fixed layout EPUBs. Generally speaking, if you have a lot of images and/or graphics and interactivity in a document, you probably want to create fixed layout EPUBs. If you have text-heavy documents with a light treatment of graphics and no interactivity, then reflowable EPUBs generally work best.

13.2   Formatting Graphics

Raster images such as Photoshop files need to conform to specifications consistent with device readers. As is the case with reflowable EPUBs, you should check the content host's web sites for guidelines, especially when using photos in your EPUBs.

13.2.1   Prepping Images

Images should be saved in only one of two formats: JPEG and PNG. As a matter of rule, use JPEG over PNG unless you have any transparency. PNG files take longer to render on device eReaders than JPEG files.

The other consideration that you have with images is the file resolution. Content providers such as Apple require you to keep images at less than 2M pixels. Therefore, when you open a file in Photoshop, view the rulers and change the unit of measure to pixels (or points). Alternatively, you can choose Image ➤ Image Size and examine the file size. You can also examine the document size in the Photoshop status bar. If you multiply the horizontal and vertical values shown on the Photoshop rulers, you get the total number of pixels in the photo. If the number is over two million pixels, you need to downsample or change the physical size of the photo. In Figure 13-3, you can see the visible rulers in an open Photoshop document, and when you multiply the horizontal and vertical values, the image exceeds two million pixels. Also note that the document size reports the horizontal and vertical pixel amounts. The total number of pixels is also reported in the Image Size (Image ➤ Image Size) dialog box.

Figure 13-3. *Multiply the horizontal and vertical values to determine the total image resolution*

When using cover images and rasterizing the first page in a document for the cover, you want to choose 150ppi as a default option. 150ppi is the best trade-off for retaining visual quality and keeping the file size low. (For more information on rasterizing cover images, see the section "Exporting to Fixed Layout EPUB Format" later in this chapter).

> ■ **Note** Unless you use any other program for creating EPUBs, InDesign takes care of file conversions and downsampling for you, depending on the file format to which you export.

13.2.2 Applying Object Styles

In Chapter 12, I talked about creating styles for everything in your document. We looked at creating object styles when adding effects, transparency, and drop shadows. Fixed layout EPUBs are much more forgiving than reflowable EPUBs when it comes to adding styles. You can get away with applying effects, transparency, and drop shadows without creating object styles.

Styles make sense when you're in a design mode. If you need to edit text and object attributes, or you have many pages of text and many images, it's always a good idea to create styles. However, styles are not necessary for rendering a fixed layout EPUB.

13.2.3 Working with Transparency

When creating reflowable EPUBs, you may recall that you cannot add live text over images and you cannot add a frame with transparency over an image unless you rasterize all of the components and create a single graphic. Once you rasterize the text, it can no longer be searched and it is not live text.

With fixed layout EPUBs, you can add text over an image and you can add transparency to a frame appearing over an image. You needn't worry about anchoring objects, because the layout you see in InDesign is honored in the fixed layout EPUB. As you can see in Figure 13-4, a frame with transparency and text appears over an image and the text is live.

Figure 13-4. *You can add text and transparent objects over images and the text remains live in the fixed layout EPUB*

13.3 Working with Interactivity

All of the features I talked about in Part III work beautifully in fixed layout EPUBs. Since this book is about interactive digital publishing, we want to harness all that InDesign provides us by adding interactive elements in our publications. As you know from Chapter 12, adding interactivity in reflowable EPUBs is limited, and sometimes you need a workaround to add some interactivity to your EPUBs. With fixed layout EPUBs, you can use all of the InDesign features for creating interactivity and you don't need any workarounds.

13.3.1 Creating Bookmarks

Adding bookmarks to a document can help you when creating a table of contents. With reflowable EPUBs, which I talked about in Chapter 12, you use paragraph styles when having InDesign generate a navigational TOC. In a fixed layout EPUB, you may not have chapter heads or even text on certain pages, but you want the pages to be part of the TOC. When you generate a table of contents, you can use bookmarks for the source, as I explain later in the section, "Creating a Navigational Table of Contents."

ADDING BOOKMARKS TO YOUR DOCUMENT

To add bookmarks to your document, do the following:

1. **Open the Bookmarks Panel**. Choose Window ➤ Interactive ➤ Bookmarks. The Bookmarks Panel opens, as shown in Figure 13-5.

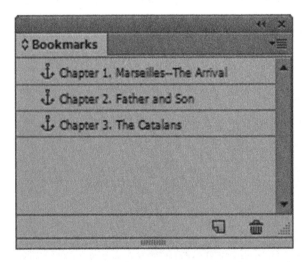

Figure 13-5. The Bookmarks Panel populated with bookmarks

2. **Navigate to the page where you want to add a bookmark.**
   You need to create all of the bookmarks in your document manually.

3. **Create a new bookmark.** Click the Create new bookmark icon at the bottom of the panel or open the Bookmarks Panel menu and choose New Bookmark. The bookmark appears in the panel as *Bookmark 1* for the first bookmark. The text is highlighted so that you can type a descriptive name for the bookmark.

4. **Continue navigating through the document and adding bookmarks.**
   Scroll through your document and add a bookmark for each page that you want to appear in your table of contents.

Later in this chapter, in the section, "Creating a Navigational Table of Contents," we'll look at using the bookmarks for the source when creating a navigational table of contents.

13.3.2   Creating Hyperlinks

You can use hyperlinks to link to pages within a document, to e-mail accounts, to online URLs, and to text anchors.

CREATING HYPERLINKS

To create a hyperlink, do the following:

1. **Select text or an object and open the Hyperlinks Panel (Window ➤ Interactive ➤ Hyperlinks).**

2. **Click the Create new hyperlink icon or open the panel menu and choose New Hyperlink.**

3. **In the New Hyperlink dialog box, choose the item you want to link to from the Link To drop-down menu.** For a page link, choose Page, as shown in Figure 13-6.

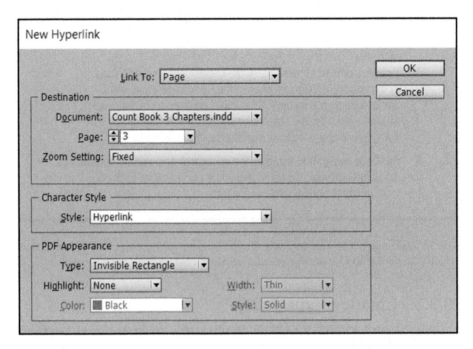

Figure 13-6. Choose Page from the Link To drop-down menu to link to a page in the document

4. **Click OK and the hyperlink is set**. When you export to fixed layout EPUB, tapping the link on a device opens the destination page.

13.3.3 Using Rich Media

Video and audio can be added to fixed layout EPUBs, very similar to the way you add audio and video to reflowable EPUBs. Although some eReaders may support audio formats other than MP3, and some video formats such as .mov and .avi are supported on some eReaders, you should plan on converting all audio to MP3 and video files to MP4 or M4v with H.264 encoding. Eventually, some eReaders may drop support for older formats and adopt the newer standards.

Fixed layout EPUBs support autoplay except on iOS devices. Apple disabled autoplay back in iOS version 6. Therefore, the user needs to tap the video to play it.

13.3.4 Using Animations

All of the animations covered in Chapter 8 are supported in fixed layout EPUBs. What you see when using the EPUB Interactivity Preview Panel generally is the same result that you find in a fixed layout EPUB. No workarounds are required when using animations, and all of the animation presets work fine in fixed layout EPUBs.

13.3.5 Using Multi-State Objects

The multi-state objects covered in Chapter 9 are all supported in fixed layout EPUBs as well as nested MSOs.

CREATING A POP-UP

One handy button action that's not entirely related to an MSO is using the Show/Hide button actions. This action is helpful when you want to create a pop-up view of an image, a text frame, or an MSO. To create a pop-up, follow these steps:

1. **Open a page in InDesign with an image.** I use an image here to illustrate how we might use a pop-up. You can use another layout, but an image works well for this example.

2. **Create the pop-up.** In my example, I use a text frame filled with a color and add a little transparency. In the top-right corner, I added an X to represent a close box, as shown in Figure 13-7. Group the objects.

Figure 13-7. *A pop-up created over an image*

3. **Create an icon in the lower-left or right corner atop the image.** This icon represents a button to alert the user that something occurs when tapping the button.

4. **Convert the icon to a button.** Open the Buttons and Forms Panel and select the icon image. Click the Convert to Button icon to create a button and name the button. In my example, I use Show Popup for the button name. Don't add an action yet to the button.

5. **Convert the pop-up frame to a button.** Select the pop-up and click the Create new button icon in the Buttons and Forms Panel. Add a name for the button. In my example, I named the button *Popup*, as shown in Figure 13-8.

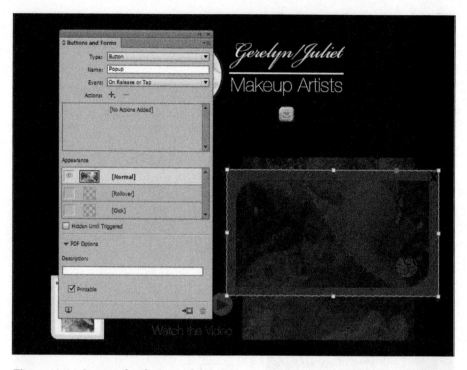

Figure 13-8. *Convert the object to a button*

6. **Add a button action.** Select the second button (named Popup) and click the plus icon to add an action. From the Actions drop-down menu, choose Show/Hide Buttons and Forms. In the list below the Actions drop-down menu, you see the two buttons. This button shows the icon and hides the pop-up. Therefore, click the default X adjacent to the button name (Popup) and click the icon adjacent to the name so that a backslash (\) appears over the eye icon. Click the Show Popup icon adjacent to the name and click the box until you see the eye icon. These actions hide the pop-up and show the icon button, respectively.

7. **Add a second button action.** Select the button (Show Popup) and Show the Popup and the Close buttons, as shown in Figure 13-9. In my example, I also have a transparent screen to dim the video in the layout.

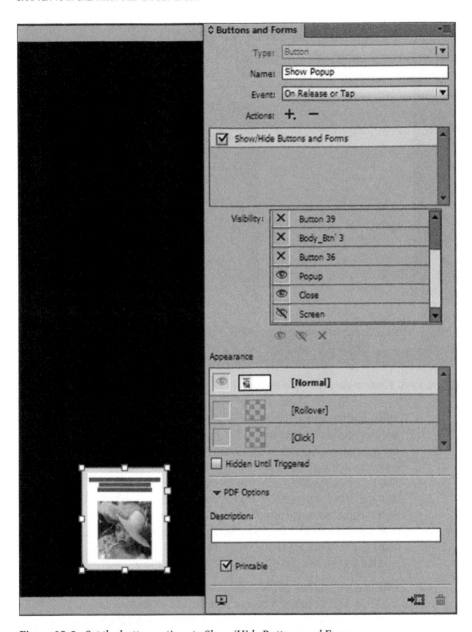

Figure 13-9. *Set the button actions to Show/Hide Buttons and Forms*

8. **Open the EPUB Interactivity Preview and test the buttons.** You should see the pop-up appear when you click the button icon, as shown in Figure 13-10. To close the pop-up, click the Popup button. The Popup button icon will appear.

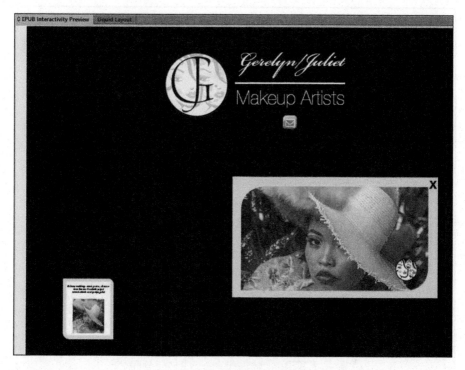

Figure 13-10. The pop-up shown in the EPUB Interactivity Preview window

13.4 Creating a Navigational Table of Contents

A table of contents isn't necessary for fixed layout EPUBs. eReaders that can display fixed layout EPUBs generate thumbnails of each page. As you swipe through a document, you see thumbnail images at the bottom of your device. However, if you have a long document, you may want to create a table of contents.

When you create a table of contents in reflowable EPUBs, you use paragraph styles and use the TOC style option. With fixed layout EPUBs, you may have new chapter pages that don't have text. You may have animations or images in locations where you want to break up the document for logical divisions. To create a table of contents when paragraph styles are impractical, you may want to create bookmarks and use the bookmarks for your TOC style. (To create bookmarks in an InDesign document, review the section, "Creating Bookmarks," earlier in this chapter.)

After creating bookmarks, choose File ➤ Export (or press Ctrl/⌘+E) and choose EPUB (Fixed Layout) for the format. In the General settings in the EPUB – Fixed Layout Export Options dialog box, choose Bookmarks from the Navigation TOC drop-down menu, as shown in Figure 13-11.

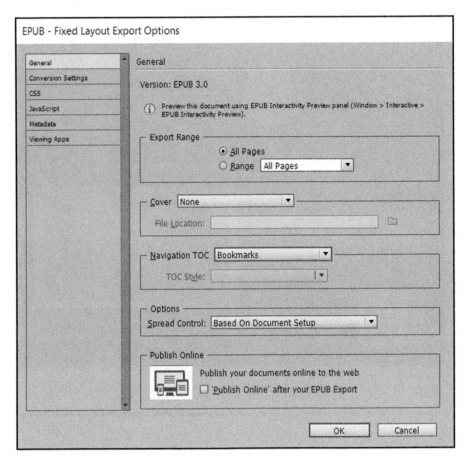

Figure 13-11. *Choose Bookmarks from the Navigation TOC drop-down menu*

Click OK. The file is exported to a fixed layout EPUB. When you open the contents page, you find a table of contents built from the bookmarks, as shown in Figure 13-12.

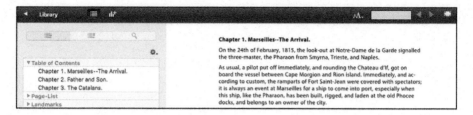

Figure 13-12. *TOC page in a fixed layout EPUB*

13.5   Working with Fonts

You don't have a choice as to whether to embed fonts in a fixed layout EPUB. InDesign makes the choice for you, and you don't have an option to disable font embedding in the Export to EPUB (Fixed layout) options. InDesign embeds TrueType and OpenType fonts in fixed layout EPUBs. Fonts in the older PostScript font format cannot be embedded.

13.5.1   Understanding Font Licensing

Since InDesign embeds the fonts you use in your fixed layout EPUB, you need to do a little research to determine whether you can legally use them this way. You might purchase a font for $24.95, but the font you buy may only be licensed for print documents. When you search through a font foundry's web site, you can find licensing requirements for uses in web pages, EPUBs, PDFs, and so forth. The same font that you purchased for $24.95 may cost you $200-$500 for embedding in an EPUB. Moreover, you may also find that the license for an EPUB might allow you to use the font only one time in one EPUB. Some of this gets really absurd, and your best practice is to stay away from those font foundries that charge exorbitant fees—especially for single EPUB usage.

Your best bet is to use Adobe Typekit fonts. All of the fonts available for desktop use on Typekit with your Creative Cloud subscription can be legally embedded in EPUBs without any additional charges.

13.5.2   Using Acceptable Font Attributes

When you begin a project, it's a good idea to export a variety of character combinations to a fixed layout EPUB to be certain that the characters you use translate properly to the EPUB. Some advanced OpenType character attributes don't export to EPUB, some do a partial job, and others fail miserably. For example, discretionary ligatures don't export to a fixed layout EPUB, and the result is much different than the page layout in InDesign. Manual kerning doesn't work, nor do OpenType fractions.

As you can see in Figure 13-13, the original type set in InDesign (left) shows some type attributes that were missed in the EPUB document (right).

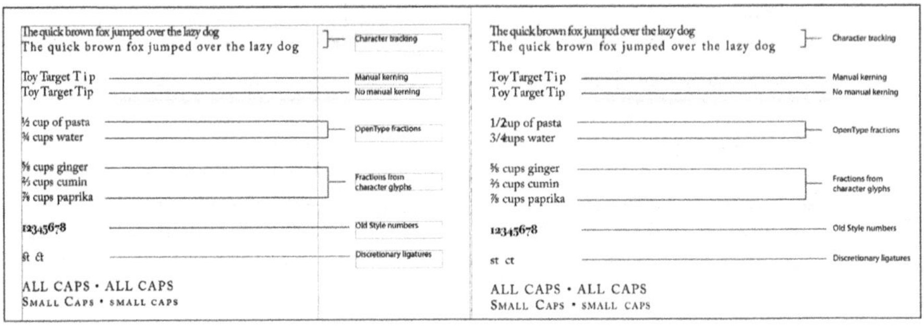

Figure 13-13. *Type set in InDesign (left) and exported to fixed layout EPUB (right)*

Old Style numbers export fine in InDesign CC 2015. If you use an earlier version of InDesign, old style numbers won't export properly. The first set of fractions is derived from OpenType. The second set of fractions was set using the character glyphs.

13.6 Exporting to Fixed Layout EPUB Format

To create a fixed layout EPUB, you export the file much like you export files for reflowable EPUBs. Choose the File ➤ Export command or press Ctrl/⌘+E and choose EPUB (Fixed Layout) in the Save as Type (Windows) or Format (Macintosh) drop-down menu.

The EPUB – Fixed Layout Export Options dialog box opens at the General pane, as shown in Figure 13-14.

13.6.1   Using General Export Options

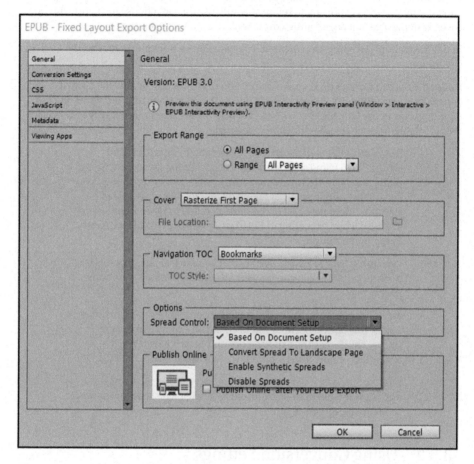

Figure 13-14. *The General pane in the EPUB – Fixed Layout Export Options dialog box*

A few things differ in the general export options in fixed layout EPUBs compared to reflowable EPUBs. In the Export Range, you can choose a page range. The Cover options are the same as when exporting to reflowable EPUBs. You can choose to export with no cover, rasterize the first page for the cover, or choose an image for the cover.

In the Navigation TOC drop-down menu, you can choose Bookmarks for the TOC generation.

Under the Spread Control drop-down menu, you have choices for how the spreads appear in the resulting EPUB document. Choices that you make here are written to the metadata tags in the OPF file that governs the page views, also known as the *viewport* in the HTML file. Your choices include the following:

- *Based on Document Setup*: Use this setting to export to fixed layout EPUB using settings that you make in the Document Setup dialog box (File ➤ Document Setup). In the Document Setup, you can choose single pages or facing pages. You also specify page size and orientation. All of the settings made in Document Setup are used when exporting to EPUB using the Based on Document Setup menu option.

- *Convert Spread to Landscape Page*: If you have facing pages as the document setup, you can convert all spreads to single landscape pages.

- *Enable Synthetic Spreads*: If you have a document set up as single pages, this option permits you to create an export with facing pages. This forces the exported document to create facing pages regardless of how the document was set up.

- *Disable Spreads*: If you have a document set up as facing pages and want the EPUB to be exported as single pages, use this option to break the spreads apart.

13.6.2   Using Conversion Settings

Click Conversion Settings in the left pane, and the right pane shows the conversion settings, as shown in Figure 13-15.

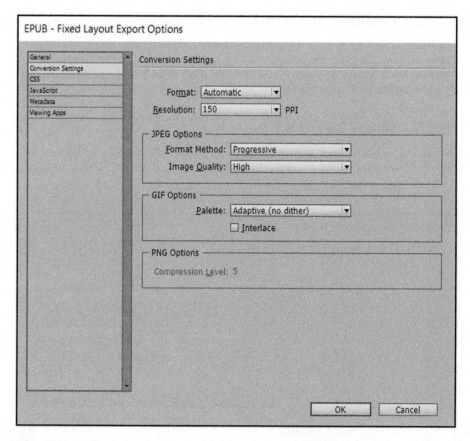

Figure 13-15. *The Conversion Settings pane in the EPUB – Fixed Layout Export Options dialog box*

Conversion settings are all about how you want to handle images. As a matter of practice, use Automatic for the Format and choose 150ppi for the Resolution. For JPEG images, choose High for the Quality. Don't worry about GIF options. You should only use JPEG and PNG for fixed layout EPUBs.

13.6.3   Using the CSS Pane

When you click CSS in the left pane, the right pane changes and really doesn't provide much for making options choices. InDesign takes care of writing all of the CSS for you, and you don't need to worry about choosing to emit CSS or not. There is a button you can click to add a style sheet to the export, but it would be rare for you ever to use it. As a matter of practice, leave the CSS options at the default when exporting to fixed layout EPUB.

13.6.4   Adding JavaScripts

InDesign generates its own JavaScript for fixed layout EPUBs. If you have a JavaScript that you want to add to the file, you can do so by clicking JavaScript in the left pane and clicking the Add JavaScript button to add the script. Unless you're a competent JavaScript programmer, leave this dialog box at the default.

13.6.5   Using Metadata

The Metadata pane is where you provide metadata for fields like the file title, creator/author, creation date, publisher, reproduction rights, and the document subject, as shown in Figure 13-16.

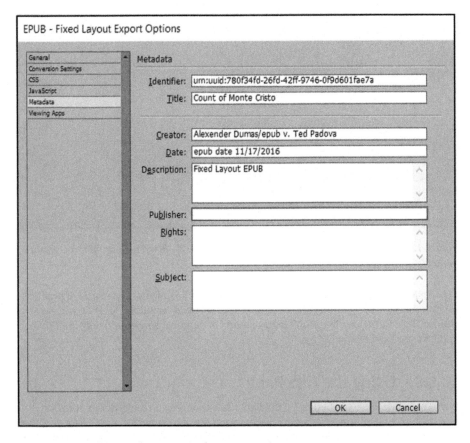

Figure 13-16. *The Metadata pane in the export options*

Leave the Identifier field alone. InDesign generates its own identifier. This is not where you would add an ISBN number. Fill in the text boxes and provide information before you send the EPUB to a hosting service.

13.6.6   Targeting Viewer Apps

The last pane in the EPUB – Fixed Layout Export Options dialog box is the Viewing Apps pane. You choose viewing apps very similar to the way you did when exporting to reflowable EPUBs. Choose the viewing apps on your desktop computer, and when the file is exported, it automatically opens in the selected app(s).

13.6.7   Validating EPUBs

InDesign is very good at exporting valid fixed layout EPUBs. If you export a document to a fixed layout EPUB and no errors are reported, you can be very certain that the EPUB is a valid document and meets standards established for EPUBs.

If you edit any of the HTML or CSS documents, you should run the EPUB through an EPUB validation application. For more on validating EPUBs, see Chapter 12.

13.7   Viewing Fixed Layout EPUBs

Normally, when you export to any EPUB format, you should preview the document on a desktop viewer first. If the document appears fine, you offload the file to a device and preview the document on multiple devices before deploying the file to a content provider.

Whereas you have many choices for reflowable eReaders viewing on desktop computers and devices, there are fewer fixed layout viewer choices. You can, as of this writing, view fixed layout EPUBs in the Readium extension for Google Chrome, Apple iBooks, and Adobe Digital Editions (version 4.0 and above). Fixed layout EPUBs can be converted to Kindle KF8/MOBI, but if you create interactive documents, you lose a lot of the interactivity.

New developments occur rapidly in the eBook world. Thus, there may be some other worthwhile viewers available to you by the time this book is published. For now, you can use Apple iBooks (desktop and device versions) or Adobe Digital Editions to view fixed layout EPUBs. On Windows and Android systems, you can use Adobe Digital Editions (ADE) on Windows and Android devices.

All of the interactivity that you add to fixed layout EPUBs can be viewed in iBooks and ADE on your computers and your devices.

Additionally, Kobo Readers provide equal support for viewing fixed layout EPUBs.

13.8   Summary

In this chapter, we looked at exporting to fixed layout EPUBs and observed all of the interactive features that you can use with fixed layout EPUBs. As you observed, your interactive documents are much more versatile with the fixed layout format than with the reflowable EPUB format.

In the next chapter, we look at another method for using a variety of interactive features in documents when we export to Adobe Publish Online.

CHAPTER 14

■ ■ ■

Discovering Adobe Publish Online

Adobe introduced Publish Online with InDesign CC 2015 originally known as Publish Online (Preview) during the development period. Don't underestimate this wonderful new addition to InDesign and the marvelous things you can do with it.

You can either repurpose an existing design targeted for print, or you can create a new document. In either case, you can take advantage of almost all of the interactive features I discussed in previous chapters. You don't need a special viewer, and the content and interactivity can be seen on just about every device, including smartphones, tablets, notebooks, laptops, and desktop computers.

When you finish creating your work, you can share your documents with anyone, by embedding the document on a web site or blog, hosting a URL link, e-mailing links to friends and colleagues, posting the work on Facebook, or sharing it on your Twitter account.

In this chapter, I cover how you create documents for Publish Online and how you can share your work.

14.1   Using Interactivity with Publish Online

The InDesign interactive features I covered in previous chapters are all supported. You can use animations, media, multi-state objects, buttons, and hyperlinks (URLs, e-mail, page destinations, TOC markers, index markers, and cross-references hyperlinks). Not supported as of this writing are some of the things that you can do in Acrobat PDFs, such as changing layer visibility or adding JavaScript to buttons. These limitations are within InDesign and Publish Online needs to be exported directly from InDesign. Hence, if you can't create it in InDesign, it won't work in Publish Online. In addition, since Publish Online is written using HTML5 and JavaScript, SWF files are also not supported.

Many of the features found in the Overlays Panel are also not supported. Unfortunately, things like scrollable frames and using web content are not available at this time.

© Ted Padova 2017
T. Padova, *Adobe InDesign Interactive Digital Publishing*,
DOI 10.1007/978-1-4842-2439-7_14

Some of the things that you can do with Publish Online that aren't supported in fixed layout EPUBs and Interactive PDF documents include the following:

- *Multi-page spreads*: You can create spreads with more than two pages. When viewed in Publish Online, you can have the spreads animate with motion. For example, you can use a panorama image to auto-scroll across the screen.

- *Multiple page sizes*: InDesign supports creating documents with different page sizes. The online document maintains the size of the individual pages.

- *Interactive Google maps*: You can insert HTML code in an InDesign document that displays an interactive Google map. The interactivity with the map is lost in fixed layout EPUBs and Interactive PDF files, but you can use an interactive Google Map in your Publish Online documents.

- *Adobe Animate files*: Formerly known as Adobe Edge Animate, Adobe Animate takes animations to a new level. Adobe Animate is similar to Adobe Flash in that you can create very impressive animations. The files are written in HTML5 and JavaScript so that they play on all platforms. When you export a file from Animate, you choose the Adobe Deployment Package (.oam) option in the Publish Settings (File ➤ Publish Settings) dialog box. The OAM file can be imported in InDesign and published as an online document. OAM files from Adobe Animate are supported with Publish Online and fixed layout EPUBs. They are not supported in Interactive PDF.

14.2 Using Publish Online

Of all the document-creation options that you have in Adobe InDesign, using Publish Online is the easiest method for creating digital publications. Just a simple menu selection opens the Publish Online Options dialog box, where you make a few choices and then click OK to send the file off to Adobe's server. Anyone using any kind of device on any operating system can view your creations. No special readers are required since all of the content is viewed in a web browser.

Unlike all of the other document exports that you have available in InDesign, once you publish a document using Publish Online you don't have access to the saved file. The file is sent to Adobe's server where it resides until you delete it. What is reported back to you is a URL that you can copy and use as a hyperlink in a web site or a blog site, share via e-mail, or share directly with your Facebook and Twitter accounts.

■ **Tip**   Keep your published online documents clean. If you're not using some documents, delete them from Adobe's server. Help Adobe keep its storage burden to a minimum.

14.2.1   Publishing a Document

You first need to create your digital publication as you would for any other kind of export. One thing that Publish Online offers you is publishing Google interactive maps. Let's start with creating a link to a Google map and then look at publishing the document.

14.2.1.1   Adding a Google Map to a Document

To add an interactive map to your document, log on to Google Maps and search for a map location. In my example, I use Costa Rica as a destination, so we type Costa Rica in the Search Google Maps text box and click the Search icon. When you arrive at the map location, open the menu (top-left corner in Google Maps) and click the Share or Embed Map link.

When the screen shows you options for Share or Embed Map, click Embed Map, as shown in Figure 14-1. Text in the text box is highlighted. Press Ctrl/⌘+C to copy the URL.

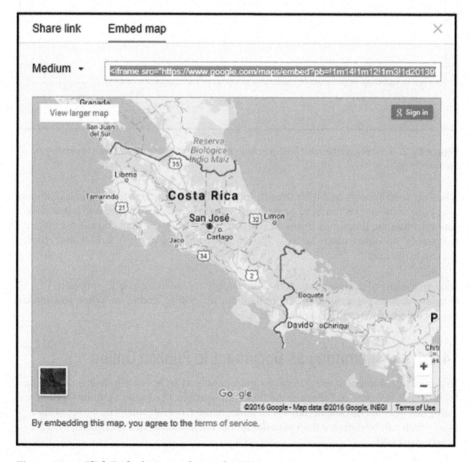

Figure 14-1.   *Click Embed Map and copy the URL*

Open your InDesign Document and choose Object ➤ Insert HTML. You'll see a long line of code. Locate the width and height in the code (see Figure 14-2) and edit the values to match the size that you want the map to occupy in your document. Click OK and wait a few minutes until you see the map appear in the center of the document.

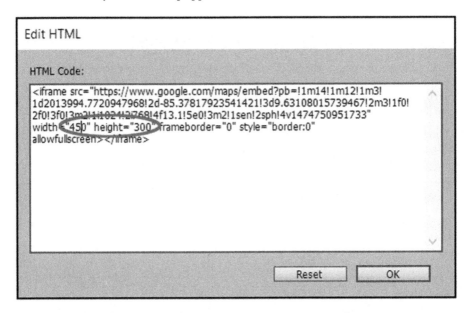

Figure 14-2. Edit the width and height values to the size you want the map to occupy in the document

When the map appears in the document, you can use the Selection tool to move it around your page. If the map is too large or too small, check the rulers at the top and left sides of your document to determine the exact size you want. Delete the map and choose Object ➤ Insert HTML again, paste the URL, and edit the width and height. Click OK and check the size of the map.

You can use any of the other interactive elements that I have discussed in previous chapters, such as animations, MSOs, rich media, hyperlinks, and so on. When you finalize the document, you're ready to publish it.

14.2.1.2 Submitting as Document to Publish Online

To publish the document using Publish Online, choose File ➤ Publish Online or click the Publish Online button at the top of the InDesign window. The Publish Online Options dialog box opens. The default panel is General. In the General Panel, you can provide a Title, which can be different than your document file name, and a Description (see Figure 14-3).

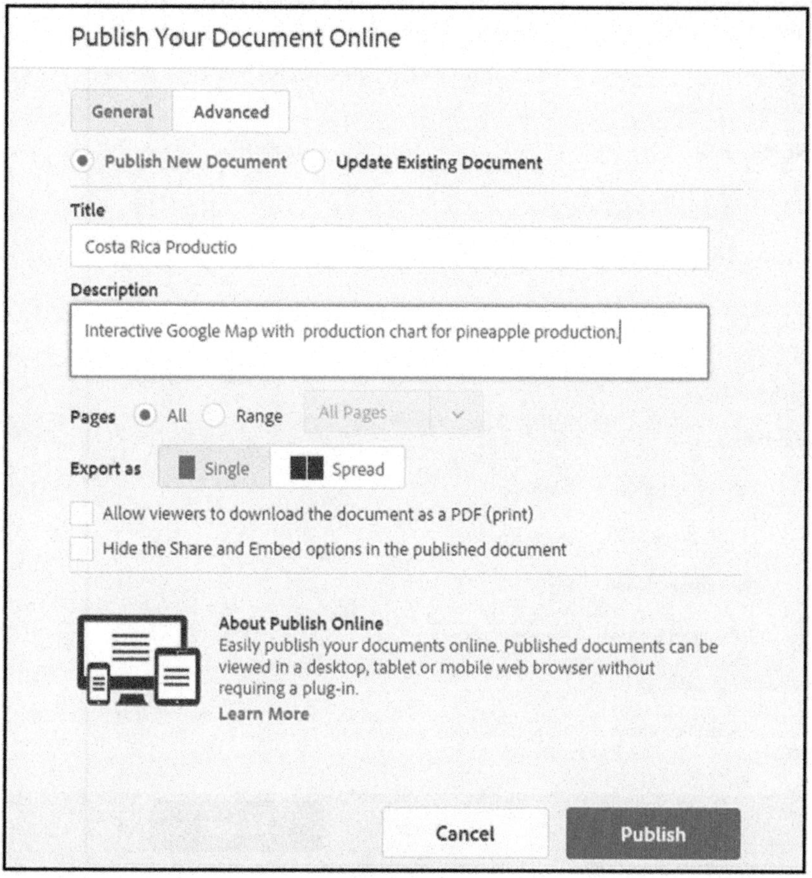

Publish Your Document Online

General   Advanced

● Publish New Document   ○ **Update Existing Document**

Title

Costa Rica Productio

Description

Interactive Google Map with production chart for pineapple production.

Pages ● All   ○ Range   All Pages   ∨

Export as ■ Single   ■■ Spread

☐ Allow viewers to download the document as a PDF (print)

☐ Hide the Share and Embed options in the published document

About Publish Online
Easily publish your documents online. Published documents can be viewed in a desktop, tablet or mobile web browser without requiring a plug-in.
Learn More

Cancel   Publish

Figure 14-3. *Type a name for the Title and a Description*

You can publish all pages or a range of pages by making choices among the available options. You can export the document as pages or spreads by clicking the respective radio button.

The second panel in the Publish Online Options is Advanced. Click Advanced in the left column to open the Advanced Panel, as shown in Figure 14-4. At the top of the panel, you make choices for the cover thumbnail image. This image is used as the one when someone shares your content on social media. You can choose the First page in the document for the thumbnail image, or you can scroll through the pages and select the page that you want to appear as the thumbnail. If you want to use an image file, click Choose Image and then click the folder icon to navigate your computer and choose a GIF, PNG, or JPEG image.

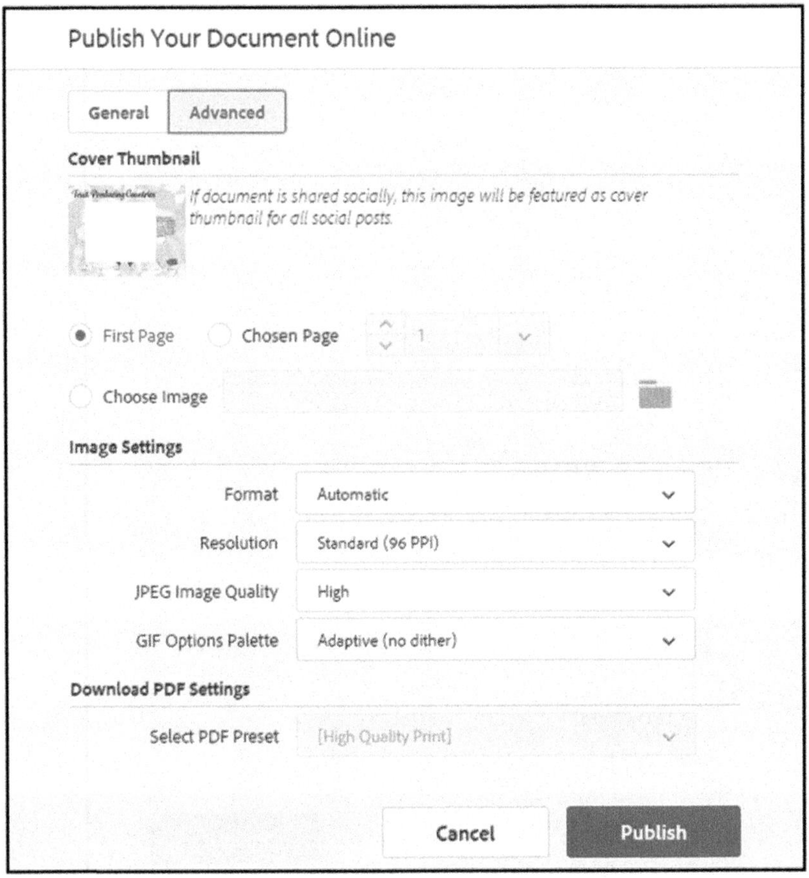

Figure 14-4. Click Advanced in the left pane to open the advanced options

In the Image Settings area, you can choose one of the three supported formats or leave the default at Automatic for InDesign to select the formats automatically. Use the Automatic choice unless you have any particular reason to convert all images to one of the acceptable formats. Automatic will optimize the performance.

For Resolution, you can use 96ppi for a lower-resolution document, or you can choose HiDPI for higher-resolution images. If your document is long and contains many images, the download time will take longer. You might try testing different options and finding the option that works best for your design.

For JPEG Image Quality, choose High as a standard, as you would do for most EPUB documents. For GIF options, if you have any gradients or shades of color in the file, choose Adaptive. If you have solid colors, your best choice might be Web.

After all of the options have been set in the Publish Online Options dialog box, click OK and your file is uploaded to Adobe's server. If the upload time is long, you can continue working in InDesign.

When the upload finishes, you see the Publish Online screen, as shown in Figure 14-5. Here you can make several choices that include the following:

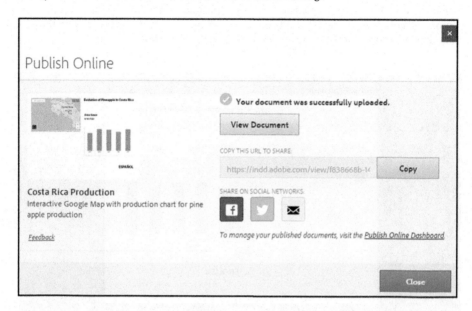

Figure 14-5. *When the document completes the download, the Publish Online screen appears where you find several choices*

- *View Document*: Click the View Document button, and your document is loaded into your default web browser. On the Mac, the file is loaded in Safari (assuming Safari is the default browser). On Windows 10, the file is opened in Microsoft Edge. If Edge isn't installed, the file opens in Internet Explorer. If you use Windows 10, you may need to toggle your applications and open Edge to see the file. On the Mac, the Safari window opens on top of the InDesign window.

- *Copy*: If you want to copy the URL, click the copy button and the URL address is copied to your clipboard. You can paste the copy in a text editor if you want to use the link later in a web page or blog site.

- *Share on Social Networks*: Click the Facebook icon, Twitter icon, or E-mail icon to share on the respective site. If you choose E-mail, your default e-mail client opens a new message window with the description of the file placed in the e-mail subject line and the file name and URL added to the message box.

  If you share to Facebook or Twitter, you are prompted to log in to your account before proceeding.

- *Close*: Click the Close button to dismiss the window.

14.2.2   Changing View Attributes in Published Documents

When you click View Document, you see your published content along with some buttons that offer viewing and sharing options. In Figure 14-6, you see the icons at the bottom of the screen for the options. These include the following:

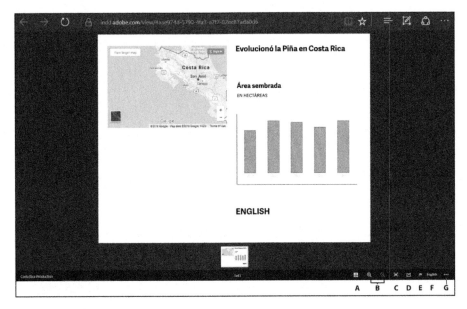

Figure 14-6. *When viewing a publication, you find several buttons that control viewing and sharing*

A. *Toggle Thumbnails*: The default view is no thumbnails shown at the bottom of the window. In Figure 14-6, I clicked the Toggle Thumbnails button and all page thumbnails are displayed at the bottom of the browser window. Since this document contains only a single page, you see only one thumbnail. To return to the default view, click again on the Toggle Thumbnails button.

B. *Zoom buttons*: Click the magnifying glass with the + symbol to zoom in on the document. Click the magnifying glass with the – symbol to zoom out.

C. *Full Screen*: Click this button to enter full screen mode. Click again to exit full screen mode.

D. *Share*: Click the Share button to open a window where you can copy the URL, share to Facebook or Twitter, or add to a new e-mail message.

E. *Report Abuse*: When you click this button, a window opens where you can make an abuse complaint for options in a menu that contain Defamation, Pornography, Abuse, Copyright, or Other. A name field appears where you type your name, an e-mail field for adding your e-mail address, and a comment box to describe the complaint further. After completing the information, you click the Submit button and the complaint is sent to Adobe.

■ **Caution**   Adobe monitors complaints and tries to make an effort to protect end users against receiving illicit and unlawful content. When creating content, keep in mind that you want to keep it clean and comply with copyright laws.

F. *Language*: The pop-up menu contains language choices. Click the button to open the menu. Two options include:

- *Embed*: This option generates an "embed code," which allows you to embed the Publish Online document in another web site. Click Embed and a window opens that offers you several choices for the sizes of the document and an embed code. The embed code is similar to the code used with Google Maps, which I discussed earlier in the section, "Adding a Google Map to a Document." You can edit the width and height in a text editor if the default sizes do not meet your needs.

- *Turn OFF Volume*: Click this button to turn off sound in the document.

14.2.3   Using the Web Dashboard

Managing your online content is handled with a separate menu command in InDesign. Keep in mind that when you upload a file using Publish Online, you have no means for editing the file or updating. You need to delete the file and upload a new file every time that you make a change in your InDesign file or simply replace an existing file with a new edited file.

To delete files and manage them in InDesign, choose File ➤ Web Dashboard. When you choose this command, your published documents appear in your default web browser. You must be logged in with your Adobe ID in order to see the files.

Along the left side of the screen you see the list of published documents sorted according to the date last published. When you mouse over a document, a Delete button appears on the right side of the browser window, as shown in Figure 14-7. Click Delete and the file is removed. If you want to open a published document, click on the document thumbnail.

Figure 14-7. *When you mouse over a publication, a Delete button appears*

14.3   Summary

In this chapter, you learned how to export files for Adobe Publish Online services. You learned how to export an interactive document, view the results, and use the web dashboard for monitoring files. You also learned how to publish your files to Facebook and Twitter accounts and how to copy URLs to use with web sites.

In the next chapter, we look at creating Interactive PDF files.

CHAPTER 15

■ ■ ■

Creating Interactive PDF Files

Portable Document Format (PDF) files can be viewed on all devices. Every mobile phone, tablet, and computer has some sort of PDF viewer. On desktop computers and laptops, the free Adobe Reader software program is the dominant PDF viewer. On mobile phones and tablets, there are a wide range of viewers available for free and/or for purchase.

Regardless of the PDF viewer you use, PDF files typically display documents exactly as they were created, including images, text formatting, and font embedding. The downside of using PDFs is that several interactive features are not supported on mobile phones and tablets. On desktop computers and laptops, you get a much broader range of support for interactive features.

In this chapter, I talk about exporting to Interactive PDF files from Adobe InDesign, adding interactivity, and performing several tasks adding interactivity directly in Adobe Acrobat. All Creative Cloud users can download Adobe Acrobat. If you aren't a Creative Cloud subscriber, then you need to purchase Adobe Acrobat or another PDF editing program. No editing opportunities exist in the free Adobe Reader application.

15.1 Preparing the Acrobat Workspace

If you're a user of Creative Cloud applications and you haven't used Adobe Acrobat, the first time you see the Acrobat user interface, you may wonder if the application was actually developed by Adobe Systems. All of the Creative Cloud applications as well as Adobe Photoshop Elements use a very similar UI. However, the Adobe Acrobat team goes its own way, and Acrobat doesn't conform to the standards for UI design that you find in all of the other Creative Cloud applications.

15.1.1 Creating a Custom Interface

In Adobe Acrobat, you should create a custom workspace that enables you to select various tools quickly, which you'll use with Interactive PDFs. To begin, open Adobe Acrobat. You don't need a document open in the Document pane.

© Ted Padova 2017
T. Padova, *Adobe InDesign Interactive Digital Publishing*,
DOI 10.1007/978-1-4842-2439-7_15

Click Tools at the top-left corner of the window, as shown in Figure 15-1.

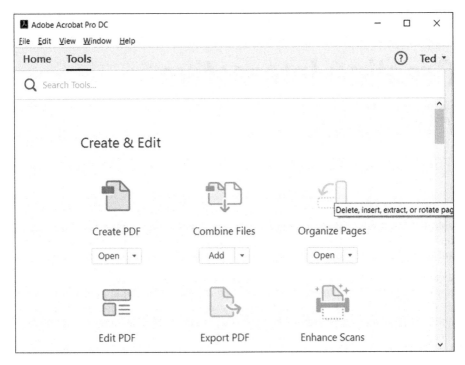

Figure 15-1. *Click Tools at the top-left of the Acrobat window to open the Tools window*

Drill down the Edit PDF category and click Add. Click Open, and the editing tools appear in the toolbar at the top of the Acrobat window, as shown in Figure 15-2.

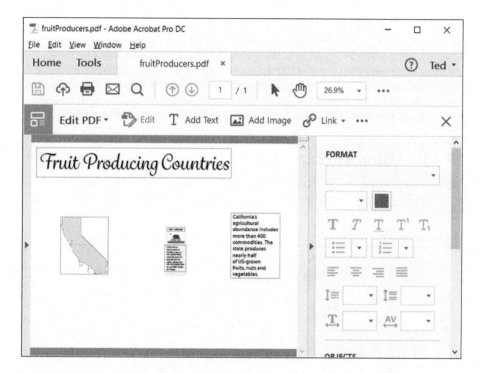

Figure 15-2. *Click Edit to edit the text in the document*

The tools that you open appear in the right pane, and they are accessible when you open additional PDF files.

15.1.2   Setting Preferences

Acrobat has a huge number of preference settings that you can select in the Preferences dialog box. To open the preferences, select Edit ➤ Preferences (Windows) or Acrobat Pro ➤ Preferences (Mac), or press Ctrl/⌘+K.

There's one preference item that you should change in the General pane as you get started. Click General in the left pane and locate the top item, Use Single Key Accelerators, to access tools. Check the box. This will allow you to use keyboard shortcuts to access tools when in Adobe Acrobat.

Creating the custom interface and setting one preference item gets you started with a minimal set of tools and preferences for working on Interactive PDF documents. As you move along in editing PDF files, you may want to add more tools or change additional preferences. These are choices for personal use. Return to the menus and make choices depending on the kind of work you want to do with Adobe Acrobat.

15.2   Exporting to PDF from InDesign

When you choose File ➤ Export in InDesign, you have two different options for the type of PDF to which you want to export. At the top of the Save as Type (Windows) or Format (Macintosh) menu in the Export dialog box, you find Adobe PDF (Interactive) followed by Adobe PDF (Print). For interactive documents, you obviously need to use the Interactive option. If you want to export a PDF document for print, then use the Print option.

15.2.1   Using the Export to Interactive PDF Dialog Box

When you choose File ➤ Export or press Ctrl/⌘+E and select Adobe PDF (Interactive) and then click Save, the Export to Interactive PDF dialog box opens, as shown in Figure 15-3.

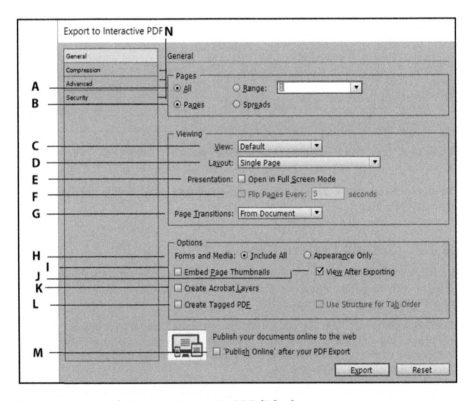

Figure 15-3. Open the Export to Interactive PDF dialog box

In the dialog box, you have several options, including the following:

A. *Page Range*: If you want to export a range of pages, click the Range radio button and type the page numbers. Something like 3–5 for exporting pages 3 to 5.

B. *Pages/Spreads*: For single page layouts, use Pages. If you have facing pages and want the facing pages to be viewed in the final PDF as a single wide page, click Spreads.

C. *View*: From the menu, you can choose different zoom options. If you want an entire page to fit on the screen, choose Fit Page. All users will see the entire page in the document pane regardless of the screen size.

D. *Layout*: If you choose Default from this menu, the PDF view adheres to the preference options on each computer. Users can set the preference options to view PDFs as single page documents or as continuous. (When you scroll the pages, you see the top of the next page as the bottom of the previous page scrolls out of view.) If you always want your PDF documents to be viewed as single pages so that when users scroll pages they snap to the next page (or any other layout view), select the option in the menu. When an option other than Default is selected, the Layout view overrides individual computer preferences and forces all users to see your PDFs in the same layout view.

E. *Open in Full Screen Mode*: Full Screen Mode is a view where all of the PDF viewer UI elements, such as toolbars, menus, scroll bars, and so on are hidden from view. The downside for opening PDFs in Full Screen Mode is that users see a warning dialog box that they have to dismiss every time the PDF is opened. Unfortunately, this is a necessary evil due to a number of security measures that Adobe employs to prevent PDFs from altering your computer without you knowing it.

F. *Flip Pages*: If you export with Full Screen Mode enabled, you can have the PDF turn pages automatically. You determine the interval by typing a value in the text box.

G. *Page Transitions*: Transitions occur when you move through pages. You can choose to honor any page transitions contained in the PDF or select from a number of different transition effects in the menu.

H. *Forms and Media*: Click the Include All radio button to include any media files and form fields that have been placed on your InDesign pages.

I. *Embed Page Thumbnails*: Always disable this option. Never check it. Thumbnails in a PDF document show you thumbnail images of each page when viewing the layout in the Pages pane inside the Navigation pane. Since Acrobat 6, thumbnails are generated on the fly when you open a PDF document. If you embed page thumbnails, it adds more overhead and the final file size is larger.

J. *View After Exporting*: If you want to open the exported PDF document in an Acrobat viewer (either Adobe Acrobat or Adobe Reader) automatically after the export is complete, check this box.

K. *Create Acrobat Layers*: Of all of the types of interactive document types, PDFs are the only ones that support layers. If you have a multi-lingual document, as one example, you can use all of the graphics and images on one layer and create text on individual layers. You can then use buttons to permit readers of your document to change layer views.

L. *Tagged PDF*: Click Create Tagged PDF so that users of screen readers can read through your document. Click the Use Structure for the Tab Order, which inherits the tab order of things like form fields.

M. *Publish Online*: Check the box to add the document as a Publish Online file. (For more information on Publish Online, see Chapter 14).

    • *Compression*: Make choices for the type of compression, JPEG Quality, and Resolution for images contained in the document.

    • *Advanced*: Choices include either displaying the File Name or the Document Title and a choice for Language.

N. *Security*: Click the Security button to open the Security dialog box. You can add password protection for opening the PDF, limit editing of the PDF, or both.

15.2.2   Preparing Layouts in InDesign

When working with Interactive PDF files there are some special treatments that you need to make and some interesting results you can achieve. In this section, I offer both. You'll find some best practices to use with Interactive PDFs that you don't need to worry about when creating fixed layout and Adobe Publish Online documents.

15.2.2.1 Thinking Outside the Box

One interesting effect that you can create with Interactive PDF files is designing a document with objects or images breaking the page border. This can only be accomplished with PDF documents, and the only program that can produce the result is Adobe InDesign. In Figure 15-4, you see a PDF page displayed in Acrobat. Notice the pineapple on the left side of the page. It breaks the page border. This is similar to an out-of-bounds effect, which you can create with Adobe Photoshop Elements.

Figure 15-4. Only Interactive PDF documents can have elements that break page borders

BREAKING THE PAGE BORDER

You may have a bicycle moving off screen, a soccer player kicking a ball, a surfer riding a wave, or some other design element where you want to add a little dimension to the final document. It's a rather easy task that we step through here:

1. **Place an object on a Master Page.** You must have the object that breaks the border placed on a Master Page. Open the Pages Panel and double-click the Master Page that's used for the other design elements on the page.

2. **Be certain that the center point of the object is within the page boundary.** You must have the center point inside the page boundary. If you want a small element outside of the page boundary, create a frame with no stroke and no fill inside the page area and group it with the small object. The center point of the grouped object must be inside the page area.

3. **Convert the object to a button.** Select the object and open the Buttons and Forms Panel. Create a new button for the object. Don't worry about assigning an action, you just need to be certain that the object is a button.

4. **Export to Interactive PDF.** Choose File ➤ Export (or press Ctrl/⌘+E) and choose Adobe PDF Interactive. If you check View After Exporting, the PDF opens in the default PDF viewer. From here, you need Adobe Acrobat to finish off the job.

5. **Lock the button.** If a user clicks and jerks the mouse click, the button may move and be contained completely within the page area. To prevent this from happening, right-click the button with the select Object tool to open the pop-up menu. (Press R on your keyboard to access the Select Object tool.) Choose Properties from the menu. By default, the General Properties dialog box opens. At the bottom-left corner, check the box for Locked, as shown in Figure 15-5.

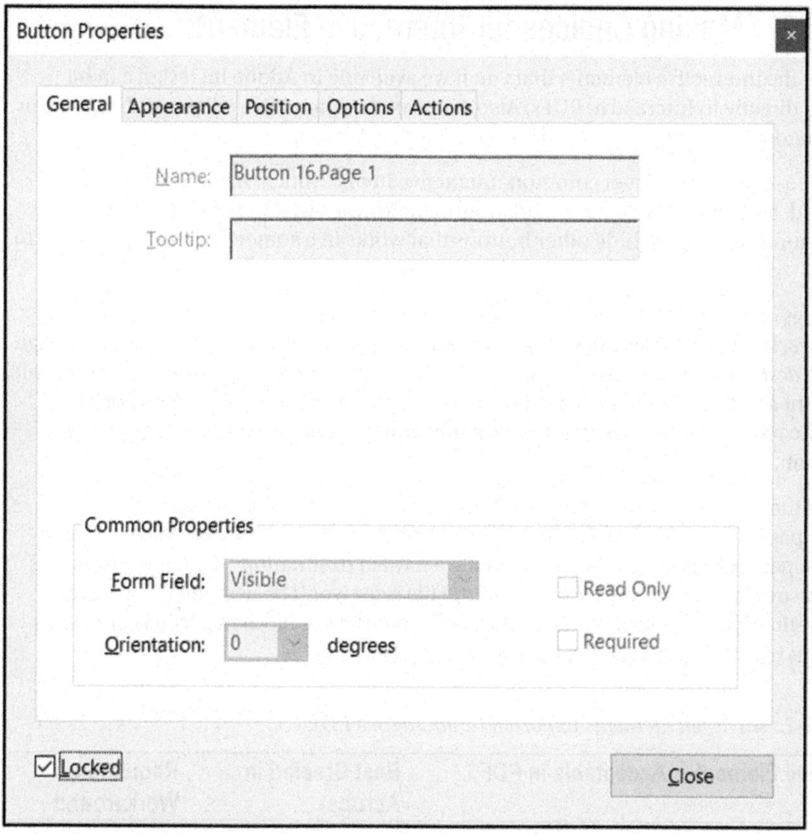

Button Properties   ×

General | Appearance | Position | Options | Actions

Name: Button 16.Page 1

Tooltip:

Common Properties

Form Field: Visible   ☐ Read Only

Orientation: 0   degrees   ☐ Required

☑ Locked   Close

Figure 15-5. *Lock the button to prevent accidental movement*

6. **Adjust the user interface (optional).** If you don't want the document opening in full screen mode, you can hide some of the interface options. Choose File ➤ Properties or press Ctrl/⌘+D. The Document Properties dialog box opens. Click the Initial View tab and choose the options in the User Interface Options area that you want to hide. You cannot hide all three interface options. Typically, the items that you want to check are Hide Menu Bar and Hide Toolbars. Ideally though, if you create a design with objects breaking the page borders, you might want to choose to view the files in full screen mode.

15.2.2.2 Making Choices for Interactive Elements

Not all of the interactive elements that you have available in Adobe InDesign can be exported directly to Interactive PDFs. Also, some of the interactive elements that you can create in Adobe InDesign are best handled in Adobe Acrobat.

In Table 15-1, you see a list of common interactive items. Notice that MSOs are not supported, and you can't create a workaround for MSOs—well not entirely. You can create buttons that show/hide other buttons that works in a somewhat similar manner to an MSO.

Two things of which you may want to take special note are hyperlinks and cross-references. In Adobe InDesign, when you create hyperlinks or cross-references, InDesign creates a *destination*. In Adobe Acrobat terms, these are *named destinations*. For example, if you want a button where the action is set up to view the next page, previous page, or specific page, InDesign creates a destination and you set the event to move to the destination.

Contrast the InDesign destination with Adobe Acrobat. In Acrobat, if you want to navigate pages, you can set up a button to go to next page, go to previous page, or go to a specific page and there is no need to create a named destination. Named destinations add some overhead to your PDF files, and the file sizes won't be as small if you have many destinations in your document. As a best practice, create all hyperlinks and cross-references in Acrobat to keep the file sizes as small as possible.

Table 15-1. *InDesign Elements Exported to Interactive PDF*

Interactive Element	Acceptable in PDF	Best Created in Acrobat	Requires a Workaround
Animation	No*		Requires workaround
Animating tables	No*		Requires workaround
Buttons	Yes	Create in Acrobat	
Cross-references	Yes	Create in Acrobat	
Hyperlinks	Yes	Create in Acrobat	
MSOs	No		No workaround
Overlays	No		No Workaround
Rich Media	Yes, with some limitations (Many mobile PDF viewers don't support video playback in PDF files)		

Can create a workaround to display the animations

15.3   Creating Hyperlinks in Acrobat

As noted in Table 15-1, you want to leave all hyperlink and cross-references to Acrobat and not create them in Adobe InDesign. You have two choices for creating navigation buttons: you can use a button or a link.

15.3.1   Using Buttons for Page Navigation

Buttons have advantages over links in that they can be duplicated over multiple pages. Therefore, if you want to create a button that sends the user to the next page, you create one button with the button action and then duplicate it across multiple pages.

> ### CREATING AN INTERACTIVE BUTTON
> ### FOR PAGE NAVIGATION

To create an interactive button for page navigation, do the following:

1. **Open a multipage document in Acrobat.**

2. **Create a button on the first page.** Click the button tool and draw a button in the location where you want the button to appear.

3. **Add a button fill (optional).** If you have a symbol or icon on the page, you don't need to create a button with an appearance. If you don't have any indication that the navigation will move on a button click, you need to create the button in some fashion so that it's obvious to a user that the element is a button. You can choose to fill the contents of the button with a color or you can add a graphic to the button. The minute you create a button, the Button Field Name window opens over the button. Type a name for the button, such as Go Next, and then click All Properties.

4. **In the Button Properties dialog box, click the Appearance tab and click the Fill Color icon.** Choose No Color from the pop-up menu. Click the Options tab. In the Layout menu, you can choose to have a Label and Icon, Label Only, or Icon Only. In this example, we'll use Icon Only.

5. **After selecting Icon Only, Acrobat has a bit of a bug in that you can't choose an icon unless you first change the Behavior.** Choose Push from the Behavior menu, and then the Choose Icon button becomes active. Click Choose Icon, and the Select Icon dialog box opens. Click Browse to open the Open window and navigate your hard drive to find the icon that you want to use. Click in the Open window and click on Open (see Figure 15-6).

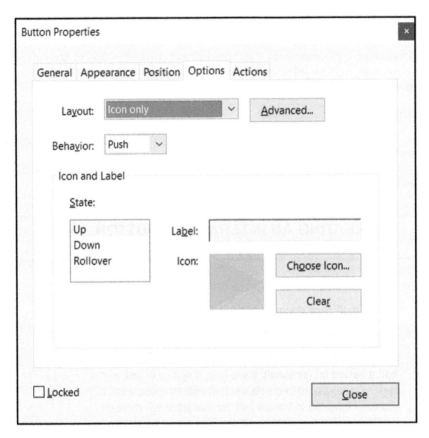

Figure 15-6. Locate the object that you want to use for the button face and click Open

You have some choices in the Advanced window for positioning the icon in the button field.

6. **Click Advanced in the Button Properties Options tab to adjust size and scaling**.

7. **Set the action**. While still in the Button Properties dialog box, click the Actions tab. Choose Execute a Menu Item in the Select Action menu and click Add. The Menu Item dialog box opens. Locate the View-Page Navigation-Next Page item and select it. Click OK and dismiss the Button Properties dialog box by clicking the Close button.

8. **Create a second button**. Follow the same procedure found in Steps 3 and 4 to create a second button. For this button, choose View-Page Navigation-Previous page in the Menu Item menu.

ALTERNATIVE TO USING THE EXECUTE MENU ITEM ACTION USING JAVASCRIPT

As an alternative to using the Execute Menu Item action, you can add a simple JavaScript. In the Actions tab, choose Run a JavaScript from the Select Action menu. Click Add and the JavaScript editor opens. Type the following:

```
this.pageNum++;
```

Click OK and the JavaScript is added to the button. To navigate to the previous page, type the following code in the JavaScript Editor:

```
this.pageNum--;
```

If you want to navigate to a specific page in the document, type the following code:

```
this.pageNum=5;
```

JavaScript is zero based, therefore this code will open page 6 in the document. JavaScript is case-sensitive, so be sure to follow the capitalization exactly as shown.

■ **Note** JavaScripts for page navigation and other custom JavaScripts should be used with desktop PDF viewers only. JavaScripts are not recognized by most mobile PDF viewers.

1. **Duplicate the buttons.** If you created the buttons on the first page, right-click the NextPage button. Choose Duplicate Across Pages from the menu. In the Duplicate Field dialog box, click the From radio button, type 1, and then the last page in the text boxes (see Figure 15-7). For example, if your document has 20 pages, type 1 in the first text box and 20 in the second text box. Do the same for the Previous button. On the first page, delete the Previous page button. Move to the last page in the document and double-click the button to open the button properties. Click Actions, select the Execute a Menu item, and click Edit to edit the action. Choose View-Navigation-First Page.

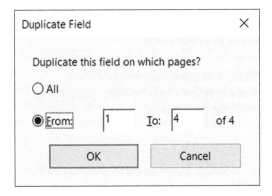

Figure 15-7. *Enter the page range in the Duplicate Field dialog box*

2. **Click Close in the Button properties and click the buttons to be certain that they work properly.**

■ **Note** You need to use the Hand tool to click the buttons. Press H on your keyboard to access the Hand tool.

15.3.2 Linking to URLs

If you want to link from URLs in text, you don't need to do anything in InDesign. Adding URLs in InDesign just creates more overhead in the PDF documents. Most PDF viewers will automatically open URLS that are included in the text if they are typed as follows:

http://www.mycompany.com or www.mycompany.com, where mycompany.com is the URL to which you want to link.

15.4 Changing Layer Views in Acrobat

Being able to change layer views adds a new dimension to interactive documents, and it is something that is only available with PDF documents. In Acrobat terms, layers are referred to as OCGs (Optional Content Groups). You might use OCGs as a workaround for multi-state objects in documents where you have multiple languages or any other kind of interactivity anywhere you want to change objects, images, and/or text views on a page.

In Figure 15-8, you see a document viewed in Full Screen Mode in Acrobat. The current view shows the document with Spanish Text. Over the word *English* is a button. When the user clicks the button, the images and graph remain the same but the text changes to English.

Figure 15-8. *Click the English button, and the English layer comes in view*

15.4.1   Setting Up the Layered File in InDesign

In a new InDesign document, you add three layers in the Layers Panel. In this example, I use two layers for languages and one layer for images/objects. If you create a similar design, name the layers Object, English, and Spanish, or whatever you want to appear on the other two layers. Content that stays static and viewed on all layers can be placed on the Objects layer.

If you want an icon or text for the area where you add a button, create those on the two layers where you add buttons to change the views.

After completing the design, export to Interactive PDF. Be certain to check Create Acrobat Layers in the Export to Interactive PDF dialog box (see Figure 15-3).

15.4.2   Creating Buttons to View Layers

When you create buttons that appear on top of each other, you need to add three different action types. You need to hide the button after you click it, you need to show the second button, and you need to change the layer view. All form fields appear on all layers, so you can't hide a layer and hide the button too. The buttons remain on all layers, so this can get a little confusing if you don't follow the steps precisely.

When you open a PDF containing Acrobat layers, the Layer's Panel opens in the Navigation pane (far-left side of the document). Click the Layers icon in the Navigation pane to open the panel. Adjacent to the file name you will see a tiny triangle to the left. Click the triangle to open the layers, as shown in Figure 15-9.

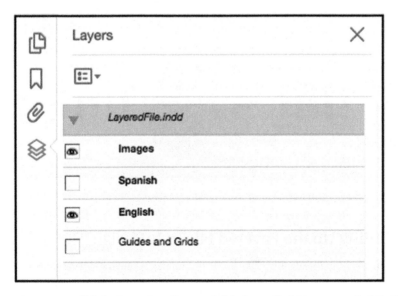

Figure 15-9. Click the Layers Panel icon and click the small white square to the left of the file name

You need the layers in view in order to proceed with creating buttons.

ADDING BUTTONS TO CHANGE THE LAYER VIEW

To add buttons that change the layer view, do the following:

1. **Create a button**.

2. **Click the Button tool in the toolbar and drag to open a rectangle over the area where you want the button to appear**. Name the button. In this example, create the button over the word *English*.

3. **Create a second button and name the button**. Move the second button away from the first button so that one is not atop the other. This will make it easier to assign attributes and test results.

4. **Double-click the first button to open the Button Properties**. If you have text or an icon on the page, click the Appearance tab and set the Fill to None.

5. **Add an action**. Ultimately, the buttons are placed in the same space. Therefore, by default one button will hide the other. You need an action that hides the current button, then shows the second button, and finally displays the respective layer.

   In the Actions tab, choose Show/Hide a Field and click Add. The Show/Hide Field dialog box opens. Currently, you're working on the

English button, so you want to show the Spanish button, as shown in
Figure 15-10. Make the choice and click OK to dismiss the dialog box.

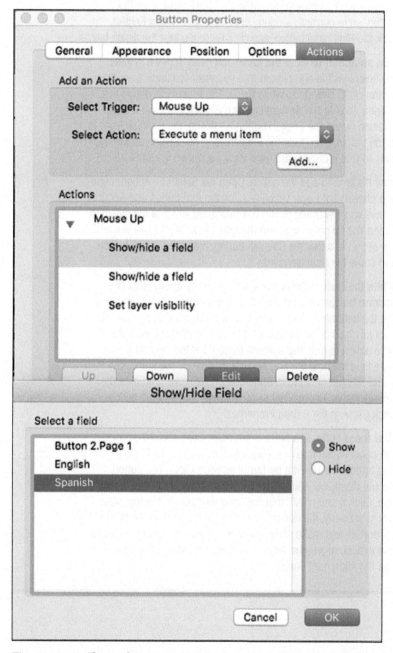

Figure 15-10. *Choose the appropriate attributes in the Show/Hide Field dialog box*

6. **Add a second action to the same button**. While the Action tab is still in view for the first button, create another action to Show/Hide a field. This time you want to click the English item (the button we're currently working on) and hide it. Select English, click the Hide radio button, and click OK to dismiss the dialog box.

7. **Add an action to view the layer**. You need to place in view the layers visible and hidden that you want to inherit from the button click. Therefore, while the Button Properties dialog box is open, look to the Navigation pane and click the eye icon on Spanish (when the English button is clicked, the Spanish layer is made visible). Also hide the English layer by clicking on the eye icon so that it disappears from view, as shown in Figure 15-10.

   Now it's time to add the action. Open the Select an Action menu and choose Set Layer Visibility. Click the Add button and Acrobat shows you a warning dialog box informing you that the selected action will be set to the current state. Click OK and the actions are set up to show the Spanish button, hide the English button, and show the Spanish layer.

8. **While the Button Properties dialog box is open, click the second button and be sure that the Actions tab is visible**. Set the actions similarly to this button. You want to reverse the options choices for the Show/Hide buttons. Set the first Show/Hide action to hide the Spanish button. Set the second Show/Hide field to show the English button. Change the layer view in the Navigation pane to Show the English layer and hide the Spanish layer. Choose Set Layer Visibility and add the action. Click Close in the Button Properties.

9. **Test the results**. The buttons are apart from each other on the page, which makes it easier to test the results. Click one button and see if it performs as you expect. The button should disappear and the second button should be ready to use. Click it and check that the layer visibility and button view works properly. If it doesn't, you need to go back to the Button Properties and make some changes. When everything works as you expect, move one button on top of the other (click-drag or use the Alignment Panel).

CHANGING THE LAYER VIEW USING JAVASCRIPT

A much easier way to handle the button action is to use JavaScript. The following script only needs to be on one button, and it will change the layer view each time the button is clicked. The script that you add to run a JavaScript action is as follows:

```
var docOCGs = this.getOCGs();
for (var i=0; i < docOCGs.length; i++)
{
        if(docOCGs[i].name == "Spanish")
        {
                docOCGs[i].state = !docOCGs[i].state;
        }
        if(docOCGs[i].name == "English")
        {
                docOCGs[i].state = !docOCGs[i].state;
        }

}
```

You can easily copy the text here and add it to a document where you want to toggle the layer views. Just be certain that the names in quotes match your layer names.

15.4.3 Creating a License Agreement

One interesting thing that you can do with Acrobat layers is to have the opening page of the document display a license agreement. On the opening page you have a license agreement with two buttons. If the user clicks Do Not Agree, the button forces Acrobat to close the file. If the user clicks Agree, then the layer view changes to reveal the document content and dismisses the license agreement. In Figure 15-11, you see such an agreement on the opening page of a PDF.

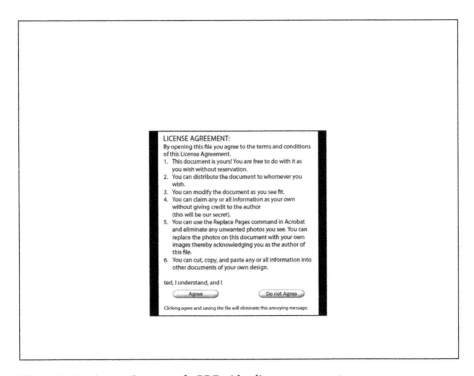

Figure 15-11. An opening page of a PDF with a license agreement

Basically, the button just changes layer states when the user clicks the Agree button. In order to protect your content, you need to secure the file with Acrobat Security. Press Ctrl/⌘+D to open the Document Properties window and click Security. In the Security Settings tab, choose Password Security from the Security Method drop-down menu. Choose Password Security and the Password Security – Settings dialog box opens. In the Permissions area, open the Changes Allowed menu and choose something like Commenting, filling in form fields, and signing existing signature fields, as shown in Figure 15-12. This prevents users from accessing the Layers Panel in the Navigation pane and only permits adding form field data, comment notes, and signing the existing digital signature fields.

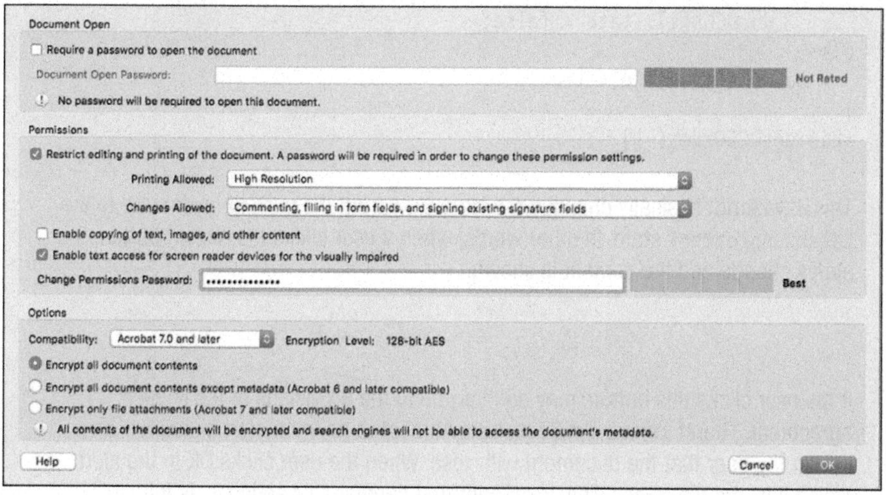

Figure 15-12. *Choose commenting, filling in form fields, and signing existing signature fields*

The caveat in creating such a document is that since the file is secure, after a user clicks the Agree button and opens the content layer, saving the file does not change the layer visibility. The file will always open with the license agreement, and the user needs to click Agree each time the document is opened.

CREATING A LICENSE AGREEMENT

Look at Figure 15-11. This is how I created the license agreement:

You need to start with a file in InDesign that has a minimum of two layers. In my example, I have one layer showing the content on 101 pages. The license agreement is on the second layer on page 1. There is nothing on this layer for the remaining pages.

I exported the file to PDF and checked Create Acrobat Layers in the Export to Interactive PDF dialog box.

Adding the Accept Button

I created a button for Accept with the button tool. I then added the following JavaScript to the button:

```
var docOCGs = this.getOCGs();
for (var i=1; i < docOCGs.length; i++)
{
        if(docOCGs[i].name == "LicenseAgreement")
```

```
        docOCGs[i].state = false;
else
    docOCGs[i].state = true;
}
this.setOCGOrder( [] );
```

This JavaScript basically changes the state view from the current layer state to the `LicenseAgreement` state. In other words, when a user clicks the Accept button, the states change and the content is shown.

Adding the Do Not Agree Button

If the user clicks this button, they don't agree to the provisions of the license agreement. Therefore, we simply instruct Acrobat to open an alert dialog box and inform the user that the document will close. When the user clicks OK in the alert dialog box, the file closes. The JavaScript that handles this action is as follows:

```
var msg = "Okay, this document will close";
app.alert(msg);
this.closeDoc();
```

Don't be concerned if you're not a JavaScript programmer. Just create a button and choose Run a JavaScript for the button's action. Click Add and type the code you see here for the buttons. For the Accept button, the only change you need to make is the line containing "LicenseAgreement." This is the name of the layer in the file. If you use a different layer name, just type that name between the quote marks.

For the Accept button, the message is shown between the quote marks in the second script. You can change the message by typing your own text. Just be certain that your message falls between the quote marks, and the remaining code is added to the JavaScript action exactly as you see it here.

■ **Caution**   You need to add security to the PDF file so that a user can't manually show and hide layers.

15.4.4   Working with Multiple Layers

Take a look at Figure 15-13. There are four buttons on the right side of the document. These buttons are used to change layer views for the house plan on the left side of the page. When a user clicks fixtures, the fixtures disappear. Click Fixtures again and the fixtures reappear. This setup is like a multi-state object where the buttons go to different state views.

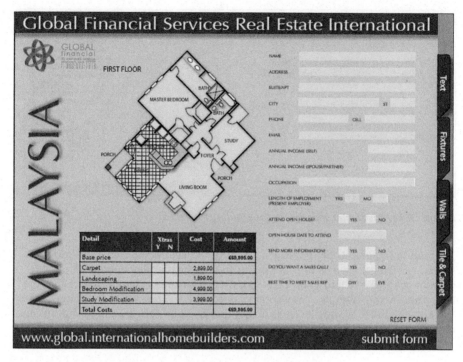

Figure 15-13. *Buttons show/hide different views for the house plan*

You can use the Set Visibility Button action to assign different layer views to the buttons. Doing so requires opening the Layers Panel, viewing the desired layer view, and setting the action. A much easier method is to use a JavaScript.

The code for showing/hiding the Text layer is as follows (see Figure 15-14):

```
var docOCGs = this.getOCGs();
for (var i=0; i < docOCGs.length; i++)
{
        if(docOCGs[i].name == "Text")
        {
            docOCGs[i].state = !docOCGs[i].state;
        }
}
```

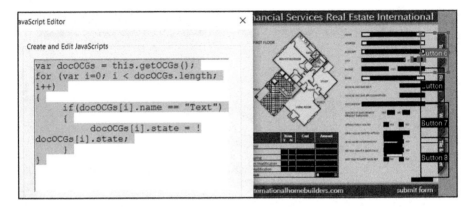

Figure 15-14. *JavaScript code for showing/hiding the Text layer*

The third-to-last line of code is a switch that turns the layer view on/off. Once you get the code working for one button, replicating the code for the other buttons is easy. Just copy the code, paste it into a Run a JavaScript action for another button, and change the layer name. In this example, the layers are named *Text, Fixtures, Walls,* and *Tile & Carpet.* You just replace "Text" with the name of the other layers for each button. By copying and pasting JavaScripts, you can quickly move through setting up the button actions.

15.5   Using Media in Interactive PDFs

Acrobat supports a variety of media formats. The best formats to use are .mp3 files for audio and H.264 encoded M4V and MP4 files, as I discussed in Chapter 10. You have two methods for using audio and video in PDF files. You can export from InDesign documents that contain audio and video, and you can add audio and video files using the tools in Acrobat. In most cases, you'll want first to place the files in InDesign and export to Interactive PDF.

In Acrobat, you can choose to view video files either in the location that they appear in the document, or you can view videos in a floating screen. To enable floating screen view, right-click the Select Object tool on a video and choose Properties when the context menu opens. In the Properties dialog box for media, you can open the Launch Settings tab (shown later in Figure 15-15) in the Edit Video dialog box and choose Play Content in Floating Window.

Buttons that you create in InDesign for play, pause, stop, and so on all work in PDF documents. Controllers also work the same way that they do in Fixed Layout and Adobe Publish Online documents. If you prefer, you can create buttons for managing video in Acrobat. In the Actions tab for buttons, you have several choices for the version of the Acrobat viewer handling your document, including the following:

- *Multimedia Operation (Acrobat 9 and later)*: Use this option for PDFs viewed in Acrobat or Adobe Reader version 9 or later.

- *Play Media (Acrobat 5 compatible)*: This is an old standard and something you probably won't use.

- *Play Media (Acrobat 6 compatible)*: Use this action when you know the viewers of your document work with Adobe Reader (or Acrobat) version 9 or earlier.

Sometimes it may be helpful to alert users that they must use a version of Acrobat or Adobe Reader of a certain version number or later. If your documents are best viewed in version 9 of Reader/Acrobat, then you can add an alert dialog to your file. The alert dialog will open only if someone is using a version older than the one that you specify. This is a simple JavaScript that you can add to your document when it opens. We call JavaScripts that appear when a document opens *document-level* JavaScripts.

Before writing the JavaScript, you must access the Document JavaScripts dialog box. Click tools in the upper-left corner of the Acrobat window and locate the JavaScript button. Click Open and the tools are loaded into the Acrobat toolbar. Among the tools, you will find Document JavaScripts. Click this button to open the Document JavaScripts dialog box, as shown in Figure 15-15.

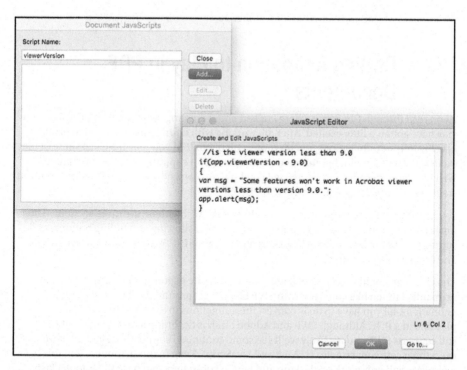

Figure 15-15. *Click Document JavaScripts to open the Document JavaScripts dialog box*

Type a name for the script and click the Add button. The JavaScript Editor opens (also shown in Figure 15-15). Type the following code in the JavaScript Editor window:

```
//is the viewer version less than 9.0
if(app.viewerVersion < 9.0)
{
var msg = "Some features won't work in Acrobat viewer versions less than
version 9.0.";
app.alert(msg);
}
```

In this code, the first line of text is a comment line and not executed. The second line of code examines the version of the PDF viewer in use. If the viewer is older than version 9.0, the message field is executed. In this case, an alert dialog box opens and says what you see in parentheses in the code. The last line of code instructs Acrobat to open the alert dialog box.

If you include some content in a PDF file that only works properly in a certain version of the PDF viewer, you should include similar code in a Document Level JavaScript.

For more on working with media, see Chapter 10.

15.6   Getting Animation to Play in PDF Documents

If you read through Chapter 8 where I talked about creating animations in InDesign, you may have gotten a little excited. After all, working with animations in InDesign brings a new life to your publications and it's quite a bit of fun. But you may have lost some of that excitement when I said that Interactive PDF files don't support InDesign animations. Well don't fret, because I'm here to tell you how you can get all of the animations that you create in InDesign to play in Interactive PDF files.

You probably noticed in the Buttons and Forms Panel that there are three sections. The top section includes page navigation, going to a URL, showing and hiding buttons, and support for sound and video. The next section says SWF/EPUB Only. Here is where you find support for animations.

The clue that you have here is that animations can't be exported to PDF, but they can be handled much like you work with SWF files. To get around the lack of support for animations, all you have to do is convert the animations to SWF and they will then play fine in a PDF. Although SWF and Adobe Flash is declining in usage, Acrobat DC still supports SWF and it's likely we'll see some continued support for a while before everything gets converted to HTML5 and JavaScript. Keep in mind, though, that this technique will only work on desktop and laptop computers that have the Adobe Flash Player installed. It will not work on mobile phones or tablets.

PLAYING AN ANIMATION IN A PDF

To play an animation in a PDF, follow these steps:

1. **Create a PDF document with Animation**. You can use any one of the 48 different presets in the Animation Panel. For more information on using the presets, see Chapter 8.

2. **Choose File ➤ Export or press Ctrl/⌘+E**. Choose Flash Player SWF from the Save as Type menu (Windows) or Format menu (Macintosh).

3. **Set the attributes in the Export SWF dialog box, as shown in Figure 15-16**. Uncheck Generate HTML. Be sure that the Include All radio button is selected in the Interactivity and Media area. Click Transparent for the background. (Note that the SWF will not be transparent in the PDF. You'll need to make an edit in Acrobat once in the PDF document). Click OK.

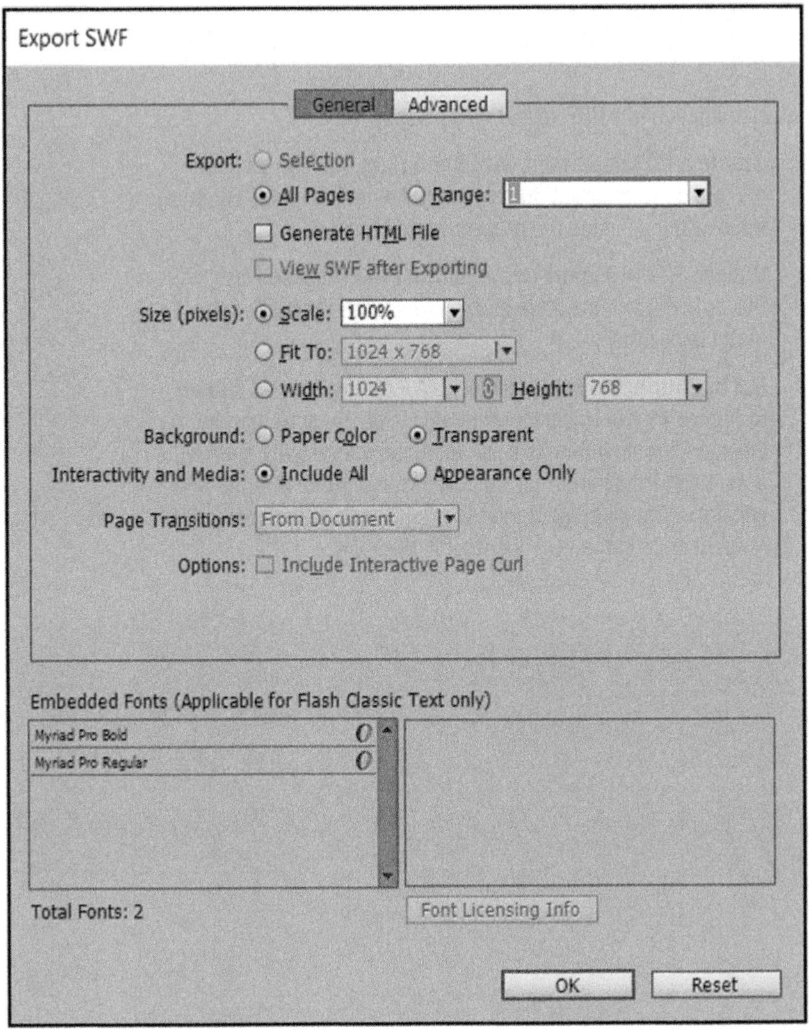

```
┌─────────────────────────────────────────────────────────────────┐
│ Export SWF                                                        │
│                                                                   │
│                         ┌──────────┬──────────┐                   │
│                         │ General  │ Advanced │                   │
│                                                                   │
│            Export:  ○ Selection                                   │
│                     ⦿ All Pages      ○ Range:  [1        ▼]       │
│                     ☐ Generate HTML File                          │
│                     ☐ View SWF after Exporting                    │
│                                                                   │
│     Size (pixels):  ⦿ Scale: [100%    ▼]                          │
│                     ○ Fit To: [1024 x 768  |▼]                    │
│                     ○ Width: [1024   |▼] [⟦⟧] Height: [768    ▼]  │
│                                                                   │
│        Background:  ○ Paper Color   ⦿ Transparent                 │
│ Interactivity and Media: ⦿ Include All  ○ Appearance Only         │
│                                                                   │
│   Page Transitions: [From Document   |▼]                          │
│                                                                   │
│          Options:  ☐ Include Interactive Page Curl                │
│                                                                   │
│                                                                   │
│  Embedded Fonts (Applicable for Flash Classic Text only)          │
│  ┌─────────────────────────────┐  ┌──────────────────────────┐   │
│  │ Myriad Pro Bold         O ▲ │  │                          │   │
│  │ Myriad Pro Regular      O   │  │                          │   │
│  │                             │  │                          │   │
│  │                         ▼   │  │                          │   │
│  └─────────────────────────────┘  └──────────────────────────┘   │
│  Total Fonts: 2                   [ Font Licensing Info ]         │
│                                                                   │
│                                    [    OK    ]  [  Reset  ]      │
└─────────────────────────────────────────────────────────────────┘
```

Figure 15-16. *Set the attributes for exporting to Flash Player SWF*

4. **Open a new InDesign document and place the SWF file.**

5. **Select the SWF file you just placed and open the Media Panel.** Check the checkbox to Play on Page Load.

6. **Choose File Export or press Ctrl/⌘+E and choose Interactive PDF from the Save as Type menu.**

7. **Review the results.** If you check View after Exporting, the file opens in Acrobat.

8. **Click the Select Object tool (R) and right-click on the SWF file**. The Edit SWF dialog box opens, as shown in Figure 15-17. Choose Properties from the menu. In the Edit SWF dialog box, be certain that the Enable When menu option is set to "The Page Containing the Content Is Opened". Click the checkbox for Transparent Background and click OK. Save the file.

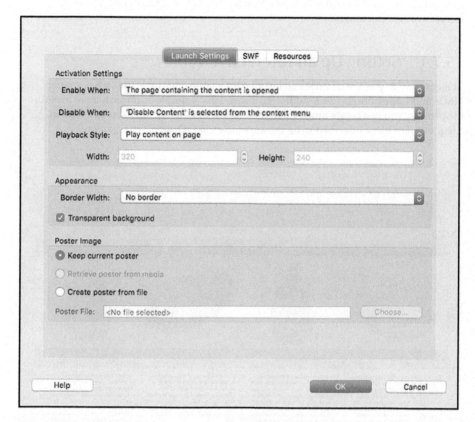

Figure 15-17. *Enable Transparent in the Edit SWF dialog box*

The animation now plays when the PDF is opened.

15.7 Exporting Interactive Tables

As you know by now, any of the button actions that you set up in InDesign in the SWF/EPUB Only area are designed for viewing in SWF files. If you create an interactive table with MSOs and buttons to view states, then obviously you need a workaround to view the interactivity in a PDF export.

> **Note** This type of interactivity can only be seen in PDFs on desktop and laptop computers that have the Flash Player installed.

The way that you set this up is much like exporting PDFs with animations. You need to export a SWF file from InDesign, then import the SWF, and finally export it as an Interactive PDF document.

15.7.1 Setting Up an Interactive Table

In Figure 15-18, you see an InDesign layout with a table. This table uses a few simple MSOs and some buttons to view different states. I use a simple example here to explain the process. You can create much more complex designs using MSOs, as I explain in Chapter 8. For more information on creating tables in InDesign, see Chapter 5.

Figure 15-18. *The InDesign table layout shows fruit images in four table cells*

The four table cells showing the fruit images are MSOs. When you look at the Object States for the first cell, you see just two states. One state shows the banana and the other states show a map, as shown in Figure 15-19, for the MSO in the first table cell.

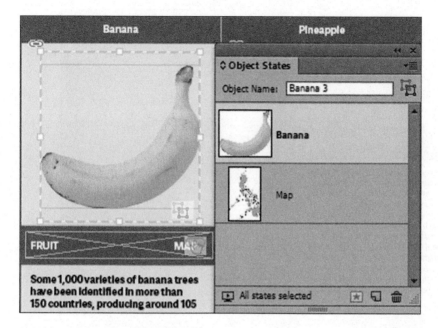

Figure 15-19. *The first of four MSOs*

A single button appears over the text below the images. In the Buttons and Forms Panel, choose Go to Next State for the button action, as shown in Figure 15-20. Only a single button is needed for each of the four cells. One click shows the map and a second click returns to the fruit image.

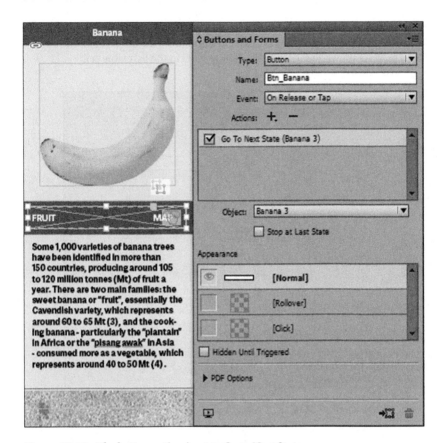

Figure 15-20. *The button action is set to Go to Next State*

After adding MSOs and button actions, copy the table and buttons and paste them into a new InDesign document. When you paste the table and buttons, you may find that the buttons lost the Go to Next State actions.

You need to reset the actions in the Buttons and Forms Panel. Preview the design using the SWF Preview Panel and be certain that clicking the buttons changes the states. When everything works, choose File ➤ Export (Ctrl/⌘+E) and export the file as Flash Player (SWF).

Delete the table and buttons in the original file. You may want to save a copy of the document and call it something like Fruit_No Table.indd. With the table and buttons deleted, choose File ➤ Place and place the SWF file.

15.7.2   Exporting to Interactive PDF

After placing the SWF file, choose File ➤ Export (Ctrl/⌘+E) and select Adobe PDF (Interactive). Check the View After Exporting checkbox, and click OK in the Export to Interactive PDF dialog box.

The file opens in your default PDF viewer. You should use Adobe Acrobat as your default viewer so that you can edit the PDF file.

When you first see the document in the PDF viewer, you probably see a Flash icon in the top-left corner of the screen with nothing else appearing on the page, as shown in Figure 15-21.

Figure 15-21. *The default view of the InDesign export*

15.7.3   Adjusting Properties in Acrobat

Click the Select Object tool in the Acrobat toolbar. If the tool is not available, press the R key on your keyboard to access the tool. You must have the General Preferences in Acrobat set to use single-key accelerators in order to use keyboard shortcuts to access tools.

Right-click the SWF overlay and choose Properties from the context menu. The properties adjustments for the SWF file open. In the Launch Settings tab in the Edit SWF dialog box, choose "The Page Containing The Content Is Opened" from the Enable When menu (see Figure 15-22).

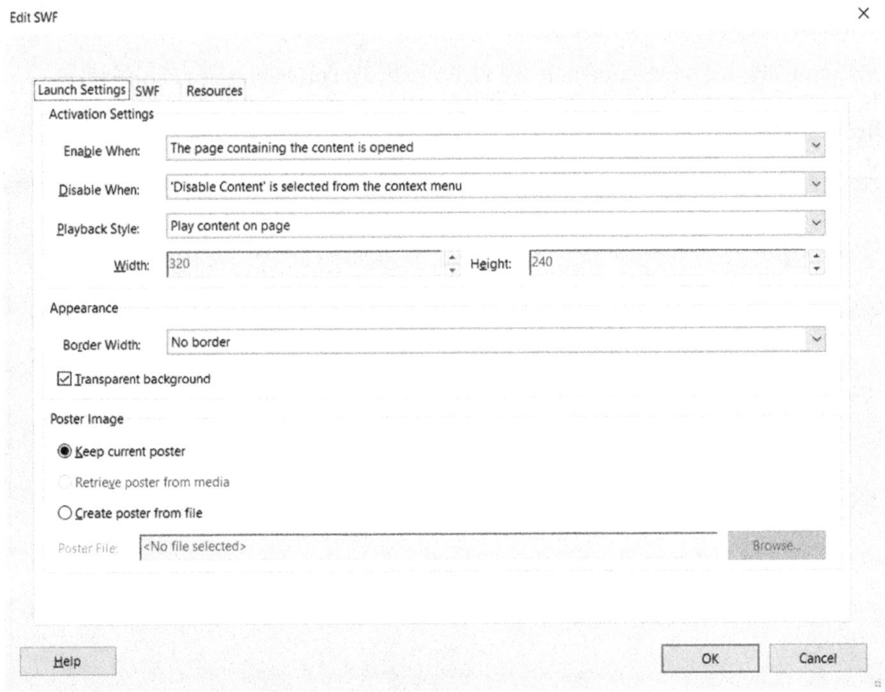

Edit SWF   ✕

Launch Settings | SWF   Resources

Activation Settings

Enable When: The page containing the content is opened   ⌄

Disable When: 'Disable Content' is selected from the context menu   ⌄

Playback Style: Play content on page   ⌄

Width: 320   Height: 240

Appearance

Border Width: No border   ⌄

☑ Transparent background

Poster Image

◉ Keep current poster

○ Retrieve poster from media

○ Create poster from file

Poster File: <No file selected>   Browse...

Help   OK   Cancel

Figure 15-22.   *Choose "The Page Containing the Content Is Opened" from the Enable When menu and check the box for Transparent Background*

Enable the checkbox for Transparent Background and click OK in the Edit SWF dialog box. Save the file and reopen it in Acrobat. When the SWF file is played upon opening the page, you should see the SWF overlay transparent and the background around the table in view, as shown in Figure 15-23.

Click the buttons and the object states should change.

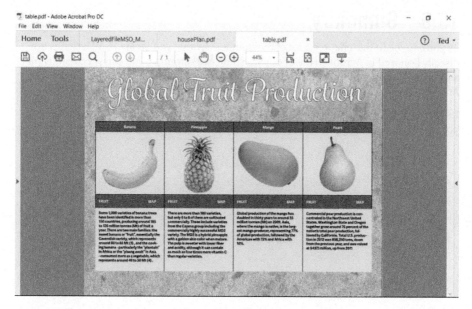

Figure 15-23. *After reopening the file, you should see the SWF overlay transparent*

15.8 Working with Multi-State Objects in PDFs

Exporting documents with multi-state objects doesn't work in Interactive PDF files. However, you can follow the same path as when you exported animations to get buttons advancing states in MSOs, and you can also get nested MSOs working fine in Acrobat PDFs on desktop computers.

As with preparing files with animations, you first need to export all of the layers containing buttons and MSOs to a Flash Player (SWF) file. Import the SWF file in the InDesign document where you have background and other design elements and export to Interactive PDF.

When the file opens in Acrobat, open a context menu with the Select Object tool and choose Properties. In the Edit SWF dialog box, choose "The Page Containing the Content Is Opened" from the Enable When menu and click the Transparent Background checkbox. Save the file and reopen it in Acrobat.

Click the buttons to show different object states, and if you use a nested MSO, click buttons to advance states in the nested MSO. For more information on working with multi-state objects, see Chapter 9.

15.9 Summary

As you can see in this chapter, a lot of the interactivity that you create in InDesign is not directly honored in Acrobat. However, with some workarounds, you can successfully play animations, work with multi-state objects, and create various assets and JavaScripts in Acrobat to help you achieve your desired objectives with Interactive PDF files.

In the next chapter, we look at some tips for helping you set up and create interactive documents in InDesign.

PART V

■ ■ ■

Tips and Techniques

CHAPTER 16

■ ■ ■

Tips for Creating Digital Publishing Documents

You can create better designs for all of your digital publications by following a few tips and considerations for laying out documents and finalizing them. All of the tips here are free, and it won't cost you any extra money—they're just some food for thought.

16.1   Edit Images in Adobe Photoshop

There's nothing like a beautiful image on a page. Graphics attract reader attention, and they keep the viewer focused on your message. Graphics need to be crisp, clean, and "pop" on a page.

All photos, especially those shots taken outside a studio, need a little correction—even those images taken with high-end digital cameras. You can open images in Photoshop's Camera Raw converter and apply edits to do the following:

- In the Basic Panel, adjust color temperature.

- In the Basic Panel, make adjustments for exposure and contrast.

- In the Basic Panel, make adjustments for highlights and shadows.

- In the Basic Panel, make adjustments for saturation, clarity, and vibrance.

- In the Lens Correction Panel, use a camera profile and make a lens correction.

- Use the Straighten tool and straighten the photo so that it's not skewed against the horizon.

- If you *must have* a photo that you can't improve in RGB mode, convert it to black and white or create a high-key photo and apply a sepia tone (see Figure 16-1).

© Ted Padova 2017

T. Padova, *Adobe InDesign Interactive Digital Publishing*,

DOI 10.1007/978-1-4842-2439-7_16

Figure 16-1. *Original image on left. The same image on the right after converting it to grayscale, creating a high-key image, and applying a sepia tone*

16.2   Create Thumbnail Sketches

Software developers continually market sketch programs for tablets, hoping to dominate the market. Recent studies show that more than 66% of graphic designers still prefer the old-fashioned method of using a sketchpad and No. 2 pencil.

When developing a new concept, free your mind by sitting on the beach, resting on a mountain, taking a bicycle ride, or doing any other activity that helps you relax. At the end of the day, create 50 thumbnail sketches in about 2.5-inch squares. Draw them quickly and use stick people if you're not an artist. You'll probably hate all of the drawings (see Figure 16-2).

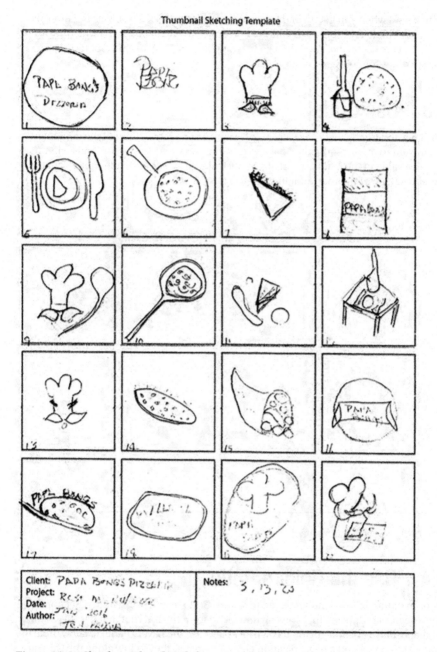

Figure 16-2. *Sketch out thumbnails for a new concept*

Go to bed, and when you get up in the morning, review your sketches. Pick out three or four that you think have some possibilities and draw out some roughs. Pick out the design that you think will work best and then go to your computer and begin creating graphics and assembling your design.

16.3   Use Grids

Create a master grid on a Master Page in InDesign. As you move through the document, you may want to modify individual page grids. Choose Layout ➤ Margins and Columns and enter a value in the Number text box in the Columns area. Drag ruler lines from the top ruler to create horizontal guidelines (see Figure 16-3).

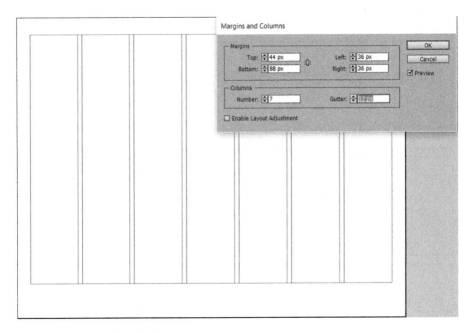

Figure 16-3. *A seven-column grid.*

16.4   Use the Golden Ratio

Patterns in nature follow a path referred to as the "Golden Ratio" or "Golden Section." Locate a vector art drawing that you can download from the Internet that has the Golden Ratio shape. Place the drawing on its own layer and use the Layers Panel to show/hide the drawing. As you work on a page, position elements so that they follow along the Golden Ratio path. You can flip the Golden Ratio template and rotate it clockwise or counter-clockwise depending on your layout (see Figure 16-4).

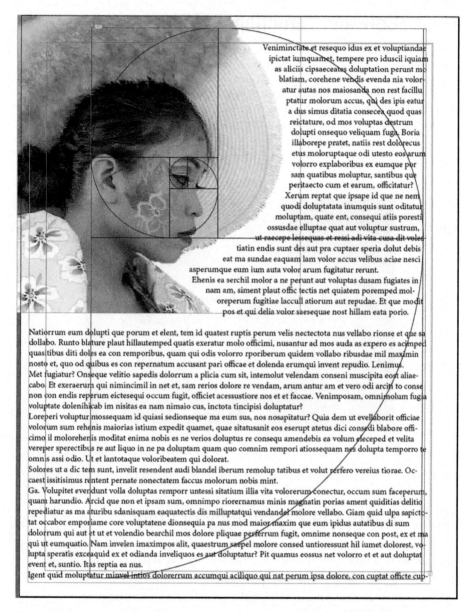

Figure 16-4. *The Golden Ratio on a layer helps position elements on a page*

The Golden Ratio may not be appropriate for every page, but it can help in many layouts. Try it on document pages, and it can give you some clues for nudging text frames and objects.

16.5   Consider Direction and Movement

Each page in a layout should *bring the reader into the page*. Large bodies of text aren't interesting for a reader. You need to add some tricks to make the page more interesting. Add whitespace and objects and position elements so that they keep the reader's attention on the center of the page. With images, have photos of individuals viewing the center of the page and not off the page. With text, you can mix alignments so that the text alignment implies a direction toward the center (see Figure 16-5).

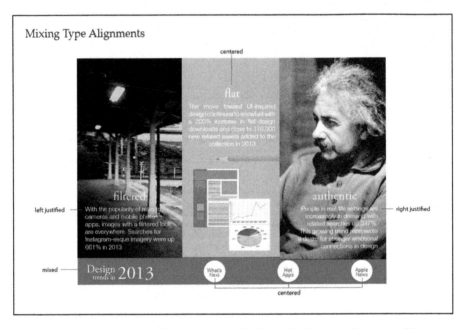

Figure 16-5. *Text and image alignment can help the reader focus on the center of the page*

16.6   Learn the Psychology of Color

Color is used creatively to capture a mood or sentiment in a design. When choosing colors, be aware of the kind of mood or sentiment that the colors represent (see Figure 16-6).

- *Warm colors*: Red, orange, and yellow. These colors represent happiness and enthusiasm, and they represent a sense of power and energy.

- *Cool colors*: Blue, purple, and green. These colors represent calm, stability, and professionalism. They create trust.

- *Complementary colors*: These colors are opposites on the color wheel. For example, red and green are complementary colors.

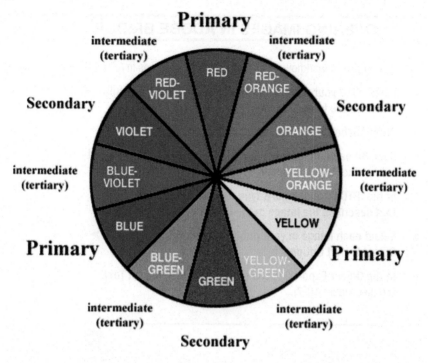

Figure 16-6. *Color wheel showing primary and complementary colors*

16.7   Use Font Harmony

Just as color creates moods and sentiment, font choices equally contribute to the emotion of a design. Choose fonts that help you deliver your message and that work well together. You can find a lot of information about typography by searching the Internet. Search for fonts that work well together. In a web browser, search for *type fonts that work well together*, or similar searches. You often find articles that offer 10-20 suggestions for font combinations. Convert articles of interest to PDF documents and keep them handy when you are creating new design projects.

If you have no design experience, stick with perhaps the ten top typefaces that work well together. As you learn more about typography, you can broaden your font choices.

16.8   Add Metadata in Adobe Bridge

Alt tags in digital publishing documents are especially important for people with visual challenges who depend on screen readers to read digital content. All of the objects and images in a design should have a description of each graphic.

OPENING IMAGES IN ADOBE BRIDGE

You can speed up your workflow by opening all of your images in Adobe Bridge.

1. **Place all of your photos and vector art images in a single folder before importing them into InDesign.**

2. **Open Adobe Bridge and navigate to your images folder.**

3. **Click on each image and open the Metadata tab on the right side of the Bridge window.**

4. **In the IPTC Core category, type a descriptive body of text that describes the image in the Description field.**

5. **Select each image in your publication and choose Object ➤ Object Export Options.**

6. **In the Object Export Options dialog box, click the Alt Text tab** (see Figure 16-7).

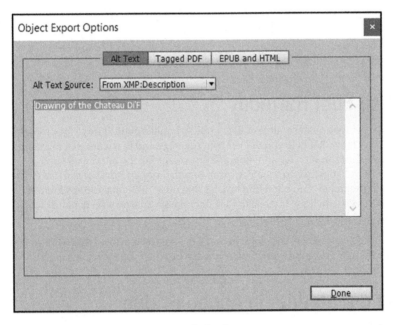

Figure 16-7. Object Export Options dialog box

7. **Open the Alt Text Source menu and choose the From XMP-Description option.**

8. **After all the images and objects have been tagged, export your file**.

16.9 Use InDesign Scripts

InDesign scripts can be a huge help when creating layouts. You can speed up your work progress by installing and running scripts. There are a number of InDesign scripts available by searching the Internet, both free and for nominal purchase prices.

While poking around the Internet, log on to www.indesignsecrets.com. The InDesign Secrets web site has a wealth of information dedicated to providing tips and techniques to InDesign users. The InDesign Secrets web site also has many articles on InDesign scripts, and some scripts are available for download.

USING INDESIGN SCRIPTS

Once you download a script, you need to install it in the correct folder.

1. **Open the Scripts Panel in InDesign.** You have two locations for InDesign scripts: an Application folder and a User folder. Select the User folder.

2. **On Windows, choose Reveal in Explorer to locate the Scripts folder. (On the Macintosh, choose Reveal in the Finder.)** The folder opens on your desktop.

3. **Copy the new scripts that you want to add to the folder, or create a new folder inside the User folder and copy the scripts that you want to add** (see Figure 16-8).

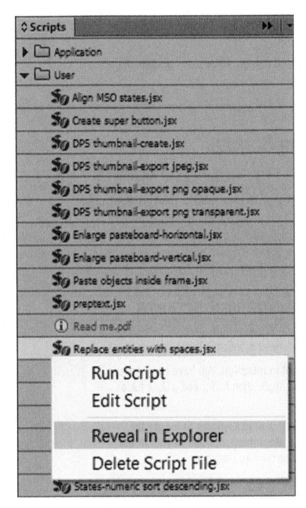

Figure 16-8. *Open the Scripts Panel and select User. Open the Scripts Panel menu and choose Reveal in Explorer (Windows) or Reveal in Finder (Macintosh)*

16.10 Package Files

While working on a document, you may lose track of your images and other assets that you import into InDesign. If you change file locations for assets, InDesign reports missing links when you open the document.

After you finish a publication, let InDesign help you organize all of the content in your publication. Choose File ➤ Package. In the Package dialog box, review the summary information and click Package. InDesign informs you of the name of the folder where the contents will be added. You can accept the default folder or change the folder name. Click

Package in the last screen, and the InDesign file, all of the assets, and all of the type fonts are added to one folder.

You can delete the original folder and use the packaged folder when you want to make edits. Since the fonts are also copied to the folder, you won't have any missing font issues when you revisit the document.

16.11   Summary

In this chapter, you learned some design tips to create better layouts for your interactive documents. The more you know about design and typography, the more professional your documents will appear.

In the next chapter, we look at some project ideas.

CHAPTER 17

■ ■ ■

Additional Project Ideas

You may have some professional need to create a digital publication, but it's much more fun to use InDesign's tools for a wide range of documents that you can publish and share with colleagues, friends, family, and your coworkers. The more you use the methods described in this book, the more applications you'll develop for creating a number of documents, not just for professional use but for recreational use as well.

17.1   Write Your Autobiography

Many people often say, "You should write a book." Individuals often think that their past experiences are so interesting that they should record those events in a publication. If you've ever thought about writing such a book, now is the time.

You can create a reflowable EPUB and add photos, audio, and video to develop an interesting story. It may not be something a publishing house will pick up and extend into a Tom Hanks or Jennifer Lawrence movie, but you'll probably get a lot of accolades from those who know you.

Begin your writing career with a personal story and share it among friends and family.

17.2   Create a Children's Book

Think of a story that might interest your children or family members and plan out an interactive book. Children's books have lots of pictures, and when you add animation and audio, the kids will play with it on tablets all day long (see Figure 17-1).

© Ted Padova 2017
T. Padova, *Adobe InDesign Interactive Digital Publishing*,
DOI 10.1007/978-1-4842-2439-7_17

Figure 17-1. *Book cover for a children's book*

Don't worry about being a great artist. Some cartoon characters don't look at all like DC Comics drawings. You can begin by searching the Internet for animal character drawings and people. Download some image files and use them as templates in a drawing program like Adobe Illustrator. If it's not for public distribution, you don't need to worry about copyright issues. Modify the drawings to make them a little different than the images you downloaded and you're just fine.

Take the image files and import them into InDesign. For text, review some children's books and get an idea for how much text appears on a page for a given age category. With younger children, a single line of text is all you need.

Animate objects with motion paths and introduce sounds. You can download royalty-free sounds from many web sites on the Internet. What's most important is coming up with a story that would be of interest to children and perhaps deliver a message.

When you finish the design, create a fixed layout EPUB and load it on a tablet. It may take a bit of work, but the children will enjoy it for some time. Watch out though, as they may ask you to write more books.

17.3   Create an EPUB Cookbook

This is a great way to catalog some of your favorite recipes. Include the traditional ingredients list, prep time, and cooking time, and you can also add videos. Take videos when you're in the kitchen preparing some of your favorite dishes. Optimize the videos in Adobe Media Encoder and place them into an InDesign document.

This project could be in development over time. Keep your file handy, and when you take a new video, add it to the document along with the text and photos. When you're ready to publish, export the file to a fixed layout EPUB. It might make a nice Christmas gift for some friends who love your meals.

17.4   Create a Christmas Card

Speaking of Christmas (or any other occasion), you might want to look at creating a greeting card. You can add video, photos, and audio to a card and share the card with all of those on your Christmas list.

Publish the document using Adobe Publish Online. Send an e-mail containing the URL to people on your list so that they can view your greeting card.

17.5   Share an Event Invitation

You may have a social meeting, a company picnic, an invitation to a party, wedding, or anniversary, or some other special occasion to which you want to invite selected friends and family. The invitation will get a lot of attention when you add animation.

Create an Adobe Publish Online document and share the URL with the individuals you want to invite to the occasion.

17.6   Publish an Event on Facebook

If you don't need to limit the audience for a particular event—for something like a sports tournament, soccer game, children's play at the local elementary school, political rally, or other such event—you may want to get the word out to a lot of people.

Create an animated document that is designed with some pizzazz. Make it interesting so that people will want to see it several times.

Publish the document using Adobe Publish Online and share the file on your Facebook timeline. Review your Facebook account periodically and see how many Likes you get.

17.7   Create an Animated Business Chart

If you work for a company, sit on a board of directors, or lend assistance to a friend who wants a creative business chart, use the Animation features in InDesign and create a well thought out design that clarifies information in the chart.

You can create animated bar charts, exploding pie charts, animated line charts, and any other thoughts you may have on how the chart should appear.

Copy the animation to a new document and export it as a SWF (player) file. Import the SWF file in an InDesign document and export it to Interactive PDF. You can show the chart on a laptop or send the PDF to other users.

17.8   Use a QuickTime VR Movie in a Document

To create a QuickTime VR movie file, you need a program to stitch photos together that eventually produce the movie file. Use a program like Pano2VR, which you can download from `http://ggnome.com/pano2vr`. You can use the program in demo mode without purchasing it to try it out. In demo mode, the resulting file displays with a watermark. If you purchase the program, the watermark disappears.

Take several photos in a 360° view and stich them together in Pano2VR. You might want to take photos inside a house that you want to put on the market. When you produce the movie file, place it in InDesign and export it to Interactive PDF.

You can click and drag the mouse to scroll through a 360° view of the movie file.

17.9   Stitch a Panorama File in Photoshop

Take several photos of a panorama scene. Use a tripod and overlap the shots about 25 percent. Set the camera on the tripod in a portrait mode and take a series of shots.

Open all of the photos in Adobe Photoshop's Camera Raw dialog box. Select all of the photos in the filmstrip on the far-left side of the screen, and from the drop-down menu, choose Merge to Panorama or press Ctrl/⌘+M. Open the merged photos in Photoshop, crop, and downsample as desired.

Place the panorama image in InDesign and choose Convert Spread to Landscape in the Fixed Layout Export Options General pane in the Options menu.

17.10   Share Multiple URLs via Dropbox

If you have several documents created with Adobe Publish Online, you may want to access them easily and routinely offer the file links to others. In order to keep track of the files and the URLs, create a plain text document with each URL.

Place the document in your Public folder on Dropbox, and users can request the URL addresses, or you can direct users to download the file(s). When they open the document in a text editor, they just need to click a URL to access a file. This can be for Fixed Layout, PDF, or Adobe Publish Online documents. For Fixed Layout and Adobe PDF files, you need to upload them to your public folder on Dropbox.

17.11 Summary

In this chapter, I offer some project ideas. You can start with one of these projects and then use your imagination to come up with ideas for projects that you want to tackle. InDesign is so powerful that the only limit is your own imagination. If you can imagine it, more than likely you can create it in InDesign.

If you're new to InDesign and/or creating interactive documents, hopefully this book has helped to you get started. The more you practice, the better you will become at mastering Adobe InDesign.

I encourage you to poke around the Internet and look at www.InDesignSecrets.com for tips, tricks, and helpful instructional guides for using InDesign. Also, look at www.epubsecrets.com for helpful information on creating EPUBs. Another source for great information is http://creativepro.com. On this web site, you learn many tips and techniques for using InDesign as well as helpful ideas for creating designs and using type.

It is my sincere desire that you will find the information contained herein helpful and worthwhile. If you have any questions or remarks, send me an e-mail at ted@tedpadova.com.

Index

© Ted Padova 2017
T. Padova, *Adobe InDesign Interactive Digital Publishing*,
DOI 10.1007/978-1-4842-2439-7

▓ T

Get the eBook for only $4.99!

Why limit yourself?

Now you can take the weightless companion with you wherever you go and access your content on your PC, phone, tablet, or reader.

Since you've purchased this print book, we are happy to offer you the eBook for just $4.99.

Convenient and fully searchable, the PDF version enables you to easily find and copy code—or perform examples by quickly toggling between instructions and applications.

To learn more, go to http://www.apress.com/us/shop/companion or contact support@apress.com.

CPSIA information can be obtained
at www.ICGtesting.com
Printed in the USA
LVOW02s2356230417
531918LV00001B/1/P